D1329674

"Music of the Highest Class"

"Music of the Highest Class"

Elitism and Populism in Antebellum Boston

Michael Broyles

Yale University Press

New Haven and London

Designed by Sonia L. Scanlon
Set in Galliard type by DEKR Corporation,
Woburn, Massachusetts.
Printed in the United States of America by
BookCrafters, Inc., Chelsea, Michigan.

Library of Congress Cataloging-in-Publication Data

Broyles, Michael, 1939–
Music of the highest class : elitism and populism in antebellum
Boston / Michael Broyles.
p.   cm.
Includes bibliographical references and index.
ISBN 0-300-05495-5
1. Music—Massachusetts—Boston—19th century—History and
criticism. 2. Music and society.   I. Title.
ML200.8.B7B76   1992
780'.9744'6109034—dc20   92-12422
CIP
MN

A catalogue record for this book
is available from the British Library.

The paper in this book meets the guidelines for permanence
and durability of the Committee on Production Guidelines for
Book Longevity of the Council on Library Resources.

10 9 8 7 6 5 4 3 2 1

To Nina

Contents

Contents

Chapter Nine

Developments of the 1840s: Retraction   235

Chapter Ten

Bands, Opera, Virtuosi, and the Changing of the Guard   269

Chapter Eleven

Boston and Beyond   306

Appendix 1

Instrumental Musicians in Boston, 1796–1842   313

Appendix 2

Individual List of Instrumental Musicians in Boston, 1796–1842   335

Notes   341

Works Cited   365

Index   377

Acknowledgments

I am indebted to many scholars for their advice, information, encouragement, or enlightening discussion. Among them are Richard Crawford, Jurgen Thym, Paul Machlin, James Mohr, R. K. Webb, William Austin, Katherine Preston, and Daniel Preston. I would especially like to thank Pamela Fox, who shared both information and insights from her own Boston research, which picks up roughly where mine ends.

A historian's work is only as good as his sources, and I wish to thank many librarians in the Boston area, Diane Ota and Giuseppe Bisaccia of the Boston Public Library, Natalie Palme of the Harvard Musical Association Library, and all the staff of the American Antiquarian Society and the Harvard University Archives, in particular Joanne Chaison of the American Antiquarian Society.

Work on this project was made possible by a senior fellowship from the National Endowment for the Humanities and as a Research Associate at the American Antiquarian Society. I wish to thank both organizations for their support. Parts of chapters 4, 7, and 9 originally appeared in a somewhat different form in the *Journal of the American Musicological Society*. I thank the journal for permission to reprint this material, and the editor of the journal at the time, William Prizer, for many helpful suggestions. I would also like to thank the music editor at Yale University Press, Harry Haskell, and his colleague Otto Bohlmann for the many ways they improved the product. Needless to say, they could only work with what they were given, and shortcomings are mine, not theirs.

Finally, I want to thank my wife, Nina Fedoroff. She is a tough but fair editor and has suggested many ways to improve the prose.

Introduction

This book seeks to explain the emergence of a fundamental duality in our musical culture: the distinction between what is commonly called classical music and all other kinds.[1]

In the early nineteenth century the notion appeared that some types of music were enriching and morally superior. From that a canon or pantheon of composers and compositions developed. Orchestral music occupied a special place in the pantheon, and Handel, Haydn, Mozart, and Beethoven came to be revered. The pantheon has grown since then, and it has been challenged. But the fundamental idea has remained. For good or ill, the presence of a cultural hierarchy based on it is an ineluctable fact of American musical life today. It is taught in our schools; it is marketed by our musical institutions; it organizes our record stores; it dominates the airwaves, as the very profile of radio stations is based on an elaborate classification of musical types. Notions of classical versus popular music in particular are embedded in our thinking. The specifics change as styles come and go, and the terms themselves are frustratingly elusive when scrutinized. But one division remains relatively constant: classical music is in a category by itself. It is surrounded by an aura of respectability that gives it, rightly or wrongly, a special mystique.

The most common current definition of this musical duality, which has characterized our thinking about music for more than a century, distinguishes between a "cultivated" and a "vernacular" tradition. It has been described in many ways. In the best-known formulation, Wiley Hitchcock, writing in 1969, although not the first to use those terms, distinguished "a vernacular tradition of utilitarian and entertainment music, essentially unconcerned with artistic or philosophical idealism," from "a cultivated tradition of fine-art music significantly concerned with moral, artistic, or cultural idealism."[2] For a time this distinction seemed appropriate. But since Hitchcock's discussion, ideas about what constitutes the two traditions have rendered the terms less suitable.

The cultivated tradition was originally based on European art music and idealistic concepts of progress and moral improvement. It was justified by a vocabulary consisting of such terms as science, taste, progress, and gentility. It was overtly Platonic: certain types of music possessed a moral value beyond mere entertainment. It was concentrated in urban centers, and it significantly affected the nature of the musical institutions that thrived there. It ultimately touched all aspects of American musical life, imposing on music making a valuative hierarchy that has not escaped even the most vernacular musician. A song like Chuck Berry's "Roll Over Beethoven" clearly depended on an awareness of this hierarchy. The attitudes that the cultivated tradition spawned remain in force even to this day.

In a broader context the duality has been considered part of the differentiation between high and low culture. A high culture–low culture distinction has existed for centuries in Western music. Usually the contrast was political and economic: court music differed from the music of the market place, cathedral music differed from the music of the parish church, aristocratic opera differed from folk play. These distinctions were recognized, and the merits of different types of music relative to their settings were accepted. In late nineteenth-century America the distinction became ethical, although with political (specifically class) implications. The cultural hierarchy was redefined principally through a new set of moral associations attached to high culture. High culture came to stand at the apex of a pyramid of cultural types because it was morally pure and edifying. As a result, by the late nineteenth century certain literary and artistic products were viewed with a sacred reverence. Paul DiMaggio described this tendency as the "sacralization of art." Lawrence Levine, who later explored its historical background more fully, called it the "sacralization of culture."[3]

According to both Levine and DiMaggio the tendency was scarcely in evidence until the second half of the nineteenth century. By then the high culture–low culture distinction was firmly in place. The most popular musician in late nineteenth-century America, for example, John Philip Sousa, was never considered on a par with even the most pedestrian symphonic conductor. Sousa conducted a band, an ensemble devoted to entertainment. A symphony orchestra, however, was at the very center of high culture. Thus Theodore Thomas, conductor of the Chicago Symphony Orchestra, avoided vulgar talk, "questionable" plays, and immoral books, because "a musician must keep his heart pure and his mind clean if he wishes to elevate, instead of debasing his art."[4] And Fritz Scheel, implored by the Board of Directors of the Philadelphia Orchestra to lighten his programs for financial reasons, responded: "I stand for art; as long as I am conductor of the Philadelphia Orchestra waltzes will not be played on a symphony program."[5]

By going back into the nineteenth century when cultural categories were less definitive, Levine and others have presented a historical framework from which they argue for abandonment of hierarchical distinctions. For Levine, as well as Gilbert Chase and Charles Hamm, the assumptions of a high culture–low culture duality have limited both our vision of art and our ability to discuss it. Their argument is one that historians have frequently made: our thinking is governed by a set of assumptions that we too often take for granted. But when we place these assumptions into historical perspective, their hollowness will become more apparent.[6]

The attitudes that these writers question have softened considerably in recent years, at least in music. Few listeners today avoid certain types of music because they are corrupting. True, some music may offend. This may be because of a political message, either overt, as in the anarchic themes of punk rock, or more subtle, as in the antifeminist themes of some country music. But the more fundamental notion that some types of music are morally superior to others is no longer compelling. That the Kronos String Quartet can perform Béla Bartók's Fourth String Quartet and Jimi Hendrix's "Purple Haze" on the same program suggests how far we have come in freeing ourselves from cultural stereotyping.

Yet while many listeners may disavow a cultural hierarchy, the idea of a pantheon has remained. The values that gave rise to the hierarchy persist. Both the Kronos String Quartet's programming of "Purple Haze" and the lyrics to Chuck Berry's "Roll Over Beethoven" are based on those values. Each depends for effect on the juxtaposition of relatively alien elements in the cultural hierarchy. An audience for whom a duality no longer mattered would miss much of the satire of Chuck Berry's lyrics and the apparent incongruity of the Kronos' performance.

Rock drummer Stewart Copeland's experience in the world of opera reflects the continuing presence of the cultural duality. Copeland described his introduction to opera as follows: "I went to see *Salomé*. Complete failure to connect. . . . I was stuck in this seat with this pounding, turgid music going 'arg, arg, arg.' I didn't understand the concept of a fat lady who can sing. I hated the sounds she was making. I don't remember who she was. A major fat lady." Soon thereafter he went to see Wagner: "Everything turned. Suddenly I was around the corner and I said, "Let me hear that fat lady again."

I quote Copeland because his first trip to see *Salomé* occurred *after* David Bamberger, general director and artistic director of the Cleveland Opera, had approached him to write for the Cleveland Opera. Bamberger was candid about the venture: he wished to attract an audience that normally did not attend opera. He hoped to revitalize opera composition by bringing in a fresh face. The opera premiered in October 1989, and was not a critical success. According to Donal Henahan of the *New York Times,* the opera failed not because it was too radical but because it was too traditional. Rather than introduce some of the dynamism of rock, Copeland tried too hard to imitate nineteenth-century grand opera. A hodgepodge of clichés resulted. Copeland, successful and solidly en-sconced in the rock tradition, was apparently intimidated by the pan-theon.

Why the values of a sacralized high culture remain so powerful needs to be examined. And in spite of much that has been written about the different musical traditions in the nineteenth century, how this cultural duality came about still awaits explanation. The two questions are closely related. Not only are the emergence and growth of the duality histori-cally traceable, but, as it is a historical phenomenon, understanding its roots provides important clues to its presence today.

The concept of music as a moral force is at least as old as Plato. But there is little evidence that music was generally accepted in America as more than entertainment throughout the seventeenth and eighteenth centuries. A duality did not exist in music because the concept of high culture did not extend to music. Thus before cultural distinctions could be made about different types of music, the premise of the cultivated tradition itself had to be established. As a consequence this book is less about the duality or the divergence between two points of view than about the emergence of a second point of view—that music could be enriching. It is primarily concerned with when, where, how, and why an idealist concept of music emerged in America. This aspect of Amer-ican musical life has provided a relatively distinctive stamp to American musical developments, and its persistence has profoundly shaped Amer-ican musical institutions.

Once the tenets of the cultivated tradition were accepted, questions about whether some music was morally superior to others followed naturally. They continue. Other questions arose: What music fits into what category? What does the notion of enrichment itself mean? Today, as symphony orchestras broaden their repertoire, as certain types of jazz and rock music are accorded the status of "art" (a term loosely used and seldom defined), questions of definition are raised again and again. Sometimes they are articulated as such, sometimes not. Fundamental questions about the ultimate purpose and potential of music in terms of both society and the individual nevertheless underlie them.

The programming of the Kronos String Quartet as well as Bamberger's attempt to form an operatic bridge to the world of rock disclose a fundamental rethinking of the cultivated tradition since Hitchcock's formulation. In the late twentieth century, the term *highbrow* has an elitist connotation, at variance with the democratizing tendencies of American culture. The result, however, has simply been an abandonment of the term, not of the tendencies that define high culture. Highbrow, high culture, and the cultivated tradition have become terms with which our society is not entirely comfortable. But musical idealism is still equated with the term *art*. Like *classical music*, the terms *art* and its derivative *artist* are used loosely and without precise definition. Lawrence Kramer limits his *Music as Cultural Practice, 1800–1900* to art music composed between 1798 and 1888. Kramer is aware of the limitation; he points out that he did not intend to be exclusionary but chose to deal with a specific body of music. I am not objecting to Kramer's decision. What I find significant is that he felt no need to define further what he meant by art music. Kramer assumed the term to be a common one, generally understood by the sophisticated musical audience to whom his book is addressed. But during the past several decades experimentalists in all of the arts have exploited the ambiguity associated with the term by consciously and systematically challenging the very concept of art itself. There is, nevertheless, just as in Kramer's thought, a recognition both by the public and by the practitioners themselves that what certain composers or performers are doing is art. The work of the Beatles, Dizzy Gillespie, Cole Porter, Josh White, Mel Tormé, or Ella Fitzgerald, for example, transcends entertainment and is considered within the realm of art. I cite musicians who established their reputation in the past, because the determination of what is art or artistic as opposed to what is merely entertainment in the contemporary world is often controversial. Yet this distinction persists and it very much affects the worth we attach to musical activity.

Musical idealism served the purposes of high culture for much of its history in the United States, but such idealism need not be limited to high culture. This recognition, although mostly tacit, underlies the shifting and at times confusing standards of American musical culture today. The idea of the pantheon is not dying out. Rather, its application is broadening, as more diverse groups are pressing for membership in it. Musicians in many styles have consciously attempted to redefine their music in terms of art. This happened to jazz in the early 1940s, with the advent of bebop. Jazz musicians went from being popular stars, like

Benny Goodman or the Dorsey Brothers, to being withdrawn, remote, and contemptuous of their audience. They became nineteenth-century bohemian musicians. The transition involved several factors: economic changes brought on by the Second World War, the recording ban between 1942 and 1944, and racism. But bebop musicians did consciously distance themselves from their public, emulating in their own manner the romantic stereotype of an artist. The same evolution is under way in rock, with publicly perceived differences between top-forty rock and a group such as the Fugs.

The distinction between the cultivated and the vernacular traditions, while having historical value, no longer serves to distinguish music as art from music as entertainment. We seek to embrace folk, ethnic, and popular art as a counter to the divisive tendencies of high culture. Yet we do it within the premises of art, applying the ideals of the cultivated tradition to other traditions. And we do it uncertainly, bringing many of the prejudices of high culture with us. The result can be dissonant, creating conflicting concepts about art, culture, and idealism. The result can be ponderous, attaching a seriousness and hidden meaning to music that is meant to be nothing more than good-time fun. But the result can also be stimulative, allowing new forms and styles to emerge unbound by the limitations of previous conceptualizations. The nineteenth-century pantheon has been growing ever since its inception. John S. Dwight, writing in the late nineteenth century, had difficulty allowing the pantheon to extend beyond Beethoven, and he absolutely would not recognize Wagner. Even Brahms troubled him. The quasi-religious associations that Dwight and others attached to high culture severely limited consideration of many vibrant musical types. The extreme ethnocentricity that characterized this vision of the pantheon not only has no place in the global, diverse world of the late twentieth century but is also inherently contradictory to the concept of art at its purest, which was Dwight's goal.

I do not propose any universal answers to what the term *art* means in the late twentieth century, or to the nuances by which musical idealism is explained and propagated. The duality between music as art and music as entertainment still exists in American culture, even though the ground under each has become more elusive. I believe that if we understand how a musical idealism arose in America we can better understand what it does and does not mean today, what it applies to, and how it has shaped our perceptions about music. We can better judge the place of music in American society and address music's political and social ramifications. Finally, we can better distinguish our own preferences. Answers to many of these questions have tangible consequences. At the personal level they influence our attitudes, our social life, and even our beliefs. At the institutional level they directly affect both private and public patterns of patronage and financial support.

The development of a musical idealism in America occurred in several stages. It was shaped primarily through reforms and attempted reforms that began just prior to the Great Awakening, an evangelical movement in New England in the early eighteenth century. It then reached a climax with the hymnodic reformers of the early nineteenth century and extended to encompass the secular through the transcendental-romantic movement. Even with the transcendentalists, however, the puritan influence is manifest. American musical culture owes much more than is usually granted to this puritanical heritage. And the reforms of the early nineteenth century were more than simply religious movements. They were responses to fundamental changes in the nature of American society, changes that touched all aspects of American life, both secular and sacred.

Several shifts of attitude toward music occurred in eighteenth- and early nineteenth-century America. Prior to 1800 music was considered entertainment. Its sensuous, passionate qualities were recognized, although sometimes in a negative context (especially in New England). Its bacchanalian qualities could lead one to lewd and lascivious conduct, particularly while dancing. It could possess one, diverting one from important tasks. In church unrestrained singing threatened the authority of the clergy as well as the decorum of the service.

The positive moral effects of music began to be recognized around 1800. At first this recognition was limited almost completely to sacred music. Church-music reformers realized that the right kind of music could help establish the proper atmosphere for the church service just as the wrong kind of music could destroy it. An extended debate began about what constituted proper and improper music, and many of the ideas advanced were later transferred directly to secular music.

The idea that secular music could reflect positive as well as negative moral values began to take hold only in the 1830s and 1840s. Instrumental music, because of its abstract nature, posed a special problem. Its very abstractness, however, became an asset. Unfettered by text, it could be elevated to a plane of moral purity and universality that no vocal music could match. Transcendentalism, which emphasized such abstract thought, was particularly sympathetic to this line of reasoning.

Most scholars consider the decisive triumph of European art music in urban centers in the nineteenth century one of the critical turning points in the development of an American musical aesthetic. And almost without exception they trace this development to early nineteenth-century hymnodic reformers who sought to replace the music of late eighteenth-century psalmody with that written in a more "correct" or "scientific" style. The terms *correct* and *scientific* are the reformers' own, and European music served as their models. From the position of the hymnodic reformers the elevation of European art music, particularly symphonic music, to the apex of a pyramid of musical values was a natural evolutionary step. In 1882 Louis Elson noted the direct connection between psalmody and symphonic music in Boston:

> Orchestral music in old Boston practically began with the old Academy of Music, founded in 1833 by Messrs. William C. Woodbridge, Lowell Mason and George J. Webb. . . . At the end of nine years good work, it was resolved to change the character of the institution, and that "instead of continuing its vocal concerts, in which it cannot do more or better than its neighbors, the Academy has concluded to engage the best orchestra it can afford, and give classical instrumental concerts." This proceeding meant a great deal. It practically sealed the fate of psalm singing as the chief music of Boston, and substituted the symphony for the weaker music which had obtained up to that time.[7]

Elson's characterization of psalmody as the weaker music summarizes the bias of his generation. More broadly, the change in public preference from psalmody to symphony can serve as a metaphor for musical developments in urban areas in the nineteenth century. Events in Boston in the 1830s were particularly crucial to those developments. First, from the time of Lowell Mason and John S. Dwight to the Second New England School of composers Boston provided a large degree of musical leadership for the country. Second, the perception of Boston as the leader in aesthetic issues, encompassing but not limited to music, was prevalent in the country even before *Dwight's Journal of Music* appeared in 1852. And finally, the specific issue of psalmody to symphony was played out with clarity and consistency in Boston, where the two types of music assumed an unparalleled role in the musical life of the community. Nowhere else is the evolutionary development from psalmody to symphony more clearly documented in its direct impact on specific institutions. And nowhere else were the participants more aware of its significance. Mason and Dwight, as champions of psalmody and symphony, respectively, reflected the development specifically in their activities and writings.

Elson's comment also reflects the importance attached to the symphony by the late nineteenth century. Since no writer in the nineteenth century believed that all instrumental music was morally uplifting, the issue became what instrumental music was, and why. The response favored the symphony. Romantic thoiught had glorified the symphony, and this thinking extended to America. In addition, aesthetic ideas with roots deep in the American religious experience elevated the abstract over the concrete in musical choices. One senses a certain hindsight justification in the writings of those involved, but the propagandist efforts of early nineteenth-century writers on behalf of symphonic music worked. By the mid-1840s the symphony orchestra was considered on a different artistic level from other instrumental ensembles, and the symphonies of Mozart, Haydn, and especially Beethoven had begun to assume a status never before accorded instrumental music.

This development raises another set of questions that have concerned both musicians and historians for more than a century. To what degree does American musical life correspond to that of Europe? Is high culture in America an extension of European culture or has America found its own musical voice? Or does this issue no longer matter in the global society of the late twentieth century? Answers to many of these questions can be found in the historical framework from which the cultural distinctions emerged. I shall show that, while American musical culture does closely follow European patterns and models, it was shaped by values and historical events that have no European counterpart. These values have been fundamental in defining American society. As a result, America's musical life today is unique. Many aspects of American musical culture, from the most tangible consequences of patronage and financial support to the most basic personal attitudes about music and music making, can be understood only when their specifically American roots are uncovered.

The increasing predominance of European music in urban areas in the nineteenth century has been viewed with either approbation or dismay. To some scholars of an earlier generation, this development raised standards of taste and provided America with a musical culture equal to that of Europe. More recent scholars found the price too high. A burgeoning musical tradition native to America was eradicated. The newly imposed musical standards that followed were considered elitist, inconsistent with what America was all about. As a consequence of the ideological positions engendered by a European hegemony, some historical distinctions have been blurred. We need to disentangle the presence of European music and musicians, the association of European music with elitist values, the question of intrinsic musical worth, and the broader issue of national identification as manifested in music.

Nineteenth-century reformers believed that musical developments followed a relatively straight line of progress, in which newer music was qualitatively better than the music it replaced. That we no longer link evolutionary change (in music) with the certainty of improvement has formed the central basis by which the aesthetic attitudes of the reformers have been faulted. The concept of progress as espoused by the reformers was so historically suspect, however, that historians have been able to critique it without fully realizing many of its complexities. For instance, questions of religion and class are sometimes confused. The notion that music is edifying, a central thesis of the reformers, is frequently associated with an elitist attitude toward musical types and styles. A more accurate understanding of the time is possible if musical developments in the eighteenth and nineteenth centuries are viewed within the context of two sets of tensions: one between a populist and an elitist attitude toward music, and another between a conceptualization of music as entertainment and music as a moral force. The assumption that a writer or musician will lean in the same direction in relation to both tensions has undermined many interpretations of this period. Failure to take into account both has been an even more common fault. In the early nineteenth century the two tensions were sometimes complimentary (as in Dwight), frequently caused internal conflict (as in Mason), and always intermixed. The historical evolution of this period suggests a dual oscillation between the two sets that is not always in synchrony. Complex phases were created, from which musical attitudes consistent throughout urban America emerged. The nature as well as the singularity of these attitudes can be understood only when these different phases are traced. The presence of the two tensions and their unfolding is a central factor in explaining the history of this time.

Parallel developments in Europe and America in the early nineteenth century have further clouded the national or the transatlantic aspect of this question. The concept of a canon of instrumental music, centering first on the works of Haydn, Mozart, and Beethoven, appeared in both Europe and America. In many respects the canon was similar in both areas. The same composers were admitted into it, the same organizations, the symphony societies in particular, assumed leadership and then guardianship of it, and the audience profiles of each area have common characteristics. The similarities as well as the widespread musical interchange between Europe and America argue for the existence of a single transatlantic musical culture throughout much of the nineteenth century.

Yet these similarities have also concealed marked differences between the musical worlds of Europe and America. The establishment of this canon took different routes in America and Europe. It came via different institutions and was in response to different intellectual currents. As a consequence, its manifestation when it did mature had a different effect on society. In America the canon and the symphony society were not only inexorably linked, but the canon itself provided justification for the symphony society. Together they created a hierarchical attitude toward music in which aesthetic value was subordinate to moral value. The recognition that certain types of music were better than others became divorced from individual aesthetic feeling. In the gaudy world of late nineteenth-century ostentation, the classical canon furnished a showcase for those who wished to demonstrate a connection with the artistic while feeling they were accomplishing an ethical duty. A person in such circumstances need not have a clue about the inner nature of the music or feel any direct response from it. That it was morally superior was sufficient ground for supporting it. And European music seemed all the more exotic because it was three thousand miles removed and had by the late nineteenth century come to represent the same foreign element that had so troubled Mason when he went from England to the Continent in 1837.

This attitude, which created an ambivalence in the American mind about music, had a singular if not deleterious effect. A career such as Charles Ives', in which tragic elements commingle with the most quintessentially American, is both representative of and peculiar to America. The eccentric individualist has a long history in American music, from William Billings and A. P. Heinrich through Ives to Harry Partch, John Cage, and Conlon Nancarrow. While his individuality is much respected, those forces that drove him into the isolation from which it sprang have not always helped to build a stronger musical culture.

In America the canon developed against a political background that pitted the most fundamental ideas of the early republic against newer attitudes toward taste, which tended to be hierarchical, authoritarian, and elitist. Early nineteenth-century advocates of the development of a musical art, including the hymnodic reformers, felt that music must have a democratic basis to develop in America. This was consistent with the republican spirit prevalent at the time. A musical aesthetic based on an elitist attitude about taste emerged only after a long struggle that the reformers ultimately lost. That struggle was centered in Boston and has gone largely unnoticed in musical scholarship. Its effects, however, were profound. The dichotomization of musical culture into classical and popular can be traced directly to it.

To explain the establishment of American musical culture as a struggle between democratic-leaning versus aristocratic-leaning class groups would oversimplify both class stratification in antebellum America and the actual course of the formation of musical attitudes. The process occurred in several steps, in which some of the participants held positions that seem internally contradictory. Thus the hymnodic reformers could argue strongly for improvement of taste and the betterment of individuals through music that was morally superior, yet hold the most democratic views about music for the people. At the same time, many members of the socioeconomic elite argued the importance of populist musical institutions in a democratic society, while believing just as fervently that control of such institutions could not be in the hands of the practitioners.

Many perceptions about the nature of instrumental music can be traced to ideas about music and religion, and much antebellum writing about secular instrumental music is saturated with rhetoric derived from religion. As a historical phenomenon religion influenced not only culture; in its complexity it affected many other spheres as well. Class and religion were related but not congruent. One overlay the other, and each created a set of attitudes that directly affected musical developments.

My principal thesis is that American musical culture, in spite of its close ties to Europe, developed a distinctive profile as a result of certain cultural forces, intellectual traditions, and political developments whose evolution was unique to America. These are Puritanism and its offspring, Evangelicalism; psalmodic reform and its progeny, the singing school; the frontier and the reaction that its life-style produced in the East; and attitudes toward class and democratization. None of these forces is exclusively American. Even the frontier only replicated a pattern that had occurred a few centuries earlier in parts of England and Scotland. The interactions and offshoots they engendered, however, created a framework that had no European equivalent. When viewed as a direct product of this framework the special nature of American musical culture becomes more apparent, and its course of evolution can be better understood.

The develoment of a cultural hierarchy, particularly in music, began in Boston in the 1830s. While New York had become the concert capital of the United States by the middle of the nineteenth century, Boston maintained an intellectual leadership in music throughout the nineteenth century. Numerous articles in nineteenth-century journals attest to Boston's preeminence in providing a new musical aesthetic in America.[8] The Puritans had built a society nurtured and sustained on rhetoric. This tendency later translated into literary movements, which did not ignore music. A series of remarkable journals, some literary and some devoted exclusively to music, emanated from Boston in the nineteenth century. The most important of these for musical developments were the *North American Review,* the *Euterpeiad,* the *Musical Magazine,* the transcendental journals, the *Dial* and the *Harbinger,* and finally *Dwight's Journal of Music.* In them New Englanders argued at length about the relative merits of different types of music and the place of music in society. Through these journals and through lectures by Bostonians, new ideas about the nature of music spread nationwide.

The contributions of Bostonians were not purely theoretical, however. The emergence of a dualistic musical culture pivoted around a redefinition of instrumental music that occurred in Boston between 1830 and 1840. It was prompted as much by the efforts of pioneering institutions to present instrumental music to the Boston public as it was by the members of those institutions to explain their endeavors. As late as the early 1830s psalmody still prevailed in Boston. Secular instrumental concerts could not be sustained. But by the early 1840s the day of the psalmodic reformer was essentially over. At least two symphony orchestras and one chamber-music series were in place. The significant historical fact about musical activity in Boston in the 1840s is not the extent to which psalmody and sacred-music was resisted or accepted but the extent to which it was ignored. By then instrumental music was generating an audience and a critical literature that explained its purpose and provided justification for its existence. Ironically those institutions that had spearheaded the reform of sacred music now led the change.

Documents of this shift are plentiful, detailed, and specific. The principals provided sufficient explanation of their motives for us to understand not only what happened but also why it did. The issue is demonstrably related to class and religion. I shall sketch a scene of a Boston in the 1820s and 1830s torn by two principal social factions. Each represented important but very different segments of society. Each was interested in promoting its own type of music. But in the end each needed and used the other as the overlap of their interests ultimately overcame the divergence of their positions. The overlap did not last long, as one faction was fading and the other ascendant. Out of that overlap, however, an American musical aesthetic was forged.

Chapter One

Boston's Place in the American Musical World

Musical life in Boston changed profoundly in the half-century between the founding of the theater in the 1790s and the proliferation of secular concert organizations in the 1840s. These changes emerged from the dominant themes of New England life: religion, rhetoric, and class. A rising secularism forced psalmody, the prevailing music early in the century, to give way to instrumental genres. Rhetorical arguments about music convinced many Bostonians that music merited the same serious consideration as literature. Patronage shifted as the upper class, formerly aloof from public musical activities, assumed control of some of the most important concert organizations in the city.

In many ways the changes mirror American society. In other ways they are unique to Boston. In spite of Boston's exceptionalism, however, they had a profound impact on the direction of American music. For in defining its own musical culture, Boston provided an ideological framework for the rest of the country. Bostonians accepted secular music only after some resistance and only by coming to terms with their own puritan heritage. That process sparked a considerable debate, in which Bostonians defined an idealistic vision of music that ultimately prevailed nationwide. The shape of high musical culture that has dominated America since the late nineteenth century can be traced directly to Boston in the 1830s and 1840s, when the symphony replaced the psalm.

Boston's influence on American culture in the early nineteenth century far outweighed its demographic and geographic importance. Boston was dwarfed in size by both New York and Philadelphia. New York grew dramatically after the opening of the Erie Canal in 1825: in 1800 it had a population of 61,000; by 1840 it had grown to 312,000. Boston was by contrast still a small town; its 1800 population of 24,937 had increased to 93,383 by 1840. This put it in fourth place, smaller than New York, Philadelphia, and Baltimore. All four American cities, however, were much smaller than the largest European cities. By 1800 London had a population of more than a million, and Paris more than a half-million. Also, Boston was reasonably isolated. As the northernmost large city in the country, it was relatively removed from the mid-Atlantic hub of Baltimore to New York; to reach a southern city like

Charleston or Savannah required a journey of a month or more. When Lowell Mason went from Boston to Savannah in the fall of 1812, it took fifty-five days. On average he was able to cover slightly less than twenty miles a day.

As Mason's account vividly illustrates, travel between cities before the railroad was difficult and time consuming. Boston's isolation may have been somewhat greater than that of other cities because of its location and unique cultural heritage, but it was not untypical. Travelers throughout America were forced to use the same bad roads that had existed in colonial times, and water travel was little better. The three-day stagecoach journey from Philadelphia to Baltimore, a distance of ninety miles, cost about twenty-one dollars, a huge sum in 1800. Since communication depended on the same means of transportation, it too was slow and uncertain. Mail service was so bad that it was little used. In 1800 the post office delivered approximately 2,900,000 letters, about one letter per person per year.[2] Communication would not improve dramatically until the development of the railroad and the telegraph.

Thus problems of travel and communication impeded the development of a national cultural outlook and encouraged separate regional musical profiles. Boston was not bucking a trend or challenging other cities for national leadership in music in the early nineteenth century, mainly because no one city stood out as the musical capital of the United States. Regionalism was promoted too by the sparseness of formal secular musical activity. Compared to later in the nineteenth century, concerts were relatively infrequent, and to consider one city the envy of others because of its concert life exaggerates the importance of concerts during the early Federal period. Public support for professional performing musicians was so weak that the struggle for the acceptance of music was historically more important than the relative breadth of concert activity in different cities.

Limited concert possibilities dispersed musicians up and down the East Coast. Because they could not earn a living from concerts, almost all musicians who came to America in the early Federal period were forced to establish varied careers in one city as both orchestral and solo performers, as leaders of musical organizations, as teachers, as publishers, and as music dealers. Some even moonlighted in unrelated vocations. A musician tended to remain in one place only so long as he could find support. Thus, for example, George K. Jackson arrived in Boston in 1812, having worked his way up the East Coast without finding prospects to his liking. After establishing himself first with the Brattle Street church and then the Handel and Haydn Society, he remained in Boston. Gottlieb Graupner came to Boston because his wife, Catherine Hellyer, was a member of the Federal Street Theatre company. He quickly found a niche as an extremely competent orchestra musician, from which he expanded into several other spheres of the musical business, including publishing. Musicians followed similar patterns in other cities: Alexander Reinagle and Benjamin Carr in Philadelphia and James Hewitt in New York, although he also spent several years in Boston.

Musical activity in 1810 did not run the gamut from simple vernacular song to elaborate high-culture productions as it did later in the century. Although music from the most unpretentious folk songs heard on the street to formal concert presentations existed, the difference between what was heard on the street and in the concert hall was not great. A formal concert was as likely to include a popular ballad, a catch, or a hymn as a concerto or symphony. In the theater the audience often demanded what was sung on the streets and expected the orchestra to play tunes yelled from the audience. Music was entertainment. It was pleasure, generally unselfconscious, unexamined, and lacking any moral imperative beyond providing enjoyment. Secular music was simply not associated with high culture.

Few considered the possibility that music could make one better; those who did, restricted their thoughts to church music. There were of course writers and music lovers who maintained that some kinds of music were of higher quality than others, but the Platonic notion that music was a means of enrichment, and that society should pay attention to secular music as a way of creating better, more moral people, was foreign. And because the music profession was still in its infancy, distinctions between professional and amateur performers were much less clearly drawn than they were later. Music was largely informal, presented in settings that allowed easy interchange between performer and listener, at times blurring the boundary entirely.

Vocal music predominated in most cities. Much of it was sacred, although it was frequently performed in secular settings. Participation was more common than passive listening. Psalms were sung at home, if for no other reason than the tunes were familiar and well liked. The singing school was found throughout much of the country, although it was more popular in New England than elsewhere. And even though psalmody was taught at the singing school, the school itself was essentially a secular, social activity. Usually meeting on a weekday evening, it was attended primarily by young men and women, not least for the obvious social benefits.

From top to bottom American musical society had a strong British flavor. It is hard to know precisely what the stevedore working on the docks or the housewife cooking a meal on an open hearth sang, but we know that a thriving trade in broadside ballads existed in most cities. The broadside ballad was a single sheet of text sold on the streets for a penny or two. In content and distribution it resembled what was sold in England. The songs could be topical or traditional; they could be about recent events, such as the War of 1812, more distant events, such as the revolutionary war, or personal stories of love, deception, and daily turns of fate. The broadside contained no music, only the suggestion that a certain well-known tune be used. The ballads were intended for the "vulgar," as the publisher Isaiah Thomas noted in 1814 about a collection of three hundred that had appeared in Boston during the previous four years.[3]

Somewhat more respectable to men like Thomas were collections of songs that began to appear around 1810, although they differed from the broadside ballads more in presentation than in musical content. Music was composed anew specifically for the text, and a full musical score was published. Most of these collections originated in the British Isles, the most important coming from Ireland. Thomas Moore published his first set of *Irish Melodies* in 1808, and it quickly became popular on both sides of the Atlantic. G. E. Blake of Philadelphia, unhindered at the time by copyright restrictions, duplicated the first volume within a year, and by 1811 twelve of Moore's songs appeared in the *Boston Musical Miscellany*.

Collections like Moore's bridged the gap between street balladry and the parlor song. By the late nineteenth century the parlor song had become the epitome of middle-class middlebrow gentility, a genre replete with sentimentality, moralism, and mawkish pretense. In 1810 the parlor song was in its infancy because the parlor, with its piano over which the lady of the house presided, was limited to wealthy citizens who could afford a piano; and the moralism that the parlor song preached remained only vaguely defined. Although many songs of the early nineteenth century did have a moral, the virtues of the parlor, instilling seriousness, sobriety, propriety, and decorum, were in the process of formation. And before the parlor song could assume its moral function, the idea that secular music could carry a message of edification and enrichment had to be accepted. In that sense the parlor song as a middlebrow phenomenon could exist only as a spin-off from the musical idealism that created high musical culture. Such idealism had not yet crystallized in America in 1810.

Music in the theater resembled the street ballad. The theater in America was a British institution, managed by Britons who presented British plays featuring British actors. Operas were common in the theater, but most were the English ballad operas of the eighteenth century. When Italian opera was performed, it was presented in English adaptations that diverged considerably from the original. The libretto was often rearranged, characters were changed or dropped, new tunes were added, and original arias removed. The theater was designed to attract all elements of society, and audiences were anything but restrained and decorous, frequently hurling objects at members of the cast and the orchestra. Because of the rowdy quality of the theater, it had a generally unsavory reputation in early Federal America and was at times considered a place where respectable women did not go.

The modern symphony orchestra as an institution did not exist in America. Orchestral music was presented at concerts, but often by hastily arranged ensembles, whose instrumentation ranged from haphazard to outlandish and whose performance level was frequently abysmal. The essential problem was a lack of competent instrumentalists. Whatever professional instrumental players were available were usually connected with a theater, the only organization that could offer regular employment. The most serious problem was a lack of string players. From the revolutionary war on, the tradition of the military band was strong in America, and Americans grew up familiar with and playing wind instruments. Although the term *band* was a generic one, referring to any combination of strings and winds, to an American in 1810 an instrumental ensemble most often meant a military band, not a symphony orchestra.

The association of band instruments with the militia and the piano with the parlor resulted in well-defined gender stereotyping. In families that could afford a piano, girls were expected to learn to play it. Young men interested in instrumental music were expected to play a wind instrument. The flute was the most popular and most acceptable instrument, followed closely by the clarinet. Brass instruments were common but not as popular, and interest in the other woodwinds was slight, partly because of the difficulty of mastering a double reed. There was little overlap between expected male and female performance roles. Although a young man might occasionally learn to play the piano or the organ, young women simply did not play wind instruments. When tracing all professional and amateur instrumental players who performed publicly in Boston between 1796 and 1842 (see Appendixes 1 and 2), I found no reference to a woman playing a wind instrument, either in public or in private.

String instruments had two common functions in early nineteenth-century America. The violin or fiddle was associated with dancing, and the bass viol or cello accompanied hymns in church. Dancing was a favorite pastime of early Federal America, even in Boston. Dancing masters used a fiddle as accompaniment, and there was only a single fiddler to provide the music at many dances. Sometimes the music would be more elaborate, performed by a small band whose composition reflected available instrumental forces more than any defined standard. Dances often followed concerts that featured an orchestra, with the dance advertised as part of the evening's entertainment. Many dance tunes familiar to fiddlers today were played then. Reels, jigs, and hornpipes were popular; waltzes too were played, although the waltz craze was still about ten years away. In fact, the repertoire and style of current old-time country fiddling probably represents the closest continuous link that we have to the sounds and style of early Federal music.

Only a few of the wealthiest churches had organs in 1810. Accompaniment to singing, where it was not proscribed, consisted of a small ensemble that often contained flutes and clarinets. The instrument that anchored the singing, however, was the bass viol, which was a somewhat oversized cello with a short neck. The bass viol added a bass line, providing a harmonic foundation. The part was often improvised. Lowell Mason, who grew up playing the cello and clarinet, once referred to "catching" the accompaniment on the bass viol. Less often the bass line would be played by instruments like the bassoon, or even the ophicleide or serpent. The latter two were brass instruments that are no longer commonly used.

Musical activity in America changed dramatically in the 1830s and 1840s. A different type of professional musician, the touring virtuoso, began to appear, and a concert circuit emerged, encompassing the principal cities and sometimes extending far into the hinterlands. Two changes in American society made the development of the concert tour possible: increased travel and commerce between different sections of the country, and increased audience interest in virtuosic performance. A boom in turnpike building lasted from approximately 1810 to 1820, after which the newly developed steamboat spurred a rush to build inland waterways. Then the railroad boom began in the 1830s, opening up space in a way that no other development did. Unlike waterways, railroads could be laid anywhere, and unlike turnpikes, which followed older roads, they increased speed dramatically. When the Philadelphia-Wilmington-Baltimore line opened in 1838, it cut the three-day stage ride from Philadelphia to Baltimore to less than five hours.

Getting to a town, however, did the virtuoso little good if no audience was interested in hearing him. Significant changes in public tastes closely paralleled the development of more efficient means of transportation. Tempting as it is to attribute the greater acceptance of instrumental music to increased accessibility to the virtuoso, the situation was more complex than that. Before the virtuoso could influence the course of American concert life, audiences had to become amenable to his offerings. The status of instrumental music itself had to improve. The virtuoso actually did much toward that end, but fundamental changes in attitudes about music were necessary before audiences could become receptive to the dazzling feats of the virtuoso. How and why that happened is what this book is about.

As musicians crisscrossed the country, concert activity developed a sameness from city to city. George Knoop, Leopold Herwig, John Nagel, Leopold Meyer, Louis Rakeman, C. Kossowski, Henri Viextemps, and Ole Bull, for instance, all gave concerts in both New York and Boston in the early 1840s. Boston musicians like James and Edward Kendall and William Keyser performed in New York, both as virtuosi and as leaders of ensembles. The concert circuits also promoted the settlement of musicians in different cities. Herwig chose to remain in Boston after playing there, and when the Germania Society's orchestra decided to disband in 1854, many of its members chose to settle in Boston because of the enthusiastic reception the orchestra had received.

The development of the virtuoso circuit was part of a broader tendency toward cultural standardization that occurred between 1820 and 1850. Writers were aware that the cultural life of the principal American cities was becoming more uniform. The *New England Magazine* referred to this development in 1835. An anonymous article stated that with the repeal of the antitheater law in Boston in 1792, the lessening of puritan antipathy toward the theater, and the greater intercourse between Boston, New York, and Philadelphia, a "uniformity of taste and fashion in regard to manners and amusements was the natural consequence."[4]

Musical events in Boston and New York in the early 1840s in particular paralleled each other. Not only did the same virtuosi appear in both cities, but similar musical organizations came to the fore. Each city established its first successful symphony orchestra during that time; the Boston Academy of Music orchestra and the Philharmonic Society of New York. The Boston Academy of Music, which had been leaning in the direction of instrumental music since 1835, gave its first predominantly orchestral concert on November 14, 1840. The academy's orchestra performed its first Beethoven symphony, No. 1, on February 13, 1841. On March 27, 1841, it performed Beethoven's Fifth Symphony. The Philharmonic Society of New York, the current organization, gave its first concert on December 7, 1842, performing Beethoven's Fifth Symphony. Since Beethoven symphonies were considered the core of the musical canon in the nineteenth century, scholars have found their performance an important measure of a city's musical sophistication.

These dates suggest that Boston and New York were neck and neck in the race to establish a musical culture based on classical instrumental music. The fact of a performance is less important than its reception, however, if the question is the development or the awakening of attitudes toward specific types of music. In developing audience support for instrumental music Boston was considerably ahead of New York. The performance history of Beethoven's Fifth Symphony, in particular, illustrates the importance of considering a performance's context. The Fifth was performed first in New York, on February 11, 1841, in a concert sponsored by the German Society of New York. It was essentially a German event, played to an audience consisting mostly of German immigrants; George Templeton Strong commented that the place was "jammed with Dutchmen like a barrel of Dutch herrings," and that he "scarcely saw an Anglo-Saxon physiognomy in the whole gallery."[5] The first Boston performance of the Fifth Symphony took place two months later, presented by the Boston Academy of Music, whose concerts attracted the principal supporters of music in the city. More important, the academy repeated the performance a week later, and altogether played it nineteen times during the following six years.[6] It was this repetition that established the work with audiences. When Christopher Pierce Cranch reviewed a performance of it by the Philharmonic Society of New York in the 1844–45 season, he observed that it had been some time since he originally heard it in Boston, and that hearing it again was an even greater experience, "for a great work like this needs to be heard many times to be fully appreciated."[7]

John S. Dwight considered the repetitions of Beethoven's Fifth Symphony a pivotal event in the history of music in America. In his review of the Boston Academy of Music's concerts during the 1844–45 season, he claimed that "the history of Beethoven in Boston" dated from the "performance and subsequent frequent repetition" of the Fifth Symphony by the academy, and that these performances established a "living bond of union between audience and performers, an initiation into a deeper life."[8] Years later Dwight twice alluded to those performances; in the *Atlantic Monthly*, he claimed that "the first great awakening of the musical instinct here was when the C-minor Symphony of Beethoven was played [by the Academy of Music]."[9] In the *Memorial History of Boston*, Dwight considered the importance of the Beethoven performances by the Boston Academy of Music Orchestra: "But it will readily be seen that early experience of seven years' exposure to Beethoven programmes must, in spite of all shortcomings in performance, have set Boston well on the way to an appreciation of the best in music. Many can remember how eagerly these concerts were sought, how frequently the audience was large, and what a theme of enthusiastic comment and congratulation these first fresh hearings of the great masters was."[10]

The importance of considering reception in assessing musical activity can also be seen in the respective fates of string-quartet concerts in New York and Boston. The first series was given in New York in 1843, but it had little impact; the presenters were hard-pressed to sell tickets, and no similar series was attempted again until 1849. The Harvard Musical Associations string-quartet concerts in Boston did not begin until 1845, but they were successful; they were followed by two more quartet series in the 1840s and generated enough interest in string chamber music to encourage the formation of other ensembles, such as the Mendelssohn Quintet Club.

It may be argued that Boston could boast a concert life comparable in quality to that of New York and other cities in the first half of the nineteenth century. Although Boston lagged far behind in some areas, such as opera, in other areas, such as choral performance earlier in the century and instrumental performance later, the principal musical organizations in Boston presented better, more innovative, and more widely received performances than musical organizations anywhere else in the country. Throughout the nineteenth century many writers recognized the importance of Boston as a musical center. Some of the statements, such as Dwight's in the *Herald* in 1888, in an article entitled "Boston a Musical Center. Her Claims of Pre-eminence Not an Empty Boast," are hardly unbiased. Dwight referred to "the Hub's acknowledged supremacy as an art, literary and musical center" and to "Boston's unique position among American cities," while defending the musical sophistication and enthusiasm of Boston audiences.[11] Henry Cleveland argued that the Boston Academy of Music did more to advance the cause of music in ten years "than the New York Opera could have effected in ten centuries."[12]

Cleveland, like Dwight, was a Bostonian and a member of the Harvard Musical Association. But the *Musical Review and Record of Musical Science, Literature, and Intelligence*, published in New York, announced that it was going to watch events in Boston closely. "Boston professes to take the lead of all other cities in the Union, but in devotion to music and in the institutions for its perpetuation and improvement," partly because of "the strong hold which the Bostonians have gained upon the public confidence in regard to musical attainments."[13] And in England the *Musical World*, in an article that for the most part spoke disparagingly about music in America, referred to Boston as "the emporium of Music; where it [music] is cultivated with the real zeal for the welfare of the art." The *Musical World* observed also that Bostonians considered their musical attainments equal to those of London, and it referred to the Boston Academy of Music "under the conduct of Dr. Mason." Since Lowell Mason had been in London in May, June, September, and October of 1837, it is not hard to speculate where the *Musical World* got its information.[14]

Statements such as these, however, do little more than give some credence to Bostonian claims of importance, although they do suggest that musical activity and audience sophistication in Boston was not far behind those of other cities. The importance of Boston as a national influence on American music, however, resided in another sphere: the intellectual consideration of music. The intensity, sophistication, and range of the debate that New Englanders in the Boston area waged over the nature and purpose of music in American society was unprecedented. From this debate, which I shall trace in ensuing chapters, came ideas that not only provided the institutional framework within which music would be presented but also shaped the attitudes of many Americans nationwide about what music was and how it should be approached.

Music was debated in both literary and musical journals, and New Englanders far outstripped the rest of the country with their contributions. Fourteen of the thirty music journals that appeared in America between 1818 and 1845 were published in Boston; nine were published in New York, and three in Philadelphia. As table 1 indicates, as many musical journals were published in Bellows Falls, Vermont, during that time as in Philadelphia. Yet the total number of journals published is not an accurate record of the extent to which music was broadly and seriously discussed, because only a few of these publications actually entered the debate about the nature of music in America. Many were specialized journals, dealing with just one aspect of music, such as the *Juvenile Minstrel* and the *Singer*, which dealt with music education and children's songs, or the *Boston Musical Gazette* and the *Musical Review*, which purported to be broader but served mainly to discuss church music from the Presbyterian-Congregational hymnists' point of view. Other journals, such as the *Lady's Musical Library* and the *Seraph*, were simply collections of music, with little or no commentary.

The two most important journals published during the first half of the nineteenth century were the *Euterpeiad; or Musical Intelligencer*, edited by John Rowe Parker, which began publication in 1820, and the *Musical Magazine*, edited by Theodore Hach, which began in 1839.[15] Both originated in Boston. Although the journals reprinted material from Europe, both also considered serious criticism and evaluation of concerts integral to their purpose. Such criticism, by nature implying standards, served to educate the public toward a more sophisticated understanding of music. Accused of being too critical, Hach published a lengthy article in 1840 explaining his position. He justified taking a "high standard" through an idealistic conception of the musical art, claiming that the critic must "have art, pure art alone in view, as the ultimate object of what falls under his notice." He admitted that an interest in music had only recently appeared in America, and he found this cause for vigilance: with the rapid expansion of music, "erroneous habits and views" had to be opposed and music had still to be freed from many predjudices.[16]

Other journals that attempted a critical treatment of music were either less sophisticated in their writing or plainly derivative. The *Lyre*, for instance, published in New York in 1824 and 1825, borrowed most of its articles particularly from European magazines. Almost all editors did that, including Parker and Hach, but little else about music appeared in the *Lyre*. Some concerts in New York, especially by the New York Choral Society, were reported; most of the many secular concerts were not. General articles on music or the philosophy of music were mostly recounts of ancient views, either what Plato and Aristotle said or what the Bible says of the effects of music. The *Lyre* lacked editorial vision; its editors provided no statement on what they believed music and its potential to be, and the articles do little to clarify that. Derivative journals include the New York *Euterpeiad* of 1830 and the *Literary and Musical*

Table 1
American Musical Journals Between 1818 and 1845

Title	Year	Place
Literary and Musical Magazine	1819	New York
Weekly Musical Visitor	1819	New York*
Euterpeiad; or, Musical Intelligencer	1820	Boston
Lyre	1824	New York
American Minstrel	1828	Providence, R.I.
Theatrical Censor and Musical Review	1828	Philadelphia
Euterpeiad	1830	New York
American Musical Journal	1834	New York
Family Minstrel	1835	New York
Musical Magazine	1835	New York
Musical Library	1835	Boston
Musical Library	1837	Not located*
Boston Musical Gazette	1838	Boston
Musical Review	1838	New York
Seraph	1838	Boston
Musical Magazine	1839	Boston
American Journal of Music	1840	Boston
World of Music	1840	Bellows Falls, Vt.
Juvenile Minstrel	1840	Boston
Singer	1840	Boston
Philadelphia Journal	1840	Philadelphia**
Musical Almanac	1841	Boston
Musical Reporter	1841	Boston
Musical Advertiser	1841	Boston
Musical Cabinet	1841	Boston
Lady's Musical Library	1842	Philadelphia
World of Music	1843	Bellows Falls, Vt.
Orpheus	1843	Boston
New York Musical Chronicle and Advertiser	1843	New York
Musical Album	1844	New York

*Announced but probably did not appear.
**No known copies.

Magazine of 1819, which actually preceded the original *Euterpeiad*. The *Euterpeiad* of 1830 was a direct descendent of Parker's journal and was founded by Charles Dingley, who had assumed editorship of the earlier *Euterpeiad* in 1823. The Philadelphia *Literary and Musical Magazine* was modeled on the British *Quarterly Musical Magazine and Review*. In its last year it took to borrowing directly from Parker's *Euterpeiad*, a fact that probably hastened its demise.

As table 1 indicates, the journals were not distributed evenly throughout the period. There is a twelve-year hiatus in the publication of musical journals in Boston, from 1823, when Parker's *Euterpeiad* folded, until 1835, when the *Musical Library*, the house organ of the Boston Academy of Music, appeared. The *Musical Library* survived for only one year, after which no other journal appeared for two more years. Then between 1838 and 1843 eleven music journals surfaced in Boston. During the hiatus in Boston, music journals flourished in New York, but after 1838, when publication activity resumed with vigor in Boston, no critical journals for the general population were published in New York.[17] It is not coincidental that several writers, including Samuel A. Eliot, Dwight, and Hach, referred to the years between 1838 and 1843 as the time in which the Boston public became aware of the higher forms of music. It was then that musical idealism also became associated with instrumental music, forming attitudes that still govern American musical culture today.

Although no musical journals were published in Boston between 1823 and 1835, important and influential articles about music nevertheless appeared in Boston during this period. Boston was teeming with literary magazines, and they frequently carried articles about music. Literary journals that discussed music included the *North American Review*, the *Christian Examiner*, the *Boston Monthly Magazine*, and the *New England Magazine*. Later, in the 1840s, the transcendental journals, especially the *Dial* and the *Harbinger*, published important articles on music. Many were lengthy and carefully thought out statements on various aspects of American musical culture. They attained a level of discourse about music unequaled elsewhere in the country. Indeed, the most important statements about music between 1830 and 1845 were made not in musical journals but in literary journals.

The appearance of musical discourse in literary magazines contributed to the growing prestige of music during this period. Literature and rhetoric had been the cultural staples of Puritan society, and throughout much of the nineteenth century literature had a status matched by no other art form. For many of the elite in Boston, literature was the only art form in which it was considered proper for a member of the upper class to engage. The visual arts were beginning to be accepted, but music still carried a stigma of impropriety, which it would not lose until the founding of the second New England school later in the century. And because the prestige of the literary journals far exceeded that of any musical journal, articles on music in literary journals did much to enhance the status of music.

The debate about music in literary journals indirectly supports one of the principal arguments that Dwight and the Harvard Musical Association advocated in the 1840s, that music *was* literature. This argument became explicit only with the attempts of the association to establish a professorship in music at Harvard, but it was implicit from at least the early 1830s, when members of the Pierian Sodality, an undergraduate musical organization at Harvard, sought to have music recognized as an academic discipline. The argument that music merited the same consideration as literature was reinforced throughout most of the 1830s by the willingness of the literary journals to publish articles about music and, more important, by the nature of the discourse in the articles, many of which approached music as if it were literature.

Transcendental journals did much to spread an idealistic concept of music. The *Harbinger*'s principal purpose was to promote the ideas of Associationism and later of Fourierism, a type of utopian society, but given that its editor was John S. Dwight, it is not surprising that a musical column soon appeared. In the first of his "Musical Review" articles, Dwight surveyed the status of music in the United States, and made it clear that he was thinking of the people of the United States as a whole. He spoke of a "Musical Movement in this country" and observed that "our people are trying to become musical." Dwight defined the Musical Movement within his framework of music as a universal abstract language and considered the appearance of such a movement as evidence of the emergence of an even broader social order, of a universal humanity.

Important discussions about music occurred in lectures as well as journals. There is no modern parallel for the popularity of lectures in antebellum America, and some New Englanders, such as Ralph Waldo Emerson, derived much of their income from them. Addresses about music by Lowell Mason and Samuel A. Eliot in the 1820s and 1830s, and the many lectures sponsored by the Harvard Musical Association in the 1840s, were important cultural events in Boston. Most of the more important lectures were subsequently published, either in magazines or independently, assuring an even greater exposure for the lecturer's ideas. New Englanders also carried their vision of music to other parts of the country via the lecture circuit. When Dwight gave a series of lectures on music in New York in 1846, he stirred considerable interest, although critical response was mixed. The *New York Tribune* ran a laudatory ten-inch front-page article on them.[18] It was owned by Horace Greeley, who supported Associationism, a nineteenth-century utopian socialist philosophy; and since Dwight was one of its chief spokesmen, publicizing his lectures furthered Greeley's own interest in the movement. Other newspapers were less kind. The *Courier and Enquirer* panned the lectures mercilessly. Calling them "disorganizing doctrines of the worst stamp," the reviewer asserted that Dwight's presentations would have been 'dangerous had they not been repulsively dry, and tedious"; they reiterated too much his theory of unity and wandered too far from the topic, music. Dwight also spoke of Associationism, and was castigated by the reviewer for connecting Beethoven's symphonies with his views of "spurious transcendentalism." The reviewer concluded, however, that the lectures were harmless, because "the few who were there who are not already bitten with the progress mania were well able to see its tendencies and avoid its fallacies."[19]

According to private accounts, Dwight's remarks were well received. Dwight himself claimed that they "produced a deep impression and were received with enthusiasm." Lydia Maria Child, well aware that Dwight's vague and poetical manner of speaking was best geared to the "select few," was nevertheless surprised that many in the audience responded positively and enthusiastically to his message. Parke Godwin spoke of the delight with which the audience received the lectures.[20]

Most of the reports agree that Dwight's vision of music was new and different. Dwight argued his theory of the religious nature of music, something by then well-known in Boston. For New York audiences, however, it was virtually unprecedented. The *Tribune* praised them for their content and uniqueness: "Mr. Dwight's lectures mark an epoch in the musical history of New York; for, although we have had the opportunity of hearing so much fine music, it is perhaps the first time that we have had a clear and wise assertion of the dignity and compass of the art."[21] Godwin also commented on their refreshing character and wished that New Yorkers were more attuned to Dwight's spiritual doctrine.

Behind the efforts of Dwight, Eliot, Mason, Hach, and the many others who wrote and lectured about music in antebellum Boston was the premise upon which musical reform had been based since the early eighteenth century: that the desired type of music be taught. Education was at the heart of the cultivated tradition, and in the broadest sense Boston's role in the emergence of musical idealism in America derived from its pioneering efforts in education. The theme of education underlay the principal efforts of Mason and of Eliot, president of the Boston Academy of Music, and was explicit in the thought of Dwight. In one sense there was a long tradition behind musical education, but in another sense it was a new idea in the early nineteenth century. Musical instruction in performance was relatively common from the mid-eighteenth century, first in the singing school and later in the lessons given in piano to girls and in wind instruments to boys. By 1800 a few conservatories had been established, but these were an extension of private or group performance lessons. The notion that the population at large could become musically literate was entirely new. It was the goal of both Mason and Eliot and the driving concept behind the Boston Academy of Music. There were no parallels in the country to the Boston Academy of Music, which was founded in 1832, and no precedents for the adoption of music as a part of the curriculum in public schools, which occurred in Boston in 1838.

Education ran deep in Boston culture. Although Jefferson had first proposed a publicly supported education system in Virginia in 1779, Massachusetts was the first state to adopt a law mandating public schools. In 1789 the Massachusetts legislature passed a law requiring towns of fifty or more families to maintain an elementary school for at least six months a year, and towns of two hundred or more to provide a grammar school in which classical languages were taught. This law was only an extension of a colonial ordinance passed in 1642 that required each community to provide for the education of children. Massachusetts could take credit for many other firsts in education in the nineteenth century: the first publicly controlled high school, the first modern school committee, the first state board of education, and the first normal school to train teachers.

Massachusetts' pioneering efforts in education had a great effect nationwide. Many states emulated the Massachusetts model in their own educational reforms. This is especially true after 1837, when Horace Mann became the first secretary for education in the state of Massachusetts and in the country. Mann used his position, which gave him a considerable forum but little actual authority, to argue the cause of education. His brilliance and eloquence gained him an audience far beyond the borders of Massachusetts.

Mann grew up hearing the sermons of Nathaniel Emmons, who preached an extreme and horrific form of Calvinism: man was depraved, with the majority damned and consigned to eternal torments; even to yearn for salvation was evidence of will and hence confirmation of depravity. These sermons and the harsh school that he attended left an indelible mark on Mann. As a consequence he later turned to Unitarianism, and when the opportunity arose to become secretary of education, he gave up a lucrative law practice and a promising political career to serve humanity in the broader sense, as well as to combat the fanaticism of extreme Calvinism in the schools. As secretary of education Mann lectured extensively, not only in Massachusetts but in other states as well. "He collected copious data about the status of education, which he published in Annual Reports. The Annual Reports were read nationwide and probably did more to reform public higher education in the United States than any other single set of documents."[22] Mann's career was consistent with the Unitarian emphasis on human service, and Mann himself summed it up in his final public statement: "Be ashamed to die until you have won some victory for humanity."[23]

Mann quickly recognized the efforts of Mason, who had not only demonstrated that music could be taught to all children successfully, in private or public schools, but had also organized the mechanism to spread this principle nationwide. Mason led a series of conventions on the teaching of music that began in 1834 with twelve teachers in attendance; by 1851 the number of teachers had grown to approximately 1,500.[24] In 1845 Mann began a series of Teacher Institutes and invited Mason to participate. Mason's successful demonstration of his methods formed the basis for a relatively warm relationship between the two men, and probably did much to solidify the place of music in education.[25]

No other musical development was as directly traceable to a geographic area as the spread of music education nationwide was to Boston. Yet music in the schools was only one manifestation of a drive to elevate the status of secular music. Through journals, lectures, public education, and private organizations, Bostonians argued vigorously that music should be taken seriously, and that its cultivation benefited society far beyond providing entertainment. Bostonians disagreed about the purpose of cultivating music, who should benefit from it, and what types of music should be supported. They all argued, however, from the premise that music could be used for moral enhancement as well as serious enjoyment. The establishment of that premise, which ultimately became the basis of high musical culture in nineteenth-century America, was Boston's principal contribution to American music.

Chapter Two

Sacred-Music Reforms in Colonial and Federal America

Between 1720 and 1830 sacred-music reform swept New England. It began just prior to the Great Awakening, embraced the vogue of the fuging tune, and culminated in the ultimately successful efforts of the Presbyterian-Congregational reformers. The reforms started when New England was a theocratic, Puritan colony and ended when disestablishment of all denominations was a reality and America had embarked upon Jacksonian democracy. The reforms had a limited state objective, to improve the quality of music sung in church, but encompassed the most fundamental political issues of authority, democracy, individualism, and class. The reforms focused upon church music but had affected secular music as well before the close of the eighteenth century.

The reform efforts resonated long after the movement had spent itself by the end of the 1830s. Its ideals were subsumed by a new generation who used them to provide the aesthetic grounds for justifying art music. Although issues of class and conceptualizations of society had much to do with the ultimate triumph of European art music in urban centers in the United States by the late nineteenth century, the premise of musical duality in America, that some types of music were morally superior to others, was derived directly and consciously from the sacred-music reform movement.

This movement did not unfold as a single event but in three relatively discrete historical episodes: first, Puritan ministers in the early eighteenth century attempted to reform church singing; second, American composers adopted the fuguing tune from England, creating a vogue for similar pieces; and third, Presbyterian-Congregational hymnists in the early nineteenth century sought to introduce a more devotional style of church music into the service. The three developments were related: the efforts of the Puritan ministers led to the inauguration of singing schools, through which the fuguing tune was propagated, and the fuging tune itself aroused the ire of the Presbyterian-Congregational reformers, who considered its use in church emblematic of all that was wrong with sacred music.

So long as secular music did not interfere with more practical pursuits, the Puritans were tolerant, even indulgent, of it. Puritan society was a passionate society, and its passions included music: we have many accounts of the lustiness with which the Puritans sang; we know that some Puritans played musical instruments and that dancing schools flourished in Puritan Boston, a sure sign of musical activity. Puritan leaders, it is true, were concerned about dancing, but about the abuse of practices such as dancing rather than the practices themselves. In a famous tract on dancing published in 1684, the author admitted that dancing, music, and singing were not wicked in themselves but were "commonly abused to lasciviousness, and that makes them to become abominable." He distinguished sober dancing done in moderation from "lascivious dancing to wanton ditties and in amorous gestures and wanton dalliances." He condemned only the latter.[1]

Yet music was peripheral to Puritan culture. Although there is little indication of antimusical sentiment among the Puritans outside the church, evidence of secular musical activity is scarce enough to suggest that it was either uncommon or unimportant. There were also no professional musicians.[2] The challenge of carving a civilization out of a wilderness left little time for artistic pursuits beyond entertainment. Puritans disapproved of frivolity almost as much as lasciviousness, and secular music, lascivious or not, was considered essentially frivolous. In 1661 Leonard Hoar wrote a letter of advice to his nephew Josiah Flynt, a Harvard student. Hoar discouraged Flynt from spending too much time with music, not because it was immoral but because it might have distracted him from more important activity. It was fine for women to pursue music, but in Puritan New England men did not have that leisure:

> Musick I had almost forgot. I suspect you seek it both to soon and to much. This be assured of that if you be not excellent at it its worth nothing at all. And if you be excellent it will take up so much of your mind and time that you will be worth little else: and when all that excellence is obtained your acquest will prove little or nothing of real profit to you unless you intend to take up the trade of fidling. Howbeit hearing your mother's desires were for it for your sisters, for whom it is more proper and they also have more leizure to look after it: For them I say I had provided the instruments desired.[3]

The Puritans did not have the same easygoing attitude about musical activity inside the church as outside. The role of music in the service was first and foremost a theological question, which meant that it was taken very seriously. Puritan theology proscribed all but the simplest psalm singing in the service, thus assigning music a minor role. The effect of music upon the service remained a matter of consternation to many clergy who, by the early eighteenth century, felt that psalm singing had become chaotic, a potentially disruptive element in an otherwise tightly controlled ritual. While the indulgence of individual passion was viewed harshly in the rigid, hierarchical, and ideologically controlled society of the Puritans, outside the church only its excesses needed to be controlled, as the anonymous tract on dancing acknowledged. It was a different matter inside the church. The clergy were the political as well as the spiritual leaders of the community, and much of their authority derived from the impression they made in the pulpit. They considered individual emotional expression in the church service a challenge to their ability to control the service, and hence a threat to the social hierarchy itself.

The focus of the clergy's displeasure about church music was the "old way of singing." The term refers to unaccompanied congregational singing, in which a leader read or chanted the text and then led the singing of each line. The parish clerk or deacon was entrusted with the text and the precentor with leading the singing. Commonly they were the same person. Because the precentor usually had little or no musical training and in consequence lacked prestige and status as a musician, the congregation tended to go its own way when the psalm was sung. The tempo became extremely slow, many extra notes and ornamental figures were added, and even the most rudimentary ensemble deteriorated. Singers would not even progress through the tune together. As a result, any clear sense of the tune was lost, and the tunes themselves tended to revert to basic maquams or melody types.

It is not clear when the old way of singing was introduced into America. Scholars have determined that a drift toward it is common wherever unaccompanied congregational singing is practiced. A similar evolutionary pattern appeared on both sides of the Atlantic: psalm singing progressed from the lively to the slower, from the "Geneva Jigs" and hornpipes to the long, extended phrases of lining out, and from the crafted melodies of the *Ainsworth Psalter* to a more rustic folk style.

Older interpretations held that the Pilgrims arrived with considerable expertise in congregational singing, and that as the religious fervor of the earlier generations declined, so did the ability to sing complex tunes. This theory appeared in the late seventeenth century and persisted into the twentieth. It was based both on testimony and on the specific psalters that were imported. Describing the singing at the departure of the Plymouth Pilgrims from Leyden, Edward Winslow stated that many were very expert in music.[4] They brought with them the *Ainsworth Psalter*, which contained thirty-nine long, relatively complex tunes in a variety of meters. The Boston Puritans brought Sternhold and Hopkins' *Whole Booke of Psalms* and Ravenscroft's *Psalter*. The Sternhold and Hopkins, which first appeared in 1562, was the most common psalter in Elizabethan England and was musically simpler than the Ainsworth. The bulkier Ravenscroft contained ninety-seven tunes. In 1698 the ninth edition of the *Bay Psalm Book*, which was the first book containing music printed in America, included thirteen tunes, with little metrical variety. According to the tune-count theory the *Bay Psalm Book* in its simplification reflects a considerable decline in musical standards.[5]

The presence of the Ainsworth or even of the Ravenscroft is no proof, however, that the majority of the tunes found in the psalters were actually sung. Evidence suggests precisely the opposite. Editions of the Sternhold and Hopkins that appeared in England after 1600 contain so many misprints that many of the tunes are unusable. The tunes, misspellings and all, were simply copied by one printer after another, even though they had apparently dropped out of use. Thomas East, in his second edition of *The Whole Booke of Psalmes* (1594), admitted that only four tunes were in common use in most English churches.[6] The movement toward the old way of singing was thus well under way in England by 1600. Since the Boston Puritans came from England, there is no reason to suppose that their congregational singing would be very different. But even if the Pilgrims were in some ways musically superior to their English brethren, there is no evidence to indicate that more tunes were in use in America than in England.

Some direct evidence suggests that the old way of singing was widespread even before the middle of the seventeenth century. In 1647 John Cotton published a famous treatise, *Singing Psalms a Gospel Ordinance: or a Treatise wherein are handled these 4 particulars*. In it Cotton argued that psalm singing was a duty, that psalms were to be sung by all in a "lively voyce." He also recommended lining out: "It will be a necessary helpe, that the words of the Psalme, be openly read beforehand, line after line, or two lines together, so that they who want either books or skill to reade, may know what is to be sung, and joyne with the rest in the duties of singing." The exact state of psalm singing in the church is not clear from Cotton's treatise. Cotton was undoubtedly familiar with lining out, but whether he was advocating a technique not yet common or describing current practice is uncertain. That he bothered to write the treatise at all indicates that, at least in his mind, all was not well with music in the church.

There is no question that the old way of singing was common in American churches by the early 1700s, when clergy began to speak out against it. Cotton Mather was especially alarmed about what he heard in his church. In 1716 he observed that "the Psalmody in our Assembly must be better provided for." Over the years he returned to that point frequently in his diary and letters. In 1718 he noted that "the Psalmody is but poorly carried on in my Flock, and in a Variety and Regularity inferior to some others; I would see about it." By 1721 he had become an outspoken critic. On March 13 he wrote, "Should not something be done towards the mending of *Singing* in our Congregation?" On June 5 he commented, "I must of Necessity do something, that the Exercise of *Singing* the sacred *Psalms* in the Flock, may be made more beautiful, and especially have the *Beauties of Holiness* more upon it."[7]

Mather did do something. In 1721 he published *The Accomplished Singer. Instructions first, How the Piety of Singing with a True Devotion, may be Obtained and Expressed; the Glorious God after an Uncommon Manner Glorified in it, and His People Edified. And then, How the Melody of Regular Singing, and the Skill of Doing it, according to the Rules of it, May be Easily Arrived unto.* This treatise marks the beginning of the first concerted attempt to reform psalmody. In it Mather began by assembling many biblical references, to establish that singing was pre-scribed in the Bible. He then stressed that it was the duty of everyone to sing "spiritual songs." Such activity brings a little bit of heaven to earth: "By our *spiritual Songs* we may now after some sort begin *Heaven on Earth*." Mather believed that psalmody united the people with the angels in heaven: "And Oh! How much of *Heaven* have hundreds of thousands found coming down into their Souls, while they have at-tempted thus to come into a Consort with the *Angels* there."[8] He condemned the old way of singing as an *"Odd Noise,"* an *"Uncouth Noise,"* a *"confused noise,"* and a *"Degeneracy,"* because people have *"Ri-diculous Ideas."* His concern, however, was not simply aesthetic. "GOD *is not for Confusion in the Churches of the Saint*; but requires, *Let all things be done decently.*"[9] By this Mather meant regular singing, or singing from notation. Moreover, he placed psalm singing squarely within the framework of the service and asserted it was the duty of the minister to oversee (and control) it.

Mather was not the only minister to be concerned about the state of psalmody. Between 1721 and 1725 a flood of sermons, pamphlets, and tracts appeared defending regular singing and denouncing the old way. Thomas Symmes and Thomas Walter each wrote two tracts and Josiah Dwight one. Peter Thacher, John Danforth, and Samuel Danforth published a joint essay. Other tracts appeared anonymously. Walter's *Grounds and Rules of Musick Explained* was endorsed by fifteen ministers including Increase and Cotton Mather, Joseph Sewall, and William Cooper.[10]

These publications differed considerably in style, ranging from Mather's dense, learned prose, filled with biblical allusions, to Symmes' folksy dialogue between a minister and a neighbor. But the arguments were similar in all of them: psalm singing was a duty, an exercise in piety, and everyone, including women,[11] was expected to participate to the best of his or her ability. When the old way "was the only way then that was of the best of one's ability. But now that the new ways exists [singing by note], one should not sing the worst he can. Thus those that used the old way should change."[12] Everyone should sing the new way.

One treatise that stood apart in some respects from the others in the debate between the new and the old ways of singing was Thomas Walter's *Sweet Psalmist*. Walter considered music a passage into the innermost soul. This led him to consider its theological implications, which he enumerated:

1. It creates a most blessed Serenity and quiet Calm in the Soul of the Worshipper.

2. Music is of good use to suspend and cure the evil and malign Influences of Satan on the Soul.

3. Music happily serves to fix the Mind upon religious Objects, abstracting the soul from every Diversion.

4. Music is of good Use in Religious Worship, to excite and improve suitable and proper Actions, according to the Diversity of Subjects, about which it is employed.[13]

An element of Platonic idealism is present in Walter's ideas. He believed that music had the capacity to move the individual, to shape his innermost being. This idea was to be a central thesis of nineteenth-century reformers of both sacred and secular music. For it to be voiced in early eighteenth-century America, however, was unusual. Most of the treatises of the time viewed music strictly in public terms, and it was evaluated almost exclusively according to its role and effectiveness in the context of the externals of the church service.

The reformers generally succeeded in imposing regular singing, at least on the congregations in Boston. In a 1723 letter to Thomas Hollis, Cotton Mather observed: "A mighty Spirit came Lately upon abundance of our people, to Reform their singing which was degenerated in our Assemblies to an Irregularity, which made a Jar in the ears of the more curious and skillful singers. Our Ministers generally Encouraged the people, to accomplish themselves for a Regular singing, and a more beautiful Psalmody. Such Numbers of Good people, (and Especially young people,) became Regular Singers, that they could carry it in the Congregations."[14]

Mather and others strove to reform psalmody across New England through the publication of their many pamphlets. By Mather's own admission, however, the success that he and other clergy had in effecting reforms in Boston did not extend to the countryside. Resistance was strong. Members of country congregations cried popery and devil worship. Some ran out of the meetinghouse at the beginning of regular psalmody. Others even attempted to secede and form a chapel of the Church of England, believing it better to associate with the Church of England than to submit to regular singing.

Advocates for regular singing were equally zealous in their claims. Rev. Hugh Adams attributed a skirmish in which four Indians were killed in his parish to the adoption of regular singing, citing a passage from the Bible in which a victory was gained by Jehosophat after he had appointed singers to go before his army.

In 1724 an anonymous pamphlet entitled *A Pacificatory Letter about Psalmody, or Singing of Psalms* appeared in Boston. It was unique in its balanced attempt to mediate between the advocates of regular and the old way of singing. Evans attributed it to Cotton Mather, which others have found highly improbable on stylistic grounds.[15] In my view, the writing has neither the learnedness nor the measured density of Mather's prose. It has a folksy, modest quality and easygoing tolerance not characteristic of Mather's publications. As the title implies, the writer sought a middle ground in the controversy. He argued that the tunes themselves were not divine. They were the creation of man, and for that reason they were what man makes of them. He lectured both sides about the intransigence of their positions. He urged those upholding the old way not to be too "*stiff and wilful*" in their opinions: "What, are you so well accomplished, so perfect, as to have no need to learn or amend? Are you so well already, that it's impossible to change or alter our way of Singing, in any measure for the better?" He counseled those favoring regular singing not to be "vainly or proudly conceited of *their own Skill or Attainments.* . . . What Rule or Authority have you to impose your own way on others? If you like one tune, may'nt they as well like another?" He implored both sides to be concerned more about the good of the whole than any particular part.

The overall tone of the *Pacificatory Letter* and the various specific aspects of singing it addressed confirm how high passions were about the reforms. The charges on each side were to echo throughout the eighteenth century: the advocates of the old way were set in their ways and unwilling to accept anything new. The advocates of regular singing, who were mostly young people, were arrogant about their abilities and contemptuous of the older tunes. Furthermore, they were more interested in glorifying themselves than contributing to the overall good.

As all of the writers on the controversy indicate, the disagreement was in large measure a generational dispute. It had all the characteristics of a youthful rebellion: the young favored the new way, regarding the old way as out of date and no longer sufficient; older people favored the old way as part of the tradition with which they had grown up. The clergy threw their weight and prestige behind regular singing, but the passion with which they argued for it suggests that more was at stake than that.

Indeed, it was the very authority of the clergy that was at stake. Thacher and the Danforths explicitly recognized that undisciplined, free, improvisatory singing was a direct challenge to the position of the clergy. In response to the question whether those who "purposely sing a tune different from that which is appointed by the Pastor or Elder to be sung, are not guilty of acting disorderly," the answer was emphatically affirmative:

> The HOLY GHOST having made Regular Pastors and Elders, the Overseers of the Churches, and the Teaching and Ordering of GOD's House, under the Great LORD of the Church, belonging to them, (it being committed to them by the LORD,) such certainly act disorderly, and contemn the Authority of the SON of GOD, which those over them in the LORD, are invested withal, who when they order one tune to be sung, will purposely sing *another*: and wilfully to disturb the harmony of the Church in the Worship of GOD in singing, is a Prophanation.

The position of the clergy in the service was a crucial and sensitive one, not just because the political authority of the clergy stemmed from their dominance of the service, but because Puritan culture glorified their role, preaching. The Puritan clergyman was without question a daunting figure who utterly dominated the church service. Weisberger painted a vivid portrait of a Calvinistic minister:

> When he [the Puritan clergyman] appeared in company in a "full-bottomed, powdered wig, full, flowing coat, with ample cuffs, [and] silver knee- and shoe-buckles," he was a majestic sight. He not only served his congregation; he ruled it. When he climbed into the pulpit on Sunday in his long black gown and white neckbands, he looked every inch God's lieutenant. There was no quarter either for Satan or for the congregation. It was supposedly considered a privilege, after two hours of sermon, to watch the hoarse and perspiring divine turn over the sandglass to begin one more.[16]

The sermon was the centerpiece of the service, and anything that distracted one from it was a serious threat. The old way of singing did just that. The uproar and backlash the clergy unleashed when they attempted to reform singing indicates that congregations relished the singing of psalms. Reports by clergy about how their congregations sounded reinforce that conclusion. Walter described tunes that are "now miserably tortured, and twisted, and quavered, in some churches, into an horrid Medley of confused and disorderly Noises."[17] As we have seen, Mather noted much the same. At the very least Walter and Mather depicted a congregation whose robust participation was far removed from the stony silence that many nineteenth-century accounts chronicle. Yet psalmody did more than create an unpleasant sound; it allowed the congregation to challenge the clergy for emotional control of the service. In the early eighteenth century congregational singing seemed utterly divorced from the Puritan religious experience, and as the tunes became more extended, as the deacon or precentor continued to lose control, and as ornamentation became more elaborate, the singing of psalms assumed less the character of community religious expression than of individual emotional display.

Thomas Symmes' complaint that the purpose of singing psalms was to please God, not to make "*Pleasing Impression . . .* on your *Animal Spirits,*" only confirms that the latter was often the effect of psalmody. By emphasizing that the singing of psalms was a religious duty, and dismissing pleasure as a criterion, Symmes in effect endorsed the authority of the clergy: he rejected individualism, feeling that the singer should suppress his musical instincts and certainly not seek to gratify them. Walter's reference to "confused and disorderly Noises" suggests a concern with the decorum of the service, as does Mather's condemnation of the old way of singing as an *"Uncouth Noise,"* a *"confused noise,"* and a *"Degeneracy"* and his attribution of this problem to the *"Ridiculous Ideas"* of the singers. The enthusiasm with which Puritan churchgoers threw themselves into the singing of psalms may have been a direct response to the suffocating effect of the large doses of Calvinism they had just endured. Within the service psalms seemed at the very least to have been an outlet, an opportunity to vent feelings in a generally repressive and emotionally constricting environment. As such, psalm singing was a crack in the emotional bulwark of Calvinistic life. Psalmody was subversive. This point was not stated openly in the early eighteenth century but was confirmed by several writers at the end of the century, who acknowledged that improper music at the close of a service often completely obliterated the effect of the most solemn sermon. We shall consider these statements in more detail after examining the next development arising from the effort to reform psalmody, the introduction of the fuging tune.

By defining the musical conflict as the old (improvised) way of singing versus regular singing (from notation), the eighteenth-century clergy could claim great success in their reforms. The clergy's position was: teach the congregation to sing from the psalm books, sticking with the tunes as presented by the authorities, and there would be a stop to the chaos, anarchy, indeed the almost bacchanalian license with which parishioners sang. Musical literacy became an end in itself. By the late eighteenth century improvised singing had been curtailed in most places, and the congregations were intimidated by trained choirs. Yet while regular singing was a laudable and sufficient goal in the 1720s, it engendered later problems. Although essentially all the choral music available in 1720 was suitable for the service, what the clergy did not anticipate was the possibility that church music itself could be written with bacchanalian license.

The demand for musical literacy created by the clergy's reforms were met by the singing school. Singing schools were independent organizations, sometimes sponsored by a church, sometimes not. They grew directly out of the reform movement, but they almost always existed outside of the church. They normally met one evening a week, usually in rented rooms that were often in taverns, whose owners were eager to gain further business. The singing schools were especially popular with young people, who looked upon them as a chance to socialize with the opposite sex. They were usually conducted by an itinerant singing master, who eked out a precarious living through the fees from the school and the sale of music to the scholars. The teacher, not surprisingly, sought to provide music that would be popular with members of the school. He found precisely what he wanted in the fuging tune, which had been popular in England. Here was a genre that was nominally sacred, dependent upon literacy for its performance, and immediately appealing. And it was all the more attractive because it was high-spirited, foot-stomping music, more in character with the music that the early eighteenth-century church fathers wished to suppress rather than encourage. That it was considered in bad taste was a religious issue that had little to do with aesthetic questions. It served congregations by providing an emotional outlet to counter the stultifying effects of Puritan orthodoxy, its acceptance smoothed by the close ties that it retained to an older folk idiom. Its life was extended by several American composers of considerable talent who carried it well beyond where it had been when it came to America.

By the late eighteenth century many clergy were concerned about the singing school. As early as 1720 Symmes had worried that young people might be "too light, profane and airy" while attending singing school. In 1778 Rev. Ebenezer Parkman called the singers' behaviour "abomidable," and William Bentley referred to a seduction that occurred at a singing school in Salem in 1791. Bentley observed public "invectives against Singing Schools as corrupting Morals" and admitted that singing schools might contribute to the evil. He was an ardent supporter of music, so this was difficult for him to admit. In his history of church music in America, Nathaniel D. Gould, who was a singing master early in the nineteenth century, recounted in detail the singing school as it existed from 1770 to 1800. He noted that the participants saw the school as an amusement rather than a serious attempt to improve church music, and he described the singers' "eagerness to meet each other for chit-chat" during recess. Since singing schools often met in taverns, the barroom was readily available—and "common civility and justice required that a proper respect should be shown to the keeper of the tavern." Gould also described a second role of the singing master. He would often be prevailed upon to get out his violin and provide music for dancing. Andrew Law, writing in 1797, succinctly confirmed Gould's description: "I viewed also the general character of singing Masters as not favourable to religion."[18]

The career of William Billings, universally considered the outstanding composer of the fuging-tune movement, indicates to what extent the clergy had lost control of this genre. Billings taught many singing schools but never once held a church position. Although he devoted himself to the creation and publication of psalmody, his entire career took place outside the church. His creative efforts went into publications that, while purchased by churches for their choirs, were intended primarily for singing schools. Billings spent most of his life in Boston, and as late as 1798 still listed himself in the city directory as a "Singing Master."

Although the development of the singing school was a natural outgrowth of the importance attached to musical literacy in psalmodic reform, its success wrested control of church music from the clergy's hands. The choirs determined what was to be sung, and their choices were most often based on musical, not religious, considerations. They naturally drew from the repertoire they had learned in the singing school. Most surprising, however, was the response of the clergy to this turn of events. Having lost control of sacred vocal music to the singing school, the clergy made no attempt to regain it. In contrast to the fierce battle about psalmody waged earlier in the century, they voiced little opposition to the rising tide of secularism that characterized the fuging-tune movement. The clergy dissociated themselves from psalmody. They tolerated it at best and tried to ignore it as much as they could. They lacked the desire to fight the kind of fight the earlier Puritan ministers had waged.

Resignation or an unwillingness to speak out leads to an absence of historical evidence. At best we sense an uneasy silence on musical topics from the church fathers of the late eighteenth century. Voices from the early nineteenth century, however, attest to the difficult position that the earlier clergy were in. When the early nineteenth-century hymnodic reformers began their crusade to improve the devotional quality of church music, they confirmed the clergy's displeasure about the direction that church music had taken as well as the sense of resignation that many clergymen adopted toward music in the second half of the eighteenth century. In 1808 John Hubbard observed: "Many respectable clergymen in New England, have been almost determined to omit music in public worship. To their great sorrow, they have observed, that the effects of a most solemn discourse were often obliterated, by closing with improper music. We cannot doubt the correctness of this idea."[19]

Gould vividly described the situation in churches in the late eighteenth century. His *Church Music in America* has been maligned as a historical document almost since its publication in 1853. But as Richard Crawford recently observed, Gould's book—however unsystematic as history and however loose with facts—is a valuable source about late eighteenth- and early nineteenth-century attitudes toward church music, because Gould was there.[20] He was the only person to attempt to chronicle the development of the church music of that time from an insider's point of view. Gould called the period of the fuging tune a "dark age." Devotion had disappeared in music largely because ministers and the more religiously oriented had lost control of the music of the church. According to Gould, ministers and other church members, who should have had a voice in this aspect of worship, allowed music to be "wrested from them," to be performed and managed by those "who apparently had no higher object in view than to please, astonish and amuse." Ministers and the devotional members of the church could only look on, "sometimes grieved and sometimes vexed." But they had so lost control that finally "hearers had well-nigh given up all interest in the subject, and settled into indifference."[21]

The problem of clerical frustration about music persisted well into the nineteenth century. When Mason delivered an "Address on Church Music" in Boston in October 1826, he charged that "even Christians seem to be unmindful of its importance as an act of religious worship, that all too often the music of the church, like that of the theater, is employed only to give variety to the performances, and to relieve the mind from a too constant attention to the subject."[22] Mason then artic- ulated a common fear among ministers and the devout:

> In vain will the minister expect, after having spent his whole strength in a faithful sermon, and labored earnestly and affectionately for the salvation of his people . . . to deepen the impression as he closes the service of the day by singing a psalm or hymn. Rather will he have reason to fear for the effect of the closing exercises, and tremble lest the state of anxious feeling, which, under God, he has been enabled to call forth . . . will be in a great measure dissipated by an exhibition of musical talent, or a flourish of clarinets and bassoons, or flutes of viols, *or a brilliant display of execution on the organ* just as the congre- gation are about to disperse.[23]

Caleb Emerson delivered a discourse on music to the Handellian Music Society at Amherst, New Hampshire, on September 13, 1808. He not only strongly opposed improper music in church but also confirmed the direction that church music had taken in the eighteenth century. He sarcastically asked whether the Sabbath was meant for religious devotion or amusement. If you wish to give it over to amusement, "Go on, then . . . but be consistent. Banish prayer, and the preaching of evangelical truth—instead of attending to the solemn realities of eternity, let your ears be delighted with the seducing fallacies of those who will *prophecy smooth things*—let mirthful music cheer your hearts, and drive every serious thought from your minds." He then examined music as practiced in most churches and came to the conclusion that it was designed not for worship but for "profane revelry."[24]

It had become apparent that Calvinistic theology offered no alternative vision of music to combat the appeal of the fuging tune. Although the reformers could marshal strong arguments against uncontrolled bacchanalian singing in the service, they were unable to provide satisfactory justification for a better type of music. By the late eighteenth century the clergy had little choice but to retreat and ignore the problem, because music remained far from central to the service. The difficulty, however, far transcended the nature of the service. It lay in Calvinism itself. Two aspects of Puritan culture and Puritan religious thought worked against a solution. First, the three-hour sermons of the Puritan minister exemplified the verbal orientation of Puritan society. Puritan society was held together by rhetoric, an art that was deeply respected and that left little room for any contributions from music. Second, the emotional content of eighteenth-century Puritan theology, with its emphasis on guilt, was at best opposed and at worst antithetical to the singing of psalms.

Any consideration of Puritan influence upon American music must take into account the rhetorical basis of Puritan culture. Only rhetoric, of all the arts, flourished in Puritan New England. As we have seen, music was considered a frivolity outside the church and barely tolerated in it, and the visual arts were virtually nonexistent. Even portraiture, the most pragmatic of the visual arts in the seventeenth and eighteenth centuries, is scarcely represented. The necessity to carve a society out of a wilderness created an urgency about frivolity. The Puritans had plenty of time and energy, however, for rhetoric. Hundreds of treatises and pamphlets poured from their pens. Rhetoric held together both the body politic and the social covenant. Puritan society was based upon a tightly controlled, rigorously logical vision of man and the universe, which could only be conceived and explicated verbally. Neil Harris observed the unusual sequence of Puritan society: "Before Americans made pictures they used words."[25]

Rhetoric could be highly personal in Puritan America. In histories, personal narratives, and poetry it could determine and influence mood at the most private level. In Jonathan Edwards the intellect and the emotions constantly vied for ascendency, yet even in his most emotional moments he sought words to reflect or support his feelings. At his moment of conversion, when he first became aware of the sense of God's divinity suffused throughout him, he turned to the book of Canticles as "a fit expression for his mood."[26]

Early in the eighteenth century Edwards delivered a series of sermons that reveal two reasons that psalmody and Puritan liturgy were not compatible. First, the rhetoric in the sermons was so powerful that music could add little. Edwards graphically depicted the fate awaiting all but the elect, as some of the sermon titles suggest: "The Eternity of Hell Torments," "The Torments of the Wicked in Hell, no occasion of grief to the Saints in Heaven," and the most famous, "Sinners in the Hands of an Angry God." Vernon Parrington referred to them as "notorious minatory sermons" that "sank deep into the memory of New England, and for which it has never forgiven him."[27] In them Edwards demonstrated the power of words in a society in which images depended upon verbal description. Second, the content of the sermons left little place for psalmody. The sermons may have been extreme in their vividness and emotionalism, but they were orthodox. Calvinism was unremittingly bleak in its standard themes of the torments of hell, the helplessness and depravity of man confronted with a stern of judging God, and the austerity and misery of life both on earth and in eternity for those not specially chosen. It is difficult to imagine the religious sentiments of Calvinism set to songs of praise.

When revivalists began to grapple with the dichotomy between Calvinism and evangelicalism, the incompatibility of psalm singing and Calvinistic theology was laid out in the open. The awkward theological position of preachers who attempted revivalism within the restrictions of Calvinistic theology made the issue especially acute. The Calvinistic revivalist had around his neck the great albatross of the doctrine of the elect. If salvation was preordained and available only through the grace of God, then there was little room for moral choice and not much point in provoking conversion. If the evangelist could not offer salvation, his sales appeal was limited. Calvinistic revivalism did, however, find a place for conversion. While salvation was still left in the hands of God, Calvinistic revivalism could prepare the candidate for its acceptance. Calvinistic revivalism was a lengthy process in which the sinner eventually became sufficiently convinced of his own guilt for salvation, if available, to occur. "Conviction of sinfulness" was the initial step in conversion, and fear and despair were the initial desired emotions. Only after a protracted time in such a state could "assurance" be forthcoming, and then only to the elect. The role of the minister was thus not to grant assurance but to prepare the way for it, should it be available. Instantaneous conversion was not possible, and the evangelist could not approach candidates with the promise of salvation. While both Calvinistic and Arminian[28] revivalism played upon the candidates' sense of guilt, in Calvinism guilt was the be all and end all; instilling it was the complete task of the Calvinistic evangelist. Guilt and songs of praise were not compatible, as Charles Finney recognized.

Finney was one of the most phenomenally successful evangelists in the nineteenth century. Intense and magnetic, he instituted controversial new measures like the protracted meeting and the anxious seat. He would wear down a community with daily meetings lasting from sunrise to midnight. He placed a bench in the front of the revival hall on which those concerned about salvation could sit. The entire weight of the congregation as well as Finney's own bullying rhetoric could thus be trained on those persuaded to occupy the bench, or anxious seat. Theologically, Finney represented a transitional phase in the movement away from Calvinism. He did not adhere strictly to the doctrine of the elect, but he did maintain the older notion that salvation was a gradual process engendered by instilling in the convert an overwhelming sense of guilt. He stressed "the total moral, voluntary depravity of unregenerate man." Scholars had claimed that both Thomas Hastings and Joshua Leavitt, compiler of *The Christian Lyre*, sought to have Finney adopt their tune books, but Finney was not interested.[29] It mattered little whether the music was in the rustic folk style of Leavitt's compilation or the more proper European style of Hastings'. The reasons for Finney's indifference had to do with his idea of the function of music: "A great deal of singing often injures a prayer meeting. The agonizing spirit of prayer does not lead people to sing. . . . Singing is the natural expression of feelings that are joyful and cheerful. The spirit of prayer is not a spirit of joy. It is a spirit of travail, and agony of soul, supplicating and pleading with God with strong cryings and groanings that cannot be uttered."[30] Finney also pointed out that "common singing dissipates feeling."[31]

With the decline of Calvinism around 1800 a new tone surfaced in American writings about music. A steady stream of tracts denouncing the older style of psalmody and urging Americans to embrace new standards of taste began to appear. The period from roughly 1800 to

1830 saw the most sustained, intense, and ultimately effective attack upon prevailing standards of church music in the history of American music. Unlike earlier ones, the new calls for reform were voiced by musicians rather than clergy. As a consequence, the reform movement of the early nineteenth century had a musical sophistication and emphasis that the earlier attempted reforms did not.

One of the first spokesmen for the new attitude was Andrew Law. Beginning in 1793, he roundly criticized American psalmody, particularly for its rough and harsh character. He compared it unflatteringly with European music: American music was "in reality faulty," especially in its emphasis upon the "perfect cords." European compositions by contrast "aim[ed] at variety and energy by guarding against the reiterated use of the perfect cords." To Law the problem was rooted in performance: composers were forced to compensate for the harshness of the Yankee singing style by frequent use of perfect intervals. The results were tunes that were "all sweet, languid and lifeless."[32]

Law devoted the remainder of his life to the improvement of public taste. His efforts were largely futile, however, in part because he allowed himself to be sidetracked by a subsidiary issue, the development of a special notation. In 1803 he printed his *Art of Singing* in a new shape-note notation that dispensed entirely with the staff in an effort to "lessen the burden of the learner."[33] Shape-notes later became common in American hymnody and were even used by Mason,[34] but they almost always appeared within the framework of regular staff notation and so could be considered aids to learning to read music. Law's system, however, was totally divorced from the staff. It was a substitute for regular music reading rather than a means of learning it. Law's system was too constrictive, too removed from anything resembling the norm to be accepted. Unfortunately for Law, promoting this system became a crusade for him.

A more determined and more pointed broadside against the prevailing psalmodic style was launched by John Hubbard in 1808 with his *Essay on Music*, which David McKay and Richard Crawford regard as "the major tract of the movement to reform American psalmody."[35] Hubbard condemned literal imitation in music as puerile, arguing that music, like the other arts, imitates nature. Like many eighteenth-century theorists, he drew up a list of aesthetic categories, but his was unusual: the sublime, the beautiful, the nervous, the concise, the dry, and the bombastic. After citing two examples, from Handel and Pergolesi, of the sublime and the beautiful, he passed over the other categories to the bombastic, which "consists in laboured notes and strains, disconnected from any exalted ideas; or in attempting to communicate some low idea which cannot be expressed by notes." Hubbard despaired that American composers had been particularly fruitful in producing such works and cited the fugue [fuging tune] as the principal culprit. A "perversion," the fugues "cannot affect the heart, nor inform the understanding." The essential problem is that it renders the text unintelligible, violating the nature of vocal music, which is to "communicate ideas."[36]

Although both Law and Hubbard found the fuging tune objectionable, their objection did not constitute a national or nationalistic issue. Scholars have long recognized that the fuging tune existed on both sides of the Atlantic. While it underwent its most extensive development in America, it was neither isolated nor unique. William Tansur's *Royal Melody Complete*, published in England, enjoyed considerable circulation in America and served as a model for William Billings' *New-England Psalm-Singer*. The conflict between the fuging tune and more "respectable" types of church music falls to an extent within the British context of the tension between parish psalmody and cathedral practice. This context is only beginning to be understood, as the tradition of parish psalmody has only recently begun to receive proper scholarly attention.[37]

It would be false, however, to consider the Presbyterian-Congregational reformers' objections to the earlier church-music style as part of a class conflict three thousand miles across the Atlantic. This is belied by the tone of acute urgency that permeates the reformers' writings. For writers like Law and Hubbard the threat posed by the earlier style was real, specific, and immediate. Their approach was determined primarily and overwhelmingly by religious factors and had little to do with ethnic, national, or regional distinctions; even aesthetic considerations per se were secondary. Yet the reformers' efforts cannot be consigned to ecclesiastical history. They were a logical response to a time when religious change in America was at the heart of historical developments, and the results not only reflected but also contributed significantly to the cultural mainstream of antebellum America.

The reformers' aesthetic entailed a unified approach to musical choices that was entirely consonant with the times. They advocated the use of "correct" or "scientific" harmony and preferred simple tunes. They avoided tunes from certain types of secular sources and abhorred unrestrained emotionalism. Probably more has been written about the use of correct or scientific harmony than about anything else the reformers advocated. Scholars have connected the reformers' concern over that point to the demise of the fuging tune in America. In that guise it is a red herring. The rejection of the fuging tune in both America and England in the early nineteenth century was closely tied to two other issues, which are related but not identical to the question of scientific harmony: the use of organs and the manner of singing. Since the organ could dictate the tune, rhythm, and harmony to the congregation in a more authoritative manner than was possible otherwise, the old way of singing seldom survived its introduction. Both Temperley and Crawford found a direct correlation between the appearance of an organ or other keyboard instrument and the demise of the old style.[38]

The manner of singing directly affected chordal preference. As we recall, Law perceived a causal relationship between the style of singing and the intervals used by composers. Law understood that the open intervals of country psalmody were particularly conducive to the rough vocal timbres with which it was normally sung. Should you teach someone to sing in a proper and less harsh manner, the compositions themselves would no longer be acceptable: "But sing the sweet-corded tunes of this country make [sic], in sweet toned voices, and they will immediately cloy, sicken and disgust."

William Bentley confirmed that Law practiced what he preached. Bentley, a minister in Salem, Massachusetts, kept a detailed diary, and his entries about musical events reveal him as musically astute. On May 23, 1776, he heard one of Law's singing schools perform. Bentley was impressed and surprised by the overall effect, especially the softness with which Law's students sang: "He aims to have his music very soft . . . many of the voices do not accent the notes so as to enable the ear to distinguish the strains from soft murmurs." Bentley was also impressed with the good order and decorum of the hundred-odd singers. Seriousness, decorum, and a tightly controlled style of singing were, at that time, unusual.[39]

The manner of singing was particularly important to the progressives. Many reformers after Andrew Law advocated smooth singing. Thomas Hastings, William Bradbury, and Lowell Mason all stressed it in both their writing and their choral directing. In *The Musical Magazine* that Hastings edited between 1835 and 1837 each issue had a "PRACTICAL" section, which was devoted principally to 'details which relate to the formation, management, and employment of the human voice in vocal enunciation."[40] In his 1826 address Mason stressed the importance of a good tone, and the necessity of cultivating it. When he was in Europe for the first time in 1837 he was often disappointed by the sound of the choirs of congregations. Congregational singing elicited such epithets as "miserable," "poor," "barbarous," and "wretched." Choirs fared little better. He described an anthem of Dr. Croft's performed in the Sunday service at Westminster Abbey as "poorly done—the choir was inefficient. The harsh tone of the Boy's Soprano was disagreeable."[41]

Given a connection between harmony and vocal timbre it is not surprising that the reformers concentrated so heavily upon this aspect. This concentration is reflected first in the singing-school movement and then in the entire musical-education movement, which attempted to instill a smoother vocal style. It is also consistent with certain beliefs of the reformers about the nature of the church service, to which I shall return later.

The reformers' preference for simple tunes has sometimes been overlooked, but the reformers were absolutely clear that they preferred simple, down to earth tunes and had no antipathy toward some of the older melodies. Hastings stated in his preface to *The Sacred Lyre*, "The old standard melodies, though found under almost every possible variety of arrangement, are still deservedly popular, and in presenting them at this time, the Editor feels that he is acting in obedience to the call of his friends and patrons, as well as in accordance with his own convictions of duty."[42] This sentiment was echoed by other writers, yet it seems inconsistent with the reformers' desire to avoid tunes from certain types of secular sources. Conversely, the reformers' use of European sources has in itself been criticized, and their bowdlerization of them has only affronted those to whom European composers seemed a fitting model. While the preference for simple tunes might explain bowdlerization, why turn to Europe in the first place? And, finally, their aversion to unrestrained emotionalism has been seen as a part of the sectional strife that characterized much of early America, in this case pitting the more restrained and dignified urban East against the rougher and rawer rural West.

As we saw in Hubbard's essay, it was the fuging tune that drew the most virulent criticism from the Presbyterian-Congregational reformers. The vogue of the fuging tune lay entirely between the early eighteenth-century church-music reforms of the Puritan clergy and the reforms growing out of nineteenth-century evangelicalism. Ironically the reform movement of the early eighteenth century allowed the fuging tune to flourish; the clergy encouraged the principal institution in which it was propagated, the singing school, and the popularity of the fuging tune was in one sense a direct confirmation of the success of the clergy's reform attempts.

The striking difference between the laissez-faire attitude of the late eighteenth-century clergy and the zeal of the nineteenth-century reformers leaves a lot of unanswered questions. There seems to be historical forces at work beyond those of music and religion per se when we consider the reformers' fanaticism on certain points, the acute sense of urgency in their writing, their restricted aesthetic outlook, their phenomenal success when so many earlier reforms had failed, and the immense influence that they exercised over later American musical developments. Since musical reforms grew out of evangelical considerations, however, American evangelicalism forms a logical starting point to examine the context within which the Presbyterian-Congregational reformers operated.

Eighteenth-century evangelicalism was Anglo-American. Its two principal leaders, George Whitefield and John Wesley, operated on both sides of the Atlantic, although it may be argued that their success rates were not similar on each side. Nineteenth-century revivalism was almost exclusively an American phenomenon. Europeans who witnessed the revival fervor in nineteenth-century America were puzzled and alienated by it. Frances Trollope, in her essay *Domestic Manners of the Americans*, painted a devastating portrait of a revival meeting. She depicted in graphic terms the anxious seat and its effect, particularly upon young girls. She observed that most of the followers who came forward were young girls, and she described with revulsion the hysteria and the Freudian overtones with which they were manipulated.[43]

One of the most extensive European descriptions of the American revival fever was Andrew Reed and James Matheson's *Narrative of a Visit to the American Churches*. Reed and Matheson, calling the revivals "the great religious phenomenon of this country," attempted to understand their purposes and motivations. They were generally sympathetic to revivals, so long as they were conducted with "the discreet, humble, and persevering use of those [regular] means."[44] But they found the "New Measures," such as the anxious seat and protracted meeting, offensive. They equated the success of revivals with the attitudes of the American people toward them: revivals succeeded in large part because the people expected them to succeed.

Nineteenth-century revivalism was peculiar to America because it was responding to fundamental changes in American society, changes that had no European counterpart. What distinguished the reform movement of the early nineteenth century from earlier attempted reforms was an unprecedented sense of urgency felt not just about religion but about society as a whole. This urgency was precipitated by a newly awakened possibility of individual choice. The historian Robert Wiebe has characterized the changes in American society in the early nineteenth century as a "revolution in choices." As Calvinistic theology weakened and a new sense of space opened up to Americans, a desire for personal freedom and individual choice erupted in the American consciousness. It was a new and exhilarating experience. Wiebe has described this movement as an evolutionary process that began in 1803. In the early stages those advocating individual freedom remained relatively close to older values; they tested them, pushed where they could, and gradually overcame established barriers. By 1820 the movement was in full tide, and by 1825 it had become a "self-fueling process that propelled the participants as fast and as far as their impulses drove them."[45]

The growth of individual choice stemmed partly from the breakdown of the older patriarchal model of the family, which had governed American society up to the end of the eighteenth century. Although the term *patriarchal* refers to any family system in which an adult male retains authority and control, I am using it here in the older sense, to mean an extended family structure in which the patriarch governed even the adult males. This structure contrasts with the nuclear-family model, in which the males struck out on their own when they reached adulthood. Within marriage the adult female still had to defer to the authority of the male, but her position changed in two ways: she had more freedom in her marriage choice (although making the choice itself immediately circumscribed her freedom), and within marriage a new responsibility was placed upon her: to prepare the children for the moral choices they would have to make.

These new developments "laid the groundwork for America's democratic society." Individual choice meant individual responsibility. Suddenly the young man was on his own, at the mercy of forces and temptations that would test his moral fiber. To a society not long nurtured on such freedom, it was a stark and fearful prospect. Social institutions like the family and then the church underwent fundamental restructuring, to provide support for the individual. The changes were replicated at the larger levels of society. From that development a new "democratic society" emerged in the 1820s. Communities, the states, and the nation itself became part of this pattern. "By the 1840s what originated in family life had been elaborated into a complete democratic culture."[46]

These changes placed new burdens and obligations upon religion. The old rules were gone. Earlier Americans had "relied as a matter of course upon superstructures: a national administration, a centralized banking system, the Constitution, an enlarged version of the patriarchal church."[47] But the new society, centered upon the family, placed an unprecedented burden on individuals to make their own moral choices, and concern about this burden mounted as vast numbers of young men left their homes to seek work or fortunes. The extent of that concern is reflected in the flood of tracts or manuals that appeared offering advice and moral guidance to young men. Many were written by clergymen and teachers who feared that the young man would be led down the road to perdition by the allures of the city, where a cast of deceitful characters, led by "confidence men" and "painted women," awaited him.[48]

The patriarchal Calvinistic church of the seventeenth and eighteenth centuries had offered a predetermined formula for salvation, so that the individual was not even responsible for his own soul. The patriarchal church was also backed by law. As late as 1818 the state of Connecticut still recognized Congregationalism as the official state religion, bestowing upon it (among other powers) the right to tax. In Massachusetts complete disestablishment did not occur until 1833. The new church could no longer depend upon its authority to control public and private morals. And it had a new obligation. America's highly independent, mobile population of the early nineteenth century made the winning of souls as critical as the securing of public virtue. Since the disposition of the individual soul was no longer preordained, salvation itself was at stake. Individual moral choices would not only determine the conduct of a person's life, with significant ramifications for the social structure as a whole, but would also have implications for eternity.

The rise of hymnody and the success of the reformers are directly related to the emergence of moral choice as an important issue in American society. Although evangelicalism is central to this point, the point far transcends evangelicalism. The real issue driving hymnodic reform was not Calvinism versus evangelicalism but the broader one of individual choice, which influenced life well beyond strictly religious decisions. The significance of individual choice was not its presence but rather its newness. For those living in the early nineteenth century the freedoms loosed by this new force were mysterious and frightening, and many leaders and intellectuals greatly feared their consequences. In *This Sacred Trust: American Nationality 1798–1898*, Paul Nagel emphasized the sense of dissolution and degeneracy that troubled many Americans in the early nineteenth century. He concentrated upon national leaders who were searching for a national character, and whose message was similar to that of the religious leaders: America was a land of Mammon, doomed because of its transgressions and lack of conscience. Some intellectuals, like Noah Webster, were extremely pessimistic and discouraged by events. Others, like Horace Mann, stressed the importance of moral education to control unrestrained and destructive passions in society: unless man's passions were controlled through education in righteousness, "licentiousness shall be the liberty; and violence and chicanery shall be the law."[49] Mann considered moral education to be "the primal necessity of social existence. The unrestrained passions of man are not only homicidal, but suicidal; and a community without a conscience would soon extinguish itself."[50]

Within the context of the fears engendered by the new freedoms of individual choice, the aversion of the Presbyterian-Congregational reformers to the unrestrained emotionalism of frontier hymnody is not surprising. To many in early nineteenth-century America the frontier itself seemed to represent uncontrolled emotional license. For centuries Europeans had perceived the peripheries as a place where restraint on violence, wildness, and brutal exploitation could be ignored. Only because the frontier had moved to America did it seem uniquely American. The American response was unusual, however. According to Bernard Bailyn, a "state of self-conscious gentility incompatible with the violence and extravagance and disorder of life in a marchland" arose early in America, and the juxtaposition of the two, "the intermingling of savagery and developing civilization," formed an important counterpoint in American culture.[51] The clash between frontier and Eastern urban hymnody in the nineteenth century is a direct manifestation of the sectional differences. It must, however, be kept in perspective: the emotionalism of Western hymnody appeared so ominous because the eighteenth-century patriarchal model had broken down, and Eastern leaders feared what choices the individual might make under the new freedoms.

In a society that seemed to have lost its traditional religious foundations, the moral imperative of education was particularly acute. If society could no longer depend upon itself to police its population morally and religiously as the eighteenth-century Calvinists had done, all aspects of persuasion had to be brought to bear to ensure that the individual himself made proper choices and stuck with them. Accordingly, aesthetic issues were indeed religious issues. It is in this milieu that we find the emergence of hymnody. The position of the reformers was that music had no greater end than moral persuasion. Hymns were an important part of the arsenal of securing and maintaining individual choice, and it was essential that they be consistent with a proper devotional spirit. Secular music was not inherently bad, but fostering the proper individual choice in religious issues was much more important than any aesthetic considerations.

An overriding concern about the devotional aspect of music explains several of the reformers' positions that some musicologists have found troubling: the rejection of the fuging tune, the hostility of the reformers to certain types of secular music, and their preference for European tunes. All three points are closely related. The reason that the reformers chose European tunes was religious: good tunes were necessary in the battle for persuasion, but where to find them? The real question was where *not* to find them. The principal theme running through the reformers' comments was that tunes must not only be singable, lest they be ignored, but also be of the proper spirit. At the very least they must be absolutely free of profane allusions. Charles Zeuner, in *American Harp*, observed, "Church music ought to be the most perfect in character and style, and ought always to be free from unhallowed associations; and its dignity and solemnity ought to be constantly guarded and as far as possible religiously preserved from all derogatory influences and corrupt and debasing tendencies."[52] In 1805 the anonymous compiler of *The Salem Collection* linked musical decadence with spiritual corruption: "The currency of inferior music cannot fail of being the subject of deep regret with every lover of harmony, as well as with the serious possessor of Christianity; for it cannot be denied, that most of our modern psalmody is not less offensive to a correct musical taste, than it is disgusting to the sincere friends of publick devotion."[53] John Hubbard deplored even more trenchantly the use of secular tunes: "From the midnight revel, from the staggering bachanal, from the profane altar of Comus they have stolen the prostituted air, and, with sacrilegious hands, have offered it in the temple of JEHOVAH. The air of a catch, a glee, a dance, a march, or a common ballad is very improper for the worship of the Most High."[54] Thomas Hastings left no doubt about why he rejected secular songs; he specifically equated their use with their associations: "Foolish song tunes can never be set to religious words without offending very person of good taste. The foolishness in this case is inseparable from the music, especially where the song has been previously known."[55]

European sources provided a storehouse of tunes that congregations would not be likely to know well enough to bring to mind secular associations. Although questions of taste and science were not trivial, they were secondary to the more important issue of source and association. Style did matter, as Hubbard observed, but even that frequently had a religious aspect; the original secular text of a hymn might not be known, but if the music itself recalled undesirable secular activity, like "the midnight revel" or the "staggering bachanal," then it was unacceptable.

The fuging tune was evaluated from the same perspective. Its rejection was part of the larger attack upon what was considered an inappropriate style of church music prevalent in the late eighteenth century. Once again the essential issue was neither taste, science, nor national origin; the essential issue was suitability for worship. The fuging tune was not appropriate for church principally because it did not have the proper devotional spirit. In 1838 *The Boston Musical Gazette* reported: "Most of the American composers, that immediately followed Billings, seem to lack the necessary, sacred inspiration. . . . There certainly cannot be anything reverential, solemn, and comporting with sacred worship, in musical jingle; yet all their compositions were of that cast. There was nothing in them of the serious and sacred character which we find in the psalmody of native Americans of the present day, viz. Ives, Mason, and some others."[56] At approximately the same time the *Musical Magazine* observed: "A few years afterwards [after the use of melodies of Williams and Tansur] came the fuguing style which called forth many censures, and excited many just fears for the preservation of devotional influence."[57] Gould, in his history of church music, summarized the situation: "The [fuging] tunes were admired in proportion to the popular taking character of the melodies, or to the wonderment with which the different parts were introduced, entangled, bewildered, evolved, and at length brought out in safety; amusement took the place of edification and worship. Congregational singing was, of course, hushed,—their harps were hanged upon the willows. Devotion fled, and admiration occupied her place."[58]

The intensity with which these reformers clung to their positions was partially due to the reluctance of society to accept the view that music was indeed part of the worship service. The number of tracts, sermons, and resolutions that continued to articulate this point into the 1840s indicates the difficulty with which the idea was accepted. It was so new and so radical that even the clergy resisted it. The author of an article in the *Musical Magazine* entitled "The Abuses of Sacred Music" listed seven abuses, which included both the use of inappropriate music in the church service and an inappropriate style of singing. The final abuse placed much of the blame upon the clergy who, in their inattentiveness and even disruptiveness when the choir was singing, clearly did not lead by example:

> What then must be thought of a clergyman, we ask with due reverence to the sacred office, and submission to the worthy incumbent, what most [sic] be thought of the clergyman . . . who treats the public praises of Zion with marked indifference and disregard? What should we think, if, whlie [sic] another was offering prayer, he were to be seen listless, inattentive, looking over his hymnbook or sermon, beckoning to the sexton, receiving written notices, leaving his pulpit to whisper to a member of the congregation, making arrangements for subsequent exercises, requesting the assembled to change their seats, as at seasons of communion?[59]

This same theme was echoed in a "Lecture on Sacred Music" delivered by Rev. Sylvester Eaton in Paterson, New Jersey, on August 11, 1835. Eaton argued that sacred music cannot be sung with the proper interest and expression unless the singers themselves feel what they sing; indifference is one of the principal evils attendant to sacred music, and that the minister, who often examines his sermon or turns over the leaves of the Bible when the hymn is being sung, is one of the chief culprits.[60] In 1836 Frederick Freeman repeated the same charge about the pastor's role in the singing of psalms:

> I have been frequently surprised, after hearing the clergyman say, "Let us sing to the praise of God," to see him comfortably sit down again, and not open his mouth; and in those churches where it is the custom to have pulpits large enough for several persons, it is no uncommon thing to see the worthy gentleman in busy conversation, while the people are singing. Does not their conduct say: "You may sing to the praise of God, I myself never studied music; I have a voice to pray and preach, but no voice to sing; while you sing praises to God, I will look over my sermon, or look for my text."[61]

The role of music in church was the topic of a convention held in Bennington County, Vermont, in June 1835. At this convention the following resolutions were passed: "1. *Resolved*, As the sense of this Convention, that sacred music is a part of divine worship, the importance of which, to the prosperity of religion, has been greatly and sinfully disregarded; and that in this sense ministers and churches have taken the lead. 2. *Resolved*, That the proper view of this part of divine worship is that which treats it in all respects, as much an act of devotion as prayer: and as requiring, both in those who lead as performers and those who join as fellow-worshipers, the same devoutness, reverence, sincerity, and activity of affections toward God."[62] In May 1836 this issue was again raised by a "Mr. Williams of Pennsylvania," who, after defining sacred music and its analogous relation to prayer, called for reform and attempted to provide some guidelines, the first of which argued that "it must be felt that instead of being a mere interlude in the services, praise is as really a part of divine worship as prayer; and that instead of being the least solemn portion of the service, there is no other part which requires so much silence, solemnity, absorbed attention and elevated devotional feeling as this."[63]

Two similar resolutions were passed at a meeting called in October 1841 to create a national music convention. This meeting, which referred to a membership of 201, was led by William Reed of Berlin, Maine, T. B. Hayward of Boston, G. J. Webb, M. S. Parker, G. W. Greatorex, T. Whittemore, and A. J. Locke. It met at the facilities of the Handel and Haydn Society in Boston. The first resolution expressed disapproval "in particular, of combining light, frivolous, vulgar or profane pieces, with sacred, in these concerts; and of employing, in executing sacred music on such occasions, men of openly immoral or intemperate habits." The second reaffirmed that "vocal music, or Psalmody, is a most important part of public worship; and consequently that proper means should be used to make it . . . an effective aid to devotional feeling, and to the great purposes of public worship."[64]

The entire tune-selection process, with the European thrust and rejection of certain types of eighteenth-century American music by the Presbyterian-Congregational hymnists, was neither national nor primarily aesthetic but almost strictly a religious issue. It surfaced when it did not simply because of changed religious activity but because American society itself changed profoundly in the early nineteenth century. In the following chapters we shall see many examples of the effects of the efforts by the Presbyterian-Congregational reformers to upgrade the position of hymnody in American churches. The impact that the Presbyterian-Congregational hymnists had upon the American musical aesthetic only reflects the magnitude and historical significance that the emergence of evangelical revivalism had upon nineteenth-century America in general. Yet the attitudes of these composers and compilers reveal much to us about the mind-set that dominated American life in the first half of the nineteenth century—a mind-set in certain ways alien to us today, and in other ways still with us.

Chapter Three

Lowell Mason: Hymnodic Reformer

Nowhere is the importance of the sacred-music reform movement to American musical developments more graphically illustrated than in the career of Lowell Mason. Along with Thomas Hastings, Mason was the most influential of the hymnodic reformers and remained dedicated to the cause of sacred music throughout his life. His influence extended far beyond that of Hastings, however; he was involved in more aspects of music, and his advocacy of the hymnodic reformers' philosophy of music reached a wider audience. He was the most famous hymn composer of the nineteenth century, when hymns had greater distribution than popular secular songs. He was the most successful and well-known compiler of sacred-music anthologies, which enabled him to propagate his ideas through lengthly polemical introductions. A pioneer in the field of music education, he also used national teacher's conventions that he organized to spread further his philosophy.

Mason's impact was so vast that many twentieth-century scholars consider him the most important American musician of the nineteenth century. The three standard histories of American music, which provided the basic interpretive framework for the past generation of musicologists, all consider Mason one of the critical figures in the shaping of American musical culture. Gilbert Chase, in *America's Music from the Pilgrims to the Present,* states that "of all musicians active in the United States during the nineteenth century, Lowell Mason has left the strongest, the widest, and the most lasting impress on our musical culture," a comment quoted by Hitchcock in *Music in the United States.* More recently Charles Hamm, in *Music in the New World,* characterized Mason as "a man who had as much impact on the musical life of nineteenth-century America as any other person."[1]

In addition to Mason's publications and conventions, which provided him with a national forum, his activities were intimately bound up with the musical development of Boston. He held commanding positions in the city's two most important musical organizations, the Handel and Haydn Society and the Boston Academy of Music. When music was first introduced into public schools in 1838, he assumed control of it, becoming the country's first superintendent of music. The period of

Mason's active involvement in Boston's musical life, from 1828 to 1845, was precisely when the most important changes in musical attitudes occurred in Boston. It was when, to paraphrase Louis Elson, psalmody lost its primary hold on the Boston public, and symphony was established.

In this chapter I shall examine Mason's early career and publications, principally as a hymnodic reformer. Since Mason was a typical hymnodic reformer, understanding his views and the motivations behind them allows us to comprehend more clearly the reform movement itself. It also allows us a better grasp of the musical milieu of Boston, his home base. In addition, there are historiographical as well as historical reasons for attempting to ferret out Mason's attitudes about sacred music. Mason's historical importance has been recognized, but his historical position has, I believe, been misunderstood; and it is in the area of his motivations and objectives in psalmodic reform that Mason needs reevaluation. His activities with the principal musical organizations of Boston will be discussed in later chapters.

Lowell Mason is one of the most controversial figures in the history of American music. He was charismatic, energetic, and opinionated. Always a cautious man, he combined a mission borne of the most lofty ideals with a hardheaded business acumen that jealously guarded prerogatives and assets. His contributions, like those of many other strong personalities, have been the subject of bitter disagreement. He has been considered a hero, a villain, an upholder of taste, a destroyer of standards, an anti-American, a suppressor of American indigenous music, and the founder of an American national musical culture.[2] In 1846 Jesse Aiken wrote: "Mason's publications alone have furnished the churches with a rich variety of music, arranged and harmonized in a style of unequalled beauty and sublimity, and characterized by a chasteness, simplicity, and facility of expression, and all that is adapted to dignify and elevate the character of devotional song."[3] At about the same time an anonymous reviewer of Mason's *Sabbath Hymn and Tune Book* (circa 1850) wrote: "No one has done so much as he, in his day and generation, to extend the practice and lower the taste in sacred music."[4]

Even recent scholars have been split about Mason. No one writing on nineteenth-century American music has been able to ignore him, however. Mason's influence is now judged, on balance, deleterious. The positive effects of his contributions to education were offset by his efforts to improve church music. He succeeded in psalmodic reform, but the price of success was too high. The European orientation of his psalmody not only eradicated an indigenous American music but also created an atmosphere in which a stilted correctness eclipsed originality or inspiration, and in which European music was considered inherently superior to American.[5]

To place responsibility on Mason for the European bent of concert life in the United States later in the century is to suggest an influence far out of proportion to his accomplishments. The American music that he "eradicated," the fuging tune, was as European in origin as his own "improvements." And Mason was hardly the instigator of psalmodic reform. The fuging tune had been thoroughly discredited, and calls for a better or at least different psalmody had sounded well before he entered the field. Hubbard's *Essay on Church Music* dates from 1808, and Hastings' *Dissertation on Musical Taste,* the most substantial treatment of the subject, was written in 1822. Predating all of Mason's professional activities in music, they roundly attacked the style of the fuging tune.

Mason was more a reactor than an innovator. Acutely sensitive to popular currents, he anticipated with almost prescient genius what the American public wanted. He had a special knack for being in the right place at the right time and, even more important, for sensing when to go on. He never stayed in one position for more than seven years, even when there was no apparent reason for him to go or no apparent position for him to go to.[6] After guiding the Handel and Haydn Society from 1828, he announced in 1832 that, after finishing his tenure of one more year, he would not accept another term as president. Mason's focus had by then shifted to the Boston Academy of Music, but in 1832 it was difficult to determine what kind of future lay ahead for the academy. In 1837 he began teaching in the public schools. Although this was a logical extension of his work at the academy, it was a risky step.[7] There was no precedent for music in the public schools, and the Boston City Council had refused to appropriate any money for music, in spite of a positive recommendation from the School Committee. Mason gambled that by teaching for a year without pay he would demonstrate the desirability to include music in the curriculum. The gamble paid off, and he became superintendent of music in 1838. His tenure lasted only until 1845, when he was forced out in a bitter controversy.

Mason was first and foremost a product of antebellum revivalism. He underwent a typical conversion experience when he was twenty-one and lived in Georgia. His conversion was the pivotal event of his life. The entire shape and direction of his career may be traced back to it, and for the remainder of his life Mason remained resolutely faithful to it.

Yet scholars have said surprisingly little about that experience, and no one has considered its implications. Many erroneous evaluations of Mason can be traced specifically to a failure to consider how much religion motivated what he did. His historical position can be properly assessed only when his professional activities, thought, attitudes, and approach to musical issues are viewed within the context of nineteenth-century evangelicalism.

As a youth Mason was neither religious nor ambitious. His upbringing was typical of small-town, late-Federal New England. He grew up in Medfield, Massachusetts, the eldest son of a moderately well-to-do manufacturer of straw hats.[8] He displayed a notable lack of drive. Whereas his friends went off to Boston or Harvard and settled in professions, Mason took no initiatives to establish a career. He admitted later that he was "a wayward, unpromising youth . . . [who] gave little promise, save for music . . . [and] spent twenty years of his life doing nothing but playing upon all manner of musical instruments that came within his reach."

He was interested in little beyond music, except possibly dancing. He learned to play several instruments and considered the cello and the clarinet his principal ones. He attended a singing school at the age of thirteen, was leading a church choir at sixteen, and had composed his first anthem at eighteen, when he was asked to lead the Athol, Massachusetts, military band, which he considered "my first entrance into my professional life." While his musical talents were modest by European standards, he apparently amazed associates with his abilities.[9] Yet he did not even consider the possibility of a career in music.

On November 27, 1812, Mason departed for Savannah with two friends. Why he went is not clear, although he seems to have been prompted by a lack of career prospects in Medfield and a vague promise of encouraging possibilities in Savannah.[10] He stayed in Savannah for fifteen years, working in a dry-goods store and then a bank. He pursued music actively, as a teacher of numerous singing schools, as organist of the Independent Presbyterian Church, as a student of F. L. Abel, and as compiler of what would become the *Boston Handel and Haydn Society Collection of Church Music*. There is no indication, however, that Mason intended to make music his profession. On the contrary, when the Handel and Haydn Society collection was published in 1821, he specifically kept his name off the title page for fear that it would harm his banking career.

Shortly after he arrived in Savannah, Mason's conversion occurred.

Precisely when and where it happened is not clear, but it was before June 8, 1814. On that day Mason wrote a lengthy letter to his family that reflects both his state of mind and typical revival rhetoric. Mason addressed each member of his family in turn, focusing upon their specific religious needs. To his father he pleaded: "O, my Father, you know not the satisfaction I should experience from an evidence of your real conversion. Why, why will you not embrace the Saviour? . . . Stop and consider—you are already on the border of eternity—witness those wrinkles and grey hairs, which before I left Medfield were too visible not to discover old age rapidly advancing. . . . I commit you to God—whether you accept Salvation or not God will finally be glorified and his people saved, O that his glorification might be in your salvation and not in your damnation—God grant it for Christ's sake."

To his mother, who apparently was already converted, he wrote: "To you I write in rather a different language—to you I can speak of the love of God—of death of Christ—may I not say he died for us? even us? O, how unworthy are we of such goodness?" To his sister:

It is first necessary to be convinced—after that, converted. Are you convinced? Do you believe there is a God, the creator and preserver of all creatures? Do you believe that man revolted against his maker, and that after he had sinned and become exposed to eternal death— God promised that the seed of the woman should bruise the serpent's head? Do you believe that in consequence and in fulfillment of his gracious promise, in the fullness of time Jesus the Son of God, offered himself the willing sacrifice of our sins? Do you believe that his atonement was accepted of God, and is sufficient for us? . . . Are you convinced that you are lost, beyond the possible reach of recovery by yourself?

To his brothers, about whom he was particularly concerned:

What shall I say to you? To you who are wholly engaged in the pursuits of the perishable objects of time and sense?—I can but warn you to "flee from the wrath to come.". . .

My Brothers—you are rebels against God, Sinning by nature, Sinners by practice. You have broken the laws of your God, trampled on his grace—and are now exposed to eternal death. You can do nothing to recommend yourself to God—you cannot save yourselves—Christ is the door by which you must enter. . . . Religion is our only rational happiness. . . . I well know that when we are young every thing seems smiling and gay—and we rush forward from object to object in pursuit of happiness—but with a few of the crosses and disappointments of life meet us—we shall begin to learn that all is vanity.—Finally, my Brothers, come to Christ—come taste the waters of life, leave the vanities of time for the realities of eternity.

This letter, only about 10 percent of which I have quoted, could come directly from a revival preacher. It reveals a young man completely carried away by a new passion, totally possessed by his conversion experience. It also demonstrates a man with a good ear for rhetoric, important in Federal New England.

The feeling of religious fervor evident in this letter never left him. Time and again similar, although slightly less exhuberant, comments surfaced in his writings. Any consideration of Mason's later career, including his stands on various types of music and the motivations behind certain of his activities, must be reviewed within the framework of this antebellum evangelical fervor.

Mason had felt no compelling attachment to religion before he came to Savannah; later in life he admitted that he was not particularly religious in his youth. His first letter to his family from Savannah, dated January 21, 1813, is almost as long as the letter quoted above and contains a daily account of his trip detailed enough to suggest that it was taken from a journal. But there is no reference whatsoever to religion in the letter. Given the tone of the June 1814 letter, and indeed most of his later writings, it is inconceivable that he would have written such a detailed account of a long and difficult experience without employing any religious rhetoric had he held the same fervent religious beliefs. On October 20, 1814, Mason recorded in a journal: "I have been looking over this book and reflecting upon my journey from Massachusetts to Georgia. I give up myself to God, resting my soul on the merit of Jesus for salvation. O receive me my blessed Saviour for in this is my hope, my only hope."[11] The journal itself has not survived, so earlier entries cannot be consulted. Mason's June 1814 letter further supports a recent conversion. He observed that his "whole acquaintance has changed," and that "those I once knew and was intimate with, I know no more"; "my pursuits are altered, my occupations are different, my affections, and I hope my heart, changed."

Mason's conversion probably occurred in the summer of 1813, apparently after an illness. In a letter written in 1864, Mason acknowledged that "almost immediately on my arrival there, I too, as I trust, found

Him."[12] When he arrived in Savannah he was concerned about the unhealthy nature of the climate. "It is very warm here . . . and amongst imprudent people it is unhealthy (there having been a number died within a few days after having been sick but two or three days) I suppose there is about 8 or 10 die weekly. I shall not think of staying in the city next summer if I do not come home." On July 3, 1813, Mason left Savannah for a two-week voyage down the coast to the port of St. Mary's. He remained there for five weeks, aboard the boat. He then received an invitation to stay with Mr. and Mrs. Phineas Miller on Cumberland Island, where he stayed for a month. The account of Henry Lowell Mason, Lowell Mason's grandson, which was taken from Mason's journal, is not entirely clear, but apparently during the voyage, possibly on the boat itself, Mason became ill, and the stay at the Millers' was a convalescence.[13]

In her study of early nineteenth-century Southern evangelicalism, Anne C. Loveland described typical converts and the conditions that precipitated their conversion. Most were in their late teens or early twenties, usually light-hearted and carefree before their conversion. In many cases one parent was deeply involved in religion. Most often conversion followed a significant change in life, sometimes provoked by a deep personal crisis, such as a serious illness.[14] For Mason every one of the conditions was in place. He came from a partly religious family—his mother was deeply committed to religion, but his father was not (at least, not conventionally). Mason was young, drifting without any real sense of direction in a strange environment. He was worried about his health and then suffered a potentially serious illness.

While we have no specific details about Mason's actual conversion experience, it closely parallels that of Michael Floy. Floy lived in New York City, and his conversion took place some years later, in 1828. The similarities between Floy and Mason are striking. Both were approximately twenty years old when their conversions occurred, with no earlier interest in religion. Each was certain of his conversion, sticking to it for the rest of his life, and each attempted to convert his family. Both were interested in music, but neither considered it a professional possibility at the time of conversion. Floy was a nurseryman but studied "Burrowes Thorough Base," which he confessed was "a new thing to me," and Catel's treatise on harmony. Both became teachers and superintendents of their Sunday schools after their conversions.

Floy has left a vivid, almost chilling account of his conversion experience. He described how "all at once I felt a trembling all over, my teeth chattered," so violently that persons in other pews noticed. Directed by one man to kneel at the front, "the sweat and tears completely drenched my handkerchief, and my cries could be heard all over the church"; "I thought I could not live long in this state." He then heard words whispered into his ear, certain that they were whispered by no one around him, and he joyfully cried out "Glory, glory!" Floy went on to observe that "it would be the height of absurdity for anyone to say I was mistaken. . . . My feelings I can perfectly remember: I felt like a little child in every respect, helpless, innocent, docile, without guile. Of the reality of the work I have never had a doubt from that day to this, although it is now more than 5 years ago (August 31st, 1828)."[15]

Given the similarities between Floy and Mason, and the typical pattern most conversions followed, this account could stand for Mason's experience as well, although there was one important difference. Floy was a Methodist, Mason a Presbyterian.[16] In 1813 Presbyterian revivalism was just reaching the southern Atlantic coast and it is highly unlikely that Mason would have encountered any revival activity in eastern Massachusetts before 1812. When he did witness it in Georgia, it must have seemed a strange and unique phenomenon.

Congregational or Presbyterian revivalism different from frontier revivalism partly in theology and partly in methods. Presbyterian revivalists were expected to maintain a degree of doctrinal orthodoxy, which meant Calvinistic predestination. Various Western revivalists either found ways to equivocate on this point, mitigating its harshness, or rejected it altogether. Presbyterian revivalists, although fervent, never engaged in emotional excesses of frontier revivalism. This was the principal reason the Presbyterians, along with the Baptists, almost immediately dissociated themselves from the camp meeting. The Presbyterian General Assembly issued a pastoral letter in 1832 that warned ministers against "bodily agitations," "noisy outcries," and "every species of indecorum." Presbyterians were "not to listen to self-sent or irregular preachers, or to any preaching inconsistent with their doctrinal standards." The editor of the *Southern Presbyterian Review,* reviewing Daniel Baker's *Revival Sermons,* declared that "our ideas of what belongs to good taste are not met by the discourses. . . . Apostrophe, and other strong figures of rhetoric, are too freely used, and carried beyond the bounds of propriety."[17] It was fortuitous that Mason originally encountered Congregational or Presbyterian revivalism in Georgia. Since dignity, restraint, and taste were so central to Mason's aesthetics that they were probably ingrained in his personality, the Presbyterian approach would have had much more appeal.

Mason's views regarding church music evolved considerably during his lifetime but did not change radically from his earlier statements. In evaluating those views we must consider two types of sources: first, his writings and lectures about church music and, second, his musical publications. His writings encompass both public and private statements. Often the two types of sources overlap, with explanatory prefaces to musical publications providing many insights. The music itself merits close analysis, as we can glean much from what he did as well as what he said. Musical evaluation includes his original compositions, particularly his hymns, his choice of sources for his anthologies, and the nature of his arrangements.

Mason's first extended essay into the field of church music was a volume he compiled in Savannah, the *Boston Handel and Haydn Society Collection of Church Music,* published in 1822. According to Mason's eldest son, William, the collection was based upon William Gardiner's *Sacred Melodies,* published in England in 1812. A comparison of Mason's collection with *Sacred Melodies* corroborates that point only to an extent.[18] The format of the two works is similar. Both contain predominantly four-part settings, with the two outer voices at the bottom and the inner voices above. Mason, however, adds a figured bass to the lowest voices. Both anthologies are thus laid out so that two-part performance is practical; an organist lacking the skill to read four parts can play the two lowest voices alone. Mason transposes the order of the two upper voices, placing the tenor above the alto. The alto part has the highest range of any of the voices, frequently going up to A^2, and it is possible that Mason intended the alto to be sung an octave lower. The tenor in Gardiner's collection is written in the alto clef, and when Mason does borrow from Gardiner's settings, he often reverses the two parts. Mason's alto part, if sung an octave lower, would correspond to Gardiner's tenor part.

Forty-four tunes are common to both collections. This does not always mean that Mason used Gardiner as his source, however. Mason's "St. Mary's" is the same as Gardiner's "Lord What is Man!" Both use the same text, but key, meter, and harmonization are different; Mason's is in E minor, Gardiner's D minor, and Mason's is in alle breve compared to Gardiner's 4/4. The bass lines differ not just in detail but in overall contour. Gardiner's attribution for the tune lists only an "Old German Air," whereas Mason's is more specific: "An ancient German melody, by

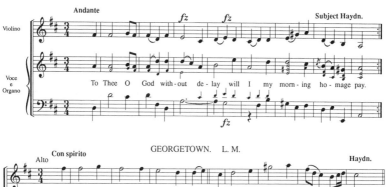

EXAMPLE 1: "To Thee O God," from Gardiner, *Sacred Melodies,* 1:124, and Mason, *Boston Handel and Haydn Society Collection of Church Music,* p. 73.

Rathiel." Mason may well have taken the tune from another source. For instance, "St. Mary's" appears in Weyman, *Melodia Sacra,* in E minor.[19]

When Mason did borrow from Gardiner, the settings were much closer. Key and meter remained the same, and usually the bass line differed only in minor details. But he almost never borrowed any setting intact, invariably rewriting the inner voices. Most of the changes involve simplification. Apparently aware of his market, Mason wrote easier lines that are usually more static and less interesting polyphonically. He also simplified in other ways. The most noticeable difference between the two collections is the much stronger instrumental orientation of Gardiner's. When Gardiner set an instrumental piece he remained much closer to the original setting: he often retained ornamentation, resulting in ornate vocal lines; he sometimes sketched in instrumental parts in small notes. Many of the settings themselves contain separate instrumental parts, ranging from violin or viola to full orchestra.[20] In using the alto clef for the tenor Gardiner probably had the viola in mind. The part itself is usually labeled with the Italian word "tenore" and occasionally with "viola." When Mason did use one of Gardiner's settings that had obvious instrumental features, he usually eliminated them. Mason avoided most of the more obviously instrumental settings from

EXAMPLE 2: "In Thee O Lord Is Mercy," from Gardiner, *Sacred Melodies*, 2:245.

Gardiner's collection entirely. It would be ludicrous for any tune-book compiler in early nineteenth-century America to think that example 2, from Gardiner's collection, would actually be practical in the United States.

The relatively small number of tune matches between Mason's and Gardiner's collections, the apparent coincidences of some tune matches, and the changes that Mason made in virtually all of the similar settings raise the question of the extent of Gardiner's influence. In a letter dated June 20, 1821, to John R. Parker, editor of the *Euterpeiad,* Mason stresses the European orientation of his collection, indicating that for several years he has been importing music from Europe, while studying figured bass under a German master (F. W. Abel). He lists the European collections to which he is indebted: Samuel Arnold and John Cullcoth, *The Psalms of David,* Thomas Costellow, *A Selection of Psalms and Hymns,* David Weyman, *Melodia Sacra,* John Whittaker, *The Seraph,* and Gardiner's *Sacred Melodies.* He singles out Gardiner's collection for special praise: "from the latter work (which is truly classical) I have selected many pieces from Haydn, Mozart, Beethoven and other celebrated composers."[21]

Gardiner's collection was probably the most important single influence upon Mason in the compilation of his collection. Arnold's and Costellow's collections are considerably earlier and Whittaker's is late enough for Mason to have had his project well under way when he first encountered them. Gardiner's *Sacred Melodies* most likely served as a model, provided inspiration for the original idea. After that Mason, well aware of the need to balance his objectives with the reality of the current American world, modified his product considerably.

In the letter to Parker, Mason stated that he wanted to supplant the *Bridgewater Collection,* which he felt no longer deserved public patronage. He was concerned that his work was too classical, that it contained "too much of Mozart, Beethoven and so forth and of consequence [is] too much chromatic." He feared that musical taste in America was not sufficiently advanced to appreciate these composers. He admitted that his work was specifically "calculated to improve in a high degree the taste for sacred music." Mason the idealist and Mason the practical businessman were both present from the start.

That Mason respected Gardiner's collection is apparent in his meeting Gardiner some years later on his first trip to Europe. His disappointment with Gardiner's attitudes toward religion suggests that Gardiner's books had meant a lot to him: "Friday, 26 May, 1837. This morning met Mr. William Gardiner of Leicester at Mr. Novello's. I was sorry to hear profane expressions from the compiler of Sacred Melodies and Judah. I had about an hour's conversation on musical subjects, but we should never agree on many things relating to Church Music."[22]

Mason never abandoned his preferences for European music. As his career unfolded, however, it became more subservient to the democratic need for music to reach as many people as possible. He wished to provide music that was dignified, chaste, restrained, and in good taste, representing a moral worldview whose propagation he considered critical to counter opposing tendencies in American antebellum society. The issue was not simply aesthetic but religious, and of the most fundamental significance.

The question of musical taste, religious need, and populism came to a head in the early 1830s. Three elements fed into it: the spread of revivalism from the West to the East and its menacing encroachment upon Boston; the growth of large musical institutions in Boston; and the popularity of revival tune books that threatened to capture a large segment of the public.

Between 1822 and 1832 Mason's career had changed completely. Mason was a relatively obscure partner in a dry-goods store in Savannah, when the *Boston Handel and Haydn Society Collection of Church Music* was published. In 1826 he was invited to give an address on church music in Boston, which turned his career around almost as much as the Handel and Haydn Society publication did. The address was published, and a group of influential citizens soon circulated a petition asking Mason to assume musical leadership of several Boston churches. The petition guaranteed him a salary of $1,500 per year, a large sum for that time. When it became apparent that he would also be president of the Handel and Haydn Society, he agreed to the offer. By 1832 his church choirs were thriving, his publications were increasingly successful, and he had moved on from the presidency of the society to help found the Boston Academy of Music.

Mason's 1826 address is important as a relatively complete statement of his philosophy on church music and as a blueprint for much that he did later. In the address Mason described music as a divine institution. Music itself is not necessarily religious, but it can serve the purpose of religion. It is a "refined species of elocution," capable of enhancing the spirit of the words being sung beyond what any recitation could do. And unless it is used for that purpose it should not be introduced into the church. To Mason musical taste is intimately connected with religious feeling, "much more . . . than is generally supposed." Singing in church should be done with the heart and be both solemn and delightful.[23]

Mason summarized church music as it then existed. He found that in spite of some improvement in recent years, church music still fell far short of what it should be: it was not cultivated as a religious exercise; its devotional quality was largely overlooked; and its purpose was usually equivalent to that of the theater, "to give variety to the performances, and to relieve the mind from a too constant attention to the subject."[24]

Music was often performed merely for its own display, a practice Mason found particularly noxious.

Most of Mason's address dealt with practical ways in which church music could be improved. He advocated squarely the use of choirs to lead the singing. He distinguished between choirs that existed for musical exhibition and choirs whose function was to lead the congregation. In the latter case the devoutness of the members of the choir was as important as their musical abilities. Mason by no means wanted to limit singing to the choir, but at the same time he was concerned about overall effect. He stressed that anyone wishing to participate in singing should have some musical cultivation and not sing in a disturbing or offensive manner. He was more interested in the cumulative effect than the use of music for expression of individual feelings. Mason also advocated the use of instruments but distinguished between their discreet use for accompaniment and their abuse through instrumental display. In the absence of an organ, which he considered the most desirable instrument for church accompaniment, he favored the violoncello, and wanted to favor the violin but could not because of its many "irrelevant associations."[25] Mason then concluded with specific examples to illustrate the importance of matching tunes with words. He also introduced an idea that would later play a central role in his career: the teaching of children. Mason envisoned the teaching of congregations to sing as part of a larger process in which every child should receive musical instruction.

The next historically significant publication for Mason was *Spiritual Songs for Social Worship*. This collection was done in collaboration with Thomas Hastings and is their reaction to American evangelicalism. When in the *Handel and Haydn Society Collection* Mason had had to deal with the problem of musical standards versus audience, he was able to do so within the British context of cathedral versus parish music. But by 1831 evangelicalism had become a more pervasive force in American society, and it had no British counterpart. Mason and Hastings could not rely upon European models to define issues as they had done in many of their previous publications. And by 1831 Mason and Hastings had both observed at close hand the new and spreading type of revivalism of Charles G. Finney, discussed in chapter 1.

In 1826 Finney conducted a revival in Utica, New York, in the church where Hastings was an elder. As editor of the *Western Recorder*, Hastings strongly supported revivalism. The *Western Recorder* was a religious weekly that included a regular column on revival activity around the country. Not surprisingly, the Utica revival was described in detail, although little was said about Finney himself. Because revivals were considered the Lord's doing rather than man's, the reports stressed the results of the revivals, tabulating the number of converts as if keeping a box score, and paid relatively little attention to the personalities of the revivalists.

Mason's contact with Finney happened later, and that it occurred at all reflects the fluid state of evangelical religion in the early nineteenth century. It came about through Lyman Beecher, Mason's pastor at the Bowdoin Street Church, who at first opposed Finney and his methods. Beecher himself was well-known as a leader of the revival movement. He had learned to use revival techniques to combat Unitarianism and to promote social reforms such as temperance. Beecher belonged to that generation of revivalists who advocated revivalism within the framework of traditional Calvinistic Congregationalism, and he staunchly opposed Western revivalism, considering it neither properly decorous nor doctrinally correct.

Beecher was probably jealous of Finney's success and fame. Many years later he claimed to have cried out in 1827: "Finney, I know your plan . . . you mean to come to Connecticut, and carry a streak of fire to Boston. But if you attempt it, as the Lord liveth, I'll meet you at the state line, and call out all the artillerymen, and fight every inch of the way to Boston, and then I'll fight you there." In his memoirs, Finney claimed that Beecher said no such thing.[26] In any event, by 1831 Beecher had changed his mind. Possibly the Unitarian threat was too great, possibly Finney's success was too much. Beecher invited Finney to Boston to join him in a series of revival meetings held in 1831 and 1832.

Beecher's alliance with Finney in all likelihood influenced Mason's thinking. As the choir director of Beecher's church, Mason must have attended some of those meetings, although there is no mention of them in any surviving documents. Given Mason's respect for Beecher and his own evangelical bent ever since his conversion in Georgia almost twenty years earlier, he no doubt supported the revival. The evidence of the hymn books bears this out. For although *Spiritual Songs for Social Worship* was ostensibly written to combat frontier revivalism, in it Mason moved much closer to the spirit of revival hymnody than any of this previous efforts would even suggest. It was a significant populist step for Mason and a practical realization of a belief Mason held throughout his life:

reaching the people with the proper religious message was more important than aesthetically correct music.

Several of Mason's collections after 1831 continued to reflect a revival influence. *The Hallelujah*, published in 1854, is closest to the spirit of revivalism, but even some of the others, such as the *Carmina Sacra* and the *New Carmina Sacra*, Mason's best-selling collections, contain individual items that have a revival tone. Mason's most well-known hymn, "Nearer My God to Thee," written in 1852, reflects very much the deepfelt, prayerlike atmosphere characteristic of early revivalism.

Although Mason was co-author of *Spiritual Songs for Social Worship*, the compilation originated with Hastings. Hastings invited him to collaborate only after the original conception and after Hastings had determined the need for such a work through communication with clergy throughout the country.[27] Once the collaboration began, however, it was totally a joint effort. It is impossible to determine from the collection itself who contributed what. Even original hymns, like Hastings' "Rock of Ages" or Mason's "My Faith Looks up to Thee," are unattributed. Authorship can be determined only from other evidence.

Hastings had developed a warm regard for Mason during the 1820s.[28] In the *Western Recorder* in 1824 Hastings referred to him as "the distinguished musician in Savannah." In 1826 Hastings confirmed that he and Mason had had a friendly correspondence for years. In 1827 he elaborated on the subject of that correspondence and indicated that they had finally met. He also hinted at future cooperation: "It may not be uninteresting to the friends of psalmody to know, that the editors of these two publications [the *Handel and Haydn Society Collection* and *Musica Sacra*] have for several years maintained a regular and friendly correspondence on the subject of uniformity in the revised harmonies of our plainest standard tunes; that a personal interview has recently been held for the same purpose; and that strong hopes are entertained of a final accomplishment of the desired object."[29]

Immediately following the publication of the first part of *Spiritual Songs for Social Worship*, Mason and Hastings became involved in a dispute with Joshua Leavitt, compiler of *The Christian Lyre*. Leavitt had a varied background, which did not include music. He graduated from Yale College in 1814 and taught briefly at Wethersfield Academy. He then studied law and was admitted to the bar in 1819. He practiced law until 1823, when he returned to Yale and completed a two-year course at the Divinity School in one year. He was ordained in February 1825. After serving for three years as a Congregational minister in Stamford,

Connecticut, he went to New York as secretary of the Seamen's Friend Society and editor of *Sailor's Magazine*. Editorship of several publications followed, including the *Emancipator*, the *Independent*, and the *New York Evangelist*, in which *The Christian Lyre* originally appeared in serial form.

Their editorial bases gave Leavitt and Hastings a forum to argue the merits, origins, and influences of their two compilations. The polemics began within the publications themselves, as each contained a lengthy introduction in which the authors stated their aims and purposes, and surveyed the state of psalmody as they saw it, particularly in relation to revivalism.

The Christian Lyre appeared first, in 1830. In the preface Leavitt maintained that many of the hymns and tunes used in church services were not suitable to revivals. *The Christian Lyre* was designed to supply that want. Throughout Leavitt opted for simplicity. He admitted that he possessed no musical skill himself, and that the collection was "not designed to please scientific musicians." He limited the number of parts to two, the tune and "a simple bass, sometimes not even that," because "the number of parts is apt to distract the attention of an audience, or to occupy them with the music instead of the sentiment." Most important, Leavitt purposely chose popular secular tunes, "the music that is most current among different denominations of Christians." This became his principal point of contention with reformers like Hastings and Mason.

Spiritual Songs for Social Worship originally appeared in periodical form, beginning July or August 1831.[30] At least three numbers were issued in 1831, and the entire collection was printed in 1832.[31] In the preface Hastings and Mason recognized as a first step the need to provide some type of religious music between psalmody, which was fine for public worship but not entirely suitable for "social and private uses, [where] something is needed more familiar, more melodious, and more easy to execution." Because most previous compilers had ignored the special needs of social meetings, as revivals were called, "a multitude of insipid, frivolous, vulgar, and profane melodies, have been forced into general circulation, to the great disparagement of the art, as well as to the detriment of musical reform." The compilers were particularly concerned about the effect of familiar secular tunes on recent converts: "Impenitent men, for example, who might be ignorant of the true principles of devotional music, would, immediately on their conversion, be found to exercise their religious feelings in such melodies as might then be at hand, whatever might be the character of those melodies, or however they might have been previously connected in the mind of others, with profane or impure associations."

That a number of the best known and loved tunes in the history of psalmody have secular origins has in the compilers' eyes complicated this problem, establishing a precedent that was much abused. The following passage, in the intensity of its rhetoric, also indicates how deeply Hastings and Mason felt about the use of popular tunes for religious purposes:

> Yet, if the lapse of three centuries has furnished among the innumerable abuses of this sort, some twenty or thirty specimens of a more favored character, it by no means follows, that in the present state of the churches, the same experiment may be safely repeated by every publisher who is unacquainted with music, directly in defiance of the fundamental principles of the art. But this very thing has been done, and the public have been extensively called upon, in these enlightened days of reform, to recognize in the current love songs, the vulgar melodies of the street, of the midnight reveller, of the circus, and the bar room, the very strains which of all others, we are told, are the best adapted to call forth pure and holy emotions, in special season of revival! In some instances too, tunes have come to us, not as old acquaintances partially recognized, but in all the freshness of their corruption, still reeking, as it were, with the impure associations which prevail in the haunts of moral pollution![32]

The compilers provided two rules of musical adaptation: (1) "whether at the time of selection, they [the tunes] possess intrinsically an appropriate character; and are thence adapted to call forth the right emotion" and (2) "whether the specimen before us, though intrinsically chaste and effective, may not, in the minds of a considerable portion of the community, be connected with profane association." This issue is easily recognizable as one of the principal tenets of the Presbyterian-Congregational reformers. It became more acute with revivalism, however, because the nature of revivals (as Leavitt, Hastings, and Mason all agreed) demanded music of a simpler, more accessible character. Since such music tended toward a popular style, the line was less clear between what was acceptable and what was not.

It was apparent to anyone involved in the field that the two tune books were in direct competition. A review of *Spiritual Songs for Social Worship* in the *Quarterly Christian Spector* specifically compared them. The anonymous reviewer espoused the philosophy of the Presbyterian-Congregational reformers, assuring his readers that the popularity of *The Christian Lyre* "need not give the friends of musical reform any just ground of alarm respecting the public taste." He welcomed *Spiritual Songs for Social Worship* because of its "more elevated and chaste" character, and because it was "freed from every unhallowed and unpleasant association."[33]

Yet *Spiritual Songs for Social Worship* is important more because it was similar to *The Christian Lyre* than because it was different. Their formats are alike: both books are small enough to be easily carried, although *The Christian Lyre*, slightly smaller, could more easily fit into one's pocket; both place the text and tunes on opposite pages, keep external information to a minimum, and omit the sources of the tunes or the texts.

The most significant departure for Mason from the *Handel and Haydn Society Collection* lay in the settings themselves. The settings of *Spiritual Songs for Social Worship* and *The Christian Lyre* are not radically different from each other, although Mason and Hastings generally used more voices than Leavitt did. Even that point is not absolute. Leavitt's harmonizations are predominantly two-part: one hundred are two-part, three are in unison, and two are three-part. Mason's and Hastings' settings are more varied in the number of voices, ranging from unison to four parts. Three parts predominate, although two-part settings appear often enough to establish it as common variant: 128 are in three parts, 26 in two parts, 11 in four parts, and 8 in unison. Six of the settings vary in the number of parts.

Beyond the differences arising from the absence of the third voice, there is little to differentiate stylistically the settings of *The Christian Lyre* from those of *Spiritual Songs for Social Worship*. This is especially apparent in five tunes that are common to both compilations. These are: "Missionary Hymn," "Mount Calvary," "Benevento," "Moravian Hymn," and "Chelmsford Melody."

"Missionary Hymn" is Mason's own tune, written originally in 1824. The versions are identical, except for the absence of a third voice. The two settings of "Mount Calvary" are very similar, with some difference in detail. Both use only two voices. Where they diverge, in the fourth phrase, Hastings' and Mason's setting seems stronger. The B-natural against the F gives a more incisive harmony, and the shape of the line itself stresses the E at the end, by moving lineally up to A, the highest note. The two keys, C at the beginning and A minor at the end, are brought out in greater relief. When the settings diverge again, in the

MISSIONARY HYMN.

MISSIONARY. 7. 6. D.

EXAMPLE 3: Mason, "Missionary Hymn," from Mason and Hastings,
Spiritual Songs, p. 44; Leavitt, *Christian Lyre*, 1:24.

final phrase, Leavitt's setting is stronger. Hastings and Mason attempt
to unify the bass through the repetition of the bass line of the fourth
phrase. The tonal situation is different, however, and Leavitt's more
straightforward repetition of A reflects it better than the slight ambiguity
created by the C-B-C movement in *Spiritual Songs for Social Worship*.

"Moravian Hymn" differs in the first two phrases and in one note in
the third phrase. In the first two phrases Leavitt's version seems superior
because of the more linear quality, specifically the two F-sharps, in
measures 1 and 4. In defense of *Spiritual Songs For Social Worship*, the
presence of a third voice does obviate somewhat the necessity of an F-
sharp in the bass. The G-sharp in the fourth phrase of *Spiritual Songs
for Social Worship* produces a better result than the E in *The Christian
Lyre*. Leavitt's version in that phrase suffers from both a static line and
a preponderance of open intervals. "Chelmsford" presents a different
situation. With the exception of a single passing note, the two settings
are harmonically identical, including the number of voices. The poetic
meter is the same common meter, but the musical meter is different, alle

MORAVIAN HYMN. C. M. D.

EXAMPLE 4: "Moravian Hymn," from Leavitt, *Christian Lyre*, p. 98; Mason and Hastings, *Spiritual Songs*, p. 79.

breve in *The Christian Lyre* and 3/4 in *Spiritual Songs for Social Worship*. Both versions work equally well. The G-sharp passing note in measure 3 of *Spiritual Songs for Social Worship* does not materially improve the harmony. The simple A–F-sharp–E movement of the bass in *The Christian Lyre* is equally effective.

As these five examples illustrate, it is difficult to claim that Hastings' and Mason's settings are musically superior to those of Leavitt. Overall, *Spiritual Songs For Social Worship* did seem to be more careful about avoiding obvious mistakes of common-practice harmony, such as parallel fifths and octaves. The presence of a third voice cannot be dismissed, as it does create a fuller and richer sound. That Hastings and Mason were willing sometimes to use only two voices undercuts any argument that they found a two-voice approach objectionable. Two-voice performances were probably more common in the early nineteenth century than the tune books indicate. As we saw earlier, Mason laid out the parts in the

Handel and Haydn Society Collection of Church Music so that organists not capable of reading all four parts could play the two outer voices. Likewise, when a bass viol created a two-voice setting, it would not be unreasonable to expect the singers to follow.

That the tune books were competing was not lost on the principals. Nor was the fact that they were similar. As editors of periodicals Hastings and Leavitt each had a forum to discuss the other's work. Leavitt's principal charge was not that *The Christian Lyre* was superior or more suited to the country's taste, but that *Spiritual Songs for Social Worship* was an imitation. Hastings retorted that the influence was the other way around. He claimed to have a letter in which Leavitt admitted that the format of the books—pocket-size, with music and text printed on opposite pages—and "the general arrangement of matter" were modeled on Hastings' *Juvenile Psalmster*.[34]

Hastings' claim is misleading. The two books were similar partly because (as their prefaces acknowledge) they both drew from the same model, Asahel Nettleton's *Village Hymns for Social Worship*, and its musical companion, *Zion's Harp*, which was published in 1824. Nettleton was a leader of the moderate Calvinistic revivalists, and his hymns were specifically designed for use in revivals. *Zion's Harp* provided the music to go with these hymns. It was published in the same format as *The Christian Lyre* and *Spiritual Songs for Social Worship*, three years before Hastings' *Juvenile Psalmster*. Most of the settings of *Zion's Harp* are in three voices, and they generally reflect a more conservative and less populist style than either *The Christian Lyre* or *Spiritual Songs for Social Worship*. The three voices have more independence, and the bass usually but not always has a more linear character, producing more true polyphony. The range of each voice is wider, and the settings are more florid. The style is generally more sophisticated than in either of the later books.

Hastings insisted that he and Mason had borrowed nothing from *The Christian Lyre*. "What, then, have we borrowed from the Lyre, or its plan of publication? Nothing—absolutely nothing." He also intimated that Leavitt had approached him to collaborate:

> At the time he wrote to us, he had issued several numbers with success, while yet the work unhappily had assumed that kind of character, for which no respectable musician could have consented to become responsible.—He knew, also, that the work had great imperfections; and more than intimated at that time that he should "rejoice" to see it "superseded by another upon a similar plan," whenever it

HOME.

EXAMPLE 5: "Home Sweet Home," from Leavitt, *Christian Lyre*, p. 142.

could "be done with sufficient improvement to render a change beneficial." To his letter we returned an answer, that was kind and explicit
as his own had been to us. We could not unite with him on his own
principles; and to these he was determined to adhere.[35]

Hastings makes it clear that he and Mason part company from Leavitt
in the use of secular songs: "The whole list of secular songs, too, from
"Auld lang syne," down to *"Lowley Nancy,"* and the *"Young Man's Wish,"*
(see first volume of the Lyre), is still at their service; not one of which
do we intend to covet."[36] This is the primary difference between two
philosophies. Leavitt could take a song like "Home, Sweet Home" and
use not only the tune but also the text as the point of departure. The
results were sometimes awkward, as shown in example 5.

Historically, *The Christian Lyre* looks backward; *Spiritual Songs for Social
Worship* looks forward. The chief difference between the settings of *The
Christian Lyre* and *Spiritual Songs for Social Worship* is the greater predominance of open sounds in *The Christian Lyre* that results from the
presence of only two voices. *The Christian Lyre* thus has more of the
flavor of the earlier American hymnody that Law and others railed
against. It also reflects an older folk style in its greater use of tunes in a
minor key: 27.7 percent, as opposed to 9.5 percent in *Spiritual Songs
for Social Worship*.

But what does *Spiritual Songs for Social Worship* look ahead to? It is

EXAMPLE 6: "Go Forth on Wings of Fervent Prayer,"
from Mason and Hastings, *Spiritual Songs*, p. 176.

scarcely more European than *The Christian Lyre*, even though it avoids
the obviously popular secular tunes of the day as a source, draws on
European melodies, and has a fuller sound, avoiding obvious harmonic
mistakes. Most of the three-part settings in *Spiritual Songs for Social
Worship* are much closer in character of the two-part settings of *The
Christian Lyre* than to the more elaborate four-part settings of the *Handel
and Haydn Society Collection of Church Music*. Mason and Hastings generally use a bass line that is relatively stationary, or moves in predominantly root position or within arpeggiated chords. The third voice is
usually an alto that follows the melody in thirds and sometimes sixths,
deviating only when maintenance of the interval would result in an
undesired harmony. The harmonies themselves are simple, staying close
to tonic, dominant, and subdominant. The percentage of tunes in a
major key is even higher than in the *Handel and Haydn Society Collection
of Church Music*. Dotted rhythms are common, and phrases are short
and clear. The settings not only have a markedly folk character but also
resemble closely the type of rural gospel music that emerged later in
nineteenth century, as illustrated in example 6.

  Mason's willingness to publish settings of this nature is entirely consistent with his career. He was prepared to embrace a populist style of
church music if it would further his cause of moderate evangelical
religion. Yet his accommodation of different musical styles should not
be confused with a laisez-faire attitude in which any music was satisfactory. Mason was fully committed to nineteenth-century notions of progress, believing that the older style of hymn tune was musically inferior
and that church music was constantly improving. In 1851 he referred

to a time fifty years earlier when "miserable musical trash which, in the form of tunes, . . . almost universally prevailed." In the preface to *The Hallelujah*, published in 1854, he spoke of the "constant progress of Psalmody in our country during the last thirty years," and admitted that even the harmony in the *Handel and Haydn Society Collection of Church Music* was not "always the most chaste and euphonious." Positive faults in the collection were avoided "sometimes at the expense of freedom and gracefulness."

In a commemorative sermon shortly after Mason's death, George Blagden Bacon summarized Mason's philosophy of church music. According to Bacon, Mason maintained two ideas about church music: "1st, That the tunes used in the churches should be such that all could sing them . . . 2nd, that they should be subordinate to the words used, should be the fit and natural expression of the words."[37] His philosophy could lead him into strange, almost contradictory directions musically. After serving as president and conductor of the Handel and Haydn Society, as director of music in several of the most important Congregational churches in Boston, and as professor and choral conductor of the Boston Academy of Music, Mason became so strongly in favor of congregational singing in church that he opposed the use of choirs, and was even uncertain about organs.

When he returned from Europe in 1852, he was engaged to supervise the music of the Fifth Avenue Presbyterian Church in New York City. James Waddel Alexander, the pastor, noted that Mason had come out against choirs. Alexander himself favored congregational singing and was delighted to discover Mason's position: "We are in an odd state as to music. Lowell Mason is our leader; but since his return from Europe he is so bent on severe, plain tunes and congregational singing, that while I am tickled amazingly, the people are disappointed. I enter no house where so many join. But I fear we cannot hold it against such odds." As for Mason's doubts at the time about the efficacy of organs in church, Alexander observed: "LM said to me the other day 'I have been an organist all my life; yet if a congregation should say to me, "shall we have an organ?" I should scarcely dare to reply "yes".'" Yet Mason did not seem to favor unaccompanied congregational singing. He was particularly interested in removing the orchestra that was apparently disruptive during the service and replacing it with an organ to lead the singing. A new organ was installed, and Mason's son William was engaged as organist while Lowell Mason continued as supervisor of music.[38]

Mason's preference for "severe, plain tunes" led him to advocate the use of chant in the Congregational service. He was not the first American musician to express an interest in chant; Andrew Law had included eight Anglican chants in his *Rudiments of Music*, first published in 1783. Chants, however, never even competed with metrical psalmody in the eyes of most Presbyterian-Congregational reformers. Mason's interest in chant may have been stimulated by his trip to Europe in 1837. On May 30 he had heard the charity children sing at St. Paul's, "about 6000 of them." He was moved by their "sublime" singing of the same chant that Haydn heard. (Haydn had written in his first London Notebook that he had heard four thousand charity children sing, and that "no music ever moved me so deeply in my whole life.") Mason referred to chant elsewhere in his diary: he commented upon the "most beautiful effect . . . produced by the organ accompaniment to the priest as he chanted some part of the service" at Berne Cathedral on August 6, and he was deeply impressed with the precise chanting at the chapel of the School for the Blind in Liverpool.[39]

Mason's most extensive exploration of chant is in his *Book of Chants*, published in 1842. The preface, in which Mason expressed his views on chant, is one of his most succinct statements of his views on music in church. Mason stated explicitly that he preferred chant over metrical psalmody because it placed greater emphasis upon the text. In chant there was "less tendency to draw attention to itself, than there is in Metrical Psalmody." Frequently "the principal object [of psalmody] seems to be to perform a pleasing air or melody; or to make the music or tune the principal thing." This was the heart of Mason's philosophy. "Nothing is more to be deprecated in church Music, than the constant tendency to mere musical display or exhibition."[40]

Mason favored chant because it was simple and because it bore no relationship to secular music. Finding tunes free of secular association was one of the critical needs of the psalmodic reformers and the principal motivation for their use of European models. Chant was peculiarly well suited to what Mason called "genuine expression." By this he meant that it was conducive to creating a devotional atmosphere when it was sung properly. Chant was also suitable for the entire congregation to sing, more so than metrical psalmody. Mason was not yet willing to abandon a choir; it (or at least a precentor) was necessary to lead the congregation, but, for the same effort invested, the payoff was greater with chant than with metrical psalmody. "Indeed, it is believed that with the same attention to this subject [chanting] which has usually been given to the singing of psalms and hymns, congregations may chant much better than they can now sing Metrical Psalmody."[41]

Mason's own position about music had led him into a dilemma: populism versus restraint. Music was to serve religion, and Mason's overriding concern was to reach as broad a populace as possible with the Congregational-Christian message. The congregation had to be an integral part of the service, so one had to resist musical processes that distanced the participants from the presenters or made hierarchical distinctions within the church body. A choir that sang while the congregation sat in silence established an unacceptable separation among the church members. Yet a congregation that was allowed to set its own direction and standards teetered on the brink of unbridled emotionalism. This lesson had been apparent from the Great Awakening to the camp meeting. In the nineteenth century the loosening of passions threatened the structure of society itself; taste and decorum were integral to the Congregational outlook. Mason believed that he had found the way to blend these two conflicting tendencies through chant. Chanting was both devotional and practical, that is, well within the reach of American congregations.

Lowell Mason, Thomas Hastings, and other psalmodic reformers had an immense impact upon American music because they spoke so directly and sympathetically to their time. They were first and foremost populists; although they firmly believed that some kinds of music were better than others, reaching the people with their religious message was more important than any musical leanings. Their populism was important to their success. The Presbyterian-Congregational reformers were the last generation for whom populism and classically oriented musical ideals could co-exist. Mason's followers divide into two directions. His sons carved careers in classical music: William studied with Liszt and became a successful concert pianist and member of the Boston musical establishment; Daniel Gregory and Lowell, Jr., founded the music publishing firm, Mason Brothers, later to become Oliver Ditson; Henry, with Lowell, Jr., helped found the piano and organ company, Mason and Hamlin. Mason's grandson Daniel Gregory Mason became a composer, professor of music at Columbia, and staunch upholder of the highbrow tradition. Lowell Mason's pupils and protégés, however, moved into popular music. After Mason's generation a musical career had to go beyond hymnody. William Bradbury stayed closest to the Presbyterian-Congregational-hymnist tradition, manufacturing pianos and compiling Sunday-school books that were immensely successful.

More than any other composer, George Root was Mason's musical heir. Root studied with Mason but later turned away from composing music that was too European. He was not a hymnist but a composer of popular secular songs, although he did write large-scale cantatas and other vocal works. Root justified this position straightforwardly: "I should be wasting my time in trying to supply the wants of a few people, who are already abundantly supplied by the best writers of Europe." He then began to compose "people's song," popular songs that had much in common musically with the songs of Stephen Foster, as Root himself acknowledged. His evolution as a composer in no way negated his own musical background, however. He sought a middle ground, a style that was simple but dignified, accessible yet correct, natural and crafted. These same principles governed Mason's aesthetic philosophy, although each composer realized them in quite different ways. Root admitted that it was easy to write correct music; it was far more difficult to reach inside the people with music that stayed in their hearts.

Like Mason, Root was keenly aware of the marketplace. In his study of the role of the marketplace in American culture, Richard Crawford discussed the "emergence of the middle-class American home as a center of musical performance and a prime target of the music business." Crawford found that this coincided with the beginning of Root's song composition in the 1850s, after he had left Boston in 1844.[42] While in Boston, under the tutelage of A. N. Johnson and Lowell Mason, Root had continued the singing-school tradition. As a businessman Mason never left that tradition, but he also adapted to the times: when secular music became more popular in the 1830s, he responded with compilations of glees. Root followed the marketplace into areas Mason did not enter, but he must have learned much about marketing his musical wares from Mason.

Crawford also observed the apparent contradiction in Root's activities: "pedagogical authority and control" (his teaching career) and "compositional deference" (his composing of simple songs that anyone could absorb). Root thus landed simultaneously on both sides of Crawford's authenticity-accessibility duality. Root's position in this regard is so close to Mason's that it is hard not to conlude that this was another lesson he had absorbed from Mason.

Root knew his music was stylistically close to Foster's. It is also close to Mason's, and this tells us much about Mason's style. For in spite of Mason's insistence upon correct harmony, the supremacy of European models, and musical dignity, he drew upon the same simple, easily

EXAMPLE 7: Stephen Foster, "Old Folks at Home"; Lowell Mason, "Nearer My God to Thee"; George Root, "Hazel Dell."

accessible resources and formulas that Root and Foster did. A comparison of three successful songs, or two songs and one hymn, illustrates just how similar the music of these composers is: Foster's "Old Folks at Home," Mason's "Nearer My God to Thee," and Root's "Hazel Dell." All three are strictly diatonic and have similar ranges: "Old Folks at Home" and "Hazel Dell" precisely one octave range, and "Nearer My God to Thee" a ninth. And even though the surface melodic shapes are quite different, all three are remarkably similar in underlying melodic movement. The first phrase of each melody consists of two parts. The first part of each tune begins with movement from the third scale degree down to the tonic, although it happens differently in each case. "Old Folks at Home" repeats the 3-2-1 motive twice, and "Hazel Dell" actually moves upward to 5, which is the most prominent note, before dropping to 1. "Nearer My God to Thee" has the most direct 3-2-1 movement. Each tune then concludes the first part of phrase one by rolling prominently to the subdominant chord, emphasizing the minor third between 1 and 6. The second half of the first phrase is nearly identical in all three songs: 5-1-3-2 for "Hazel Dell" and "Nearer My God to Thee," and 5-3-1-2 for "Old Folks at Home." The first part of the second phrase repeats identically the first part of the first phrase, followed by a full cadence based upon a 3-2-1 melodic descent.

Both "Hazel Dell" and "Old Folks at Home" repeat the first two phrases before going to the bridge, or b section. And both smooth out the syncopation near the end of the first phrase to four quarter-notes in some of the repetitions. The bridge of all three stresses the subdominant melodically: "Hazel Dell" moves directly to the fourth scale step; "Nearer My God to Thee" moves from 5 to 6, emphasizing 6 both rhythmically and as the melodic apex; "Old Folks at Home" descends over the subdominant chord to the fifth scale step. All three tunes then repeat the first two phrases.

Much of what I have described is nothing more than standard clichés for popular music of the mid-nineteenth century. It nevertheless illustrates that Mason could and did write in that style, and that his compositions, independent of his writing about music, were so close to the popular idiom to be at times indistinguishable from it. We see the beginnings of an unusual duality with Lowell Mason. Mason the advocate and Mason the composer are two radically different personalities. This has led to a misinterpretation about Mason by many later writers. His advocacy of cultivated, dignified, European-based music has been wholeheartedly embraced by defenders of high culture and lamented by writers with populist leanings. His compositional career, however, has been an embarrassment to those same defenders of high culture, something to be explained as a lack of training and opportunity at best or as evidence of a mediocre musician at worst.

Yet there is no inconsistency here. When Mason's work is examined from the point of view of antebellum America, the two sides of his activity conform perfectly to his time. Attitudes about high and low culture had not yet hardened, religious factors mattered more than purely aesthetic ones, and an incipient musical idealism, sired by Puritanism and born of evangelicalism, was forming, to remain within the provenance of religion for much of its early growth. Only to later generations was the dichotomy between idealism and populism apparent. Even when the ideals of the church-music reformers first penetrated the secular musical world, advocates of new standards of value for secular music sought to reach the population at large with their ideals, as we shall see in future chapters.

Chapter Four
Class and Concert Life in Early Nineteenth-Century Boston

In 1823 Adam Hodgson divided the population of the United States into three classes. The first class consisted of the old revolutionary-war heroes, "who hold a sort of patent of nobility, undisputed by the bitterest enemies to aristocracy." Many of this class were educated in England and resembled the English gentleman "of the old school." Few were left, and they were old; the class itself was about to die out, as Tocqueville also noted. The second class contained the leading politicians, the wealthier merchants, the more prominent lawyers, and generally the more respectable members of the professions. The third included everyone else. This group differed, however, from the corresponding class in England, "by greater acuteness and intelligence, more regular habits and reading, a wider range of ideas, and a greater freedom from prejudices, provincialism, and vulgarity."[1]

Hodgson's definition varied somewhat from later notions of upper, middle, and lower classes. Both of his first two classes comprised what would normally be considered the upper class, or elite, and his third class did not distinguish between the middle class and working class. This raises the question of the existence of a middle class in early nineteenth-century America. The term itself was seldom used. From the eighteenth century on, many references were made to the middling sorts, middling ranks, middling interests, and sometimes middling classes. Recent scholars, like Stuart Blumin have considered whether these references constitute an actual class, as opposed to a rank or station in a hierarchical social scheme, and have argued persuasively that by the early nineteenth century they did. Both Blumin and Sean Wilentz, who documented the emergence of the working class in the nineteenth century, differentiate the middle class from the working class. By the early nineteenth century members of the middle class had begun to distance themselves from both the working class and the upper class, and these distinctions applied to music as well. In a lecture on the music profession delivered in 1841, Timothy Haywood argued that painting and sculpture, because of their expense, must "look to the rich for patronage and encouragement," but music must look for support to the "middling classes, which in fact compose the great body of the people." As we shall see, some of the musical organizations in Boston tended to divide along class lines, with their members making a conscious distinction between the middle and the working classes.[2]

Especially important for explaining musical developments, however, is Hodgson's differentiation of two upper classes, because each class attempted to use music for its own political agenda. Spiritual and political heirs of the older gentry in particular sought to use music to create a republican vision of American society, a development that has been virtually ignored by scholars. Although the effort ultimately failed as a political stratagem, the process itself had important historical consequences: it convinced broad segments of the upper classes to support public musical activity for the first time, and it represented the first concerted attempt to place instrumental music at the center of American cultural life. It also created a set of paradoxes for which the only solution was the subversion of the republican vision. When the socioeconomic elite in Boston began to support secular musical activity in the 1840s, they did so from a very different political perspective, with the result that radically new attitudes about music became the norm. Later developments, which are sometimes considered the beginning of an elitist attitude toward art music in America, are directly related to this change of direction. Overall, musical activities in Boston, such as concert attendance, membership in musical organizations, and patronage itself, closely followed class lines.

The socioeconomic elite of the nineteenth century differed from the Colonial gentry in one profound way in particular. Most of the gentry believed deeply in republican values; most of the socioeconomic elite did not. Republicanism had many meanings in revolutionary America, as scholars have recently determined, but certain core political principles characterized the mainstream varieties. The theoretical basis of early Federal republicanism was an egalitarian society, at least in terms of opportunity. Equality of opportunity meant a relatively homogeneous society. The organic model, which had transformed the conceptualization of both art and science in the eighteenth century, was applied to the body politic as well. Because the community was an organism, all its members wre linked to each other, the actions of one affecting all the others. The state was "one moral whole," in which individual interests would yield to the public good. Hierarchy would exist, but a commonality of social purpose would insure rule by the public. For the

Colonial gentry, government was by consensus; those at the top of the hierarchy were best able to govern. Their position in the hierarchy validated that, and they expected the rest of society to recognize it. The republic was considered open enough, however, that, with proper training, members of the lowest class might be elevated to become leaders of society. Jefferson suggested that each year twenty bright boys from the lowest element of society be educated for leadership at the state's expense. As Robert Wiebe observed, Jefferson meant this as no challenge to the social structure.[3]

While few, if any, members of the gentry wished to abolish the social hierarchy, a flagrant display of wealth or social pretension was considered incompatible with republican principles. Artificial, as opposed to natural, distinctions between individuals were to be opposed, talent alone determining one's position in the social hierarchy. Birth did not determine gentility in America, but those who rose to the top were expected to conform to the same model of gentility as Samuel Johnson's native-born gentleman. Wiebe defined the qualities for the colonial gentry as courage, resolution, moderation, dedication, and control.[4] By the early nineteenth century, the Emersonian qualities of individualism and self-reliance had been added to the list.

Even in the earliest days of the republic, the republican notion of a homogeneous society was purely an ideal. Already by 1776 republicanism "possessed a decidedly reactionary tone," and many members of the colonial gentry were beginning to have doubts that the majority were "the safest Guardians both of public Good and private rights."[5] By the early nineteenth century the Colonial hierarchy was in disarray; American society had changed: industrialization had radically altered the relationship between employer and employee; new religious movements had responded to a new relationship between the individual and the social structure; vast new lands in the West had stirred the American imagination with new vistas of mobility. And by the 1830s new waves of immigration were raising serious questions about even the possibility of a homogeneous society.

Unlike the Colonial gentry, who attempted to reconcile their ideals of a democratic, homogeneous society with their conviction that they belonged at the top of a well-defined hierarchy, the nineteenth-century socioeconomic elite had few reservations about their right to a privileged position. The new elite were politically antidemocratic, socially insular, and at times pretentious about their wealth. When Harriet Martineau traveled in the United States during 1834 and 1835, she pointedly distinguished the "real aristocracy of the country" from the socioeconomic elite. The real or natural aristocracy could as easily be found "in fishing-boats, in stores, in colleges chambers, and behind the plough" as in "ball-rooms and bank-parlours." The socioeconomic elite were vulgar, their ostentation and affectation odious. Her greatest contempt was reserved for their antidemocratic attitudes and aristocratic pretensions; in Boston she even heard some of them openly advocate a monarchy. It is not surprising that she called Boston "as aristocratic, vain, and vulgar a city . . . as anywhere in the world."[6]

Not all members of the Boston socioeconomic elite fitted Martineau's characterization. Many considered it inappropriate to emulate European aristocratic styles. They realized that America was different. When Francis C. Lowell traveled to Europe, the "great corruption of the highest classes" did not escape his notice; neither, however, did the corruption of the lowest classes. Amos Lawrence was concerned that his son would bring home from Europe "foreign fancies" which he felt were "inapplicable to our state of society."[7] It is striking that even though most of the socioeconomic elite isolated themselves by living in Beacon Hill, they nevertheless chose to build relatively unpretentious homes.

The feeling that American life was unique, shared by many members of the socioeconomic elite, was a residue of their Puritan heritage. Part of that heritage, the work ethic, caused many upper-class Bostonians to view European aristocratic life-styles as not only affected but also indolent, an especially serious charge. When Silas Pickney Holbrook complained about the ball as an activity of the leisure class, his concern was with the conflict between it and the world of work. He observed that a ball in London would normally begin at ten in the evening, which would present no hardship on those who attended, as they normally slept all day anyway. In Boston, however, it was ludicrous for those who had to work—practically everyone—to emulate this aristocratic activity. Holbrook depicted as "preposterous" in American society one who "is obliged to hold himself in a strait coat and silk stockings; when he longs for slippers and night-gown, or he is bound to be civil when he has a greater tendency to be sleepy."[8]

Although puritan values remained strong among the socioeconomic elite, most members were liberal in religion, frequently being Unitarian. They also retained much of the older patriarchal family system.[9] Businesses often included members of the extended family, and family groups tended to live within close proximity. The new elite built houses in the Beacon Street area or in certain suburbs, an act that not only symbolized their material success but also reinforced their insularity. Their sons usually went to Harvard, which was not just a bastion of Unitarianism but by 1830 had become "almost wholly an elite institution"; according to Ronald Story, Harvard was the prime consolidator of the urban upper class in antebellum Boston.[10] What musical interest the socioeconomic elite had was as patron of secular music.

The middle class, while generally not wealthy, engaged in professions that offered ample opportunities for advancement. Politically they were pragmatic, motivated more by local issues than ideology,[11] and reserved their ideological bent for religion, usually fervent evangelicalism. They considered the nuclear family critically important, much more so than the extended family. They were interested in psalmody and musical organizations in which they could participate.

The religious element is one of the most important and unique aspects of class structure in antebellum Boston. While Unitarianism was found throughout the city, it was identified primarily with the elite. Members of the working class with a Unitarian doctrinal orientation tended toward universalism, which was less intellectual and more immediately appealing. Congregationalism, the principal denomination in Boston, was supported primarily by the middle class. It had an Eastern, urban, evangelical orientation, which differed considerably in tone and theology from the revivalism of the West, although many members embraced it with the same dedication (if not emotionalism) of Western converts. Not all members of the middle class were congregational evangelicals of course, but very few of the socioeconomic elite were. This religious distinction is important because well into the 1830s the principal musical developments in Boston were connected with sacred music. As we shall see, musical organizations and support followed religious lines.

The middle class did distinguish themselves from the working class or the mechanics. (In the early nineteenth century the term *mechanic* meant laborer.) The distinctions were sometimes subtle and could be quite exclusionary. In 1827 Frances Trollope was surprised that at a ball in Cincinnati the gentlemen, although "exceedingly smart," were the same men she had seen in city shops. She could not, however, find one particularly beautiful girl she had noticed before, and was told: "You do not understand our aristocracy, the family of Miss C. are mechanics." When she remarked that the young lady had been educated at the same school as those present and that her brother had a prosperous shop in town, it was explained to her that "he is a mechanic; he assists in making the articles he sells; the others call themselves merchants."[12]

Trollope's account further reveals the thin line between the socioeconomic elite and the middle class. Precisely when merchants moved from one to the other was never clear; neither was the application of the term *aristocracy*. The Eastern evangelicalism of the middle class further obscured these lines. A desire to reach as much of the population as possible was combined with a code of conduct that incorporated values of restraint, dignity, and decorum, which corresponded closely to those of the Colonial gentry. They also caused both groups to share a common fear of the religious bacchanalia they saw in the West.[13]

With the industrial revolution in the early nineteenth century, the working class assumed a more definitive shape, and historians have only recently begun to uncover its values, social structure, and changing relationship to other classes. While this class played less of a role in establishing musical attitudes in the early part of the century than the middle and upper classes, its presence in Boston musical circles is important for two reasons: first, the status of professional musicians varied somewhere between the middle class and the working class, depending on the nature of the individual's work; and, second, some actions of certain organizations can be explained only by taking this distinction into account. For instance, the Boston Handel and Haydn Society has been portrayed as a working-class organization. Yet, as we shall see, evidence suggests that it was in fact middle class and carefully guarded its position in that respect, either dismissing or discouraging mechanics who wished to join.

The middle class rather than the socioeconomic elite were the heirs to the democratic attitudes of the colonial gentry. Although the middle class became associated with the "priggery" of gentility later in the nineteenth century when the values of the gentry acquired a hollow character,[14] early in the century the middle class frequently held positions bordering on populism. This orientation was related to their evangelical fervor and the fears precipitated by the revolution in choices brought about by the new mobility and individualism. It also reflected a recognition of the fluid character of American society.[15] It was thus quite different from the paternalism of the Colonial elite.

The cultural activities of the Boston socioeconomic elite suggest an ambivalence about the democratic ideals of the founding fathers. On the one hand the elite created institutions that would separate them from other elements of society. The Boston Athenaeum and the Massachusetts Historical Society fit that category. In each case membership and privileges were tightly controlled, and conformity in thought was demanded. When Bronson Alcott, for instance, differed too much from orthodox beliefs in 1837, his privileges at the Athenaeum were revoked.[16] The socioeconomic elite were keenly aware of their privileged status and saw themselves as guardians of culture. Nowhere are both points more clearly articulated than in the declaration by the incorporators of the Athenaeum: "Let men of leisure and opulence patronize the arts and sciences among us; let us all love them, as intellectual men; let us encourage them, as good citizens. In proportion as we increase our wealth, our obligations increase against the pernicious effects of luxury, by stimulating to a taste for intellectual enjoyment; the more we ought to perceive and urge the importance of maintaining by manners, manners by opinion, and opinion by works in which genius and taste unite to embellish the truth."[17] On the other hand many members of the socio-economic elite continued to maintain eighteenth-century republican principles. Some envisioned the arts as a unifying social force, accessible to all members of society. This belief persisted into the 1840s, and writers and lecturers discussing music articulated it with great clarity.

The elite's concept of cultural stewardship did not extend to music; as a consequence, public musical activity existed for at least one hundred years in Boston before any regular or sustained patronage from the upper classes developed. With neither the financial nor moral support of a segment of the community that both controlled great resources and did much to set the cultural tone of the society, concerts remained a risky venture well into the 1840s. Various musical organizations did enjoy brief success, but, except for the Handel and Haydn Society, none was able to secure the financial basis to sustain itself for long. And, as we shall see, the Handel and Haydn Society succeeded because of a financial windfall from a totally unexpected source, unrelated to traditional patterns of patronage.

We know that public concerts occurred in Boston from at least 1731, although they were sporadic until 1760. In the 1760s secular concerts became more frequent, and subscription concerts began in 1761. After 1770 concert activity was such that rival musicians or organizations at times simultaneously competed for support.[18] Unfortunately information about eighteenth-century concerts is sketchy and incomplete, when it exists at all. Most of it comes from advertisements in contemporary newspapers. The advertisements seldom list the programs and at times do not mention even the sponsoring organizations or the performers. Reviews are nonexistent, except for concerts that were part of special festivals or commemorations. Even the accounts of the festivals often speak of them only in general terms. It is more difficult still to determine the composition of the concert audiences, although scattered references do occur.

Information about musical societies is even more elusive. Many appeared in Boston in the eighteenth century, but few survived long. The Musical society, probably the most important musical organization prior to 1800, apparently flourished only from 1786 to 1789. After 1789 no more notices of it appeared in any of the papers. The last notice, in the *Massachusetts Gazette* of March 14, 1789, portended its demise, requesting that members pay their subscriptions so expenses could be met. Yet the Musical Society seems to have survived longer than most similar organizations, which either enjoyed a briefer tenure or left even fewer tracks. Oscar Sonneck speculated that other societies existed concurrently with the Musical Society because an announcement in the *Massachusetts Centinel* referred to the "intentions of the Musical Societies in this town" in regard to the rebuilding of the Meeting House on Hollis Street.[19] Sonneck's conclusion itself demonstrates just how inferential much of our knowledge about eighteenth-century musical activity is.

Most concerts consisted of various combinations of vocal and instrumental secular music, often followed by a dance. Military ensembles frequently took part. John Rowe described a 1769 benefit concert for "the fife-major of the 29th regiment" as providing the "best musick I have heard performed there."[20] A concert presented by William Selby in 1772 included assistance from "the band of his Majesty's 64th Regiment."[21] In 1771 Mr. Propert gave a series of three concerts at the Coffee House, on March 3, 17, and 31. Sometimes operas were presented as concerts. Sonneck mentioned a concert advertised as "A vocal entertainment of three acts. The songs (which are numerous) are taken from a new celebrated opera, call'd, *Lionel and Clarissa*."[22] Rowe's description of a performance of *The Beggar's Opera* confirms that these were concert versions of operas: "In the evening I went to the Concert Hall to hear Mr. Joan read the Beggar's Opera and sing the songs. He read but indifferently, but sung in taste. There were upwards of one hundred people there."[23]

An audience of between one hundred and two hundred was considered substantial but not unusual. Rowe commented several times on the size and composition of the crowd for different concerts, sometimes specifically, sometimes only generally. He called the audience for the three 1773 Propert concerts "a very genteel company" and the audience for the fife major's concert a "large and genteel company." Propert may have been encouraged to present his 1773 series because of the success of a 1771 concert, which drew "a good company, upwards of 200." Rowe's most detailed description of concert attendance was for a concert of Hartly Morgan "and others," which was followed by a dance. "The Commodore and all the captains of the navy here was there, and Colo. Dalrymple, and fifty or sixty gentlemen and the same number of ladies present."

Other reports confirm that an audience of between one hundred and two hundred was typical for a concert. A 1793 advertisement announcing the continuation of a concert series managed by William Selby stated that one hundred subscribers would be needed. In 1794 Mrs. Pownell gave a concert to raise money for a fire that had recently devastated Boston. She was disappointed that the house netted only $200. Yet a benefit for Josiah Flagg's widow raised $102, probably a more typical figure. In each case tickets sold for one dollar.[24] Besides London and Paris, cities with populations many times that of Boston, audiences of more than one or two hundred were rare even in Europe. And even in London and Paris, which had an established tradition of support for secular music, many concerts drew no better. To expect more from Boston would be unrealistic.

Eighteenth-century concerts sometimes combined sacred and secular music. Selections from Handel, particularly the *Messiah*, were common, and William Billings' anthems were occasionally performed.[25] Billings lived in Boston his entire life (1746–1800), and although he had little to do with the presentation of secular concerts, he was very much involved in the musical life of Boston. Concert tickets could be purchased at his shop as early as 1764, and as late as 1798 the Boston city directory listed Billings as a "singing master" on Newbury Street.[26]

In 1786 the Musical Society, headed by William Selby, gave one of the most extensive concerts to occur in Boston in the eighteenth century. For that reason it was reported relatively fully. It was a benefit for prisoners and consisted of twelve musical numbers interspersed with a church service. Sonneck speculates that Selby may have been inspired by the 1784 Commemoration of Handel in London, in which a concert with an orchestra of 250 and a chorus of 274 was presented at Westminster Abbey. The Boston concert assumed the proportions of a festival, with selections from the *Messiah* and *Samson* as well as several liturgical pieces, including the Te Deum, the Jubilate Deo, an anthem based on Psalm 95, and the doxology in a special setting composed by Selby. The performance concluded with an orchestra performing the

Overture to the *Occasional* Oratorio and "a favourite overture by Mr. Bach," probably one of the Bach sons. Selby, together with the orchestra, performed the "4th Concerto of *Amizon*, musica de capella, op. 7," and Selby performed an original organ solo.[27]

A correspondent sent a report of the concert to the *Pennsylvania Herald*, in which he claimed that parts of it equaled performances at Covent Garden itself: "The first recitative and the first song in the Messiah were sung as to have done no discredit to any capital singer at the theater in Covent Garden; but the song of 'Let the bright cherubins in burning row, etc.' in the opinion of several who had heard the oratorio of Sampson at Covent Gardenhouse, was sung, as least as well, in the Chapel Church, on Tuesday by our townsman, as they had ever before heard."[28]

The correspondent reported two other significant aspects of the concert. First, it was a mixed crowd, the church being "thronged with all classes of people," including a fairly large number of women. This implies that women did not normally attend concerts and that most concerts may have been relatively class stratified, although it is difficult to determine which classes did attend concerts regularly. Rowe's comment on "a very genteel company" at a 1773 concert and several references to "gentlemen" in concert announcements indicates that at the very least concerts were not aimed at the working or the lower classes. Since concert organizations in the early nineteenth century tended to imitate patterns of European academies in their semipublic exclusivity, the correspondent's observation probably means that the prison benefit drew from further down the class hierarchy than was normal. The second notable aspect of the concert was that the instrumental parts were well received. The correspondent commented that the instrumental performance "reflects the highest honor on the musical abilities of the gentlemen who composed the band, and he attributed the "theatrical clap" at the end to "the pitch of enthusiasm to which the excellent overture of Mr. Bach wound up the enraptured auditors."[29]

Technically, the regular concerts of the Musical Society were not public. New members were admitted when a vacancy occurred, and strangers needed the introduction of a subscriber. It is difficult to determine how exclusive such membership was. The 1789 season began with a request that gentlemen desiring to renew their subscriptions do so to allow new members to fill any vacancies that might remain. Announcements for an unidentified subscription concert series in 1790 and 1791 refer to a meeting of the "members of the subscription concerts," suggesting that membership consisted of purchasing tickets. Yet the requirement of introductions indicates that some attempt was made to screen sub-scribers.[30]

No eighteenth-century event had greater consequences for the development of musical life in Boston than the opening of the Boston Theatre on Federal Street on February 3, 1794.[31] In 1796 a second theater, the Haymarket, opened. The absence of theatrical activity in early Federal Boston was due to an antitheater law that had been passed in 1750. This law banned any sort of theatrical entertainment, stage play, or interludes in either a public or private house if more than twenty persons were assembled. The law provided penalties equally for the audience and the presenters. After several unsuccessful attempts to rescind this law, and after many various efforts to circumvent it through the presentation of "moral readings" and other ruses, the ordinance was finally allowed to expire quietly in 1793.[32]

The theater included music virtually every evening. It was the one place that both instrumental and vocal music could be heard on a regular basis. The bill usually consisted of two plays, at least one of which contained music. Sometimes operas, either eighteenth-century English ballad operas or works in English translation, were performed. There were often songs, dances, and instrumental numbers between the main pieces. Both theaters had orchestras that would play several overtures or other instrumental works before the curtain and other instrumental pieces between acts. Altogether this could include three or four symphonies, by Vanhall, Haydn, Stamitz, or Ditters von Dittersdorf. Attendees were thus treated to a virtual orchestral concert in addition to the plays. The opening night of the Boston Theatre promised:

> . . . the following distribution of the music will precede the drawing up of the curtain:
>
> YANKEE DOODLE.
> Grand Battle Overture in Henry IV.
> General Washington's March.
> The prefatory Address, by Mr. C. Powell, between the Acts.
> A Grand Symphony by Signor Charles Stametz [sic]; Grand
> Overture by Signor Vanhall; Grand Symphony by Signor Haydn;
> do. by Charles Ditters.[33]

The presence of an orchestra in the theaters had ramifications beyond introducing many Bostonians to orchestral music. Until at least 1850 instrumental concert life was too sporadic for an orchestral musician to earn a living at it. The theater, however, provided regular, steady employment promoting the presence of a core of instrumental musicians in Boston and later the professionalization of the orchestra, with both musical and social consequences. Instrumental music simply would not have developed in the manner that it did in America had not theaters been present in most large cities.

Beyond supplying an employment base for instrumental musicians, the role of the theater in the development of Boston's musical culture is problematic. It probably inhibited concert activity to an extent. Sonneck discovered that not a single concert notice appeared in the papers while the theater was open during the first season.[34] Throughout the first half of the nineteenth century the theater and concert organizations competed for the services of musicians, and because the theater provided more steady employment, concert organizations had to work around the theater schedule. The theater, however, never became the focal point of high culture in Boston as the opera did later in New York. Yet it was not purely a working-class entertainment. It continued to stir both practical and theoretical interest as a potential cultural magnet for the city. But it remained on the fringes of middle- or upper-class culture: at times it attracted considerable support from the elite, at other times it drew support almost entirely from the working class.

Considerable negative sentiment about the theater existed in Boston throughout the eighteenth and into the nineteenth centuries. It had several sources. Puritanism opposed the theater, in part because of the perceived theatricality of the Catholic Mass. In America Increase Mather referred to the theater in his "Testimony against Profane and Superstitious Customs." The act of the General Court of Massachusetts of 1750 outlawing theatrical productions found the theater objectionable for two principal reasons: it encouraged immorality and a "contempt of religion," and it "discouraged industry and frugality." The theater was thus not only profane but also frivolous. Clapp noted the "bitter feeling that existed against theater and theatrical representations" at that time and attributed it specifically to Puritan sentiment. When the Federal Street Theatre burned in February 1798, a letter appeared in the newspaper by an original proprietier of the Haymarket Theatre offering to contribute $340 toward demolishing the Haymarket. He considered it both a fire hazard and a hazard to the community, because "the public exhibitions there displayed have a tendency to corrupt the morals of youth, and lead them into temptations which may injure their reputation." He then urged the legislature to pass a law prohibiting the construction of future theaters.[35]

Patriotic sentiment ran against the theater during the revolutionary war. The Continental Congress passed a law forbidding any public official from attending the theater, on pain of being removed from office.[36] British-supported theater, when Boston was under British occupation during the war, further tainted the theater for many Bostonian patriots. General Burgoyne, one of the commanding British generals, was fond of the theater and arranged a few productions. At least one of these, *The Blockade of Boston*, was performed several times. Written by Burgoyne himself, this play was strongly biased toward England. Designed to show contempt for the American soldiers, it naturally aroused resentment in those committed to the patriotic cause. Since political sentiment continued to be voiced openly and emotionally in the theater throughout the early Federal period, there is no reason to think that political feeling would be any less strong during the war itself, at a time of enemy occupation. Thus it is not surprising that, given the experience of Burgoyne's productions, the ban on theater was revived when the war was over.[37] The dominance of British actors and theater managers in the early Federal period further worked against the prevailing patriotic sentiment.

The wealthy at first rallied around the Federal Street Theater. It was originally funded by selling shares, which were limited to 150 at $50 a share, with no subscriber allowed more than two shares. Charles Bulfinch was employed as architect. He designed an imposing brick building, 140 feet long, 61 feet wide, and 40 feet high, which seated 1,200. Interest in the theater was so high on opening night that scalpers reportedly received up to twelve times the ticket price.[38]

The trustees and the first manager, Charles Stuart Powell, made every effort to avoid offending important segments of the community. They entered into a delicate truce with the Church of Christ nearby on Federal Street. They agreed to close the theater on nights that the "Sacramental Lectures" were given at the church so that the noise of "Hackney Coaches, Rabble, etc." would not disturb the devotions. They also agreed not to post any playbills in or around the meetinghouse.[39] In 1798, when Bernard Dickson became manager of the theater, he further attempted to present it in a favorable light by giving part of the proceeds to charity. When tragic events occurred in Boston or other communities, Dickson arranged benefits to assist. Thus, when much of Portsmouth,

New Hampshire, was destroyed by fire, Dickson raised more than $600 for the city through a benefit.[40]

To draw the upper classes of Boston and the wary elements of society to the theater, the trustees went to considerable lengths to maintain strict decorum in the theater itself. On January 22, 1794, they published a series of regulations governing the conduct of the audiences, the actors, and the orchestra. They appointed a master of ceremonies, Col. John S. Tyler, to enforce them. He directed the discharge of carriages in front of the theater, the seating of the audience, and attempted to monitor the conduct of everyone during the performance. His efforts proved so popular that he was accorded the first benefit of the year.

Yet Tyler had a difficult time. The audience's attitude toward the orchestra was particularly problematic. The trustees had decreed that the orchestra play only the assigned pieces each night. It was instructed not to honor requests called from the audience, as was common in theaters in the eighteenth century. This apparently irritated the audiences. On February 22, less than three weeks after the theater opened, the musicians put the following advertisement in the newspaper:

> The musicians that perform in the orchestra of the Boston Theatre, assure the public that it is not more their duty than it is their wish to oblige in the playing such tunes as are called for, but at the same time they wish them to consider the peculiar poignancy of insult to men not accustomed to it. Thus situated they entreat a generous people so far to compassionate their feelings as to prevent the thoughtless, or ill disposed, from throwing apples, stones, etc., into the orchestra, that while they eat the bread of industry in a free country, it may not be tinctured with the poison of humiliation.[41]

Management apparently relented on the question of audience requests. Henry Wansey described his visit to the theater that first season: "Between the play and the farce, the orchestra having played *Ça ira*, the gallery called aloud for Yankee Doodle, while after some short opposition was complied with."[42]

Many references in the late eighteenth century linking politics and the theater reveal just how strong political sentiment was at this time. When Tyler assumed management of the theater in 1795, he prepared a lengthy verse address pleading for a respite from political bickering:

> Let Feds and Antis to our temples come,
> And all unite firm Federalists in Fun;

Let austere politics one hour flee,
And join in free Democracy of glee!

Clapp commented that "men then carried their political feelings into the
very inner circle of social life, oftentimes severing social ties on this
account, and looking upon a political opponent as we should be apt to
regard an escaped thief or marauder." Somewhat later in the poem Tyler
specifically appealed to anti-British sentiment:

In me, her captain, know me for your friend,
Your townsman,—town born, town bred—at north end;
Let British lords their haughty birth declare,
I boast of being born in—Old North Square.[43]

In spite of efforts to attract the upper classes to the theater, they never
supported it strongly. There are scattered hints that the theater was eyed
suspiciously, no doubt under puritan influence. Most noticeable is the
absence of upper-class interest in the theater as a cultural institution.
The type of support that the upper class gave to other cultural endeavors,
such as the Boston Athenaeum, the Massachusetts Historical Society, or
the *North American Review*, and even later to the Boston Academy of
Music, did not extend to the theater. True, the theater was a commercial
enterprise as opposed to the others, which were benevolent institutions
founded as cultural institutions, but theatrical production itself, including opera, was never considered in that light until almost mid-century.

A string of bankruptcies plagued theater management, a sign that
community support was never solid. Only when a noted Shakespearean
actor like Edmund Kean came to Boston, or when a special attraction
such as Master Burke appeared, was middle- and upper-class support
strong. In 1831 Master Burke's stage appearances became the rage of
Boston society. Some of the box tickets were sold for premiums at
auctions; $1,344 was paid in premiums alone for the box tickets for
seven nights. The entire receipts for his stay of slightly over one month
were close to $20,000.[44] This was at least twice the normal receipts for
a successful run. For those plays or headliners who flopped, receipts
were of course far less.

Even when acts could command no premium, sale of boxes was necessary for financial solvency. And here the Tremont Theatre, the most
important theater in Boston in the late 1820s and 1830s, had architectural problems. When the Tremont opened in 1827, prices were $1 for
the better boxes, 75 cents for third-tier boxes, 50 cents for the pit, and

25 cents for gallery. The theater itself was small, and receipts of between $300 and $600 were considered good. A packed house yielded between $700 and $800.[45] Actors' and musicians' expenses alone typically ran between $400 and $500 a week, usually closer to $500. In addition there was rent on the building, many other production costs, and the much higher fees that star attractions like Kean commanded.[46] There was little financial cushion. In comparison, the Park Theatre in New York frequently took in between $1,000 and $1,500 per performance. The Tremont Theatre earned less than the Park in large measure because it had fewer boxes: 264 in the first two tiers, as opposed to 411 in the lower tier alone at the Park. And the Tremont was designed so that the boxes in the second tier were considered inferior to those in the first.[47]

Nineteenth-century writers like William Clapp and Charles Buckingham frequently referred to earlier times when the theater was supported by middle- and upper-class society. Their nostalgic looks backward both reflected their desire that the theater attract the upper classes and confirmed that for the most part it did not. Clapp spoke of 1802 when the new manager of the Federal Street Theatre, Snelling Powell, wooed back "the long absent taste and beauty of Boston."[48] Later he referred to the high morality of the theater in 1816, "where (to borrow from a critic) the cautious guardian of female innocence may safely conduct his charge to the enjoyment of scenes which exited the glow of pleasure that is unmingled with the blush of shame." Buckingham described his time (1852) as one in which actors were held in lower esteem than thirty years before. In a tribute to Elizabeth Powell, who first appeared in Boston in 1794, he described the "palmiest days of Boston theatricals, when familiar social intercourse with those, who by their talents could furnish living illustrations of the poetical creations of Shakspeare and Otway, of Goldsmith and Sheridan, of Colman and Mrs. Inchbald, an acquaintance with Mrs. Powell was an honor."[49]

Other evidence confirms that as late as the 1830s and 1840s the theater was still considered a morally questionable place. During his 1837 European travels Lowell Mason found that his aversion to the theater did not extend to Europe, because in Europe it was not "a place where the worst characters are brought together, as the Theater is with us."[50] When a new theater was founded in 1841, it was named the Boston Museum, because of the tenuous position of theaters in Boston. To attract the upper and middle classes the directors of the Boston Museum released for publication a statement that the theater would produce "some of the most chaste and elegant productions of the French, Italian, and German drama." These would be translated by "gentlemen of high literary attainments." The management further promised that "all profane expletives and indecent allusions will be totally expunged, the aim being to offer an Evening's Entertainment of innocent mirth and rational amusement," and that "the same order and decorum that have prevailed will stil be preserved throughout the Establishment."[51]

Theatrical fare varied almost as much as the perceived moral tone. At times the theater was essentially a circus, with equestrian acts, acrobatics, and tightrope dancing. At other times serious drama with well-known actors was presented. The state and quality of the presentations differed from year to year, depending on management, the offerings, and the box-office receipts. Audience reception varied. When Kean appeared in February 1821, tickets were in such demand that they were sold at auction.[52] Kean himself shared in receipts above $1,000 a week and received one benefit. He netted $5,453.28 for two weeks, a phenomenal sum compared with standard salaries. At that time a typical star in a theatrical production would make between $30 and $60 a week, with other actors' salaries ranging down to $10 a week. But when Kean returned in May, past the normal theatrical season, audiences were so thin that he decided to suspend his engagement and leave town.[53]

In spite of puritanical prejudice against the theater and the discomfort of the upper classes with the fare and the attendant conditions, certain visionaries in Boston during the Federal period argued that the theater could be a social institution fostering the ideals of the republic. The suggested plans were unrealistic, even bizarre, but for the first time in American society writers seriously advocated the use of the performing arts as a positive political instrument. And since these plans incorporated music as an integral part of the theater, they mark the first attempt to view music as a secular political tool. The earliest writings to suggest the use of the theater as an institution capable of improving society predate by forty years efforts to use secular music independently for similar purposes.

The most elaborate moral vision of the theater belonged to William Haliburton, who published an anonymous pamphlet in 1792, "Effects of the Stage on the Manners of the People; and the Propriety of Encouraging and Establishing a Virtuous Theater: By a Bostonian."[54] The pamphlet is a mixture of fancy, satire, and moral polemic. Sonneck observed that Haliburton's vision was truly Wagnerian. Haliburton suggested that the state of Massachusetts should fund a large building to house not only the theater but also the legislature, as well as an assembly room for large public occasions, including dinners, and a military hall. The theater itself would seat 6,200: 2,000 in the pit, with three galleries of 1,500, 1,500, and 1,200. According to his frontpiece drawing, it would be round. The legislature was to ensure that it be filled with the best actors and that proper regulations governing conduct be enacted. Haliburton believed that the effect would be "astonishing" and would mark a significant historical era.[55]

Haliburton compared the theater to a temple. It "is intended to suppress vice, and advance virtue; and serves likewise to make men better, and more virtuous." He believed that by mixing the good and the bad, which would occur in his theater, the good would be encouraged further toward the good and the bad would be moved "to leave the scene with 'solemn vows of amendment.'"[56]

Haliburton was one of the first writers in America to recognize the potential moral value of secular music. His rhetoric is as grandiose as it is vague, but the intent is clear: music can move men and make them better:

> Here music lends her aid divine, softens the savage heart, awakes the sympathetic powers of love and melting pity, lifts the rapt soul to Him who educes good from evil, who sees and shelters virtue in distress. With the animating descriptions of the Stage, music combines her soft, deep-felt, retentive sounds, her enhancing powers, and thenceforth united they return with trebled energy to dwell on the fancy and govern the man when busied on the daily concerns of life.
>
> The burthen of the interludes should be the praise of the virtues of heroic souls, and all such personages as truly deserved the name of great. . . .
>
> Let sublime, affecting sentiment in the voice of manly or feminine harmony, be accompanied with some instrument or instruments capable of the full, deep, and well toned bas, as the viol, aided by the clear symphonie of the violin, tuned and executed in such manner, as only to give harmony to the human voice, and leave the sentiment at liberty, when the heart is thus attuned to take full possession of the soul, and lift it in ecstasy, to the loftiest heights of passion; or move it delighted, into the profoundest depths of softened humanity. . . .[57]

Haliburton was specific about his musical likes and dislikes. He wished to banish forever "Italian airs, trills, [and] affected squeaks and quavers." He disliked the louder wind instruments such as bassoons, trumpets, and oboes as well as the organ. He desired harmony that conformed to nature, and he preferred more delicate sounds.

Although Haliburton's polemic is more moral than political, it falls within the republican gentry's concept of a unified society. By bringing various elements of society into the theater, a single set of values would be inculcated in the population. Since the theater would be run by the state, presumably only the virtues proper to the perpetuation of the gentry consensus would be presented. Regarding the cost of this endeavor, Haliburton calculated that even with an average price of two shillings for a ticket, which he proposed, a full theater would gross $2,000. This would not only cover expenses but also leave extra money to give to the poor. Poor citizens would be admitted free as a reward for proper behavior. Haliburton never said how he expected a theater seating six thousand that presented moral dramas night after night to be filled regularly in a town of twenty thousand.

Probably no one in nineteenth-century America argued for the place of theater in a republican society with greater clarity and fervor than William Dunlap, playwright, theater manager, theater critic, and later theater historian. As a playwright he wrote plays in heroic verse. As a theater manager he discovered that in order to survive financially he must "please the vulgar or shut his theater."[58] Dunlap's proposed solution was a state-run theater. In his *History of the American Theater* he attributed part of the blame for the "deterioration of the drama" to the cupidites of managers and the absence of regulations for the theater, such as existed in France, where the national government supported drama. He suggested that if the national theater were to run in the red, the tax on "taverns and tippling houses" should be increased to fund the deficit. He proposed that every city have one state-run playhouse.[59]

Dunlap distinguished between a theater and a playhouse. He conceded that the terms were used synonymously (he was writing in 1832), but he felt that they should be quite different in purpose and character. He considered the theater of a country "its loftiest and most efficient literature, when its play-houses may be, as in England, unhappily at present, and in a less degree in America (though we hope in no respect whatever), the open marts of vice and portals to destruction."[60]

Dunlap wished to reconcile lofty aesthetic ideals with republican principles. Like many reformers in the nineteenth century, he assumed that progress was inevitable, and he saw it as the avenue to moral perfection. He also aligned himself with the social utopianism of his time, stating that moral perfectibility was the ultimate goal not just for the individual but for society as a whole. He differed from many reformers, however, in his belief that art could lead the way.

Dunlap considered moral improvement necessary for a democratic society. "The people" were the real governors in a democratic society, and art had no greater mission than to prepare them to govern wisely and morally. He articulated a highly idealistic populist vision of American theater that traced the themes of progress and perfection and stressed the importance of the arts, specifically the theatrical arts, in achieving them. He believed that the world would become democratic, and that "every source of knowledge should be opened to the governors, the people—every obstacle to their improvement removed, and every inducement held forth to qualify them for the high office they are destined to fill." Some of the population had already achieved a high level of moral perfection on their own; others "less refined" needed the help of public institutions like the theater to reach that same level. "Let us give to theatres that purity, as well as power, which shall produce the high moral purpose here aimed at."[61]

Dunlap's views of progress and perfection through art differed little from those of the Presbyterian-Congregational reformers, for whom these themes were also central. Both Dunlap and Haliburton diverged from the Presbyterian-Congregational reformers, however, in their emphasis on societal rather than religious goals, and their consequent recognition that secular art, including music, could be an important means to those goals. Even though separated by almost forty years, Haliburton's and Dunlop's visions were essentially expressions of Whig republicanism; they were calls to use culture to maintain the social hierarchy.

A state-run theater of course never became a reality in America. Dunlap's and Haliburton's views, however, were important precursors for attitudes adopted by a number of writers on music in the 1830s. These writers, discussed in following chapters, recognized the potential of music as a means of furthering republican gentry ideas of society. They were among the first to elevate secular music to a position of cultural prominence, above that of mere entertainment.

In spite of the idealistic vision of men like Haliburton and the more practical efforts of Powell and Tyler to make the theater a morally acceptable place, prejudice against the theater remained strong throughout this period. In the 1830s and 1840s this prejudice had an important effect on musical developments, for it allowed institutions and types of music outside the theater to command a more crucial role in Boston's musical life than would have been possible had the theater been more fully accepted. In other cities, such as New York, where antitheater prejudice was not as strong, opera assumed a much more central place in their musical evolution.

Secular concerts were relatively infrequent in Boston at the end of the eighteenth century and early in the nineteenth. Sonneck claimed that the newspapers recorded no benefit concerts between 1797 and 1800.[62] He missed a few, but not many. Most are clustered in a busy spring of 1798: Catherine Graupner gave a benefit on March 14, a Mr. Leaumont gave one on April 14, and Francis Schaffer followed with one on April 25. On September 13, 1797, a "Concert of Vocal and Instrumental Music" was announced. It was not strictly a benefit, but it featured Francis Mallet, Rozier, and Stone, who probably organized it. In terms of musical presentation there was little to distinguish it from a benefit.

Sonneck attributed the relative sparseness of concert activity in Boston to the presence of the theater. But ten years later, when only one theater remained, there were even fewer concerts. On September 23, 1809, a Mr. Webster performed an "Entertainment, consisting of Dialogue and Songs—called the Songter's Jubilee."[63] On April 27, Catherine Graupner had a benefit at the Boston Theatre. No particulars are available, but Gottlieb Graupner probably performed. On December 26, 1810, James Hewitt presented a "Musical Entertainment" of vocal and instrumental music. Instrumental pieces included trios and solo violin pieces. Vocal music included songs and a glee by "two gentlemen amateurs." The concert was apparently a success, for Hewitt gave a similar one January 8, 1811. On October 9, 1811, a Mr. Chambers gave a concert, advertising it as the only opportunity that the Boston public would have to hear him. The instrumental offerings were ambitious for the time, principally because Chambers had an orchestra, led by James Hewitt. Orchestral selections included an overture by Haydn (probably a movement from a symphony), the Overture to *Lodoiska* by Kreutzer, and the Andante from the *Surprise* Symphony of Haydn.

These five concerts spanned three seasons, from 1809 through 1811. Except for outdoor summer offerings, they were the only public secular concerts advertised during those years.

Summer concerts became popular during this time with the founding of the "Promenade and Concert" performances at the Exchange Coffee-House. The first occurred on May 10, 1810. It was an experiment, as the organizers admitted. But it was sufficiently successful to warrant others, and on May 19 the proprietors placed a lengthy advertisement in the *Columbian Centinel* explaining their plans and justifying the enterprise. They further described the setting in a May 23 advertisement, which also listed the program for the forthcoming concert.

The Exchange Coffee-House was a large building fifteen hundred feet in length. It contained a dining hall, a ladies' drawing room, five galleries, and a ballroom, where the concerts were held. All was "superbly decorated and illuminated," with evergreens and "variegated lamps." Food and drink were available, specified only as "a profusion of all the delicacies which the season affords." The first part of the concerts began at 8:30, the second at 9:30. The first part consisted of "popular Airs, Marches, Waltzes, etc."; the second part was the concert proper. In the intervals between musical presentations, the audience was invited to stroll through the house. Although the events were indoors, the Exchange Coffee-House resembled the outdoor gardens that provided popular entertainment in Europe and in some American cities.

Concerts at the Exchange Coffee-House were presented approximately every two weeks for most of the summer. The concert on May 24, 1810, was typical. It featured Thomas Granger and the Graupners—Gottlieb, his wife, Catherine, and daughter Catherine, who had by then become an established pianist—and a full orchestra. The management had promised that "the best musicians and singers which can be procured will be engaged," and the program reflected that decision. The most ambitious concert of the summer, however, was Gottlieb Graupner's benefit, held on June 13. The program was extensive and varied. Vocal numbers included songs by Mrs. Catherine Graupner, Mr. Bates, and Mr. Darley. They ranged from a Handel aria, "Let the Bright Seraphims," to "The Laughing Song" by Mr. Bates. The singers participated in two glees. Instrumental offerings included a clarinet concerto by James Turner, an oboe concerto by Graupner, a bassoon divertimento by Simeon Wood, and a trumpet concerto, "in which will be introduced, Pleyel's celebrated German Hymn." The trumpet player, not identified, was probably William Rowson. The first half opened with Gluck's Overture to *Medea and Jason*, and the second half with Kreutzer's popular Overture to *Lodoiska*. Both were played by a full orchestra. The concert concluded with "The Celebrated Grand Sonata, the Battle of Prague, with two Double Basses—Cymbals—French Horns—Kettle Drums—Trumpets—Cannon, etc." The first half concluded with a "Quartetto Violino" by Pleyel, an early but by no means the first instance of a public string-quartet performance in Boston.[64]

The management of the Exchange Coffee-House sought to allay any fears or backlash in the Boston community about the propriety of the endeavor. Their efforts bear witness that disapproval of musical entertainment still existed. Referring to the evenings as "refined and elegant amusements," they observed that they had long been popular in Europe and many American cities. They admitted that Boston was "equally and justly celebrated for its discouragement of those amusements which have a tendency to corrupt the morals, and debase the manners of society," and for encouraging those which are "innocent, polished, and refined." They were confident that the citizens of Boston would approve of their undertaking through their patronage, because the entertainment was designed "to unite pleasure with improvement, innocence with recreation, and the promotion of health with the amelioration of the heart and the mind."[65] As in so many other advertisements for musical or theatrical events in Boston, the sponsors of the Exchange Coffee-House assured the potential audience that the entertainment would not corrupt but improve. Entertainment void of moral lesson, no matter how innocent, was still considered wasteful frivolity.

The fate of an earlier attempt to have a summer garden in Boston may have been on the minds of the sponsors of the Exchange Coffee-House when they established their enterprise. In 1798 J. B. Baker and Charles Stuart Powell proposed to erect the Columbian Vauxhall, an outdoor garden. Baker operated a bookstore on Cornhill Street and Powell was well-known in Boston, at various times managing both the Haymarket and the Federal Street theaters. They estimated that $10,000 was needed to establish it and advertised for backers, offering two hundred shares at $50 each. The advertisement ran for several weeks, but support apparently did not materialize, as there is no subsequent mention of it. Clapp stated that it failed.[66] Baker and Powell conceived their proposal strictly as entertainment, albeit one with class overtones. They referred to it as a "species of summer entertainment" and an "elegant resort of fashionable entertainment." They sought to appease Boston's skeptical element by promising that the entertainment would "combine salubrity with amusement, and novelty with taste." But they made no attempt to provide any further moral justification, which was probably a fatal mistake. The idea that music should improve as well as entertain was to be an important principle in the latter nineteenth-century definition of high culture. Even in antebellum Boston it was a consistent theme voiced in all successful musical proposals.

The coffee-house did not repeat the Promenade and Concert experiment of 1810, possibly because support was not strong enough. Yet there may have been another reason for its discontinuance. The next year the coffee-house had a new attraction, the Panharmonicon. On June 29, 1811, the following advertisement appeared in the *Columbian Centinel*:

PANHARMONICON

This surprising and Grand Instrument, the work of the celebrated and ingenious Maelzel, of Vienna, who was employed 15 years in completing it, will be ready at the Exchange Coffee-House for the inspection and amusement of this intelligent public, on Monday Next, 1st July. To describe its peculiar excellencies is too difficult a task; it is sufficient to say, that the Wind Instruments go by a most perfect mechanism, and with such exactness as to excite the greatest astonishment. The precise and perfect time that this magnificent instrument keeps in the different pieces of music could not by any means be exceeded by the most experienced and perfect Orchestra of Professors, while the numerous and complicated Instruments which are exposed to the view playing by the effect of mechanism would amaze the most enlightened in reflecting how human ingenuity could possibly have formed an object so grand and so perfectly in its various branches. The airs which have been chosen, cannot fail to please an audience— They are selected previously from Haydn, Mozart, Steibalt, Cherubini, etc.

Tickets cost $1. Because of the "warm evening," seating was limited to three hundred.

The exhibit of the Panharmonicon apparently did not go well. On July 3 Mr. Pardy put another advertisement in the *Columbian Centinel*, in which he admitted that the machine sounded "imperfect" because of the attempt to get it going "in the shortest time possible," the "dampness which has penetrated many of its barrels," and the short time that the performer, Mr. Goodrich, had had to master it. He acknowledged the "numerous and respectable assemblage" at the first performance and promised to correct the problems. Despite this rocky start, the Panharmonicon eventually proved popular in Boston. Advertisements for it appeared regularly throughout the summer and continued for several years. On July 26, 1823, the *Columbian Centinel* announced that the Panharmonicon was to be removed, but it stayed in Boston for at least three more years, as further advertisements for it appeared until 1827.[67]

One outdoor garden did manage to thrive in early nineteenth-century Boston: the Washington Gardens, established by 1815, when James

Hewitt was the leader of the orchestra. The management advertised it as an "elegant and fashionable Garden" providing "refined amusement." A few nights after it opened, an article about it appeared in the *Boston Gazette*, probably a puff, describing the "order, decency, respectability and brilliance of the company" and praising the managers for their arrangements "to exclude improper visitors from the garden."[68]

Even though the Washington Gardens survived economically, it did not secure a reputation as a desirable place of entertainment. In 1827 a Mr. Burroughs placed an advertisement in the *Columbian Centinel* imploring the public to attend a benefit that he planned at the Washington Gardens. He admitted that his attempt to found a summer theater had failed, at least partly because he had learned too late that "a prejudice exists against the Washington Garden Theatre, which has deterred a number who would otherwise have patronized the exertions of himself and company, from visiting it." Burroughs' experience was representative; early nineteenth-century middle- and upper-class Boston audiences viewed musical and theatrical arts with skepticism and were reluctant to patronize places unless they were convinced of their moral acceptability.

Chapter Five

Private Music Making and Amateur Musical Organizations

Even though early Federal Boston had at least one theater and sometimes two, a moderately active concert life, and various summer entertainments that featured music, most musical activity occurred in other settings. As Albert Rhodes observed in 1872, when comparing the musical achievements of America and England, Americans were more interested in making music than in listening to it.[1] This was certainly true in early nineteenth-century Boston. Participatory ensembles and private music making were much more important than formal concerts that separated the professional musician from the amateur performer or the listener. The amateur-professional distinction grew only after 1820, and will be discussed in the next chapter. In this chapter I shall examine the panoply of amateur musical activity in homes, churches, taverns, and public buildings, which involved a great variety of musical organizations.

More than any other type of music, psalmody still prevailed in early nineteenth-century Boston. More people participated in church choirs and church-related singing societies than in any other organized musical activity. In addition, many attended singing schools, which frequently drew from sixty to ninety students, nearly as large as the attendance figure at many concerts.[2] Sometimes a singing master would advertise the formation of a singing school; at other times churches would petition to form one. Following eighteenth-century custom, singing schools usually lasted for several weeks, although in a few instances they became a regular establishment.

Probably the most well-established singing school in the Boston area was at Jonathan Bird's Tavern in Watertown on the Charles River, abutting Cambridge. Bird bought the Richardson Tavern in 1800, moved it to a new and better location, renamed it, and enlarged the building to thirty guest rooms and an upstairs ballroom. In the 1830s his grandsons Joseph, Jr., and Horace became well-known as singing-school teachers there, but the school itself apparently existed from the time that Jonathan Bird assumed ownership of it. More than a tavern, it served as an important inn and a focal point of Charlestown social activity. The ballroom had multiple functions: dances were held there and it housed the Union Social Library. The town took pride in the singing school, at one point voting to furnish candles and appropriate $100 for expenses.

At least three generations of Birds were actively involved in music. We do not know who originally led the singing school, but it was probably Joseph Bird, Sr. We do know that vocal music was important to the entire Bird family. Joseph's sons Joseph, Jr., and Horace studied with Lowell Mason and continued the singing school well into the 1860s. They also composed and published music, held church-music positions, gave concerts, and ran a farm. Horace's son Arthur became a well-known organist and composer, active in both Europe and America. On the recommendation of John Knowles Paine, he studied at the Royal Institute for Church Music in Berlin, and he composed many stage, orchestral, piano, and organ works. The Bird family thus made the transitions from singing-school teacher to church musician to European-trained artist much as the Mason family did.[3]

No musical organizations were more well-known in early Federal Boston than the better church choirs. Their reputation transcended religion and became a matter of civic pride. Music in the larger and more prestigious churches had a quasi-official tone, because disestablishment of Congregationalism occurred in Massachusetts only in 1833 and the church service was such a regular activity for both native Bostonians and visitors to the city. Church choirs also provided music for public occasions like celebrations and dedications, further blurring the distinction between church and state functions.

The most prestigious church choir in Boston in the early nineteenth century was the Park Street Choir, led by Elnathan Duren. Nathaniel D. Gould described the power and precision of the choir as unprecedented and attributed its success to its director, whose abilities as both a talented musician and charismatic leader Gould lauded extravagantly. Although his description must be tempered with the knowledge that Gould was born a Duren, Elnathan Duren's talent apparently was extraordinary. Henry K. Oliver, who sang in the choir as a boy soprano, recalled many years later that it was "deservedly renowned for its admirable rendering of church music." The choir's performance at the dedication of the Park Street Church in 1812 was long remembered. The choir consisted of approximately fifty singers, including a number of professional musicians and founders of the Handel and Haydn Society. In addition to Oliver, it included Gottlieb Graupner, Simeon Wood, a bassoonist, William Rowson, a trumpet player, and three original officers of the Handel and Haydn Society: Amasa Winchester, Nathaniel Tucker, and Elnathan Duren.[4]

Another important church choir was the Second Baptist Singing Society. On February 16, 1815, it gave a concert that included parts of Haydn's *Creation*, Handel's Hallelujah Chorus from the *Messiah*, the "Ode to St. Cecilia's Day," excerpts from *Judas Maccabeus*, and the Te Deum of Dettingen. This was the first time that substantial parts of the *Creation* had been performed in Boston. Between the announcement of the concert on February 10 and the concert itself on February 16, news of the signing of the Treaty of Ghent and the formal end of the War of 1812 reached Boston. A grand peace celebration was arranged, which included a lengthy choral and instrumental program. The celebration was not the same event as the Second Baptist Singing Society's concert, as Perkins states. The two events took place on different days, and the peace celebration included 250 vocal and instrumental performers, both professional and amateur, and was authorized by a committee of the legislature. Since some of the same pieces were performed at both the society's concert and the peace celebration, the Singing Society almost certainly formed the nucleus of the peace celebration's choir.[5]

The Park Street and similar choirs were Congregational, which at that time meant middle class. New England Baptists were also middle class, although the Baptist branch of New England Calvinism was less prestigious than mainstream Congregationalism. Working-class churches also had choral societies, whose repertoire and activities differed little from those of Congregational churches. One such group, the Universal Singing Choir, is of interest because its records and minutes have survived, allowing us to glimpse into the weekly operations of church choirs in Federal Boston, its activities and problems probably being typical of many others. The Universal Singing Choir was founded on January 27, 1807. It was almost certainly connected with the First Universalist Church, the only Universalist church in Boston at the time. The statement of purpose in the choir's constitution confirms its institutional connection: Article 8 reads, "The Society shall Assemble for practical improvements in Sacred Music, once every fortnight, in the Vestry, or any other place that the Society may agree upon." The society was organized with 34 members, 25 males and 9 females, but apparently had a difficult time with attendance. On January 22, 1808, the society voted to distribute the money in its treasury to the poor and dissolve, but a year later it reformed. The entries pick up again in April 1809 with the "Rules and Regulations of the new Universal Singing Choir."

The choir held social events as well as a variety of musical activities. The minutes refer to a social outing on the water in July 1809 and to a singing school, probably for juveniles, formed by Samuel Cushing in 1809. There were internal disputes over places and position. When Cushing was appointed to sit on the left of the organist, probably to lead the singing, Obijah Adams, who had previously sat there, complained vigorously. Adams admitted that he no longer attended regularly, but that he had been engaged for years with the choir, and that at his time of life he simply wished to have a seat where he could hear the music well.

The most serious problem that the choir faced was attendance. Particularly after 1813 many members, including several officers, were reprimanded for not attending, and at least one meeting was canceled for lack of attendance. Name after name was erased from the membership list for excessive absenteeism. Yet interest in singing remained high. The last pages of the minutes contain a rquest to the standing committee to form another singing school. It was signed by sixty-seven individuals. The society formally dissolved in 1816. The final record of the minutes of the trustees states: "Monday, March 11 1816 there being no business before them, voted that the meeting be desolved—Per Order Henry Turner Secy."

As the preceding examples confirm, most of the choirs and singing societies were either middle or working class. The socioeconomic elite generally remained aloof from public musical activity. Part of the problem was an almost universal lack of musical knowledge among the upper classes. Men were not encouraged to learn to play a musical instrument, and women were only beginning to confront the piano. Even in the middle and lower classes, however, only a small percentage of the men played musical instruments. The singing school had provided most of the musical knowledge that existed in late Federal Boston, and it was a predominantly middle-class organization, often connected (at least nominally) with a Congregational or other evangelical church. As a result, singing in the home often meant psalm singing, either for religious reasons or simply because the music was familiar. The socioeconomic elite rarely participated in either psalm singing or the singing school as most members of the upper class considered amateur performance inappropriate. When Samuel A. Eliot, who will be discussed below, participated in the Unitarian West Church Chapel Choir, he had to suffer the strong disapproval of his brother-in-law George Ticknor. When Eliot brought the choir to his house to rehearse, Ticknor found it reprehensible.[6] What little interest the socioeconomic elite manifested in public music was as patron, not performer.

The elite did enjoy secular music at home, although it is difficult to determine how much. One of the most active homes for music making was that of Col. William Tudor, the father of Frederick Tudor, who was later known as the "ice king," for his success in exporting New England ice to much of North America and the Caribbean. The Tudor residence was a focus of cultural activity. When the Marquis de Chastullux arrived in Boston in 1782 he was treated to a program of French songs at the Tudor home, arranged by Mrs. Tudor. They were sung by the nephew of the Marquis de Vaudreuil, commander of the French forces.[7] Mrs. Tudor's musical interest went well beyond songs. When her son William, Jr., was in Paris in 1799, he wrote her of the musical purchases he had made for her. They included "about eighty sonates of Haydn, Pleyel, Koseluch, Steibelt, Clementi, Mozart etc. fifteen overtures, the most celebrated that you have not at present, such as Pamorze, Psyche, Ballet de Paris, etc. de Telemaque, la Caravanne, etc. etc.," as well as "a number of other pieces for the piano, a small collection of the most favorite ariettes, a few pieces of Musique for a Grand Orchestre, and also a set of quatuors of Pleyel and Boccherini."[8] Altogether Tudor paid $400 for his purchases, which in 1799 was an immense sum for a private collection of music. This letter also observed that the quartets of Pleyel, although not those of Boccherini, were already known in America, one of the earliest New England references to the string-quartet literature.

How much of the music that was imported was actually used? William, Jr., feared that much of it would not be. He confirmed the rarity of good string players capable of performing a quartet. Yet he was willing to purchase symphonies as well as chamber music, apparently with the intention of their being performed. It is impossible to know how much of this music would have been played by members of the Tudor family themselves. Mrs. Tudor no doubt played the piano but was probably the only member of the family to do so. William, Jr., wrote extensively on a great variety of cultural and social topics but virtually never discussed music. Letter 6 of his *Letters on the Eastern States* is entitled "Fine Arts."[9] But except for two fleeing references to national ballads, and this to illustrate that we took even our popular airs from foreign sources, there is no mention of music whatsoever. William's brother Frederick was considered a great eccentric, so a great deal was written about him. No one observed that he had any interest in music.

The most extensive personal references to musical activity in the late eighteenth and early nineteenth centuries are found in the diaries of William Bentley, who was a Congregational minister in Salem, a musical satellite of Boston. Many of the more prominent Boston musicians regularly gave concerts in Salem, and Bentley's comments, especially about less formal musical activity, are probably representative of persons of similar station in Boston.

Bentley usually described public musical events but did occasionally refer to private gatherings. On April 29, 1793, he reported: "Mr. Atwell and Mansfield of Lynn, musicians, with me this evening. They recommended and performed the music of one Oliver Holden." In 1798 he described a visit to the family of a relative of his maternal grandmother: "The Son plays well on a Bass Viol, and the g. daughtr sings well, while the Father retains a sweet voice, even after fifty, and performs in the Meeting House. They had made the largest collection of Music I had even seen in private hands; entirely church music and all American publications."[10]

Bentley tried to encourage young musicians, both singers and instrumentalists, partly by hosting them in his home. He recorded one such evening on March 22, 1796: "This evening my instrumental music with me. The Company, Masters Macintire, and Palfrey, and Heard Becket, and a young man, name unknown. They supped with me and were encouraged I trust." That same year he visited Heard's, where a slightly larger ensemble performed: "Attended with the Instrumental music for the first time. We had one Bass Viol, one Tenour viol, and two violins and two flutes, at Heard's. The principal objection to these interviews are, that in private houses they give occasion to the too free use of spirituous liquors." Later in the nineteenth century instrumental music would be considered edifying, associated with moral purity. At this time it was still strictly for "private amusement." As Bentley's remark indicates, instrumental music not only lacked a moral component, but connoted precisely the opposite—in this case, excessive drinking.[11]

Bentley's observations suggest a relatively thin line between private and public musical activity. Music was frequently performed on closed social occasions or at private social gatherings. In 1788 Bentley recorded a visit to Cape Ann with the Association, where they "tarried over night, and were very agreeably entertained by a Band of music, and by the vocal music accompanied with female voices." In 1798 he reported a similar entertainment: "We reached Salem at after sundown and this evening was appointed to receive the little band of Music which so kindly entertained us on the last Thanksgiving day. We had 2 Bass Viols, 3 german flutes and 6 Violins, and passed the evening happily. The Company left us at 9 o'clock." In 1801 he described the Annual Meeting of the East India Marine Society, which included an elegant dinner and appropriate toasts: "The Instrumental Music was provided in Town, for the first time and consisted of the Bass Drum, Bassoon, clarinet and flute, and was very acceptable. There was no singing." William Tudor's letter also suggested the blurring between public and private music making; he looked on the collection he purchased in France, presumably for use in his home, as serving "to diversify the Concerts of Franklin Place."[12]

Bentley lamented what he considered the lack of musical interest and the low state of music in Salem, but at the same time revealed that there was considerable musical activity in his relatively small town. In the 1790s Andrew Law's singing schools drew close to one hundred students. When the New South Meetinghouse at Salem was dedicated on January 1, 1805, the celebration included a band of nineteen instrumentalists and a chorus of eighty. When a new organ was needed at the First Church in 1798, $1,000 was raised quickly by subscription. Bentley acknowledged that instrumental music was catching on in Salem in the 1790s: "The fondness for Instrumental music in Churches so increases, that the inclination is not to be resisted."[13] He attributed much of this interest to Samuel Holyoke, who not only encouraged it in churches but also formed the Musical Society in 1797 to promote instrumental music.

According to Bentley, earlier societies had not succeeded. They, however, had been attached to choirs; Holyoke's was not, and Bentley thought it stood a better chance because it was independent and private. On December 18, 1798, he recorded: "some efforts are making in this Town to create a love of Musick." Three societies were being formed to play instrumental music. One consisted of mechanics and was confined to wind instruments; another was "of a different class united key with wind instruments"; and the third was unspecified, except that it met in a large hall that was to be fitted with an organ. Bentley further noted that "other Instruments are to be conveyed to this place, and that the hall would also be used for teaching vocal music."[14] Bentley's comments about the society of mechanics is one of the earliest references to mechanics forming musical organizations, and one of the most explicit indications that class was a factor in the formation and membership of musical societies.

Bentley's and Tudor's accounts suggest that there was a great deal of informal music making in and around Boston, but are they representative? Very few records exist of musical activity in private homes. The many advertisements for musical instruction, musical instruments, and sheet music in Boston newspapers confirm that music, including instrumental performance, did occur in private homes and in informal organizations, but they give little clue as to its extent. Gen. H. K. Oliver, describing musical conditions in Boston between 1810 and 1814, asserted that "few musical instruments of any sort were to be found in private houses," and that "in the entire population of Boston, of some six thousand families, not fifty piano-fortes could be found."[15] Most of the diaries and letters of the time, the principal sources for such information, are silent about music, although this does not necessarily mean the writers were indifferent to music. Several of the most prominent men in Boston, such as Harrison Gray Otis, not previously connected to music, are mentioned in private records for their support of musical activities. Those rare diaries that discuss music extensively, such as Bentley's, suggest that musical activity was relatively fluid with regard to type, style, and class. The boundaries between sacred and secular, instrumental and vocal, and popular and serious were not distant, although (as we have seen) there was some class awareness in the composition of organizations and audiences for public performances.

In November 1800 three of Boston's leading musicians, Filipo Trajetta, Gottlieb Graupner, and Francis Mallet, announced the formation of the city's first formal, professional institution devoted to instruction in music, the Conservatory, or Musical Academy. The announcement is primarily an essay on the role and value of music, one of the earliest statements we have on how Boston musicians conceptualized secular music. As it is designed to sell the Conservatory to the public, it must be read as a calculated effort to reflect the community's attitude to music:

Music being almost an inseparable branch of a finished education, one of the most useful and agreeable arts, is (as an interpreter of the finer feelings) a necessary one.

In support of what is just advanced, the truth may be adduced from time the most remote, and amongst all nations, the most savage not excepted, Music has been known and cultivated. Besides which, its agreeable utility has been so repeatedly demonstrated by celebrated and good men, that all those who may have it in their power, must with their children instructed in an art of such general use, and which affords so copious a resource of rational pleasure. In prosperity our moments of enjoyment are heightened by Music: In adversity, it dissipates the gloom of care, mollifies the frowns of fortune, and when obliged to seek a foreign asylum, smooths the unequal paths, becomes our interpreter among a strange people, and our conductor to amiable society; but a motive of still greater consideration presents itself, that of addressing the Supreme Being, in melodious accents. These motives gave existence to the many Music Academies established in all Europe, which have been raised to the highest degree of perfection.

The advertisement recognizes the artistic value of music but gives only a hint of Platonic idealism—music can somehow tame the more savage emotions. Its emphasis is on cultivation, the development of finer feelings, and a finished education. It is aimed at upper- and middle-class families, permeated with an aura of what sounds like late nineteenth-century gentility, but with important differences. Trajetta, Graupner, and Mallet are appealing to class and refinement without the moral-laden rhetoric characteristic of such appeals later in the century. Their advertisement values music for providing secular pleasure and enjoyment yet also recognizes the importance of sacred music. The ability to learn psalmody is extolled as one of the most important functions both of European conservatories and Boston's academy. This ingenious claim may have reasured Bostonians who under the prevailing sentiment might have felt uncomfortable with so European an institution.

The Conservatory was a success, but only briefly. In June 1801 Mallet, Graupner, and Trajetta opened a second school, for young ladies, and announced a change of time for gentlemen to study wind instruments, an indication that such a clientele existed. Earlier in the year they had formed a lending library for music, but how successful it was is not clear. The Conservatory did not last beyond 1802, but not because of lack of support from the Boston community. Events in 1802 suggest some sort of personal friction among the three principals. Trajetta abruptly left Boston in early 1802, eventually to settle in Philadelphia. The Conservatory continued to expand, opening a third school in April 1802 and installing a music press. The press was probably Graupner's idea, because he remained in the music-publishing business for at least twenty-five years. But by November 1802 Graupner and Mallet had parted. Neither offered an explanation about the split or the dissolution of the institution, but each advertised for the Conservatory's pupils in the newspapers, a sign that they did not see eye to eye.

Amateur performance of instrumental music, to which Tudor's and Bentley's accounts attest, was shaped primarily by the strong wind-band tradition in America. This tradition gave a unique shading to American attitudes toward instrumental music, and as a consequence the symphony orchestra, which eventually came to embody high culture, had to follow a path different from the one it took in Europe. The military band had been the principal instrumental ensemble in America since the eighteenth century. It had been the only type of instrumental music supported by the government. By the late eighteenth century it had assumed many roles in most communities, performing not only for military functions like parades and reviews but also for a variety of public ceremonies, as well as for concerts and even dances. Many eighteenth-century concerts featured either a military ensemble per se or an ensemble in which the military band formed the principal accompaniment. W. S. Morgan's benefit at Concert Hall in Boston on February 8, 1771, for example, was accompanied by the band of the Sixty-fourth Regiment. Morgan was a violinist, and in 1774 he and a Mr. Stieglitz combined to give two benefits, one for each. The instrumental forces consisted of:

First violin, Mr. *Morgan*. German flute, Mr. *Stieglitz*. Harpsichord, Mr. *Selby*. Accompanied with clarinets, hautboys, bassoons, French horns, trumpets, kettledrums, etc. etc.

N.B. The Gentlemen Performers of the Army, Navy and of the Town, have promis'd Mr. Morgan their assistance in [this] Concert; likewise some of the best performers from the several bands of music of the line.[16]

Not only did the military ensembles assist, but the instrumentation itself was essentially that of a military band.

Military bands sometimes presented concerts on their own. When Col. John Crane's Third Regiment of the Continental Artillery was on furlough between 1781 and 1783, its band performed several concerts. The first was in Salem, on January 16, 1783. The advertisement stated that the band would play "Overtures, Symphonies, Harmony and Military Musick, Solo's, Duets on the Horns, and some favourite SONGS." The concert lasted from six until half past nine. The band proved so popular that it was asked to play in a concert to aid the poor the next week, followed by another concert in Portsmouth, New Hampshire, which Louis Pichierri claims was the "first real public concert recorded in New Hampshire."[17]

To most Americans of the eighteenth and early nineteenth centuries, instrumental music meant band music. The term *band* itself was imprecise; it meant any instrumental ensemble ranging from small informal groups to the orchestra of the Handel and Haydn Society.[18] The semantics of the term, however, do not obscure the reality of Federal musical life: wind instruments were much more common than string instruments. Most ensembles were predominantly if not exclusively wind bands. Classical violinists, as opposed to country fiddlers, were rare. In consequence, a preference for winds over strings came naturally out of the musical experiences of the late Colonial and early Federal periods.

The band movement spread rapidly beyond the militia in the early nineteenth century. Col. Crane's regimental band stayed together after the revolutionary war and became known as the Massachusetts Band, a name it had assumed when on furlough in 1783. According to Richard Franko Goldman, who has traced its history, it became the Green Dragon Band around 1812 and the Boston Brigade Band around 1820.[19] Band activity proliferated in the 1820s. Between 1825 and 1835 at least three major bands were active in Boston: the Boston Band, the Boston Brigade Band, and the Boston Cadet Band. The Cadet Band seems to have disappeared by 1830, but the other two remained active throughout the 1830s.

By the 1830s the relationship between professional bands and the militia had changed, as bands like Col. Crane's established independent ensembles. They did not completely sever their connection, however, and frequently hired themselves out to militia units that needed a band. They were no longer simply part of one particular unit but were available for whoever wished to secure their services. The Boston Brigade Band, for instance, went to Philadelphia with the City Guards in May 1833, to Nahant with the Hancock Light Infantry in July 1833, to Worcester with the Ancient and Honorable Artillery Company in August 1835, and to New York with the New York Light Guard in July 1839 and with the Hancock Light Infantry in July 1840.[20]

Bands provided music for many occasions other than military functions. According to a report in the *American Weekly Traveller,* Samuel Eliot, who was mayor of Boston in 1839, instituted band concerts on the Common during the summer. The Boston Brass Band and the Boston Brigade Band alternated with concerts twice a week. Bugbee reported that the city had appropriated money for such concerts as early as 1830, in the hope of cutting down on disorder and intemperance. One program for outdoor band concerts appeared in the *Daily Evening Transcript* of July 3, 1835, corroborating that such concerts did exist. How frequent they were and whether they persisted to 1839 is unclear, however. Bands also played for political rallies, serenades, boating events, fairs, and circuses. The Boston Brigade Band advertised that it was available for "Military Parades, Processions, Serenades, and Steamboated Water Parties." It could also "furnish several different sets of Music for Balls, Cotillion Parties, etc." Edward Kendall and L. L. Sanborn announced that the Boston Brass Band could provide "music for Cotillion Parties, Assemblies, Private Parties, etc. at short notice."[21]

Although the military band was by far the predominant instrumental ensemble, other amateur instrumental groups were formed in the late eighteenth and early nineteenth centuries. Two of the most interesting are the Pierian Sodality and the Arionic Sodality at Harvard College. Part of their historical interest lies in the information that we have about them, as the private, amateur, and frequently informal nature of this type of organization makes it particularly elusive to the historian. Detailed records are rare, and the occasional public reference to groups like the Society of Gentlemen, which formed the instrumental accompaniment for a concert in Boston in 1789, only suggests that much activity currently lies beyond historical recovery. Diaries and letters allow further glimpses, but those that discuss music are so uncommon that what they disclose is often more tantalizing than informative.

The Pierian Sodality, established in 1808, was the first organization at Harvard dedicated to the performance of instrumental music; The Arionic Sodality, formed in 1813, was the second. Thanks to several exuberant and loquacious secretaries, detailed accounts not only of what these groups did but also how they conceived of music have been preserved. From them we can understand the attitudes of the members to the place of music at Harvard and in their own lives. We can trace over a period of time their changing concepts of the role of instrumental music in particular. The Pierians' views of instrumental music were typical of their time, and their abundant minutes give us real insight into their thinking. But their story gains added importance because the Harvard Musical Association grew directly out of the Pierian Sodality and later writers have made much of the connection.

Originally separate, the Pierian and Arionic societies eventually merged. The Arionic Sodality thrived until approximately 1815. In May of that year, the membership voted to invite some members of the Pierian Sodality to join them. The offer apparently was not accepted, and there is a hiatus in the records from May 1, 1815, to November 6, 1816. The society was then reorganized with a new relationship to the Pierian Sodality. The Arionic minutes explain: "After a long suspension of the functions of this society it was at length resuscitated for the purpose of being a subsidiary of the Pierian Sodality: at a meeting of which it was resolved. That the officers of the Pierian should hold the same offices in the Arionic Sodality, in consequence of which resolution, [Thomas] McCulloch was chosen Pres't or Senior Leader [John F.] Jenkins V Pres't or Junior Leader Dorr E. [Eben R. Dorr] Secretary."

The Arionic Sodality was to remain a subsidiary organization to the Pierian Sodality, but they did not continue to share officers. Later the Arionic minutes refer to the election of officers different from those of the Pierian Sodality. For instance, John S. Dwight was elected president of the Arionic Sodality in 1829. He graduated from Harvard in 1832, and although active in the Pierian Sodality, he was never an officer of it.[22]

Both societies were small, seldom having more than eight to ten members each. According to Dwight the Arionic Sodality was a training ground for players not yet capable of performing in the Pierian Sodality. He referred to it as "the purgatory which half-fledged musicians of his own ilk had to pass through before they could be candidate for the Pierian paradise."[23] It was therefore populated more by freshmen and sophomores than upperclassmen.

The minutes of the Arionic Sodality confirm its subsidiary role. They seldom refer to the Pierians, except when some occasionally joined the Arionic rehearsals, usually to add a missing instrumental dimension, such as bass. The Pierian minutes regularly mention invitations to perform in public and to various exhibitions and serenades. Practically no such references are found in the minutes of the Arionic Sodality, unless it met jointly with the Pierian, as occasionally happened. The Pierian Sodality was clearly the varsity instrumental team at Harvard in the early nineteenth century.

The Pierian and Arionic records suggest that the members themselves were not certain about how music should be conceptualized. The minutes of both groups make it absolutely clear that their principal purpose was to have a good time. Their activities and repertoires indicate a down-to-earth, high-spirited approach to music that has little in common with the sacralized frame of mind later in the century. Music was an indulgent amusement, simply one-third of the triad, wine, women, and song. Yet a more serious tone occasionally emerges in the records, which include informal observations on music and transcriptions of poems and orations delivered by members. These writings reveal a more idealistic view of music than the activities of the societies would suggest, especially when considered in the context of both the societies' activities and other musical thought of the time.

The societies usually met once a week, on Tuesday evenings, although in some years they met only every fortnight. Each member was to copy the appropriate tune in his book every week and show up with instrument and book. Failure to do so resulted in a fine. Indecent or disorderly behavior, defined principally as playing during interludes or when not directed to, also drew a fine. Each member in turn was required to procure one tune for the society at his own expense, so that a new tune could be introduced each week. This requirement was repealed in 1829.[24]

Members apparently rotated the honor of hosting the meeting. After a brief business meeting, they played for approximately an hour or until eight o'clock, quiet time in the houses. Playing often ended with the proctor's call, and the minutes recorded one vote of thanks to a proctor who was too lazy to bother them when eight o'clock arrived. After the playing came refreshments, which consisted of brandy, wine, or punch and cigars. That part of the evening invariably involved a great deal of conviviality, including singing. In some years the refreshments were served first, in order to generate more uninhibited playing. The Arionic minutes record one particularly bacchanalian joint anniversary meeting when the conviviality apparently went too far: "Anniversary held with Pierian sodality. Gallons of punch and 150 cigars used. Mr. Cooper sang some songs which were received with great applause by the company. Also Mr. Tucker and Mr. Burton favoured the company with some songs. The evening was passed with pleasure and hilarity. But alas! The next day we all had Publices."[25] The minutes for the following meeting read: "Met at Parkers this evening a vote was passed to have punch without Brandy." For the next several years reference to punch is constant, but the minutes are silent about what was in it. For one meeting in 1821 the secretary recorded, "Nothing remarkable happend excepting drinking 5 quarts of punch."[26]

The Pierians also performed publicly, either in informal serenades or by invitation to more formal exhibitions. Serenades consisted of nocturnal outdoor performances, sometimes at the Piazza, a public square, but more often at individual houses. On March 4, 1819, the two groups "repaired to the Piazza after adjournment and played 'Hail Columbia' three times in honor of the day (inauguration of President.)" The group was "cheered with the acclamations of an attentive and enraptured multitude and encored." On July 26, 1821, the Pierians were invited to attend an entertainment at Boston's Concert Hall. Afterwards they "serenaded the people of this 'emporium' and were invited in at Mr. Rodgers the former President of the Pierian Club and at Mr. Harrison Gray Otis Jr.'s and elegantly—and generously received and treated."

The nocturnal serenades were often undertaken with specific young ladies in mind. On September 12, 1836, "we proceeded to serenade some young ladies at Captain Stevens' who were kind enough to show us that they had their night caps on and were preparing to go to bed. We then proceeded at Tuckerman's desire to serenade the Misses Whitney's, and for once gave pleasure to the young ladies who said we played in time and tune and did not make the night hideous." On May 13, 1837, "we serenaded Miss Crabbe, Miss Miles, Miss Story, Miss Phipps, and last but not least our beloved professor Beck. No sign of life was shown any where except at Mr. Pierce, but alas t'was the chambermaid who showed us her night cap. Her night gown was heaving with the contending passions which swelled her lustful breast." The minutes of April 13, 1840, contain a lengthy description of a long evening during which they met, went to Willard's tavern, then serenaded with waltzes at Mr. Foster's, where they were given drinks and invited to waltz with the ladies. Next they were welcomed at the oyster shop, where they apparently imbibed too long; according to the secretary, what happened that evening "can better be imagined than described."

The more formal exhibitions usually involved a university occasion, such as graduation or valedictory. The Pierians took these events seriously in one sense: several times they declined if they felt they were not ready or were not capable of performing well. The minutes of October 2, 1832, describe what was probably a typical job for the Boston Brigade Band. On that day the Pierians voted not to play for Exhibition Day on October 16 because they were reduced to three members. The minutes then record the surprise that occurred when the university community assembled on Exhibition Day: "All eyes were turned towards the places which the Pierians had been accustomed to occupy on similar occasions, but alas!! they were *not found—missing*; and in their stead, were to be seen looking down on the astonished spectators six strange and '*bearded*' faces, the owners of which were clad in the uniform of the Boston Brigade Band. It is said that Pres. Quincy is obliged to pay them from his own pocket, the Faculty refusing to do it on account of the *enormous expense*!!!"27

Even in these more formal settings, however, the members were more interested in having a good time and impressing the members of the opposite sex than in the solemnity of the ceremony. On Exhibition Day of April 30, 1811, the secretary recorded: "This day the Sodality performed at the public exhibition with honor to themselves, and to the satisfaction, entertainment, and gratification of an unusually numerous, respectable, brilliant, and cheerful auditory, of which the fair of our land made by far the most delightful and attractive part—who warmed the cold with their beauty, encouraged the time by the expressive sweetness of their countenances, and rewarded us musicians by their approving smiles." A similar statement occurs in the minutes of August 19, 1811. Ironically, it is the closest the records come to stating the purpose of the society: "Met according to adjournment, and played our Music.— The piece publicly performed was "*Handel's Waterpiece*"—in which the Sodality did honor to themselves. . . . It was however remarked by some of the members that we hardly did so well as usual. Allowing this to be fact—the Ladies whom the club principally wish to serve, the primum mobile of our music, were few in number, which must have damped the ardor of their humble servants."

The secretaries' own observations about the performances suggest that music was to be enjoyed in good humor and high spirits. Apparently the secretaries were charged with providing a critique of each performance. Some critiques were serious, some were tongue-in-cheek, but all brimmed with youthful enthusiasm: "our utmost expectations were exceeded, by the incomparable excellence of the performances"; "after performing most ravishing thought to adjourn"; "after playing in style superior to any thing of the kind ever before known"; "our Divertimento was performed with so much spirit, that the Secretary has no doubt, the ghost of Pleyel was somewhere in the east entry of Mass. rejoicing at the resuscitation of the Taste, which erst was wont to exist in the Academic groves of Harvard." Yet the secretaries were not indiscriminate in their praise: "Sodality met per Hilliard played very badly magna discordia erat"; "plenty of bass but rather a failure on the part of the flutes."

The repertoire of the two organizations ranged from Handel to popular airs and marches, with the latter predominating. On Exhibition Day 1819 the Pierian Sodality performed Handel's *Water Music* and an unidentified divertimento. On Exhibition Day 1821 it performed "Eveleen's Bower," "Pandean March," "Queen of Prussia's Waltz," "March in Little Book," Allemande No. 2, "March in *Battle of Prague*," "Cadet Band Waltzes," and "Paddy Cairy." The most extensive list of pieces that has survived dates from an 1831 third-flute book. It is hand-copied and consists of eighty-eight pieces overall. The principal part of the book contains fifty-four pieces; the rest of it consists of material started from the other end upside down to the first part. Some pieces are untitled and, as this is the third-flute part, are not identifiable. The following list contains all of those pieces that are titled:

Kerry's Slow March	Rieff's Quick Step
Troop	Bridesmaid's Chorus
Trivoli	geschwind Marsch
Railway March	Hunter's Chorus Weber
Grand Waltz Mozart	Yellow Haired Laddie Scotch
Sprig of Shilalagh Irish	Dance C. Richardson
Woodpecker	Oft in the Stilly Night
Di tanti palpiti Rossini	oBrin Adair
Auld Lang Syne Scotch	No. 23 Brigade Band
Bonnets of Blue	Home, Sweet Home
Pas de Double Brigade Band	Musette de Nina Mozart
Bonnie Boat	Grand March Logies
March Brigade Band	March Brigade Band
Scotch Air	We're all Noddin Scotch
Yankee Doodle	unknown Sul Margine
Allegro Troop	Hartman
Soldier's Grav	Andante
Quick Step	March in the Overture of Lodoiska
Hail!! Columbia	Washington's March
Dirge	Trans Continental March Ch.
Waltz	Waltzes
Waltz	Waltz

Since the 1831 book was a hand-copied manuscript, it was probably several years in the making and thus represents the repertoire that was played throughout much of the 1820s. In 1875 John S. Dwight had access to a book of copied music used between 1808 and 1822. The book contained several popular marches:

Swiss Guards	Valentine's Grand Slow March
Massachusetts	in C
Cadet's March	Dirge in the Oratory of Saul
Buonaparte's March	March in the Overture of
	Lodoiska

It also listed other pieces, which Dwight summarized:

Rondos by Haydn and Pleyel
The Downfall of Paris
Waltzes
A Divertimento by Pleyel
A portion of Handel's Water Music
Airs, like Robin Adair, Yellow-Haired Laddie, Fleuve du Tage,
    Aria in the Brazen Mask, etc.[28]

Samuel Jennison, who graduated in 1839, reported on the repertoire in the 1830s. He listed the following pieces:

O Nannie, wilt thou gang wi' me?
Spring-time of Year
Popular Extravaganza called Jim Crow
Roy's Wife
Kinlock of Kinlock
Most of Moore's Melodies
Oft in the still night
Come rest in this bosom
Araby's Daughter
The harp that once thro' Tara's halls
My lodging is on the cold ground [Believe me, if all those endearing
    young charms]
Fair Harvard
Zitti, zitti
a waltz in C by Mozart
Airs from Caliph of Bagdad and from Le Dieu it la Bayadere
Something by Von Weber called the Witches' Dance
Celeste's Dance
Compression of the Overture to Le Nozze di Figaro
Duke of Reichstadt's Waltz
'Buy a Broom' and waltz from William Tell
Fanny Ellsler furore
Celebrated Air by Hadyn[29]

The repertoire broadened in the 1830s but stayed essentially the same. Popular songs, dances, marches, and arrangements of better-known selections from classical European music formed the heart of it. The Pierians occasionally commissioned pieces or arrangements from local musicians. On August 19, 1811, the Pierians "*Voted* that the President apply to [Frederick] Granger for music *specifically arranged*—proper for Serenade." And in 1833 Thomas Comer agreed to arrange some tunes for the Pierians. They also had a particularly close relationship with the Boston Brigade Band. The 1831 manuscript book lists four pieces attributed to the band: two marches, "Pas de Double," and one entitled only "No. 23."

In addition to records of meetings, the secretaries transcribed three poems and one oration presented to the societies. The first poem, "On Music," by F. Pratt, was read to the Pierian Sodality on August 23, 1814, at a dinner after an exhibition. It is a mixture of youthful idealism, classical erudition, and awkward, often clumsy verse. It consists of eleven four-line stanzas, with an *a b a b* rhyme scheme. Verses as the following are typical:

When Cynthia's beams deck the sky,
And mortals have gone to their rest;
Their music can draw from the eye,
What sorrow has seldom supprest.

'Tis the tear that silently flows,
When the heart inspired with joy;
Not rising from sorrows or woes;
But from lays, that never can cloy.

When wandering tones meet the ear.
Proceeding from some distant grove;
Our minds rapt in pleasure appear
The votaries of music, I love.

Pratt's basic concept of music is classical: music essentially provides pleasure; it can enrapture; but most of all it has charm and can sooth and banish cares. The poem begins:

When grief and despair would the heart,
And in peace, no longer can rest,
'Tis music, its charm an impact,
A charm that each woe lulls to rest.

The other two poems were delivered to the Pierian Sodality in 1819. They are unattributed, but at least one was probably written by the secretary at that time, George W. Adams. They are different enough in character and style to suggest that Adams did not write both. They have one similarity: both are replete with classical allusion. The first poem, "We May Say of Our Music," conceptualizes music in much the manner that Pratt did. Music has the power to

> . . . chain the passions, soothe the soul,
> To snatch the dagger, and to dash the bowl
> From Murders hand; to smooth the couch of care
> Extract the thorns and scatter roses there.

The second poem is more bacchanalian. Classical references abound, to Cato, Venus, and Bacchus. The essential message of this poem is

> To mingle sweet pleasure with search after treasure
> Indulging at night for the toils of the day.

Reference is made to "good wine and good company." Care "in an ocean of claret is drowned." The poem closes

> Thus happy together, in spite of all weather,
> 'Tis sunshine and summer with us the year round.

On July 20, 1820, Adams delivered an oration to the Arionic Sodality, "On the Progress of Music." He recorded it entire in the minutes, and it differs markedly from the earlier poems, with only minimal allusions to classical mythology. Adams stressed the idea of progress in music and the ability of music to move the passions. His approach was historical, and the oration reflected more the general tone and sentiment of the Presbyterian-Congregational reformers than that of the two sodalities.

After observing that the members of the Arionic Sodality were "in search of the temple of Music" but "have as yet merely entered its portal," Adams attempted a historical survey of music. He began with several passages from Scripture to indicate that music was favored by the Hebrews, followed by references to Greece and Rome. To demonstrate that Greece was the land of poetry, he quoted a passage in Greek from Homer, and asserted that in Rome music "was the rule of eloquence, as well as theatrical declamation, and of common speech." Adams surveyed European music, speaking of the national musics of France, Spain, and Scotland and the various types of songs associated with them. He was harsh on England, which he claimed "alone of all the nations of Europe

. . . to have no national music." England's best music was written by foreign composers, including her national anthem, "God Save the King," which according to Adams was composed by Handel. The finest music of recent times was found in Italy and Germany, Germany in particular having given the world Handel, Haydn, Mozart, and Humler [Hummel?], as well as the waltz.

Turning to America, Adams observed that while the taste for music had improved considerably in recent years, America had still produced no original native composers. He considered the fine arts still in their infancy in America, but was confident that "as Commerce and Agriculture imprint their blessings on her soil, extend her power and increase her wealth, the Genius of Music and Apollo shall bless, with the notes of the swan, the soaring eagle of Columbia, imparting to him the power of sending far strains now grand and majestic as the roar of Niagara, now gentle and peaceful as the Dove, whose wings are covered with silver and her feathers with yellow gold and some future Handel shall arise 'untwisting all the chains that tie the hidden soul of Harmony.'"[30]

This statement is unique as an undergraduate expression of musical attitudes. But how original and how representative is it? Where did Adams get his ideas? Most of the ideas in his oration can be traced to the thought of the Presbyterian-Congregational reformers. The concept of progress in music was one of their central theses, and their ideas had been in print since the early years of the century.[31] The idea of progress itself implies a historical dimension. In drawing on biblical sources, the reformers provided a historical context for the discussion of musical evolution. Caleb Emerson, for instance, traced the history of music from Jubal, the seventh generation from Adam in the Old Testament, through David and then Egypt, Greece, and Italy into modern times.[32] The reformers also stressed national airs as "the most perfect models of melody" and compared the relative strengths of those from different countries.[33] Other writers echoed similar sentiments, especially about progress and the historical element. On January 9, 1819, John Rowe Parker had written in his column, "Euterpeiad," in the *Boston Intelligencer and Morning and Evening Advertiser* that music was progressive and that its progress could be traced for more than two thousand years. On April 15, 1820, two months prior to Adams' oration, Parker reprinted that article in his newly founded magazine, *Euterpeiad*. Parker went back as far as the Greeks in his brief historical overview, entitled "Modern Music." He addressed the question of national music in much the same manner as Adams did.[34] It is entirely possible, even likely, that the *Euterpeiad.* was the direct source and inspiration of Adams' orations.

The three Pierian poems seem entirely consistent with the character of the two sodalities. They hark back to Goliard poetry, displaying that same combination of youthful exuberance, love of music, irreverence, bacchanalian festiveness, and erudite display of classical learning. They are in the mainstream of several centuries of undergraduate rhetoric and poetry. Adams' oration in contrast stands apart. It is unique among the Pierian and Arionic documents in its historical focus, emphasis on music as a fine art, and nationalistic appeal. It confirms that these ideas were current at the time, but it does not reflect the thought or activities of the two groups themselves. All of the other evidence suggests that their members had very different attitudes toward music. Adams' oration is not even consistent with the three poems, one of which Adams himself probably wrote, and both of which, next to the oration, are the most serious statements about music in the records of the societies.

There is no evidence that Adams or other members of the Pierian Sodality carried the attitudes expressed in his oration with them into their adult lives, at least not immediately. Some twenty years later these attitudes would become much more commonplace, but most of the Pierians who settled in Boston played little part in its musical life. Adams' oration can probably be looked upon as a typical undergraduate exercise of the time, an exegesis or an essay upon a topic.

The two most important secular musical organizations in Boston between 1800 and 1825 were the Philoharmonic Society and the Handel and Haydn Society.[35] They are the only secular organizations to have survived for any length of time and to have had a public impact on the Boston musical world. Many other independent societies existed in and around Boston in the early nineteenth century: the Franklin Musical Society, the Lock Hospital Musical Society, the Norfolk Musical Society, the Essex Musical Society, the Lockhart Singing Society, at Andover, the St. Cecilia Society, the Boston Musical Association, and the Massachusetts Musical Society. In addition, the Brattle Street, Hollis, Bowdoin, Winter Street, and Park Street churches each had a musical society. Some of the societies were relatively large. The Franklin Musical Society had 120 members in 1802 and expected to grow by another forty or fifty the following year, when it hoped to secure the services of Andrew Law.[36] Unfortunately little is known about most of the societies, such as the St. Cecilia Society or the Boston Musical Association. One or two references appear in newspapers, followed by silence, suggesting that their existence might have been as ephemeral as the surviving evidence.[37]

More is known about the Massachusetts Musical Society, organized in June 1807 for the purpose of "forming a musical library and of occasionally meeting to perform and discuss the style of performing sacred music." Its members hoped to remedy the perceived lack of knowledge of musical science among professional musicians and the "vitiated style of performing that part of sacred worship." The society began when fifteen "gentlemen" agreed to contribute $2 each to purchase a collection of sacred music that included Handel's *Messiah, Judas Maccabeus,* and *Acis and Galatea,* Prang's *Twenty Anthems,* Stephen's *Cathedral Music,* and six anthems by Mozart.[38]

Judging from the contents of the collection, the choir was ambitious. The president assigned the music to be sung and led the singing. Unfortunately the group was often not capable of the music chosen, and had to substitute less difficult music. The members voted to attempt the "Hallelujah Chorus," but it is uncertain that they succeeded. At one time they contemplated public performance, but that never materialized. Finally, after twenty-three meetings with mostly discouraging results, they voted to sell their library to pay off debts and dissolve the society, which disbanded on July 5, 1810.[39]

Charles Perkins dismissed the notion that the Massachusetts Musical Society had a direct effect on the founding of the Handel and Haydn Society, as it ceased to exist five years before the Handel and Haydn Society was established. Perkins also had the testimony of George Cushing, one of the founders of the Handel and Haydn Society, that the earlier group was not mentioned in the discussions leading to the founding of the Handel and Haydn Society, and that Cushing was not even aware of its prior existence.[40] Perkins does admit that the experience gained by members in the former society probably contributed to the founding of the latter. The goal of the two organizations was similar, to improve sacred music through the performance of more complex and lofty European music. Two, possibly three, of the founding members of the Massachusetts Musical Society were founding members of the Handel and Haydn Society: Charles Nolen, the secretary of the Massachusetts Musical Society, and James Pierce. It is not clear if Asa Peabody of the Massachusetts Musical Society and the founding Peabody of the Handel and Haydn Society were the same person. It is not even clear who the Handel and Haydn Society Peabody was. At one time Perkins referred to an Augustus Peabody and at another time to an Aaron Peabody.[41] Charles Nolen also served as a trustee of the Handel and Haydn Society. One other member of the Massachusetts Musical Society, Elijah Mears, joined the Handel and Haydn Society on June 1, 1815.

The Handel and Haydn Society and the Philoharmonic Society evolved into concert organizations, but that was not the original purpose of either; from the start they were both amateur performing ensembles. Beyond that, however, they were radically different. The Philoharmonic Society was founded to perform instrumental music. It was an informal gathering of professionals and amateurs and in its early days existed for the private reading of orchestral music. The Handel and Haydn Society was established to further the cause of sacred vocal music. It was formally organized from the start and did intend public performance of large-scale vocal compositions, although that activity was not its raison d'être.

In 1837 Francis J. Grund observed that the choir of the Handel and Haydn Society consisted mostly of mechanics.[42] Writing many years later, John S. Dwight described the membership in the early part of the century as "mechanics, tradesmen, and marketmen, etc."[43] Both men may have been influenced by their own preconceptions. Grund was from Germany, where singing societies frequently were working-class organizations. Dwight was a native of New England, but his impression of the working class was mostly an idealized one connected with Fourierism and his participation in the Brook Farm experiment in the 1840s. Dwight himself was considered a lofty, dreamy, ethereal individual, not always in touch with the world about him,[44] and he moved mostly among the elite, in Unitarian and literary circles; he was, for instance, the only person related to the music profession to be admitted to the elite Saturday club.

Although the Handel and Haydn Society did have some members from the working class, it was predominantly a middle-class organization in its early years.[45] Dwight correctly observed that "'first families' were not much represented in the ranks," and explained the society's coolness to George K. Jackson's conditions of employment as class resentment: "No aristocratic English 'Mus. Doc.' could go in on equal terms in what he probably regarded as rather a plebeian movement; nor would the democratic instinct accept him for president or musical director."[46] The Handel and Haydn Society combined and selected members from various church choirs, which Perkins identified as the Brattle Street, Old South, Trinity, Hanover Street, Hollis Street, Federal Street, West, Chauncey Street, and Park Street churches. Conspicuously absent are

Table 2
Occupations of the Original Members of
the Handel and Haydn Society

Occupation	Number
Merchant	8
Attorney	2
Bank cashier	2
Clerk	2
Music	2
Schoolmaster	2
Shopkeeper	2
Tailor	2
Apothecary	1
Blacksmith	1
Building trades	1
Printer	1
Wharfinger	1

members from the Second Baptist and First Universalist churches (although two, but only two, members of the First Universalist Church did join). The class composition of the Handel and Haydn Society can be further ascertained from the occupations of the original members. Table 2 lists the known occupations of the original members.[47]

According to H. Earle Johnson, a blacksmith, a housewright, and a bricklayer tried out but were discharged. A shipwright, a housewright, and a soapboiler were admitted but soon resigned.[48] Since the one requirement for membership in the Handel and Haydn Society was a good voice, an inability to read music did not preclude admission. Unanimous approval of the board of directors, however, was required. Whatever the official reasons, the overall pattern of original membership, new admissions, discharges, and resignations suggests that members of the working class were not especially welcome.

Less is known about the membership of the Philoharmonic Society, but because of its close ties to the Handel and Haydn Society it probably had a similar profile. The Handel and Haydn Society was conceived at a meeting of the Philoharmonic Society, and the two had many members in common. When the Philoharmonic Society was incorporated in 1819, five of the six directors listed were members of the Handel and Haydn

Society. The two organizations frequently collaborated, with the Philo-harmonic Society forming the nucleus of the orchestra for the Handel and Haydn Society concerts.

The origins of the Philoharmonic Society have been the subject of considerable debate. Dwight, writing in 1881, dated it from 1810 or 1811. In 1907 Oscar Sonneck found an advertisement in the *Columbian Centinel* calling a meeting of a Philoharmonic Society on April 6, 1799. He wondered if this group was the same as the later Philoharmonic Society but stopped short of claiming that it was. H. Earle Johnson, who made the most extensive study of the society, reiterated the later founding date on the grounds that, had the society existed continuously, some notice in the newspapers would surely have appeared between 1799 and 1809, the next mention that Johnson could find. Recently Daniel Layman discovered at least one such notice, an advertisement in the *Columbian Centinel* of March 28, 1801, changing the "usual" meet-ing time of the society to the first Tuesday of April because of conflict with a concert by Trajetta's Conservatory. The Conservatory ordinarily presented concerts on the first or third Tuesday of the month; this particular concert occurred on the fourth. Layman sensibly argued that the wording indicates that the Philoharmonic Society held regular meet-ings, and that they were probably on the second and fourth Tuesdays of each month. Further indirect evidence supports the early origins of the Philoharmonic Society. John R. Parker, writing in the *Boston Ingel-ligencer* in 1817, referred to the Philoharmonic Society, "whose existence is of many years standing." In 1819 Parker called the Philoharmonic Society the "nursery for instrumental amateurs" and referred to its "use-fullness [which] has continued for nearly twenty years." In 1820 he repeated his column in his own journal, the *Euterpeiade*.[49]

The founding of the Philoharmonic Society just prior to 1799 corre-sponds with Gottlieb Graupner's arrival in Boston. All sources agree that Graupner was the founding father and guiding light of the Philo-harmonic Society, serving as its president for its entire existence. He was the leader or conductor in concerts, and rehearsals were held in his hall. Graupner came to Boston in either late 1796 or early 1797 from Charleston, where he had married Catherine Hellyer on April 6, 1796. Hellyer was an actress and singer with the City Theater in Charleston. The company itself had transferred from Boston, although Graupner was not then a member of it. On October 7, 1796, both Graupners appeared in a concert in Norfolk, Virginia. By January 27, 1797, they were in Boston. On that day Catherine Graupner appeared at the Federal

Street Theater as Lauretta in *Richard Coeur de Lion*. It was billed as "her first appearance these two years."[50] Gottlieb Graupner is not listed as part of the band in the theater's records for 1796 and 1797, but received a special payment of $45 recorded as arrears due. Graupner is listed as part of the orchestra for the following year. He had probably joined the orchestra at mid-season, 1796–1797, too late to be included in the treasurer's list. He almost certainly came to Boston with his wife.

Graupner was a galvanizing force for instrumental activity in Boston. He was proficient on both the oboe and the double bass. He had had considerable professional experience in London, possibly playing under Haydn in the famous Salamon concerts. He quickly became one of the principal leaders of musical life in Boston. Soon after arriving in Boston Graupner expanded his activities beyond the theater orchestra. At the same time, 1801, he formed the Conservatory, or Musical Academy, with Francis Mallet and Filipo Trajetta and opened a music business that sold instruments and later published music. Such activities would naturally attract instrumental players around him. There is no reason to doubt that they would establish a small, informal group before 1809. Since the April 6, 1799, announcement indicates that the society was already in existence, we can date its origins somewhere between October 6, 1796, when we know that the Graupners had not yet arrived in Boston, and April 6, 1799.

At first the Philoharmonic Society was a private group. According to Dwight it was "simply a social meeting" of "Mr. Graupner and his little knot of musical friends, mostly amateurs," who "practiced Haydn's symphonies, etc. for their own enjoyment." Thus it is not surprising that its public profile was low. The Philoharmonic Society did not present any concerts per se under its own name until 1818, although it participated in public musical presentations. The society sponsored "rehearsals," which were open to members, many of whom joined as listeners; the distinction between rehearsals and concerts was subtle. The society also appeared with the Handel and Haydn Society, with or without their presence being acknowledged; most of the early programs of the Handel and Haydn Society do not mention the orchestra. The formation of the orchestra for the Handel and Haydn Society concerts varied from year to year, but usually the society negotiated with individual players or a leader like Graupner or Louis Ostinelli, who would provide the orchestra. Since the Philoharmonic Society consisted of most of the instrumentalists in Boston,[51] that the two orchestras in large measure had the same players does not necessarily imply institutional sponsorship.

The Philoharmonic Society also sponsored or participated in benefit concerts. On June 24, 1815, a Mr. Lefolle announced a concert of vocal and instrumental music in the *Columbian Centinel*, which included a Mozart overture as well as a sinfonia and a finale by Pleyel. The Philoharmonic Society's orchestra itself was not mentioned, but the concert was announced for "the Hall in Pond street, occupied by the Philoharmonic Society." The concert was sufficiently successful for Lefolle to give a second one. This time he advertised that the concert would take place "under the Patronage of the Philoharmonic Society."

The Handel and Haydn Society was an indirect spin-off of the Philoharmonic Society. According to George Cushing, one of the founders, the society originated in informal discussions at meetings of the Philoharmonic Society, in which individuals expressed concern about the low state of sacred music in Boston.[52] From those discussions a public meeting was called of all who were interested in the subject. By April 1, 1815, at least two meetings had been held and a society formed. On that date the *Advertiser* observed "that exertions are making to form a general association, comprising the leaders and most active members of the different singing societies of the several congregations in this metropolis, for the purpose of bringing into general use the compositions of Handel and Haydn. . . . The association contemplates digesting a plan, embracing all the musical talent in this town, of the purpose of sacred oratorio performances." A formal constitution had been adopted and signed by forty-four members by the end of April. Rehearsals began in May, and the first concert was presented on Christmas evening. The chorus numbered approximately one hundred, and the audience almost a thousand. In a city of 38,248, the estimated population of Boston in 1815, that was an excellent crowd.[53]

An important question about both the Handel and Haydn Society and the Philoharmonic Society was their purpose. We know the stated public purpose of each, but what sort of vision of music or attitude about the nature of music did these organizations project? How did their members view their activities and what did they conceive music to be about?

The overlapping membership and the close ties in origins suggest a commonalty of vision between the two organizations. Because the Handel and Haydn Society was a more public and a more formal body than the Philoharmonic Society, we know much more about it. According to Cushing, the Handel and Haydn Society was born out of a concern about the state of church music in New England. The early documents pertaining to the society support him. On March 24, 1815, an announcement was made requesting performers from several choirs to meet "for the purpose of considering the expediency and practicality of forming a Society, to consist of a selection from the several choirs, for cultivating and improving a correct taste in the performance of Sacred Music, and also to introduce into more general practice, the works of Handel, Haydn and other eminent composers."[54]

On April 29, 1815, nine days after the first meeting of the Handel and Haydn Society, an article appeared in the *Columbian Centinel* describing the formation of the society. It was signed "Public Good" and was included under the section "GENERAL MISCELLANY." Although its authorship is unknown, it almost certainly was written by one of the original founders of the Handel and Haydn Society. As such it stands as the most authentic and detailed statement of purpose that we have from the original meeting.

The statement opened with a peroration on the power of the human voice to move the listener. It then discussed the effect of music and poetry when properly combined, and the defects that often occur in improper performance. Specific complaints were registered: distortion of harmony through the use of a tenor rather than a soprano for the melody; and a nasal singing style—here described as "sounds proceeding through an unnatural passage," caused by "obstruction either by compression or contraction of the mouth." These criticisms echo precisely some of the Presbyterian-Congregational reformers' observations about sacred music. There is no question that the writer had psalmody in mind throughout this opening section, referring at one point to "the pleasing, grateful and ennobling exercise of Psalmody." He considered the prophet David the creator of the union of melody and poetry. He emphasized the importance of singing in public devotion and its elevating quality: "Nothing can give to the soul of the Pious Christian so high a sense of harmonic grandeur, as an organized assembly singing with one heart and one voice their great Creator's praise, in solemn strains of poetic devotion."

In the second half of the article the writer was more specific about the Handel and Haydn Society. He recognized that considerable progress had recently been made toward improving sacred vocal music. He viewed the society as continuing and bringing to fruition that trend: "The 'Handel and Haydn Society' will combine select members from the choirs of the several congregations in this metropolis; and will extend to gentlemen—properly qualified—from the towns in this vicinity. It is contemplated to practice the compositions of such European Masters as have been most eminently great in their works of Sacred Music, and it is intended to perform Oratorios for the general improvement of the science."

When the society was incorporated in February 1816, the act of incorporation supported the church-music function of the society, stating that the society had been established "for the purpose of extending the knowledge and improving the style of performance of Church Music."[55]

The Handel and Haydn Society straddled a position between singing school and public concert organization. The presentation of oratorios was a stated objective. But the presentation itself was only a means to an end, subordinate to the ultimate objective of improving church music. Public performance as entertainment was not even addressed, probably because the ideals of the founders deemed it irrelevant. That music could be elevating was explicitly acknowledged, but only with regard to church music. Finally, the Handel and Haydn Society viewed itself at this time partly as an independent body, admitting members on their individual merit, and partly as an umbrella organization to form an all-star choir from the various choirs in town.

Although most of the sixteen persons who attended the first meeting were members of various church choirs in Boston, the connection with church choirs was never very specific, and over the years it diminished. The sacred-music mission of the Handel and Haydn Society remained for some time, however. In 1819 a committee on the subject of season tickets recommended to the board of directors that the society dispense with the performance of oratorios, except on special occasions, and observed "that those Gentlemen who may feel disposed to patronize the Society and thereby promote the improvement of the Style of performance of sacred musick, would subscribe in such number." The reason for dispensing with the oratorios was financial; as it turned out, the society was able to continue offering them. For the society to even consider eliminating them, however, indicates that it viewed its purpose as other than just public performance.[56]

Beyond the vague statement of purpose in the act of incorporation, no direct information exists about the way the Philoharmonic Society saw itself. Activities from 1819 on suggest that it did consider itself a concert organization. Its "meetings" reflect a desire to educate the public in instrumental music, but there is no evidence that such music was seen in the same lofty, idealistic terms in which sacred music was beginning to be conceptualized. Since by 1820 the Philoharmonic Society included almost all the instrumental musicians in Boston, instrumental music remained predominantly within the framework of diversion or entertainment.

Membership in both the Handel and Haydn Society and the Philoharmonic Society was limited to men. This limitation was written into the constitution of the Handel and Haydn Society; it was at least de facto for the Philoharmonic Society. It was inevitable that the Philoharmonic would have no women participants; of the 213 orchestral musicians active in Boston for even a brief period between 1796 and 1843 that I have been able to trace, not a single one was female. It was only barely acceptable for a male amateur to perform with an orchestra. Many amateurs purposely left their name off of programs. For a woman to appear in the orchestra was unheard of.

Women did sing, and the Handel and Haydn Society needed female voices. But the bylaws specified that women could not join, although they could sing in the choir by invitation. This practice did not encourage women to participate. In 1835, for instance, the chorus had approximately ninety tenors and basses, but only twenty sopranos. When Lowell Mason became president of the society in 1827, he discovered that there were no women altos, only a handful of men who attempted the alto part. Mason called the result "disgreeable." Furthermore, the sopranos could neither read music nor carry the line themselves but had to depend on tenors who sang the soprano part an octave lower. The Handel and Haydn Society never employed a soprano or alto soloist until 1830. As president, Mason tried to improve the choral sound by encouraging female altos and abandoning the practice of men singing the soprano part. He did not, however, suggest that women be given full membership.[57]

Many women learned to play musical instruments, but very few played in public. Wind instruments remained the province of men, in part through tradition and in part because of the military association. Military bands were overwhelmingly amateur organizations, and given their connection with a militia, it was unthinkable that a woman would participate. The violin was associated with dance music more than concert music. This left the piano, which many women did learn to play. The piano, however, was limited almost entirely to upper-class homes at the beginning of the nineteenth century. Its spread into the middle-class house began around 1810, buoyed by the establishment of several piano manufacturers in Boston between 1790 and 1830, whose success indicates the instrument's increasing popularity.[58]

Other industries catered to women's interest in music, a sign that women were actively involved in music. Several musical publications were aimed specifically at women: from 1796 to 1799 William Norman published, albeit irregularly, the *Musical Repertory* and the *Ladies Musical Journal*; in 1797 P. A. Von Hagen announced a monthly magazine, the *Lady's Musical Miscellany*; in 1821 John Rowe Parker retitled the second volume of the *Euterpeiad or Musical Intelligencer* to the *Euterpeiad: or, Music Intelligencer, and Ladies' Gazette*. Many musical instructors specifically sought female pupils. Newspapers carried advertisements for private instruction, musical academies, and schools that included the fine arts. At about the time Von Hagen announced his journal, he placed a lengthy advertisement in the *Columbian Centinel* "inform[ing] the Ladies of Boston, of his intention to form a musical academy." The academy was to be divided into four parts: "1. The Grammatical knowledge of Music;—2. The Practical part—3. The Vocal part.—4. The theoretical part." He made no specific mention of teaching instruments, although he stated that he had pianos for sale and instruments for lease. Many advertisements for piano lessons referred specifically to females. In 1798 B. Glann, for instance, announced that he wished "to inform respectfully the Ladies of Boston" that he was available for pupils. Other advertisements touted music as a social grace. Mr. Dearborn's Academy, announced in 1797, was devoted to the "Useful and Ornamental branches of a Polite Education," in which music was included.[59]

Some advertisements presumed a musical specialization by sex. In 1820 a Mr. Huntington advertised a Grammatical Musical School that offered singing classes for young ladies on Thursday and Saturday afternoons and for young gentlemen on the same evenings, classes in which they were taught not only singing but also how to play the flute. The Conservatory, founded by Graupner, Mallet, and Trajetta in 1800, advertised classes for girls as well as wind-instrument classes specifically for boys.[60] These advertisements reflect accurately the musical situation in Boston. Both men and women learned to sing, women mostly learned the piano, men almost exclusively learned wind instruments, and little mention was made of string instruments.

There were professional women musicians in Boston, but they performed only on voice and keyboard and in almost every case were part of a musical family. Gottlieb Graupner's wife, Catherine, was the leading female singer for the Federal Street Theater, although her success was independent of her relationship with Graupner. If anything, Graupner's career in Boston was due to her. She had already established her career, as Catherine Hellyer, before they married and came to Boston as part of the theatrical company that transferred from Charlestown. Graupner played in the orchestra with the same company, but all indications are that her career brought them there. Their daughter Catherine Graupner debuted as a pianist in Boston in 1809, subsequently appeared often in concerts, and became the first organist of the Handel and Haydn Society in 1815.[61] Another daughter, Charlotte Elizabeth Rowson Graupner, also became a pianist and organist, performing frequently in Boston. Sophie Henriette Hewitt, the daughter of James Hewitt, debuted at age seven as a pianist. She became organist of the Handel and Haydn Society in 1820, holding the position for ten years. In 1822 she married Louis Ostinelli, who had established himself as the leading violinist in Boston upon his arrival in 1818. The Ostinellis separated in 1834, and Sophie moved to Portland, Maine. Until then she performed in concerts, including her own benefit in 1831, and taught piano, harp, and voice. Francis Mallet's daughter debuted as a pianist in 1805 when she was, according to advertisements, seven years old. After she appeared on programs in 1810 and 1811, however, she disappeared from public view. Nothing is known of her subsequently.

Most women musicians, like their male counterparts, gave music lessons. Mrs. Von Hagen specifically advertised the advantage of young ladies studying with women musicians: "As motives of delicacy may induce parents to commit the tuition of young Ladies in this branch of education to one of their own sex . . . she flatters herself that she shall be indulged with their approbation, and the protection of a respectable Public."[62]

Sophie Ostinelli was peremptorily fired as organist of the Handel and Haydn Society in 1830, a move that provoked a bitter controversy among the members of the organization. The incident raises a number of questions regarding both musical standards in general and the status of women musicians at the time. Ostinelli had been organist of the society since 1819, was well-liked, and had proven herself a competent musician. When Charles Zeuner arrived from Germany in 1830, Mason believed that Zeuner had a greater variety of talents as an organist, particularly the ability to play orchestral parts on the organ. On June 2, 1830, Mason persuaded the board of directors to elect Zeuner organist at the same salary, $200 a year, they had paid Ostinelli. Ostinelli was to be dismissed. On October 14 forty-seven members of the society, led by J. K. Wise, presented to the board a remonstrance that the election of Zeuner be rescinded and Mrs. Ostinelli be reinstated. After some discussion a motion was presented that the remonstrants have leave to withdraw their petition. Mason would not allow even that, and the motion lost "by the casting vote of the President." The board then issued a statement "that while the Board entertain the greatest respect for the motives which have influenced so large and respectable a number of members of the Society to remonstrate on this subject—and while there is the strongest desire on the part of the Board to comply with the wishes of the members of the Society generally on every subject connected with the welfare . . . the Board constitutionally has the authority to select an organist." The statement then offered a more specific justification of the board's decision to replace Ostinelli with Zeuner, and in doing so revealed a lot about the problems of the society at that time. While Zeuner combined "execution with scientific knowledge," his real strength as far as the society was concerned was in orchestral accompaniment: "It has always been considered very desirable that the organist of the H & H Society . . . should be conversant not only with the organ, but with the nature and design of the accompaniment, orchestral effect and vocal music generally." According to the statement, the Handel and Haydn Society needed an organist who could keep time accurately, add "full and correct harmony," and "render the whole performance more powerful, effective and creditable to the Society."

Mason clearly had standards in mind, was obdurate in his pursuit of them, and was willing to do what was necessary to implement them. He showed these same traits at other times during his presidency, as when he pushed to have the bylaws altered to require candidates for membership to undergo an examination of their musical qualifications. Mason's stubborn insistence on standards also caused him to treat with disdain those who opposed him. The Ostinelli affair was not an isolated incident. He was sometimes so harsh on orchestral players who flubbed their parts that they would pack up and leave the rehearsal. His dispute with his close friend and associate George J. Webb in 1839 became so bitter that Webb resigned from the Boston Academy of Music. In spite of these other incidents, the Ostinelli affair does raise the question whether her being a woman affected the cavalier treatment that she received. Certainly many members of the Handel and Haydn Society were outraged over the incident and, it seems justifiably, protested the action of the board.[63]

In the second half of the nineteenth century women played important roles as patrons of music. There is some, but little, evidence that they did so earlier, too. Most public musical activity was sponsored either by the performing organizations themselves, like the Handel and Haydn Society and the Philoharmonic Society, or was organized as benefits or profit-making ventures, such as the attempts to establish outdoor gardens in the summer. Both activities were controlled by men. The two principal avenues for women patrons in the second half of the century, benevolent cultural institutions that sponsored musical activity and large-scale soirees, were nonexistent in the first case and rare in the second. Members of the socioeconomic elite simply did not participate significantly in public musical activity. Some had music in their homes, but the concerts and the great interest in instrumental music in Col. William Tudor's home were unusual. It should be noted, however, that according to all evidence Mrs. Tudor was responsible for them. There was little such activity in the Samuel Eliot home, even though (as we shall see in the following chapters) Eliot was one of the first members of the socio-economic elite to support vigorously public musical activity. Eliot's daughter, Mary E. Guild, wrote an unpublished account of her home life[64] in which she described Mary Lyman Eliot, Eliot's wife, as a well-educated woman for the time. She had studied classics, was considered a good French scholar, and had considerable knowledge of botany. She liked to entertain, and enjoyed presiding at the head of the table at large dinners. But she had little interest in music, and there was little musical activity in the Eliot home, in spite of Samuel Eliot's passion for it. The place of music in the Eliot's family life was probably more typical of the upper class in the early Federal period than that in the Tudors'.

Chapter Six

Crisis in Secular Concert Activity:
Disputes and Divergences

Until approximately 1820 amateur and professional musicians enjoyed an easy rapport. Instrumental performance occurred mostly in private, and professionals invited amateurs to play alongside them in the orchestra. The scarcity of instrumental musicians necessitated an alliance between the two groups. Even the theater welcomed assistance from amateurs to fill out the orchestra. The larger theaters, with four or five performances a week during the season, needed the reliability of a professional orchestra. Other smaller theaters did not, or could not afford it, and there the professional and amateur often worked together. Bates and Harper, for instance, actors at the Federal Street Theatre, formed a summer theater company in 1803 that played in Salem and Providence, Rhode Island. They hired Francis Schaffer, who played at the Federal Street Theatre during the regular season, to lead the "orchestra," which officially consisted of Schaffer and one other violinist. Schaffer was sometimes assisted by students from Brown University, who volunteered as amateurs. On the other side, professional musicians would sometimes sit in with amateur ensembles. Harvard's Pierian Sodality had a relatively close working relationship with members of the Federal Street Theatre's orchestra. The Pierians commissioned members of the orchestra to compose or arrange works for them, and the members of the orchestra sometimes assisted them in "exhibitions," or public performances.

Around 1820 signs of strain appeared in the cozy relationship between amateurs and professionals. Professional musicians began to seek a larger audience through public concerts, which put new performing pressure on all musicians. Professionals easily tolerated amateur musicians in a semiprivate situation. The glare of a public unsure about instrumental music, however, exposed mercilessly an amateur's lack of facility, and by association implicated the professional. The public only remembered when an ensemble played badly, not who caused it to sound bad. The professional began to have second thoughts about associating with amateurs.

Before pursuing the events that ensued because of this growing rift, we must first determine who, in a musically fluid situation as existed in Federal Boston, was an amateur musician and who was a professional. How does one categorize each group? The line between professional and amateur was clear in one sense: an amateur was not paid. Frequently an amateur did not even want his presence acknowledged, and programs often omitted amateurs' names. In another sense, however, the line was not clear. Many musicians earned their living in other trades. George Pollock, who played flute in many benefit concerts and in the Handel and Haydn Society's orchestra from at least 1817 to 1835, was a dry-goods merchant. John Hart, who played clarinet in the Handel and Haydn Society's orchestra and in the Washington Gardens, was an usher at the courthouse. William Coffin, a violinist in the Handel and Haydn Society and secretary of the Philoharmonic Society, was a cordwainer. All three received compensation for their musical services. Since most performing musicians in Federal America were forced to supplement their income in one way or another, it is moot whether they did so in music-related fields like teaching or selling musical instruments, or whether they did so outside of music, as Pollock, Hart, and Coffin did. But with changes in the 1820s, when some musicians attempted to elevate the status of their profession, the distinction between a musician who looked on his playing as a means of supplementing income and a musician who considered music his livelihood became more important.

Amateurs and professionals played side by side in both orchestras and wind bands. As we have seen, the wind band was the most common instrumental ensemble in early Federal America. Most wind bands were associated with local militia and consisted mainly of amateurs. They were popular for entertainments, both indoor and outdoor, and frequently played at dances. To capitalize on this popularity some bands, like the Boston Brigade Band, broke from direct connection with a military unit and became professional ensembles, available either wholly or in part for a variety of functions. Even those bands that retained their amateur status called on professional musicians for leadership. Lowell Mason, for example, began his professional career in music by leading a military band.[1] Orchestral ensembles in the early Federal period were created for the benefit of the musicians themselves, as no audience for instrumental music existed. The Philoharmonic Society originally fitted that pattern. It was formed so that its members could play orchestral music informally and in private. Not coincidentally (as we shall see), it went public only when the first evidence of tension between amateur and professional musicians surfaced. The society originally welcomed both amateurs and professionals. In fact, given the small number of professional musicians in Boston at the beginning of the nineteenth century, the addition of amateurs was almost a necessity if enough of the orchestral repertoire was to be covered.[2]

In 1821 John R. Parker brought the growing tension out into the open in a two-piece article in the *Euterpeiad*, "On the Association of Professors with Amateurs" (professional musicians were commonly referred to as professors). Parker admitted that the two groups seldom worked well together and that a "reigning jealousy" existed between them. He was not the first to notice the problem. A *New England Galaxy* article in January 1821, critical of a performance of the Handel and Haydn Society in January, commented that a lack of rapport between the amateur chorus and the professional orchestra was apparent to all attending. The *Galaxy* despaired of a solution: "Professional men will not harmonize with amateurs. You might as well attempt to unite two of the most opposite qualities in nature, as to produce a unanimity of feeling and taste and judgement in such a case. They cannot, or rather they will not, coalesce. To which side the want of a spirit of accommodation is to be imputed, let every one judge for himself."[3]

Parker tried to explain the causes of the friction between professionals and amateurs, and he suggested remedies. He thought the difficulties centered on public concerts, or exhibitions. The professor was more interested in the music itself, the amateur in exhibiting his own powers. The amateur was content with less because he knew that he could plead that he did this only for amusement. He ever delighted in the making of music and expected the professor to do likewise. The professor, however, regarded the amateur with contempt and tended to be irritable about his attempts at performance. The professional feared for his reputation when performing with amateurs. He also felt that he could make more profit from performances unencumbered by amateur colleagues. At the same time, the professional sought the amateur's cooperation for his own ends, be they artistic, financial, or political. In addition, the ears of the professor might be more polished but they had become inured. The amateur retained his enthusiasm but did not have the technical judgment of the professor.[4]

Parker pointed out that the professor needed the amateur more than the amateur needed the professor. The amateur "looks to the professor for his science and his amusement," but the professor "is absolutely and entirely dependent [on the amateur] for the bread he eats." Parker further argued that the amateur was more able to generalize about music, whereas the professor focused more on practical music making. Parker's remedies were that the professor should learn to profit from the more general knowledge of the amateur, and the amateur should recognize and profit from the greater technical knowledge of the professor. Each should trust the other more.[5]

Parker's solutions sound somewhat simplistic because the problem was more fundamental than Parker revealed. By 1820 instrumental organizations had become interested in public performances; they were in essence seeking an audience. At the same time, instrumental music itself began to be viewed more seriously, at least in musical circles. It would be another twenty years, however, before the public would catch up with the change. This led to a rift between performer and audience. To be successful, public concerts had to interest a section of the community beyond amateur musicians, but most of the public was not ready to support secular concerts, particularly ones that featured serious instrumental music. Yet it is uncertain to what extent public apathy stemmed from differences in conceptualization between the musician and the public about the nature of instrumental music, and to what extent it can be attributed to the level of orchestral performance in Boston at the time. Both factors contributed. It is also not clear how far the professional could blame the amateur for the performance level.

The growth, evolution, and demise of the Philoharmonic Society exemplify the fate of orchestral music in Boston in the 1820s. The society was the leading instrumental organization in Boston, and for much of that period the only one, and its activities probably prompted Parker's article about the amateur and professional. Around 1819 the Philoharmonic adopted a more public posture. It had been moving in that direction since at least 1812, and possibly earlier, with "meetings" that members were invited to attend as listeners. These meetings, more like concerts than rehearsals, provide the first indication of public interest in instrumental music in Boston. But beginning in 1919 the society published more detailed advertisements of its rehearsals. The advertisement for the opening rehearsal of the season, on January 2, 1819, announced that ". . . Rice's [Ries's?] second grand Concerto, allowed to be the greatest piece that has yet been composed for the Piano Forte, will be among the performances—Gillineck's Queen of Prussia's Waltz with variations—Several songs—Chorusses from Haydn's Creation—Quartette, violin by Mr. Ostinelli—Symphonies, but a full Orchestra, etc."[6] This sounds more like an advertisement for a public concert than for a private

meeting of a society. It was not quite that, however. The same annouce-
ment stated that members could bring their friends each Satuday, as
the bylaws provided. Yet the only reason for the more detailed announcement, with all of its hyperbole, would be to draw a larger audience.

For a brief time the Philoharmonic Society enjoyed great success.
Attendance at its rehearsals was sufficiently strong for limitations to be
set. On April 19, 1819, the Standing Committee of the society published
a set of regulations on who could attend. After congratulating the
members "on the increase and unprecedented popularity of the Society,"
the committee limited attendance to members plus two guests. In 1821
the Philoharmonic moved to a new hall, the Pantheon, which, according
to the *Euterpeiad*, was 72 by 22 feet, commodious, well-lit, and "suitable
to the objects contemplated by the Philoharmonic Society." The hall
was almost always full, even though admission remained restricted to
members and those introduced by members.[7]

By the early 1820s the society was essentially an academy. Membership
was by ballot, and members paid an annual fee of $10.[8] Most members
probably joined as concert subscribers rather than performers. Control
of the society, however, still remained with the musicians. Graupner
served as its president throughout its existence, and from all evidence
he ran the society.

Another indication of a change in status to a more public organization
was the Philoharmonic Society's petition for incorporation, which was
granted by the state legislature on June 19, 1819. The act of incorporation named Gottlieb Graupner, Thomas Smith Webb, William Coffin,
Jr., Matthew S. Parker, John Dodd, and Bryant P. Tilden as directors,
with Graupner specifically authorized to call the first meeting. The
purpose of the society was listed as "extending and enlarging and improving the style of performance of vocal and instrumental music."[9]

With the increased public visibility of the society's activities, the quality
or level of performance became more critical. Technical skill, including
the ability to perform in public with some security and consistency,
became highly desirable. As professionals concentrated more on the
public presentation of their wares, a tension between professional and
amateur was a logical development. A concert that went badly reflected
negatively on the professional no matter who was to blame for the
specific problem. Accounts of concerts substantiate that the performance
level in Boston was not high. An article in the *Columbian Centinel* in
1817, signed "O," scathingly described a Handel and Haydn Society
concert: "The violins apparently played with no confidence in time or

tune, the chorus was more than once completely thrown out by them, and the efforts of the vocal performers completely paralyzed by their want of spirit. The trumpet seemed to require painful effort to give it utterance, and was frequently behind time. The kettledrums were too loud, and sometimes out of tune; and the performer on the cymbals should have remembered that he was not in the open air with a military band. In 'Surely He hath borne our griefs' the chorus was completely thrown out by the orchestra."[10] The situation had not improved much by 1821, when the *New England Gallery* referred to the Handel and Haydn Society's orchestra as "lamentably deficient in numbers or power, perhaps in both." The *Euterpeiad* corroborated this opinion with its own declaration of "unequivocal dissatisfaction of what we heard from all quarters instrumental and vocal."[11]

Not all of the problem lay in the gap between the abilities of the professional and the amateur. The professionals themselves were criticized for being at times indifferent or incompetent. In a city in which professional instrumental musicians were relatively scarce, it was almost inevitable that the level of some professional musicians would not be of the highest quality. This only exacerbated the rifts between musician and audience and between amateur and professional. Nonprofessionals, whether performing amateurs or listeners, felt they were entitled to more than inept or indifferent performances, particularly if the performer was being paid.[12]

Implicit in Parker's discussion of the tension between professional and amateur musicians was how instrumental music was to be conceived. The problem of attracting an audience and the professionalization of the orchestra were intimately bound up with fundamental premises about art and the artist. The need to have instrumental music presented by an artist was more compelling to the degree that instrumental music was defined as an idealistic force in itself. One might listen to one's friends for entertainment, but the highest artistic standards demanded a level of performance not expected of an amateur ensemble. Ironically, an amateur chorus was perfectly acceptable, as it is even today. The issue was essentially one of tradition and perception. It was assumed that an amateur singer could be taught to sing satisfactorily in a large ensemble, but an instrumental performer demanded a degree of technical expertise best left to the professional.

The Boston public was not ready to grant instrumental music the status of art for another twenty years, as we shall see. The extent to which the professional musician conceived of it as art is not clear. Some, like Louis Ostinelli, who arrived in Boston in 1818, did. Many others, trained in Europe, probably did also. Performing musicians in Boston at the time, however, recorded few of their thoughts about music. We know that many musicians later in the century did conceive of their public role as being an artist with a sacred mission. Whether they had begun to think that way in the early 1820s can only be judged through writers like Parker, who was not a professional musician but probably reflected the thought of the musical community. Their work reveals an incipient but uncertain idealism.

John Rowe Parker founded the *Euterpeiad or Musical Intelligencer* in Boston in 1820. It was the first music journal in the United States that included serious critical appraisal of music. Parker was outspoken in his editorial capacity and championed instrumental music. He lamented that it was not better accepted in Boston and sought to explain why it was not. Parker believed the principal reason to be the ignorance of the public, although he conceded that this was not the only cause.[13] Musical taste had to be acquired, and the "cultivation of Instrumental music" would produce "the most beneficial consequences."[14] He never enumerated specifically the benefits of instrumental music, although he did attempt to define the value of music in general:

Music refines and exalts our ideas of pleasure, and when rightly understood and properly pursued, is the very end of our existence. It improves and settles our ideas of taste, which, when founded on solid and consistent principles, explains the causes, and heightens the effects, of whatever is beautiful or excellent, whether in the works of creation, or in the productions of human skill. It adorns and embellishes the face of nature, it sharpens and invigorates, it polishes and civilizes the manners, and in a word, it softens the cares of life, and renders its heaviest calamities more supportable by adding to the number of its innocent enjoyments.[15]

Parker recognized explicitly that music in America was considered by the majority a "mere amusement," and that this seriously hindered its potential to have a beneficial effect. Here he faulted the professional musicians, who were their own worst advertisements. If music was to assume the level of dignity that it should in American society, the activities of the professors should reflect that sublimity. But most Americans saw little evidence that the higher qualities of the art had an effect on the character of professional musicians.[16]

Parker strongly supported the Handel and Haydn Society. His support, however, was motivated less by the desire to see sacred music improved than by the conviction that through sacred music an appreciation for other types of music, including instrumental, could be developed. His review of *The Boston Handel and Haydn Society Collection of Sacred Music* concentrated on the value of sacred music to the community in terms of cultural enhancement. By presenting the great works of genius in sacred music to the public, a "taste for its [music's] higher beauties may be acquired. . . . Greater and more lasting effects may be anticipated, therefore on the national taste, from the influence of sacred music, than from the greatest exertions of skill, in that which is devoted to mere amusement." Parker specifically argued that sacred music prepared the people to accept instrumental music; "therefore, in all countries, a taste for instrumental melody, and an acquaintance with the higher branches of the art, *must commence with sacred music*; where its adaption to the emotion intended to be awakened, is obvious to the most untutored mind."[17]

It is clear from this passage that Parker regarded instrumental music more highly than sacred. He was outspoken about what he considered good and bad music. He referred to "refined music," "music of the highest class," and "true music," as opposed to music that is "quite deficient in solemnity, dignity, and decency," or "musical trash."[18] His criteria for distinction were based on three concepts: science, progress, and taste. Unfortunately, Parker never really defined these. His usage of them was typical of his time, however, similar to that of the Presbyterian-Congregationalist reformers.

The concept of progress in particular was central to Parker's thinking. It affected both his understanding of music history and the development of individual refinement. Parker believed unequivocally that music was evolving from the simpler to the more complicated: "Music, like all other arts, is progressive, and its improvements may be traced through a period of more than two thousand years. In the time of the Greeks it was thought to be in high perfection, but we need only examine the structure of their instruments, to prove its comparative rudeness and simplicity." He then argued that while Handel, Purcell, and Corelli did much to improve music, Haydn completed the task: "Handel, Purcell, and Corelli, gave it scale, system, and arrangement; but the completion of the work was reserved for the immortal Haydn, who has . . . environed [it] with the delights of melody." To prove the point Parker cited modern harmonic innovations, including the chord of the thirteenth, "which is a compound of all the notes of the scale," and the "extreme flatted seventh," "a combination of four minor thirds" (a fully diminished seventh chord).[19]

An evolutionary bent is obvious in Parker's ideas about progress. He referred to the "declension of taste" that had recently occurred in New England churches and, when describing developments in the concert life of Boston, alluded to "several movements in the musical world."[20] On the more personal level Parker believed in a sort of musical embryology comparable to that found in evolutionary theory. An individual listener's tastes would follow a pattern of growth if only the individual were exposed to the proper kind of music. An understanding of better, hence more complicated, music had to be cultivated and nurtured.

Inherent in the concept of progress was the assumption that some kinds of music were better than others, with the implicit assumption that more recent music was better than older music. One of the great paradoxes in American musical history is that many of the strongest advocates of progress in the nineteenth century were classicists. They wished to freeze progress at the classical masters: Haydn, then Mozart, and somewhat later Beethoven. Parker belonged to that group. Advancement from the simpler to the more complex was central to his theory. Yet he found modern compositions, which were never named, too complex. He lamented that works of current favorite composers were so "full of extravagant modulations, . . . so weighted down by a mass of elaborate harmony," that they "sink into oblivion."[21]

I have examined Parker's writings in some detail because they occupy a special place in American journalistic history. Parker was one of the first writers to describe the American musical scene, and he did so with considerable insight and sophistication from a relatively powerful forum. The *Euterpeiad*, itself a pioneering and influential journal, was not, however, the first American journal to feature articles about music. Hency C. Lewis is usually given credit for that. In 1819 Lewis began publication in Philadelphia of the *Lady's and Gentleman's Weekly Literary Museum and Musical Magazine*, later shortened to *Literary and Musical Magazine*. He had struggled to publish a literary journal since 1817, and his magazine had undergone several name changes. He added a page or two of music in January 1819, when publication resumed after a three-month hiatus. Commencing with volume 4, which began on April 26, 1819, Lewis devoted the bulk of his journal to music. His purpose, according to an explanatory essay, was "to take an occasional survey of the progress, situation, and future prospect of the various branches which they may have undertaken to cultivate, as well as to ascertain their advances and positive improvement."[22]

Lewis detected an increased interest in music as a science in the United States. He cited the founding of conservatories, the establishment of many new musical societies, and the presence of many "able professors and practitioners" as evidence of that trend. He did not identify any specifically. About a month after his introductory essay he appealed to these professors as well as amateurs to contribute to the magazine. One respondent, who signed himself "D," responded enthusiastically to Lewis' call. Describing music as "this charming and important science, "D" observed that it had "hitherto been too much neglected amongst us." He went on to compliment Lewis' plan as something entirely novel and deserving approval. Wunderlich hinted that "D" may have been John Rowe Parker.[23]

Unfortunately, the increased interest in music that Lewis sensed did not extend to support of his magazine. His original plan, to publish an eight-page journal weekly, lasted two months. After that, size and frequency of issues gradually decreased. Lewis reduced the journal to four pages and published biweekly. He started a "new series" after September 13, 1819, and began to omit the date. Wunderlich surmised that the reason for this was that publication was no longer regular and Lewis was attempting to hide the magazine's coming demise. The last known issue was probably published in June 1820.

H. Earle Johnson hypothesized that both Parker's and Lewis' journals were modeled after the British *Quarterly Musical Magazine and Review*, which appeared in 1818. In the first issue of the *Euterpeiad* Parker published the customary statement of objectives, and they conform almost precisely to those of the *Quarterly Musical Magazine and Review*.[24] Parker took many articles from British journals, and since he had made several trips to England prior to 1818, he was probably familiar with the British press.

There is a better model for the *Euterpeiad*, however, supplied by Parker himself. On December 27, 1817, Parker had begun his "Euterpeiad" column in the *Boston Intellligencer and Morning and Evening Advertiser*. The column ran until March 20, 1819. It started as a regular column, appearing in the next three issues after is inauguration, but then began to run less and less regularly. For a while it appeared biweekly, with an occasional gap of three weeks. By 1819 its appearance was sporadic. The column covered a wide variety of topics, such as styles of singing, instruments, notices of various inventions like the metronome, the gamut board, the finger guides (a Schumann-like invention), but consisted mostly of a review of musical activity in Boston. It discussed both performances and the state of different musical organizations. The column was so close in content and orientation to the *Euterpeiad* that Parker used some of the material from the earlier column in the *Euterpeiad*. Thus although he did not have his own journal until 1820, the concept, general tone, and thrust of what he was to do was in place by 1817, preceding both Lewis' musical efforts in his literary magazine and the British *Quarterly Musical Magazine and Review*.

The concerns about music in America and the beliefs about the place of music in society that appear in the *Euterpeiad* are to be found in Parker's early columns. He began his first column with a general observation about the state of music in America:

> It is universally acknowledged, that MUSIC in this country is in a rapid state of improvement, and that to cultivate a true taste for the science, much information is wanted, by which Persons may become acquainted with the most remarkable musical occurrences, as well as the new distinguished authors, together with the performers, publications and performances, their style, taste, etc. in a more general manner than they have hitherto had an opportunity.—But as Music is rapidly cultivating in this country and many foreign publications and foreign virtuosos constantly arriving from Europe, I shall not confine my musical observations merely to what occurs at home, but give occasionally as much foreign information as the limits of your paper will permit.[25]

Parker's optimism was quickly tempered. By April 1818 he admitted that "the state of society in our country furnishes little aid to the progress of the fine arts, and scarcely admits of their successful cultivation."[26]

In his reviews Parker extolled performances that were scientific, chaste, and correct. He argued that singing should be a branch of education, to close the gap between regular and vulgar singing, a distinction many Americans did not understand.[27] He urged amateurs to study thoroughbass. He observed dissention in the professional circles in Boston, and regretted that Lewis, Graupner, and Jackson could not put aside their disagreements enough to appear in public together. But most of all he argued for musical idealism. In attempting to define the general standards of excellence to which one appeals when discussing music, Parker stated, "the only Music by which the mind is ever truly gratified, is such as has a direct and powerful tendency, either to enliven, soften, or to elevate the feelings."[28]

As in the later *Euterpeiad*, Parker strongly supported the Philoharmonic Society. In the *Euterpeiad* in 1820, he called it "the nursery of instrumental music in Boston," a statement that originally appeared in his column of January 9, 1819. On March 20, 1819, Parker published a long poem extolling the Philoharmonic Society in idealistic terms. The poem, "On Retiring from the Concert of the Philo-Harmonic Society," typical of many rhapsodic eulogies of the time, equated instrumental playing with art—as this small portion of it shows:

Yes, she is great! Fame did not say too much;
  Transport, surprise, delight, my breath held fast
The keys were swept by scarcely mortal touch,
  And every note gave pleasure, save the *last*.

It was not that she play'd with skilful pain,
  A forc'd, mechanical, or task-like part;
Oh no, soul, soul, rush'd onward through the strain,
  And smote, or tipped, each key with untaught art. . . .

And soon methought I saw a heavenly Fair,
  Call'd by those slender hands from midst the strings;
Her waving robe stir'd rapture through the air,
  Which fondly woo'd her measure-beating wings.[29]

The musicians of the Philoharmonic Society took their concerts seriously. The society prohibited applause, and Parker supported this move, because it distinguished the society's presentations from intentions "to excite emulation by vain applause," or "to exhibit the feats of dexterous musicians, like performances on the tight rope, which excite no feeling but that of surprise." At the same time, Parker referred to the "great pleasure" the audience must receive "in attending the diversified amusements." Instrumental music, to Parker, and probably the musicians themselves, was serious but nonetheless still amusement.

Even though both the *Euterpeiad* and the *Literary and Musical Magazine* failed in a relatively short time, the *Euterpeiad* was unequivocally the more successful of the two. After six months the *Literary and Musical Magazine* already exhibited symptoms of a fatal condition as issues became smaller and less frequent. The *Euterpeiad* lasted into a fourth year, which was unusual not just for a musical magazine but for any magazine in America before 1830. Its tenure is thus striking not because it was so short but because it was so long. And in comparison with other musical journals, the record of the *Euterpeiad* was unprecedented. The only other musical journal before 1840 to survive for four years was Benjamin Carr's *Musical Journal for the Piano-Forte*, 1800–1804, which was a collection of piano and vocal music.[30]

The demise of the *Euterpeiad* may have been due as much to Parker's own business abilities as to insufficient interest in the magazine. As a businessman Parker had a long string of failures. Until the 1820s, when he became involved in telegraphic services, he was a merchant, specializing first in household goods and then in musical items. He formed a partnership in 1803 with a man by the name of Smith and then in 1806 a partnership with Moses Poor in Scotland, to import household goods—quilts, counterpanes, carpeting, knives, forks, coffee pots, and so on. By 1812 Poor was in partnership with an Appleton in Baltimore and trying to recover $1,000 he claimed Parker owed him. In 1815 Parker went into business with his third wife's brother, John Still Winthrop Parkin. By 1817 the partnership had been dissolved, and Parkin was trying to collect money due. In April 1817 Parker formed an association with Gottlieb Graupner, who moved his inventory into Parker's warehouse. Four months later he moved it out. George Cushing, a bank cashier and a flutist, was asked to mediate between them, but declined. As late as 1840 Parker's business methods were still questionable. In a letter to Parker, E. & G. W. Blunt "order their goods returned as they decline to do business in the way Parker does."[31]

The *Euterpeiad* never had a large subscription list. Not more than sixty names of subscribers were referred to in the correspondence with printers, who also had the responsibility of mailing the issues.[32] Yet the *Euterpeiad* was widely distributed. Parker listed more than forty agents from whom it could be obtained, from Montreal to Augusta. Many copies of the journal were probably sold in bookstores or music stores, particularly in Boston; had it not been well-known in Boston itself, music teachers and dealers would not have repeatedly advertised in it. A less direct measure of the *Euterpeiad*'s influence is its use a model for many later music magazines.[33] Even Lewis' *Literary and Musical Magazine* was indebted to it. When the *Literary and Musical Magazine* was in its death throes Lewis borrowed articles directly from the *Euterpeiad*, and it began to resemble, according to Wunderlich, a "vastly watered-down Euterpeiad." Subscribers to the *Literary and Musical Magazine* had little reason to pay $2 a year when they could obtain much more for $2.50 from the *Euterpeiad*.[34]

Parker's professional involvement with music was unusual for someone of his class in Boston in 1820. He was in that gray area between the middle class and the socioeconomic elite. His father was rector at Trinity Episcopal Church, which was patronized mainly by the upper class. He was named after John Rowe, the merchant whose diary provides much information about musical life in eighteenth-century Boston. The Rowes were childless, and Parker inherited Rowe's estate upon his death. Parker himself belonged to the merchant class, although whatever wealth he had came more from his inheritance than his own success; in 1825 his sister Rebecca wrote to him, "You have had property without earning it, and every domestic comfort that money could procure you." Parker traveled to England several times on business and entered into partnership with several Europeans as well as Americans.[35]

Parker's musical thinking reflected his social position. Although he desired a better type of psalmody and lamented that much church music was "quite deficient in solemnity, dignity, and decency,"[36] Parker was more interested in secular concert music than church music. He supported the middle-class Handel and Haydn Society as a way to elicit support for other, higher types of music. A hint of Federal republicanism colors his views on that subject. He believed that only religious music provided "the means of training all classes of Society amongst us, to a due sense of the importance of this noble art." Religious music was capable of "the expression of feelings in which all ranks and classes of men feel an equal interest."[37]

Yet as strongly as Parker believed in a distinction between good and bad music, in the importance of science, progress, taste, and refinement in music, and in the need to educate all classes to better music, the concept of instrumental music as moral agent is at best only implicit in his thought. In his eyes music had a strong civilizing effect and when fully understood could enrich men's lives. It did so, however, through the pleasure it gave, no matter how rarefied that pleasure might be. Although his conceptualization of music was advanced for its time, Parker did not put music on the same idealistic plane that advocates of instrumental music in the 1830s and 1840s did. His thought was much like that of other members of the socioeconomic elite that we shall encounter later in this chapter.

Parker's struggle—and eventual failure—to keep his journal alive paralleled the fate of several organizations in the 1820s that tried to present serious concert music in Boston. The period from 1820 to almost 1840 was a time in which many attempts were made to place secular, mostly instrumental music before the Boston public, but with little if any success. With these efforts the consequences of the rifts between professional and amateur musicians and between musician and audience become apparent. In addition, a third split developed among professional musicians, who formed two warring factions for a time. The rift between professional and amateur was the least serious, and was never a complete rupture. Some amateurs continued to sit with professionals in various orchestras, and professionals, in their many-faceted ways of earning a living, continued to depend heavily on the patronage of the amateurs. The second rift, between musician and audience, proved to be more serious. The professionals had begun to alienate the one part of the community that had provided support, the amateurs, without being able to find another support base. The result was a fifteen-year hiatus in which the professional musician and the public were at odds. The split between the professional factions was more a turf war than an ideological battle, but it divided and then drained what little audience support for instrumental music existed.

The one musical organization that survived in a strong position through the 1820s was the Handel and Haydn Society. Two factors favoring it were its purpose and some windfall income. The Handel and Haydn Society was essentially a sacred-music society. The New England singing schools and church choirs had created an interest in vocal music and spread some knowledge of singing. The level of activity was higher in Boston than in New York, where a similar Handel and Haydn Society was founded in 1816 but survived for only seven years.[38] Samuel Dyer acknowledged the superior singing ability of the Bostonians in 1825, when he wrote to John R. Parker in behalf of the Philharmonic Society of New York (not the later Philharmonic) to request some singers from Boston to assist in a concert. The concert was to include Beethoven's "Hallelujah, Handel's Worthy is the Lamb, and Haydn's, The Heavens are Telling."[39] Dyer admitted that "few New Yorkers are equal to the task" and indicated that he would include travel expenses for any singers.[40]

Even though interest in psalmody remained high in Boston, many regarded the Handel and Haydn Society more as a concert than a singing organization. Complaints were voiced about members who joined only to receive tickets to the oratorios. Attendance was a problem. Neither the orchestra nor the singers were punctual, some showing up for the oratorios only to sit in the audience as listeners. The *Euterpeiad* called for a tightening of membership requirements, but little was done until Lowell Mason became president in 1828.[41]

The second element favoring the survival of the Handel and Haydn Society was luck: money came from an unexpected source. In spite of the favorable climate for psalmody in Boston in the 1820s, the society's minutes reveal that it was in serious financial trouble between 1819 and 1822. At that time it sponsored the publication of Mason's anthology, *The Boston Handel and Haydn Society Collection of Church Music*. Mason was then an obscure bank teller in Savannah, and there was no reason to expect much from the publication. Yet between 1824 and 1831 profits on it alone netted the society between $600 and $1,100 a year.[42] This amounted to roughly half of the society's revenues, enough to enable it to present several large concerts a year with orchestra. By the mid-nineteenth century the Handel and Haydn Society had become a venerable organization, connected with high culture. It is still active today.

The Philoharmonic Society in contrast did not survive as a public body beyond the mid-1820s. The last season for which there is recorded concert activity was 1825–1826. H. Earle Johnson cited November 24, 1824, as the last recorded concert of the society, but according to two entries in the *Columbian Centinel*, it continued for some time after that. A notice on January 1, 1825, indicated that a concert would take place that evening. On November 26, 1825, the society announced a full complement of concerts for the 1825–1826 season. No details were given beyond that the concerts would be held at the Pantheon at seven o'clock "every concert evening," traditionally the second and fourth Saturday's of the month. Whether the concerts actually took place is uncertain, but the publication of the announcement suggests that the 1824–1825 season was not terminated. After 1826 an occasional newspaper notice of a meeting confirms that the Philoharmonic Society still existed as a private organization. Daniel Layman concluded that it may have continued as such until Graupner's death in 1836.[43]

A "Member and Friend to the Society" issued a warning in early 1823 about what might happen to it. In a letter to the *Euterpeiad*, the friend criticized the practice of granting special favors to allow certain people into the concerts. He contrasted the present situation with that of the recent past, when one could obtain a ticket only "with much difficulty." He felt that the subscribers were subsidizing the many gratuities, with the result that many subscribers would withdraw their support. He also complained of the programs: "There is not sufficient variety in the performances, and it seems little or no exertion is made to bring forward any thing new; and we partake season after season, of the same *dish* which was served up to them who went before us."[44]

The Philoharmonic Society's demise was probably hastened by an attempt to establish a rival organization, the Apollo Society. The Apollo Society was founded in 1824, flourished only briefly, and then quietly expired. Beyond advertisements in the newspapers, little is known of it. On November 3, 1824, the society announced that its concerts would take place during the winter season on the second Tuesday of each month at Concert Hall, beginning on November 9. There is no further mention of the society in the newspapers during that season except for its final concert, which was postponed to Thursday evening because the Concert Hall was not available. A communication in the *Columbian Centinel* solicited support and exuded optimism for the new orgnization: "Its members are ambitious that their association should become every way worthy of patronage, and are determined to spare no exertions to give variety and interest to their performances. The support which the Apollo Society has heretofore received has given it the stimulus still more to merit it."[45]

The Apollo Society existed into the 1826–1827 season, although it sponsored no known concerts. On January 25, 1826, it assisted in a concert of Mr. Willis of Westpoint, who played the "Kent Bugle, Common Trumpet, Double Flageolet, and an instrument of his own invention called the vox humana." On March 18, 1826, it participated in a concert of vocal and instrumental music by Miss Ayling. The society's final recorded appearance was on December 30, 1826, when it assisted in Mr. Williamson's concert. In the latter two concerts it provided a full orchestra.

It appears that the Apollo Society was established as a rival organization to the Philoharmonic Society. The advertisements for both groups and for various benefit concerts suggest that little cooperation existed between members of the two organizations. Graupner continued to head the Philoharmonic Society, as he had done since its inception. James Hewitt, Lewis Ostinelli, Asa Warren, and A. P. Heinrich were involved with the Apollo Society, although it is not clear who, if anyone, directed it. Warren acted as secretary. A benefit concert on May 20, 1825, prominently featured Heinrich and both Mr. and Mrs. Ostinelli; Hewitt's music store was the center of ticket distribution.[46] Graupner's music store did not sell tickets for the Apollo Society, and Hewitt's did not do so for the Philoharmonic Society or for Graupner's benefit. When Heinrich gave a benefit on March 19, 1825, Hewitt played the orchestral accompaniment for a clarinet solo by James Kendall. Graupner is not listed on the program, and apparently Heinrich could not assemble an orchestra. Graupner was able to present an orchestra for his benefit on April 30, 1825, but none of the musicians associated with the Apollo Society appeared on the program.

Boston apparently could not support two instrumental organizations, as neither survived beyond two yers of competition. Sacred music, however, continued to thrive; as late as the mid-1820s Bostonians were still supporting several sacred-music societies. In fact considerably more sacred than secular concerts were presented in the 1824–1825 season. In addition to the regular rehearsals of the Handel and Haydn Society, which were in reality private concerts, the Union Sacred Singing Society presented seven concerts, the Naponset Sacred Music Society four, and the Central Universalist Society and the Second Universalist Society one each. The Handel and Haydn Society gave five public oratorios. Many of the concerts of these various organizations were substantial presentations. The concert of the Second Universalist Society on May 25, 1825, featured portions from Haydn's *Creation* and "selections from Handel, Beethoven, Mozart and others."[47] The advertisements for the concerts of the Central Universality Society on February 2, 1825, and the Union Singing Society on May 18, 1825, list the entire program. I quote them both to illustrate the scope of the offerings of these less well-known, church-related societies:

Sacred Concert

A Concert of Sacred Music will be performed by the singing Choir of the Central Universalist Society, in Bulfinch-street, on Sabbath Evening next, Feb. 6th. at half past 6 o'clock, to perform the following select pieces of Sacred Music.

Part I.

Chorus	The Great Jehovah.	Handel
Anthem	They play'd in air	Dr. Stevenson
Chorus	Lift up your Heads	Handel
Air	Star of the North	O. Shaw
Chorus	Father we adore thee	Haydn
Anthem	Child of morality	John Bray
Air	As down in the sunless retreats of the ocean	O. Shaw
Chorus	He gave them hailstones for rain.	Handel

Duet	Array'd in clouds of golden light	Shaw
Rect. and Chorus	Now the work of man's Redemption is complete	Beethoven

Part II.

Solo and Chorus	O praise ye the Lord, prepare a new song.	Haydn
Chorus	Come sweet Spring.	Haydn
Duet	Who's this that on the tempest rides	O. Shaw
Chorus	Glory be to god on high	Mozart
Air and Chorus	Rejoice O Judah	Handel M. P. King
Recit. Air etc.	Father, thy word is past	M. P. King
Chorus	The Multitude of Angels	O. Shaw
Duet	The bird let loose	
Anthem	When lost in woder	
Grand Hallelujah Chorus		Handel

Union Singing Society

Will meet at the Rev. Dr. Pierce's Meeting-House, Brookline, on Sunday Evening, the 22nd inst. at half past 6 o'clock, to perform the following select pieces of Sacred Music.

Part I.

Chorus	The great Jehovah is our awful theme.	Handel
Air	Lovely as from showers descending.	Shaw
Chorus	Come sweet Spring.	Haydn
Air	O thous who driest the mourner's tears.	
Chorus	O Father whose almighty power.	
Duett	Arrayed in clouds of golden light.	Shaw
Anthem	Give the Lord the honor.	Kent
Air	Star of the North.	Shaw
Chorus	Glory be to God on high.	Mozart

Part II.

Recitative	Father thy word is past.	King
Solo	Blow ye the trumpet.	Jackson
Chorus	A fire devoureth.	Jackson

Duett	Come ever smiling liberty.	
Chorus	Now elevate the sign of Judah.	Haydn
Air	by Mr. Williamson	
Chorus	Lift up your heads.	Handel
Air	Now heaven in fullest glory shone.	Haydn
Recitative	And God created Man.	Haydn
Air	In native worth.	
Chorus	Father we adore thee.	

One significant difference between these sacred concerts and secular concerts was their ticket price. All of the sacred-music societies charged twenty-five cents; prices for the principal secular concerts ranged up to $1. Heinrich's price structure was typical: $1 for a single person, two admitted for $1.50, and three for $2. Kendall's was simpler: $1, period. When societies offered season tickets or multiple admission on one ticket, the ticket structure could get quite complex. The Apollo Society was forced give an extra concert to mollify season-ticket holders who did not understand the terms.[48] For concerts of a more popular character the price was fifty cents. Several such secular presentations occurred during the year: the Plympton family gave a concert, program unspecified; the Lilliputian Songsters, consisting of Mr and Mrs. Clark, appeared in a concert of folk songs, accompanying themselves on the guitar and flageolet; Master Joseph and his sister performed, accompanied on the piano and organ by Miss Schaffer.

The price differentiation between concerts probably had little to do with any overt attempt to segregate different classes by pricing. The various sacred-music societies had low overheads, and because they were essentially amateur singing organizations, they were probably more interested in having an audience than in making money. A group like the Handel and Haydn Society, on the other hand, had the expenses of an orchestra to pay. We know from its records that it was constantly strapped for money, and that the cost of the orchestra was the principal reason.

In some cases ticket prices were probably related to the class composition of the expected audience. The Lilliputian Songsters presumably did not expect to draw the upper classes of Boston society, but Hewitt, Heinrich, and Graupner undoubtedly did. The socioeconomic elite did not patronize concerts much anyway. At the same time, writers were attempting to plant in the minds of Bostonians that some music was better than others, and hence more deserving of patronage. The *Euter-*

peiad had been pushing a better European music, sacred-music reform was beginning to suggest that quality was a factor in judging music, and the romantic notion of genius was gaining in public attention. Kendall, Heinrich, and Graupner were known professionals, able to convince the public that they had something special to offer. Graupner was described as an "able and highly gifted musician," who for his benefit concert had engaged "a full orchestra to do justice to the fine symphonies selected." For Kendall's benefit, some new compositions by Heinrich were announced. These were described as new and novel pieces, characteristic of "the genius and inspiration of their author."[49]

The single attempt by the socioeconomic elite to establish a concert series in the 1820s was even less successful than the attempts by the various organizations described above. On May 15, 1826, a group of nine prominent citizens circulated a printed letter to other citizens of Boston. Entitled "Circular," it reported a recent meeting called to consider instituting a "Society for the promotion of a taste for Music and the encouragement of the progress of this Science in this city." According to the letter, the objectives of the proposed society were "to promote the cultivation of the Science of Music, to afford means and present encouragement for the exhibition of musical talent, and to advance the growth and diffusion of an enlightened taste in this department of the Fine Arts."[50] Some of these terms are familiar from the Presbyterian-Congregational reformers. The writers speak of progress, Science (with a capital S), taste, and cultivation. Other words, like *enlightened* and *fine arts*, reveal a different bent, suggesting the practice of art for art's sake. Art is neither tied to a broader propagandistic goal nor viewed within the service of a specific religious objective. Pleasure and enrichment were ends in themselves.

The circular went to great lengths to justify the formation of the proposed society, whose specific aim was to promote public concerts of music. Its signers acknowledged that those to whom the circular was addressed had never patronized the arts extensively, and that "the present period is particularly unfavorable for the collection of funds for the support of any new Institution."[51] They criticized Boston in particular and the country overall for the sorry state of the arts and asserted that, for the size of its population, Boston was "singularly deficient in public amusements." The theater especially lacked quality, largely because the wealthy classes did not support it. More generally, the circular acknowledged that a taste for music and the arts was rare in Boston society.

This lack of taste for music, however, was itself a principal argument for the founding of a musical society. The signers of the circular stressed that a taste for good music was not innate but had to be cultivated. Yet they despaired of being able to improve musical taste if the finest models of the art were not available. Beyond this, they stressed that the cultivation of taste required discipline and training and specifically recommended the introduction of classes for young people, as happened in Germany; these would be not only aesthetically but also morally beneficial. "One other practice in the instruction of youth almost universal in Germany, we would be glad to see introduced into the United States, that of furnishing all classes with an opportunity of making some proficiency in music. Such as addition to our regular course of discipline would, we are persuaded, be attended with the most salutary moral influence."[52]

Throughout the circular the signers emphasized the moral and social benefits of art music. Quoting Voltaire, "L'amusement est un des premiers besoins de l'homme," they argued that amusement should be innocent and "not below the dignity of a rational creature." Since amusements will exist in society, one had better pay attention to them. "To persons who think public amusements altogether undeserving the patronage and the interest of those whose example is constantly exercising a powerful influence in society, the subscribers do not address themselves. They conceive public amusements indispensable in large societies, and they think it no trifling service to good morals, to aid in rendering those attractive which are perfectly innocent, which are of a nature to polish the manners, which are not peculiar to any sex or age, and the enjoyment of which leaves no regret behind."[53]

To implement the goal of establishing concerts, the circular proposed that each member of the society contribute $100, which would make him a life subscriber; a minimum of $10,000 would be needed. In addition to sponsoring concerts, the society would establish a fund for professors of music, who might become society associates. The professors would be compensated for their services, and in the event of their death their families would be entitled to (unspecified) compensation.

I have found two copies of the circular, one addressed to Walter Channing, the other to Professor Norton. Channing was the grandson of William Ellery, one of the signers of the Declaration of Independence, and the brother of William Ellery Channing, the most important Unitarian clergyman of the nineteenth century. He attended Harvard from 1804 to 1807 and in 1815 was appointed the first professor of obstetrics at the Harvard Medical School. He served as dean of the school from

1819 to 1947. Professor Norton almost certainly refers to Andrews Norton, who graduated from Harvard College in 1804. In 1813 he became the college librarian and in 1819 Dexter Professor of Sacred Literature at the Harvard Divinity School.

A handwritten note in Norton's copy of the circular states that William H. Eliot, the last to sign it, was its author. He was the son of the wealthy merchant Samuel Eliot and the brother of Samuel A. Eliot, with whom he was active in the West Church choir. He was also the brother-in-law of Andrews Norton. At Harvard he was a member of the Pierian Sodality, and after graduating in 1815 he toured Europe before returning to Boston. He was active in Boston politics in the 1820s and held several city offices. In 1828 he was elected to the Massachusetts legislature. While running for mayor of Boston in 1829, he caught a fever and died suddenly.

The signers of the circular and its known recipients represented a class and outlook different from those of the founders and supporters of the Handel and Haydn Society. Without exception they were from the socioeconomic elite of Boston: many had ties to Harvard and to Unitarianism; none was a member of the Handel and Haydn Society; and, as far as can be determined, none was a supporter of evangelical religion. These men were not just from the upper class; they were prominent either in their own professions or in politics. Nine of the eleven are listed in the *Dictionary of American Biography*.[54] Many were members of what has been called the Boston Associates, a group of interrelated families that "became the new economic core of blueblood Boston."[55] Nathan Appleton and Patrick Tracy Jackson built the Boston Manufacturing Company in Lowell. Harrison Gray Otis served as U.S. senator and mayor of Boston; Josiah Quincy served five terms as mayor of Boston and was president of Harvard for thirteen years. William Hickling Prescott was a prominent historian, and William Sullivan, after a career in politics, turned successfully to writing. Israel Thorndike inherited a fortune from his father's success in the shipping business, and John Collins Warren was professor of surgery at Harvard and instrumental in the creation of the Massachusetts General Hospital and the *New England Journal of Medicine*.

The signers' attempt to found the society bespeaks a European aristocratic attitude, because the society would have imitated the academies in many European towns and cities in the eighteenth and early nineteenth centuries. European academies were formed for the same purpose as that outlined in the circular and in a similar way, by prominent citizens banding together. The academies were concert societies that provided support for local musicians, sponsored touring virtuosi, and in general furnished the structural organization for secular, predominantly instrumental concerts. In some cases their performances were open, in some cases closed. Membership in an academy, however, was usually limited to the more prominent members of society.

In Europe the academies formed a link between the private concerts of the wealthier eighteenth-century aristocracy and the public concerts of the nineteenth century. Although they admitted members from both the aristocracy and the upper-middle class, the academies did not represent a break with aristocratic tradition. The middle class sought participation as a means of emulating and identifying with the aristocracy, and the academies allowed them to do so in an important and highly visible cultural activity.[56]

The signers of the circular were well aware of the European model. They compared the theater in America with that in Europe, where in many countries it was state supported, and in London where it was patronized by the wealthy. They envisioned themselves as part of a class whose obligation it was to improve the taste of the rest of the community. They disavowed being in any sense musical amateurs, thus dissociating themselves from most other musical groups in Boston. They made it clear that they were patrons, no more no less: "We do not assume the character of Amateurs in Music, because we would do something for its encouragement, any more than we claim to be men of Science, when we subscribe to a Scientific Library, or should pretend to be Connoisseurs in Painting, if we were to associate for the purpose of forming a Public Gallery. We wish it to be distinctly understood, that our object is to promote a taste, of which we do not profess to have more than others in the community."[57]

There is no record of the outcome of this proposal, which suggests that it failed. Had it succeeded, some traceable results would certainly have surfaced. The proposal may have been too ambitious, and the city not ready for it. To raise $10,000 at $100 a person required one hundred subscribers, and no musical activity in Boston had ever drawn such support from the segment of the community capable of making such a contribution. The Handel and Haydn Society, for instance, had a membership of between two hundred and three hundred in 1826, and during the 1820s drew between one hundred and two hundred outsiders per concert.[58] Most members of the audience were almost certainly friends of performers. Even if some of the founders of the projected society intended to contribute more than the suggested $100, the project nevertheless demanded relatively broad-based support, and the proposal was aimed at a segment of society that had until then shown little interest in public musical activities.

The proposal may have been prompted by the recent failures of the Philoharmonic Society and the Apollo Society. Those failures themselves were warning signs that Boston was not yet sufficiently interested in secular concert activity of a high quality. Other events within the next five years were to confirm this. The Tremont Theatre opened on November 12, 1827, with Thomas Comer as musical director, who worked principally with the singers and the chorus, and Louis Ostinelli as leader of the orchestra. The opening of a theater with an orchestra significantly affected the development of instrumental musical activity in Boston. William Pelby, the first manager and apparently the motivating force behind the construction of the theater, sought to procure an orchestra unequaled in the United States. This was no small drain on the budget of the theater. Later when Pelby was forced out as manager, one of the charges against him was that he used the orchestra to distract the public from his inability to assemble a first-rate dramatic company.

According to William Clapp, the orchestra consisted of twenty-eight musicians, which would have made it the largest orchestra ever assembled in Boston. Ostinelli and Comer were both paid $40 a week, the other musicians from $11 to $14. The orchestra may have been slightly smaller than twenty-eight, however. The members of the Tremont Theatre orchestra formed the orchestra for the Handel and Haydn Society. After trying to engage orchestral players individually in October 1828, the society contracted with Ostinelli to supply an orchestra for one-half of the net proceeds. Ostinelli of course provided the Tremont Theatre orchestra, which the Handel and Haydn Society minutes in 1829 confirm. The members of the orchestra listed on the program of the Handel and Haydn Society for January 18, 1829, the first program to include such a list, were thus probably the players in the Tremont's orchestra. There were twenty-four musicians. Lists of orchestral musicians from other concerts of this same period conform closely enough to this one to suggest the number twenty-four as the likely size of the Tremont Theatre orchestra.

Pelby's gambit worked briefly. The theater's orchestra attracted attention, and the quality of the performances was apparently high. In 1853 Clapp, who seldom refers to the orchestra or instrumental music, observed that "the orchestra at the Tremont was very good." In 1841 the

Musical Magazine, basking in the glow of newly revived orchestral activity, looked back to the late 1820s: "We have often heard that some ten or fifteen years ago we had, under M. Ostinelli's direction, very good instrumental concerts." The *Musical Magazine* may have been referring to the Tremont Theatre or to a series of benefit concerts that were given in 1831. The programs for eight of these concerts have survived, and in almost every case they list the members of the orchestra, something that had not occurred before and would not occur again in the near future. When they do not list the orchestral members they specifically mention the orchestra of the Tremont Theatre. Mr. Hanna's "Grand Concert" on April 10, 1831, for instance, referred to "all the gentlemen of the TREMONT ORCHESTRA, and . . . many other professional gentlemen of Boston and the vicinity."[59]

Three of the concerts featured a new ensemble: the Boston Band, a military band led by James Kendall. It was large, consisting of eight clarinets, one flute, two bass horns, four trombones, two trumpets, three French horns, one serpent, and two percussion, twenty-three musicians altogether. Usually the band played alone, most often an operatic potpourri but at times joined the orchestra. Edward Kendall's "Grand Secular Concert, of Vocal and Instrumental Music," on February 12, 1831, opened with Boieldieu's "Overture de L'Opéra 'Jean de Paris,'" with full Orchestra and full MILITARY BAND—first time in Boston, embracing near 50 instruments."

The programs of 1831 differed little from those of previous or subsequent years. They offered vocal and instrumental selections, of varying degrees of quality. Bishop's songs were popular. Overtures of Boildeau, Auber, and Weber were featured; Weber's Overture to *Der Freischütz* was especially popular. The program to Mr. Hanna's "Grand Concert," for instance included Weber's Overture and Auber's Overture to *Masaniello,* each performed by a "Double Orchestra." Instrumental solos were common, and they ranged from a double-bass concerto of Corelli (performed by Gear) to airs, waltzes, fantasies, and variations performed on various instruments. Beethoven appeared as the basis for a "favorite cotillion, with Variations for the Pianoforte," played by Charles Zeuner.

The emphasis on instrumentalists in the programs of 1831 is unique. Orchestral and band members had seldom been listed before, and large ensembles were stressed only occasionally in the programs. The Tremont Theatre evidently generated considerable interest in orchestral music.

This interest did not continue, however. No programs for several years after 1831 list the members of the orchestra. The programs of 1831 were a momentary aberration, the fate of orchestral music already presaged by events at the Tremont. For in spite of Pelby's attempts to sell the theater through its orchestra, and in spite of the recognition given instrumentalists in 1831, Boston audiences remained indifferent to sophisticated instrumental music. Ostinelli's programs at the Tremont proved to be too arcane for Boston theater audiences. In 1830 the new manager, Richard Russell, replaced Ostinelli with Comer as leader of the orchestra. An article in the *Daily Transcript*, possibly planted by Russell, approved:

> We now have the gratification of occasionally hearing intelligible music; something that comes down to the level of our understanding, and creates pleasant impressions without any wild and erratic attempts at astonishment. The theater is a place of popular amusement, and the first thing to be remembered by the leader of the Orchestra is, that he does not play to an assembly of musical dilettanti. . . . That was the great fault with Ostinelli; he was ambitious and erred in judgement; his object seemed less to please the public than to please himself. The consequence was that many praised, whilst few listened to his music. . . . The public requires something familiar; something national in character; something exciting; something that all can feel, and in the beauties of which all can participate.[60]

The anonymous writer was clearly aware of a duality in his musical culture. His definition of that duality, between music for the cognoscenti (dilettantes musicians) and music for the people, was not that different from the conceptualizations of the late nineteenth century, but his attitude was: he disapproved of a musician who was too ambitious, who was more interested in his art than in entertaining the public. He defined popular music as something accessible, something familiar, and dismissed originality as "wild and erratic attempts at astonishment." The idealistic aspect is totally absent. There is no suggestion that music, at least for the theater, should have any moral value beyond providing pleasure for the listeners.

Russell not only changed the leaders of the orchestra but reduced its size. A correspondent for the *Daily Transcript* complained that "in the present limited number of musicians, it is not one overture in ten to which they can give the proper effect, and in an elaborate piece of music

requiring a full orchestra, the deficiency is seriously felt." The correspondent also described the intended audience: "Mr. Comer plays
properly for people and not for the amateurs."[61] The orchestra was
enlarged to nearly its original size for the 1831–1832 season. George
H. Barrett, who took over the management for the season, also retained
Comer as leader. The instrumentation consisted of seven violins, two
violas, three cellos and double basses, two flutes, two clarinets, one
bassoon, two horns, two trumpets, one trombone, and drums, for a
total of twenty-four. This is less than the twenty-eight musicians reported
for the first year, but it is almost identical with the instrumentation of
the Handel and Haydn Society orchestra for 1829, as well as with the
size of the orchestra for the various 1831 concerts.

In 1831 several musicians formed the Musical Professional Society, in
another attempt to interest the public in secular music. The most prominent of the founders were Charles Zeuner, George James Webb, and
Gottlieb Graupner. Graupner was the first conductor. In 1831 he was
64 years old and had been the central figure in Boston musical life for
at least thirty years. He still played in the Tremont Theatre orchestra
but after 1830 assumed less of a leadership role in the community than
earlier, when he had founded and kept alive the Philoharmonic Society.

Zeuner and Webb were recent immigrants from Europe. Both were
organists and active in the Handel and Haydn Society. Zeuner had
arrived in Boston from Germany in 1831 and was almost immediately
offered the position of organist with the Handel and Haydn Society.
That the position was not open at the time, and that the offer necessitated displacing the incumbent organist, Mrs. Ostinelli, who was liked
and considered competent, suggests that Zeuner's abilities were extraordinary. Webb had arrived from England the year before. In the 1830s
he conducted many of the Handel and Haydn Society concerts and
served as its president in 1837 and from 1840 to 1841. He was one of
the original professors at the Boston Academy of Music until a dispute
with Lowell Mason in 1840 prompted his resignation.

The Musical Professional Society gave its first concert on April 27,
1831, its second and last on June 1 of the same year. The June concert
was to have been the first in a series of ten, but there is no record of
the others having taken place. Neither is there any record of why they
did not. As in the case of the Philoharmonic Society and the Apollo
Society, public activity simply ceased. The program of the first concert
was:[62]

I.

Grand Symphony (first part)	Witt
Glee: Chief of the windy Morven, with double accompaniment for the pianoforte	Calcott
Air with variations for flute	Rode
Song: Oh! Go not to the field of war	Webb
Trio Concertante for Guitar, tenor and fl.	Kufner
Andante and Minuetto	Witt

II.

Overture to the Enchanted Flute	Mozart
Variations for piano and violin on an air from Semiramis	Rossini-Meyerbeer
Song: Where the bee sucks	Purcell
Glee: In peace love tunes	Attwood
Finale	Witt

The concert itself was neither unique nor even much out of the ordinary. It was ambitious but, compared with earlier concerts, not exceptional. Secular concerts, consisting of a variety of orchestral, solo and ensemble instrumental, and solo and ensemble vocal pieces had occurred many times before in Boston. The Musical Professional Society differed from earlier groups in its purpose, as explained in the *American Traveller* of April 22, 1831. The stated aims of the society were "to diffuse a more general taste for Music of a secular character, to benefit and encourage the Professional members . . . to render their profession more generally respected by the public at large." This explanation is reminiscent of statements by Presbyterian-Congregational reformers. The Musical Professional Society, however, not only explicitly stressed secular music but also gave it a new status, viewing it as more than entertainment; the statement closed with the hope that the society would be a "source of gratification to the friends of musical improvement."

The collapse of the society's concert series may have indicated a failure to reach its objective but did not signal the end of the society. In a highly symbolic move, the society turned to the publication of collections of psalmody. In 1832 it issued "an entire (new and original) Collection of Church Music," which contained two hundred pages of psalm tunes and one hundred pages of anthems.[63] That same year it sponsored Zeuner's *American Harp* and the following year issued the *Ancient Lyre.*

The society's change in direction reflects more the mood of Boston in 1832 than the personal preferences of the leaders. Both Webb and Zeuner were deeply involved in sacred music, and each edited many collections of psalmody. Yet neither of them limited his activities to the sacred sphere, as their attempts to found the Musical Professional Society indicate. Unlike Mason, however, they were primarily musicians rather than evangelicals. They were also realistic. Webb published several collections of secular glees and was active as an educator and a conductor of secular concerts. As secular music became more important in Boston in the 1840s, Webb involved himself more with it. In 1848 he became director of the Musical Fund Society. Zeuner composed one oratorio, *The Feast of the Tabernacle* (1837), and published many secular works, including fugues, marches, variations, waltzes, polonaises, and divertissements. He remained in Boston only briefly, however. Emotionally unstable, he left in 1839 after a disastrous year as president of the Handel and Haydn Society. Had he, like Webb, remained active in Boston in the 1840s when secular music became increasingly prominent, he would probably have been involved in its growth. In 1857 Zeuner committed suicide. Graupner seems to have gone into semi-retirement after 1830; the Music Professional Society is his only known activity. He died in 1834.

Even though there were few further public attempts to establish an idealistic attitude toward secular music in the 1830s, musical leaders began to speak out more forcefully on the subject. New organizations that would later lead the struggle were being formed. Old ones were being transformed. The intellectual framework of Boston society underwent profound changes in the 1830s. Revivalism peaked, new intellectual trends arose, and class attitudes toward music changed. The following chapters trace these crucial developments, in which leadership came from two very different organizations: Harvard University and the Boston Academy of Music.

Chapter Seven

Samuel Eliot and the Boston Academy of Music

By the end of 1832 every attempt to establish secular concert music in Boston on an ongoing basis had failed. In each case the reason seems to have been a lack of interest by the public or the intended audience. Although we know little of what happened to the Philoharmonic Society, the Apollo Society, or the Musical Professional Society, their sudden abandonment of concert activity, particularly after further plans had already been announced, strongly indicates that public support was not forthcoming. It is clear why Ostinelli was displaced. Secular music was still seen within the framework of entertainment. Music that suggested more, music that challenged, or music that necessitated cultivation was unacceptable. The public might allow its taste in psalmody to be improved, but would have none of it when it came to secular music.

A fundamental shift in musical direction began in Boston in the mid-1830s. Interest in sacred vocal music declined precipitously in favor of classical instrumental music. This change is most dramatically seen in the evolution of the Boston Academy of Music. It was founded in 1833 to advance urban, evangelical, sacred music. In less than ten years it became the principal purveyor of instrumental music. By the early 1840s it had virtually dissolved its chorus. Its orchestra, consisting primarily of professionals, was recognized as the best in the city. The academy's orchestra introduced much of the classical literature, including the Beethoven symphonies, to Boston audiences. It was the first symphony orchestra to gain the support of the public, indicating an important change in musical taste.

The Boston Academy of Music was more than a symbol of change, however; it spearheaded the movement to instrumental music. It became the most important musical institution in Boston during the 1830s and early 1840s, a position presaged by Lowell Mason's decision in 1832 to abandon the presidency of the Handel and Haydn Society and devote his attention to the academy. Yet by the end of the 1830s Mason had little influence at the academy, his own star fading with the decline of sacred music in Boston. Newer leadership not only wrested control of the academy from the Presbyterian-Congregational reformers but also rallied support from entirely new constituencies in Boston, ones that had never backed music before. In the following pages I shall trace developments at the Boston Academy of Music throughout the first ten years of its existence, because the academy had a more profound and enduring impact on the course of American music than any other organization in the first forty years of the nineteenth century. Events at the academy depended greatly on prior developments: the work of the Handel and Haydn Society, the spread of musical idealism through the efforts of the Presbyterian-Congregational reformers, and the crusading attempts of earlier advocates of instrumental music like John R. Parker. But were it not for the new direction that the academy took in the 1830s, American musical culture might have had a very different profile.

The academy's original purpose was to foster the improvement of sacred music. Article 1 of its constitution reads: "This Association shall be called 'The Boston Academy of Music,' and its object shall be to promote knowledge, and correct taste in music, especially such as is adapted to moral and religious purposes." A committee later appointed to formulate more precisely the academy's objectives submitted the following list:

1. To establish schools of vocal music for Juvenile classes.

2. To establish similar schools for Adult classes.

3. To form a class for instruction in the methods of teaching music, which may be composed of teachers, parents, and all other persons desirous to qualify themselves for teaching vocal music.

4. To form an association of choristers, and leading members of choirs, for the purpose of improvement in conducting and performing sacred music in churches.

5. To establish a course of popular lectures on the nature and objects of church music, and style of composition and execution appropriate to it, with experimental illustrations by the performance of a select choir. These lectures might be extended to a great variety of subjects; such as the style of sacred poetry, the adaptation of music, the prevailing defects on this subject, and the means of remedying them.

6. To establish a course of scientific lectures, as soon as circumstances shall permit, for teachers, choristers, and others desirous of understanding the science of music.

7. To establish exhibitions or concerts.

    a. Of juvenile and adult classes, to show the results of instruction.

b. Of select performers, as specimens of the best style in the performance of ordinary church music.

c. Of large numbers collected semi-annually or annually, for the performance of social, moral, and sacred music of a simple kind.

8. To introduce vocal music into the schools, by the aid of such teachers as the Academy may be able to employ, each of whom shall instruct classes alternately in a number of schools.

9. To publish circulars and essays, either in newspapers and periodicals, or in the form of tracts and books for instruction, adapted to the purposes of the Academy.[1]

Although the first three objectives of the academy do not specify sacred or secular music, the vocal emphasis and attempt to instruct both children and adults imply church choirs. What many later assumed to have been the real purpose of the academy, to have music introduced into the public schools, is buried in point 8. Originally the academy was an extension of the singing school, whose theoretical aim had almost always been the improvement of church music. And if there was any doubt about the type of music the committee had in mind, points 4 through 7 removed it. The first annual report of the academy, delivered in May 1833, reinforced the sacred-music emphasis, explicitly stating that the academy had been founded "to devise and execute extended measures for the cultivation and improvement of sacred music."

To implement these goals, the committee strongly urged the academy to appoint a professor, "who shall occupy himself exclusively in devising and executing plans for promoting the views of the Academy; who shall act as their general Agent, and who shall be assisted by the members of the Academy, and by other agents acting under his direction, as circumstances may require." Lowell Mason was appointed, and shortly afterward George J. Webb joined him as a second professor.[2]

It is not clear what Mason's role in the establishment of the Boston Academy of Music was. Contemporary evidence cites William Woodbridge as its founder and early motivating force.[3] Yet the committee almost certainly had Mason in mind when it made its recommendation (which may have been pro forma). The first annual report opened with a description of Mason's 1826 address and the impact it had on the citizens of Boston. It then referred to the musical illustrations Mason had provided for Woodbridge's lecture on vocal music delivered before the American Institute of Instruction in 1830. Woodbridge's lecture was a pivotal event in the development of music education, in part because

Mason was able to demonstrate with his choir that Woodbridge's educational theories worked when applied to music. Mason's refusal in 1831 to accept a fifth term as president of the Handel and Haydn Society makes sense only if Mason was already involved with the academy. He did not relinquish power readily, and there is no evidence of discord between him and the Handel and Haydn Society.

According to the first annual report, the academy taught more than fifteen hundred pupils in the first year. Some were taught in rooms at Bowdoin Street Church, Mason's church, and at Old South Street Church, Webb's church. Several private schools allowed music classes on their premises: Mount Vernon School, the Monitorial School of Mr. Fowle, Mr. Thayer's school for boys in Chauncey Place, the academy in the New England Asylum for the Blind, the schools of Mr. Haywood and Miss Raymond on Chestnut Street, Miss Spooner's school in Montgomery Place, and the academy at Cambridgeport. Thus a precedence for musical instruction in schools was established from the start.[4]

Sacred music was still central to the academy's objectives in 1834. The second annual report began with a lengthy essay about the plight of music in American society. It lamented that music had been little cultivated and was associated detrimentally either with religion or amusement: "Music has been associated wholly with the solemnity, and in the apprehension of many, the gloominess of religion, or with the dangerous allurements of revelry and dissipation." The essay stressed how music and poetry were not united to produce a single effect and complained that singers in church paid little attention to the meaning of the words. It questioned whether music enhanced the devotional effect beyond what would be attained if the words were read and acknowledged that the music performed at the time frequently served to "hinder, if not wholly to dispel, devout and solemn emotions." This part of the report is precisely a summary of the standard argument of the Presbyterian-Congregational reformers for change in church music. The report also suggested the need for a series of lectures "on the nature, object and character of music, especially sacred music, and the style of performing it." It recommended that the lectures be experimental, meaning that a choir be present to demonstrate.[5]

The academy continued to expand rapidly during the second year. According to the report, classes formed specifically for music instruction attracted seventeen hundred pupils. The total number of music pupils in common schools increased to twenty-two hundred. The academy established a choir and initiated adult classes in Boston and Salem and at Harvard, with a total enrollment of five hundred pupils. Unfortunately, there is no breakdown of adult attendance by location, and no other reference to Harvard. Neither have I been able to locate an independent reference to activities of the academy at Harvard. Any inroads it made at the university would be noteworthy, because Harvard was predominantly upper-class and Unitarian and, as we shall see in chapter 9, was hostile to official musical connections in the 1830s.[6]

The direction of the Boston Academy of Music changed dramatically in its third year, 1835, when Samuel Atkins Eliot replaced Rev. Jacob Abbott as president. Eliot singlehandedly altered the course of the academy, and from his position as president became an important spokesman for music not only in Boston but nationwide. Eliot is a major figure in the history of American music, but he remains unknown to most scholars, probably because his contributions have never been investigated. Eliot came to the academy when questions of class distinction and class relationships were being seriously raised in Boston, and his work at the academy as well as his general ideas about music were intimately linked with class issues. Eliot's background was different from that of most academy members, who were middle-class Congregational evangelicals interested in sacred-music reform.

Samuel Eliot, a Unitarian, graduated from Harvard College in 1817 and Harvard Divinity School in 1820, but he declined ordination. His father's death in 1820 left him a considerable fortune, and he lived in Europe from 1823 to 1826. His marriage in 1826 to Mary Lyman, the daughter of another wealthy merchant, further increased his wealth. He was related by blood or marriage to many prominent families in Boston and held several important political positions. He was a member of the Boston School Committee in the early 1830s, served on the Massachusetts general court, and was an alderman while his brother-in-law Theodore Lyman was mayor; he himself was elected mayor for three consecutive terms beween 1837 and 1839. He served as treasure of Harvard from 1842 to 1853 and as president of the Prison Discipline Society. He also served in Congress in 1850 and 1851, declining reelection. Daniel Webster described him as "the impersonification of Boston; ever-intelligent, ever-patriotic, ever-glorious Boston."[7] In 1846 Eliot's net worth was listed at $300,000, an exceptionally large sum for the time.[8]

Eliot was one of the few members of the socioeconomic elite interested in music. The most striking aspect of his musical interest, however, was its late development. Eliot did not participate significantly in music until the death of his older brother, William Havard Eliot, in 1829. By all accounts William Eliot was the member of the Eliot family most involved in music. In his biographical compilation of the Eliot family, William Graeme Eliot described William H. Eliot as "a public-spirited man, . . . the great patron of, and active in developing the musical resources of Boston." According to George Harvey Genzmer, he displayed considerable interest in Boston's musical life.[9] William H. Eliot graduated from Harvard in 1815, and as a student was a member of the Pierian Sodality. Unfortunately little is known of his activities as a Pierian, except that he was once asked to deliver an oration but declined. In 1814 he was in charge of the choir at the university chapel. According to an account of Gen. Henry K. Oliver, who received a B.A. in 1818, Eliot not only performed the duties well but also had a clear concept of taste. He was wholly sympathetic to the musical reform movement and was apparently dedicated enough to inspire young college students. Oliver described Eliot's activities in relation to the choir in some detail:

There was also the College-choir, under charge of William Havard Eliot (H. 1815) of Boston, a gentleman of excellent musical gifts, and thoroughly interested in the improvement of the College-lads in vocal music. . . . There were at least a dozen [singers]. Mr. Eliot's exquisite taste and correct judgment protected the service from the trivial and, as now judged, irreverent fugue-music of the day (which had so long captured the untrained ear.) He turned our ears to nobler strains, . . . *Dundee . . . Martyrs . . . Elgin* . . . with other German or English chorals of solemn and hollowing power. . . . The singing in the College-chapel was excellent, and a most interesting part of the service to the three hundred and fifty persons, or so, that made up the congregation—college officials and their families, undergraduates, etc. all told.[10]

According to Samuel Eliot, William was also instrumental in persuading the members of the West Church, the Unitarian church that the Eliot family attended in Boston, to improve the quality of its music.

Samuel Eliot in contrast displayed little interest in music as a youth. He was not a member of the Pierian Sodality, and there is no record that he participated in the college choir. We do know that he sang in the West Church Choir, but we do not know when or for how long.[11] There is no other evidence connecting him directly with musical activity prior to the 1830s. When he visited Baltimore in 1819, he did send an account of music at the Unitarian church back to his sister, Catherine Eliot Norton: "I was very much pleased with the music at the Unitarian

Church; the organ is second only to that of Brattle St. if indeed it be inferior to that, the organist second only to Dr. Jackson, and a young lady who is the principal female singer of the choir, second only to Helen Davis. They sing the best tunes with much taste and skill." This letter shows Eliot to be a perceptive observer of music. It also epitomizes the nature of his involvement with music throughout his life: as a listener rather than a performer, and as someone willing to make judgments about taste and skill.

Yet even as a listener Eliot's interest in music was not particularly strong in his early years. Eliot went to Europe in the early 1820s to gain culture, "for the sake of the fine things to be seen abroad."[12] He sent back many letters, to his brother-in-law George Ticknor, to his mother, to his sister Anna (Mrs. Ticknor), and to his brother William. At least forty-eight have survived, most of them between two and five tightly written pages. Eliot described at length the museums and galleries that he visited. He was particularly interested in the visual arts, especially painting and jewelry. He only once mentioned attending the theater, and in none of the letters did he ever refer to music. This absence is not surprising in letters to recipients, such as George Ticknor, who were notably uninterested in music. But it is remarkable that Eliot made no mention of hearing any music to his brother William.[13]

William's sudden death in 1829 seems to have spurred Samuel's involvement with music, although there is no direct evidence that it did. The Eliot children were raised to be independent, and Samuel did not appear abnormally distressed by William's death. He was concerned mostly with straightening out William's estate, which was in a chaotic state, and which he undertook assiduously, at considerable time and personal expense. The fact remains, however, that Eliot became deeply involved in musical organizations and in writing about music in the years immediately following William's death.

We do not know precisely when Eliot first became interested in the Boston Academy of Music, or what originally motivated him to do so. Neither do we know how he came to be elected president, but the immediate effects suggest why he desired the position. Eliot brought with him a new agenda for the academy and wasted no time in implementing it. In his first year he hired J. A. Keller as instrumental professor, formed an orchestra through an alliance with the Amateur Society, which supplied the instrumentalists, and sought to have a larger organ installed. In his second year he hired Henry Schmidt as "Leader of the Orchestra." Schmidt, a German violinist who had studied with Spohr, had been

Table 3

Net Worth in Dollars of $100 Donors to the Boston Academy of Music Measured in 1847

Donors	Real Estate	Personal Estate
Appleton, Nathan	93,000	275,000
Appleton, Samuel	176,000	225,000
Appleton, William	153,000	200,000
Eliot, Samuel	62,000	100,000
Fiske, Benjamin	64,600	
Jackson, Patrick T.	21,000	20,000
Lawrence, Abbot	599,400	250,000
Lawrence, Amos	189,500	129,000
Lawrence, Stone & Slade		75,000
Parker, Johanthan	35,000	8,000
Shattuck, George C.	162,200	175,000
Stoddard, Charles	10,000	10,000
Tappan, John	109,000	60,000
Warren, John C.	128,900	180,000
Waterson & Pray	96,000	75,000
Williams, John D.	663,800	100,000
Musicians		
Mason, Lowell	16,000	25,000
Pearce, Shadrach S.	3,600	2,000
Webb, George J.	4,000	1,500

highly recommended by Keller, who had probably heard him in New York.[14] In 1835, Eliot's first year, the academy renovated the defunct Federal Street Theatre into a concert hall, the Odeon. Such a project required money, specifically $4,000, according to an account book of subscribers.[15] A sum of $2,300 was raised by contributions of $100 each, two of which were from businesses, and another $565 by smaller contributions ranging from $10 to $50. It is not clear where the remaining money came from.

The Odeon project succeeded because it was backed by the socioeconomic elite. Fifteen of the twenty-three subscribers who paid $100 to the Odeon project were listed in the published tax records of 1847; table 3 indicates their net work.[16] At a time when $100,000 was con-

sidered a significant fortune, this list represents an extraordinary concentration of wealth. By way of comparison I have included three of the
wealthiest musicians in Boston: Lowell Mason, George J. Webb, and
Shadrach Pearce, a bassoonist.

Eliot had entrée to the socioeconomic elite community in a way that
no other member of the academy did. The elite had not previously
supported either the Boston Academy of Music or the Handel and
Haydn Society. Only one $100 subscriber other than Eliot, Charles
Stoddard, was a member of the Boston Academy of Music, and not a
single one was ever a member of the Handel and Haydn Society. In
contrast, nine academy members were members of the Handel and
Haydn Society.[17] The society had enrolled 369 members by 1835, a
significant percentage of the musically oriented population in a town of
75,000 not noted for its interest in music.

The list of subscribers of the Odeon project also provides a further
clue as to why Eliot became interested in the academy. Three of the
twenty-one individual subscribers were signers of the 1826 circular. Two
others (Eliot and Samuel Appleton) were immediate family members of
signers, and Eliot's brother William had written the circular. Eliot may
have considered the academy a way to accomplish the goals of the
circular, for in retrospect the circular became a blueprint for Eliot's
tenure as president. The academy became a concert institution, and
emphasis shifted to secular instrumental music. The moral aims and
educational goals of the circular were fulfilled; so too was the role of
the subscribers as benefactors with no interest in music making, not
even as amateurs. The Boston Academy of Music became a practical
realization of the Boston upper-class view of musical activity.

The success of the Odeon project compared to the failure of the 1826
circular must be attributed at least in part to the dedication and energy
of Eliot. Yet the 1826 circular had an impressive list of signatories from
the socioeconomic elite, representing enough economic and political
power to create a concert organization even if there was only modest
support amongst their peers. The difference in the way these two proposals were received was due in part to fundamental social changes that
occurred in Boston between 1826 and 1835. Two of the most important
were the declining influence of evangelicalism and increased class tensions precipitated by new patterns of immigration.

Evangelicalism had peaked in the early 1830s. Charles Finney had
come to Boston on behalf of revivalism in 1832 but had had only a
qualified success, even though he generated immense interest. Finney's

"invasion" of Boston was the last grand hurrah of revivalism in New England. By the mid-1830s revivalism had begun to wane nationwide, and Finney's presence never again stirred a community as it had Boston in 1832. According to Bernard Weisberger, revivalism's original phase was over by 1835, the "voice of the revivalist" being "lost in the din of political conventions, theatrical amusements and assorted journalistic enterprises. . . . Democracy and popular culture had other agencies for their work."[18] Lyman Beecher left Boston in the same year Finney launched his revival, 1832, to found a seminary in Cincinnati. With his departure the last of the old-guard Congregational leaders was gone.

A lessening of interest in psalmodic reform came with the decline in the status of revivalism, although calls for reform extended throughout the 1830s. Psalmodic reformers continued to lobby hard for greater acceptance of the contribution that the reformed psalmody could make in the church service, while ministers continued to resist the reformers' goal to accord psalmody a status equal to prayer. But the older psalmody had long been banished from most Congregational churches in Boston, and there was little hostility to the new, at least on musical grounds. The issue was receding rapidly as a matter of central cultural concern.

One event in particular demonstrates the total triumph of the newer psalmody: the founding of the Billings and Holden Society on January 5, 1834. Its ethos was antiquarian; its purpose, to perform older psalmody. It began with a membership of 130 men and women and still had sixty-nine members, fifty-four men and fifteen women, in 1838. It gave one or two concerts a year during its fourteen-year existence and published one major collection of eighteenth-century psalmody, *The Billings and Holden Collection of Ancient Psalmody*. From 1837 through 1840 its concerts were substantial enough to include an orchestra under the direction of Ostinelli. But the society gradually declined in the 1840s. After Asa Warren took over direction of the orchestra in 1841 it was abandoned, and public concerts became less frequent. They were in any case probably peripheral to the real purpose of the society, which was to allow members to sing older psalmody. The scope of the concerts in the late 1830s, however, indicates a vigorous organization. After 1842 public rehearsals took the place of concerts, and the meeting place frequently changed, a sign of instability. The last recorded meeting of the society occurred on October 3, 1847.[19]

The Billings and Holden Society supports the premise that the battle for psalmodic reform was over in the 1830s, in spite of the interest shown in the organization. The society was consciously and overtly antiquarian. Its members considered the music of Billings and Holden representative of another time. The constitution stated that "their principal object, was the performance of ancient sacred music as represented in the composition of Billings and those who followed him." The *Daily Evening Transcript* declared that the society's purpose was to preserve "'the good old fashioned tunes,' in vogue twenty or thirty years ago, and now almost obsolete, from the introduction of more *fashionable* music."[20] The society referred to the older music variously as "Ancient Music," "Ancient Psalmody," "Ancient Sacred Music," "Ancient Church Music," and "Old Fashioned Psalmody."[21] Gould stated that "many respectable singers and musicians" founded the society "partly for amusement, and partly for the purpose of reviving old associations, and giving an opportunity for the curious, who had a desire to hear the tunes sung by their fathers, and mothers, of which they heard so much." Gould also acknowledged that some members joined out of preference for the old tunes over the new.[22] Yet not even these members tried to argue their cause in the face of newer psalmody.

Attempts at antiquarianism or turning to the past seldom occur when a new style of fighting to overthrow an older one. Only after the old has been displaced can it be viewed with either curiosity or nostalgia. The Billings and Holden Society represents that phase. Its exhibitions or concerts were essentially museum pieces; its activities as well as its single publication were exercises in historical recovery.

The Billings and Holden Society also bears witness to what extent class alignment affected the musical life of Boston. The society was a working-class organization, with little overlap in membership of other musical societies. The only known member of the Society who was also a member of the Handel and Haydn Society was Leonard Marshall, one of the few professional musicians in the Billings and Holden Society. The following are members of the society whose occupations are known:

Sumner Adams	barroom operator
John Allen	confectioner or housewright
Benjamin Applin	housewright
Thomas Austin	bricklayer
Benjamin Baldwin	Faneuil Hall Market worker
John H. Beal	carpenter
David Bryant	housewright
Daniel Copeland	mason
Robert Hayden	housewright

Joshua Lovell	housewright
Leonard Marshall	music teacher
Edmund N. Morse	pumpmaker
Evert Read	dealer in stoves
David C. Smith	Faneuil Hall Market worker
Elijah Trask, Jr.	barroom operator
Horatio G. Ware	grocer
Nathaniel Waterman	tinplater
Joseph Woodman	mason

Sixteen of the eighteen names on this list are from the working class. Of the two exceptions, a music teacher and a dealer in stoves, the latter could also be working class, depending on the nature of his business. The list is of the officers and trustees of the society, who were the only members mentioned in newspapers and hence the only ones whose membership can be ascertained. As officers, however, they are probably representative of the society. At the very least it is highly unlikely that the membership of a society whose officers were overwhelmingly working class would have a different profile.

The working-class composition of the Billings and Holden Society corroborates the view that the battle over psalmody in Boston was a class as well as a religious and musical issue. The Presbyterian-Congregational reformers, and the members of the Handel and Haydn Society and the Boston Academy of Music in its early years, were Congregational evangelicals and overwhelmingly middle-class. The membership of the Billings and Holden Society was not only of a different class but of a different religious orientation. Although the society was not formally associated with a church, it had close ties to Universalism. Many of the concerts were held at either the Central Unviersalist Church on Bulfinch Street, the First Universalist Church on North Bennet Street, or the Second Universalist Church on School Street. Both the middle and the upper classes looked on Universalism with disdain. William Bentley, a Harvard-trained minister, complained in 1809 that "it is unhappy for this rising sect that not one man of education in the County is attached to their ministry."[23] As we saw in chapter 5, Universalists participated only minimally in secular middle-class musical organizations. Although the Universal Singing Society flourished between 1807 and 1816, only two of its forty-seven members joined the Handel and Haydn Society when it was formed in 1815. Yet even that number indicates a greater social fluidity than was found in the 1830s. By the 1830s religion, class, and musical activity had become more stratified.

Irish immigration into Boston, which some Bostonians began to find alarming in the 1830s, contributed further to class stratification. Although the huge influx of Irish immigrants did not occur until the mid-1840s, considerable anti-Irish sentiment appeared already in the 1830s. The Irish posed a serious threat to the cultural homogeneity of a region not noted for cultural pluralism. Their customs seemed strange to many Bostonians, and their religion was profoundly disconcerting to evangelicals. Evangelical Congregational ministers in particular voiced concern about the Irish Catholic threat to religious stability. The most serious episode brought about by the tension between Catholics and Protestants was the burning of the Ursuline convent in Charlestown, a suburb of Boston, on August 11, 1834. The convent was deliberately torched by Boston and Charlestown workmen who feared job competition from the Irish immigrants, and a mob prevented the fire companies from reaching the scene.

The burning of the convent exposed the animosity between evangelicals and Unitarians almost as much as it did between Catholics and Protestants. Unitarians were not only tolerant of Catholicism but took advantage of its educational offerings. Many upper-class Unitarian families, disturbed by the fervid Congregationalism of the public schools, sent their daughters to be educated at the Ursuline convent. Congregational evangelicals saw this as a conspiracy between Unitarians and papists, and many Congregational ministers stirred passions with anti-Catholic sermons, which included lurid claims of girls being held involuntarily and being educated in "vile corruption."[24]

Samuel Eliot was directly involved in policing Boston during this time. Two nights before the burning, he sent his wife, who was out of town, a lengthly letter describing his activities. Tensions in Boston were sufficiently high for local officials to fear an outbreak of violence or worse. Special constables were sent out each night to help keep order, and Eliot was placed in charge of eighty of them. In describing his evening Eliot attested to the sympathy felt for the Irish Catholics by some parts of society: "At nine I was at the school house again [the impromptu headquarters for his unit], and there I staid until three, hearing rumors, (silly ones for the most part) about noises heard and lights seen, in this direction and that, but generally that every thing was perfectly quiet. I conversed with many of the Irish Catholics, who were expected to be particularly exasperated, but found them quite sound and calm, viewing the business correctly, and understanding the sympathy felt for them."[25]

Earlier that evening Eliot had been at a meeting of the Boston School Committee, which he described as "one of our tedious yet stormy sessions." The two events are not unrelated. Boston was culturally divided, and the divisions were becoming more apparent. Education was a central issue. Both evangelicals and Whig republicans like Eliot saw it as one of the means to achieving their ends. Their goals were in some ways similar and in other ways totally at odds. Both envisioned a society united by their own principles. Evangelicals sought to disseminate the moral values of evangelical Christianity, Whig republicants to maintain the social hierarchy. The socioeconomic elite looked on the proselytizing of the evangelicals with suspicion. Evangelicals expressed concern over the laissez-faire immorality of the upper classes as well as the heresy of Unitarianism. The two groups were even split on the Irish issue, at least in part because some Unitarians allied themselves with the Catholics for their children's education.

A recognition of the value of education ultimately united the upper-class Unitarians and the middle-class evangelicals, and in the process created some strange bedfellows. Eliot's concern for education was probably what originally attracted him to the Boston Academy of Music. His devotion to education had already won him the position of chairman of the Boston School Committee in the early 1830s. He and Lowell Mason, a fervent evangelical, were thus firmly united to secure the adoption of music in the public schools. Mason is usually credited with winning that battle. Eliot, however, as president of the Boston Academy of Music, chairman of the Boston School Committee, and mayor of Boston in 1837 and 1838, when the issue was formally considered, had as much to do with the introduction of music into the public school curriculum as Mason did.

It should be stressed that there is no record of enmity between Eliot and Mason. In fact, Mason frequently visited the Eliot house on academy business.[26] Mason could not have been pleased with the new directions of the academy, but he was pragmatic. The public school victory allowed him to focus his attention elsewhere, giving him a new and broader forum as the first superintendent of music in Boston and in the country.

The extent to which Eliot succeeded in reshaping the Boston Academy of Music can easily be seen in its annual reports. Each report begins with a lengthy statement both summarizing the previous year and explaining the purpose and goals for the forthcoming one. The first annual report was signed "George Wm. Gordon, Secretary." From 1833 through 1839 the reports are anonymous, but from 1835 on they were written by Eliot.[37] Before 1835 they stress the sacred-music mission of the academy; as from 1835, Eliot gradually but inexorably dissociated the Academy from sacred music.

Eliot wasted no time in making it clear that the academy was not strictly a sacred-music institution. The third annual report began with an attempt to counter "misapprehension" about its purpose, stressing that it was not limited exclusively to the study of sacred music, "as has been supposed." Eliot probably dared go no further than that at the time, however, and acknowledged that sacred music was still considered the most important type of music. Nevertheless, he urged that other types of vocal music be encouraged, especially those that tend "to diffuse a chastened cheerfulness around the domestic circle."[28]

The report referred to the desirability of introducing music into the common schools as part of general education and warned that music of a pure kind and of a correct taste had to be inculcated: "But in order that the art may produce its proper effect upon mankind, it is necessary to provide music which is of a pure character, as well as to cultivate the voice. . . . A correct musical taste, in its extended sense, comprises something more than an ear capable of appreciating sounds and their distinctions. Something of a more intellectual nature enters into its composition."[29]

Eliot emphasized public performance much more strongly in the fourth annual report, written in 1836 after his first full year as president. Describing the time since the previous report as "an era of some importance . . . in the history of the Academy," Eliot listed the several new developments: the renovation of the Boston Theatre for concerts under its new name, the Odeon; the augmentation of the choir by "large numbers of ladies and gentlemen"; the formation of an orchestra, although it still played a subordinate role, to aid the choir; an alliance with the Amateur Society, the instrumental organization that supplied the orchestra; the appointment of Joseph A. Keller as the third professor and the first instrumentalist. Eliot gave the purchase of a larger and more suitable organ for the Odeon a high priority.[30]

Eliot also listed the accomplishments of the professors. Lowell Mason instructed various types of classes throughout the city. His juvenile classes had leveled off at between eight hundred and a thousand. George Webb gave private lessons in voice and piano and "rehearse[d] with members of the choir the more difficult and delicate pieces which have been performed." George Keller formed a violin class of boys and taught music at the New England Asylum for the Blind. If we read carefully between the lines it appears that Mason's influence at the academy was on the wane. Eliot not only acknowledged openly that Mason's classes were no longer growing but publicly credited Webb with the preparation of the more difficult pieces. Mason's clout was not gone, however. Four years later Webb's better musicianship and Mason's greater fame led to a serious conflict between the two, resulting in Webb's resignation from the academy. The precise details of the conflict were never made public or even referred to in private communication. Eliot appointed a special committee to investigate the problem, but its five-page report referred to the disagreement only in general terms before siding with Mason. The report sympathized with Webb but in essence told him he would just have to live with Mason's greater fame and prestige.[31]

In the fifth annual report (1837) Eliot hinted at future plans but was reluctant to reveal them: "Plans of more extensive usefulness, and wider fields of effort have presented themselves to our minds, and these not of a visionary nature; but we have been obliged to content ourselves with merely contemplating them as objects which we should be able to compass at some future time." Apparently Eliot saw two obstacles to immediate implementation, finances and public sentiment. In Eliot's eyes, the public was not yet ready for his new ideas. But Eliot believed that "in the course of a few years there will be . . . a revolution in public opinion in relation to music." He did speak of progress with the orchestra, but was prouder of the choir, which had grown to 198, and whose members had "exhibited an unabated ardor in the art for the promotion of which they are associated."[32]

What Eliot had in mind became clearer with the sixth annual report (1838), the first in which the orchestra was the focus of his discussion. After an opening statement lamenting that too many men were too caught up in business affairs to cultivate the arts, Eliot then concentrated on the question of the orchestra. He observed that the pieces it performed met with audience approval, and that "this species of musical entertainment seems so evidently to be gaining ground in the public favor, that there is a strong inducement to cultivate it." The orchestra was composed of amateurs and had been pared down from the previous year. Eliot expressed hope that such an orchestra "might make . . . a very attractive amusement to the public. The experiment is worth the trial." He also announced the appointment of Henry Schmidt as "Leader of the Orchestra."[33]

Emphasis on the orchestra came at the expense of the choir, which apparently no longer received the attention it needed. Eliot reported that the choir had shrunk since the last report, to 177 members: 28 sopranos, 49 altos, 35 tenors, and 65 basses. Attendance at choir rehearsals was also down, to about 125. Resignations were of course expected, but the choir was beginning to atrophy from calculated neglect: "While individuals, from various causes, have withdrawn from the Choir, no measures have been taken to fill the vacancies thus made."[34]

Near the end of the report Eliot expressed concern about the activities of the academy. Public performances were a financial burden, and he warned that they might have to be discontinued until the public became sufficiently educated in music to support them. The process of education could not happen overnight, however, but "must be the slow growth of years." Yet Eliot was heartened by the progress made on the educational side, in the increased number of pupils, in the greater demand for the professors' books, and in the inquiries coming in from all parts of the country. From this he discerned "that there is a movement upon the public mind from which future and more rapid progress may be reasonably anticipated."[35] Noteworthy about Eliot's discussion is the absence of any reference to church music.

Eliot devoted most of the seventh annual report (1839) to the teaching of children, probably because the academy had achieved an important goal in 1838: the adoption of music as a subject in the public schools. Eliot also reported that Henry Schmidt, the leader of the orchestra, had been made a professor at the academy, and that instrumental music was "gaining ground in the public favor."[36]

Much of the eighth annual report (1840) dealt with the sudden resignation of George J. Webb following his disagreement with Lowell Mason, although Eliot provided no specific details about the incident. Eliot also acknowledged the contributions of the Amateur Club in providing the core of the orchestra but then, without enumerating them, admitted serious deficiencies in the orchestra. He stated that the government had given its attention to this problem, and that Schmidt had begun a series of instrumental classes, which he hoped would help remedy it.[37]

Theodore Hach's *Musical Magazine* provided more details about the changes in the Boston Academy of Music's programs and their reception. The academy began the 1839 season with lighter music, chiefly glees and madrigals, but in March 1839 changed direction to "pieces of a more solid character."[38] In a retrospective article in July, Hach elaborated further on the academy's role: "Its usefullness arises more from its general influence on public opinion in favor of music and musical cultivation, than from its musical performances. The Academy . . . found an orchestra too expensive, and therefore changed their plan to the commencement of the last season. They chose music of a lighter character, than formerly; but soon found that Glees sung in Chorus, and often times connected with insipid or unmeaning words, were insufficient to sustain the interest of their concerts; and they therefore returned to music more weighty in its character."[39]

In a review of Eliot's 1840 report, Hach discussed the state of instrumental music in Boston. He acknowledged that the academy had already attempted a union of all the instrumental professors in the city to presenting orchestral music to the public. The project had failed, for two reasons: the lack of support of musicians, who were either indifferent to the idea, feared that the effort would not be financially beneficial, or were jealous of the academy's authority; and the absence of a strong instrumental leader in Boston, someone who was not only an excellent musician but also combined the energy and tact to command the respect of the musicians.[40] Hach pleaded that the academy not give up on presenting the best instrumental music possible. He believed strongly that the cultivation of instrumental music was essential for the development of taste in America: "Without creating a taste for sterling instrumental music, all its [the academy's] efforts for vocal music will have comparatively but a minor and insufficient, and most certainly, but a divided effect. . . . The taste will never take a purely musical elevation, if not formed in part, at least, by a due appreciation of instrumental music."[41]

Earlier that summer Hach had recommended that the academy "take measures to get up an orchestra of its own," on the grounds that for the advancement of taste instrumental music should be cultivated equally with vocal music. "None of our institutions have the means for effecting this, which the Academy possesses."[42]

In 1840 and 1841 the academy did precisely what Hach had recommended, and completely reorganized its performance priorities. In the ninth annual report (1841) Eliot first referred to the progress of music and the improvement "in the style of musical performances and the knowledge and taste of both performers and audiences." He then explicitly articulated the new direction of the academy: "It was determined, at the commencement of the last concert season, that more attention should be given than heretofore to instrumental music, and that as efficient an orchestra as could be procured should be engaged. Between twenty-five and thirty instruments were accordingly secured, and were played by persons whose professional talent is well known in this city. . . . We do not think it will be considered unbecoming in us to express the opinion we most confidently entertain, that this was the best orchestra ever assembled in Boston for an entire season."[43] To concentrate resources on the orchestra, choral performance was cut back, and some singers resigned. At the end of the season the Executive Committee voted to disband the choir. The shift in emphasis was complete.

Eliot observed that the orchestra competently performed a great variety of music ranging from waltzes to symphonies and concertos. On December 5, 1840, it played Rossini's Overture to *L'Italiana in Algieri,* and on November 27, 1841, Mozart's Overture to *Don Giovanni.* On December 18, 1841, it performed Beethoven's Fifth Symphony, but not intact: the first movement ended the first part of the program; the second movement began the second part; and the last two movements concluded the concert. Beethoven's Sixth Symphony was performed in a similar manner on January 15, 1842, although it was less splintered than the Fifth had been: the first two movements ended the first part of the program, and the last three movements opened the second.

No one, including reviewers, suggested that the symphonies should be played without interruption. All were euphoric that they were attempted at all. Hach was particularly pleased with the turn of events. He considered the concerts the highlight of the musical season in Boston and praised the academy for producing "classical music by the greatest composers, in great variety, and in a better style, than the public can hear them any where else, in this city at least."[44] Since Hach was a known advocate of classical instrumental music, his enthusiasm is not surprising. But he was not alone in his commendation. The *Musical Reporter* also approved of the academy's efforts. Of the three instrumental concerts that the academy gave that winter, the *Musical Reporter* thought the February 13, 1841, concert the best. It consisted of Beethoven's Fifth Symphony, the "Base Song from the Seasons" by Haydn, a Strauss waltz, Beethoven's Overture to *Fidelio,* and Rossini's Overture to *La gazza ladra.* The *Musical Reporter* praised "the manner in which the parts of the different instruments were brought out and sustained," and lauded Beethoven's music in particular. Hach too spoke favorably of that performance: "Thus the orchestra under his [Schmidt's] direction brought out effects, which we had not known before. . . . Their last performance of Beethoven's truly grand symphony in C minor has, we doubt not, such an impression on the small, but select audience, which heard it, that they will look forward with the greatest interest to a continuation of these instrumental concerts, in the next season."[45]

The size and quality of the orchestra contributed much to the success of the concerts. Hach acknowledged that nowhere else in Boston could one hear classical music "in great variety, and in a better style," simply because the academy's orchestra consisted of all the best professionals in town. Hach was also pleased with the proportion of string and wind instruments, a problem that plagued many orchestras in Federal America. According to the *Musical Cabinet,* the orchestra in 1841 consisted of thirty-five players, "much superior, both as regards its number and the ability of its members, to any orchestra before collected in the city." It contained most of the better performers, including Lewis Ostinelli, Thomas Comer, and Asa Warren on the violin, I. Friedheim on the clarinet, and A. L. Ribas on the oboe. Ribas had only recently arrived from London, where his playing had been praised by the *Musical World.* The *Musical Reporter* listed specifically the instruments in the academy's orchestra:

4 Violins Primo	2 Clarionets
4 Violins Secundo	2 Fagottos
2 Violas	2 Trumpets
2 Violoncellos	4 Horns
2 Contra Bases	2 Trombones
2 Flutes	1 Double Drum
2 Oboes	

A triangle and side drum were also used once. This list confirms both Hach's comment about balance and the *Musical Cabinet*'s estimate of size. Whether thirty-one or thirty-five musicians, it was the largest orchestera ever assembled in Boston, even larger than the ill-fated Tremont Theatre Orchestra of the late 1820s.

The historical significance of these concerts was not lost on those who commented on them. Hach predicted that the concerts would "prepare the way to a further progress of the art." Eliot implied that the academy's efforts heralded a new age for music in the city: "We esteem nothing more desirable, in the present state of musical taste in Boston, than to establish permanently a band capable of performing music of the high character which was given at our concerts the last season. We believe the time has arrived when the appetite for such harmony will grow by what it feeds on."[46] The *Musical Cabinet* claimed that these concerts, along with the virtuoso concerts of Knoop, Nagel, and Herwig, marked "a new era in the history of music in Boston."[47] John S. Dwight, too, spoke of a "new era." Writing many years later from the vantage of an established high culture, he saw the concerts as a critical turning point not only for Boston but also for America: "The day of the Symphony in Boston has come! Beethoven enters; we have reached our second station. A new era has begun for us in music." Dwight credited Eliot fully with this turn of events, and then described the audience's reaction:

Doubtless we owe this wise resolve, this new departure, to the sagacity, the taste, the public spirit of his Honor the Mayor of Boston at that period, Samuel A. Eliot, president of the Academy throughout its whole career. . . . Many can remember how eagerly these concerts were sought, how frequently the audience was large, and what a theme of enthusiastic comment and congratulation these first fresh hearings of the great masters was. And what willing ears were those that listened? What souls were most susceptible to the new, quickening influence? To what ideas, what sympahetic phase of thought and aspiration did those harmonies appeal? Partly, of course, to those most musically taught already; partly to those trusting in authority; but largely also to a peculiar element then stirring in the intellectual and social life of this community, to minds in sympathy with what was idly called the "transcendental" movement,—that class of young enthusiasts for culture, in the freest, highest sense, with whom Emerson (although not musical) and Beethoven came in, it may be said, together.[48]

Dwight's words must be taken with his own prejudices in mind: toward Boston, toward orchestral music, toward art as "pure" and sacred, and toward Beethoven. But these very prejudices became orthodoxy in the later nineteenth century, as orchestral music in general and the symphonies of Beethoven in particular came to form the cornerstone of a sacralized high culture. Dwight was partly but not wholly responsible for that. In the early 1840s it was not at all clear that the moral dimension of instrumental music would be recognized by the American people or that symphonic music itself would be accepted.

Dwight's reference to a large audience was not correct, at least at first. When the academy first attempted instrumental concerts, it faced some rough going because they did not draw well. Eliot admitted as much in his ninth annual report (1841), and the *Musical Magazine* and the

Musical Cabinet both confirmed it. In its laudatory 1841 article on the instrumental concerts of the academy, the *Cabinet* reported that because of insufficient audience the concert series was losing money. The financial situation had become so dire by 1842 that the academy threatened to discontinue them. We do not know whether the threat worked or the educational efforts of the academy began to bear fruit, but the Boston public finally began to respond. Beginning in 1842 instrumental concerts drew larger audiences.[49] The *Daily Transcript* noted the increased attendance as well as the change in musical tastes of Boston audiences. The *Transcript* also credited the Boston Academy of Music for this development: only a few years prior, the music of Haydn, Mozart, and Beethoven, "with no other attractions offered, would hardly have drawn an audience of fifty persons. Now, we see the hall filled an hour before the commencement of the performances . . . which speaks well for the increase of correct musical taste in our good city. The Boston Academy of Music, can justly claim the honor of bringing about this great revolution in musical taste."[50]

For Eliot the increased audience support was more than a financial triumph. It was a vindication of the character of Boston's citizens. In the eleventh annual report Eliot equated a love of orchestral music with the character of a people: "It [orchestral music] is, indeed, an intellectual and social enjoyment of so high an order, it so stimulates the mind and the best feelings, that it would be a very discouraging and painful symptom of the character of our population, a symptom we are sure can never occur, if it were not highly appreciated and esteemed." The concerts of the academy offered "decisive proof that this kind of music is becoming more and more highly esteemed."[51]

By 1845 Eliot had not only transformed the Boston Academy of Music from being an institution founded to further sacred vocal music to being the chief progenitor of secular instrumental music; he was also rewriting its history. In the final report issued by the academy before it disbanded in 1847, Eliot looked back on its early years: "The end and object of our corporate being was to spread the knowledge and the love of music as fast and as far as we could. It was not limited to any particular department, nor by any thing but the bounds of the science and the art themselves. Whatever was good in them was an object of our attention and our ambition—the vocal and the instrumental, the elementary and the advanced, the sacred and secular, the scientific and the simple, music as it is performed, and music as it is to be invented and written."[52]

Eliot's ability to wrest control of the Boston Academy of Music, change its direction completely, and convince the public to accept orchestral music are important steps in the development of American attitudes toward music. They raise important questions about his motivation, purpose, and influence: What did Eliot hope to accomplish by selling orchestral music to the American public? How broad was his forum, that is, how far beyond the walls of the Boston Academy of Music did his message go? What effect did his activities have on the evolution of American musical attitudes? And why did the Boston public accept orchestral music in a way that it had never done before?

Eliot himself provided answers to these questions. He was not only a successful organizer and leader but also an important propagandist for a specific vision of music in American life. In spite of his activity in politics and many social and educational causes, he wrote extensively on a variety of subjects, including music, and frequently lectured at educational, artistic, and civic events. Between 1824 and 1861 he published twelve articles in the *Christian Examiner,* eight in the *North American Review,* and at least one in *Dwight's Journal of Music.* A number of his addresses were published as pamphlets, and he of course wrote lengthy essays for the annual reports of the Boston Academy of Music. This material has never been examined as a unit, possibly because many of the writings were anonymous, their authorship hitherto unknown in some cases. In consequence, Eliot has been ignored as an intellectual force in American music.

Two of Eliot's most important statements appeared anonymously in the *North American Review.* His personal papers confirm his authorship of the two *Review* articles,[53] as they contain handwritten manuscripts of them. There are some minor differences in wording, and they show sufficient evidence of revision to make it reasonably certain Eliot had not simply copied them from the *Review.* Furthermore, a short biographical statement that accompanied the gift of the papers to Harvard states that Eliot wrote them.

The *North American Review,* one of the leading literary journals of its time, was essentially a Unitarian publication. It originated in 1815 as part of the movement in Unitarianism led by Joseph Stevens Buckminster and Edward Everett to apply literature and scholarship to religious teaching. It was an ideal medium for Eliot, whose ideas about music closely paralleled Unitarian ideas about literature, and who personified the upper-class Unitarian in his wealth, his Harvard background, his interest in social causes, his political orientation, and his willingness for public service.

The first article appeared in July 1836, as a review of the first three annual reports of the Boston Academy of Music.[54] In it Eliot dealt with the question of cultivation and taste. He placed himself squarely within the cultivated tradition, arguing that music must be cultivated and that its cultivation was only just beginning in America: "The taste of the public, too, cannot be forced; but must be carried gradually and easily along to the highest branches of the art, or it will fall back again to the rude and unformed state from which it is just emerging."[55]

His article advanced two principal theses. The first was that musical taste is universal, not culturally bound:

It is a mistake to suppose that there is a particular style of music which is adapted to a particular period of the world. Music is a universal langauge, and what is able powerfully to affect one generation of men will not fail to affect another. . . . Palestrina had the merit and the glory of pointing out the true path in which music should walk, the true mode in which she must produce her effects; and from his day to the present there has been but one school of good music. Divided and subdivided as the schools have nominally been, correct taste of one and indivisible; and all must be conducted by her guidance, or they cease to be schools of music, and degenerate into academies of uproar.[56]

To demonstrate that the practice of music is universal, Eliot set out to trace its history. He contended that the music of antiquity, while highly expressive, was simple and natural, not scientific in the sense that modern harmony was. Eliot did state, however, that he favored expression over dry science. After discussing ancient Greek music, he concluded that we simply do not understand it. He then provided a relatively sound, straightforward discussion of Gregorian chant. (For a nineteenth-century dilettante, he was well read. Most of his information came from Burney, to whom he referred several times.) Following a lengthy consideration of Guido, Eliot jumped to Palestrina, whom he called the founder of the modern school of good taste. Palestrina was "the best composer, not only of his own, but of all preceding time. . . . He must continue to be regarded as the successful reformer of a barbarous era, and the father and founder of a better school, which, from that day to this, has been considered as the school of true taste."[57]

Eliot's second principal point was that taste is progressive. He saw musical taste increasing at an accelerating rate since Palestrina, and acknowledged that since each age has greater resources than the previous one, "succeeding times will go on improving."[58] As with many of his contemporaries, the concept of progress was fundamental to his theories.

Eliot thought that musical progress reached a pinnacle with Handel, Haydn, and Mozart. He discussed each composer at some length, in laudatory terms. He called Handel's *Messiah* "one of the best musical productions extant . . . [belonging] to the highest class of compositions."[59] With Haydn and Mozart, Eliot abandoned himself to effusions of unrestrained praise. The adjectives and phrases pile up: sublime, extraordinary, incredible, delightful, astonishing, pure, refined, boundless genius, vivid pictures, solemn grace, dignity of expression. He used these terms to describe Haydn alone, for in his eyes Mozart surpassed the capabilities of language itself. Admitting that the moderation necessary to give weight to language makes it difficult to speak of Mozart, Eliot nevertheless tried. Mozart beguiles, enchants, captivates, excites. His works display wonderful beauty, sweetness, inexpressible charm, sublimity, noble harmony, grace and delicacy. His genius was such that "one almost despairs of either doing justice to his memory, or making others sensible of his preeminent power." Finally Eliot asserted that Mozart's compositions "form a striking climax to the musical history of the last century." Mozart combined all of the best qualities of both Handel and Haydn, so that

The force of nature could no further go;
To make a third, she joined the other two.[60]

After such paeans, one anticipates with fascination and trepidation how Eliot would describe Beethoven. He mentioned him only once, in a paragraph about Rossini, in one-third of one sentence that also included an appraisal of both Rossini and Weber: "Beethoven has shown us a wonderful scientific skill, and a dark imagination, lightened occasionally by a soft half which shines the brighter by contrast."[61] Eliot clearly had a pantheon or canon of composers, into which Palestrina, Handel, Haydn, and Mozart had been admitted. Beethoven was yet outside, somewhere below Rossini and on a par with Weber.

Eliot was not pleased with the state of music in America, which to him had no history and "scarcely an existence here," America having no instrumental composers and only a few who composed songs and anthems. He found the future hopeful, however. The country was young and vigorous and rapidly increasing in wealth. Recent developments in particular boded well: the change in style in church music was a beginning; the formation of the Handel and Haydn Society was "the dawn of the spirit of improvement;" the establishment of the Boston Academy of Music was further proof of a greater interest in music.

In closing, Eliot looked at Germany. How was it possible, he asked, that five of the six composers that he mentioned near the end of the article (Handel, Haydn, Mozart, Beethoven, Weber, and Rossini) were German? How could a nation "with a language almost as unmusical as ours" have produced so many great musicians? The answer lay in education: Germany universally taught the rudiments of music to children. The equivalent in this country would be "the most important means of eliciting the now dormant taste and talent of our country." Eliot thus reiterated precisely one of the principal themes of the 1826 circular.

In his second *Review* article[62] the political aspect was more focused. Eliot wrote of revolution. He began by claiming that "a great revolution in the musical character of the American people has begun, and is, we trust, to go forward, like other revolutions, till its ultimate object be attained." Later he claimed that the Boston Academy of Music was one of the causes of the revolution.

Eliot was overtly Platonic in this article. To him music was universal, a powerful instrument that could affect everyone, and he quoted Plato's "Let me make the people's ballads, and I care not who makes their laws." To prove his point, Eliot cited three modern examples: The French Revolution, in which popular airs provided an additional impetus; the national anthem "God Save the King," whose positive effect had helped save the English monarchy, and the most recent American election, won by William Henry Harrison over Martin van Buren. Eliot was probably referring to the song "Tippecanoe and Tyler Too," but he unfortunately offered no further specifics on any of the three.[63]

To Eliot the effects of music were deeper than a temporary arousal of passions. Music has a "permanent effect . . . upon the national character." He argued that music, more than any other activity, addressed man's whole nature, his physical, intellectual, and moral aspects. To substantiate his claim Eliot listed the positive effects of music, many of which echo the 1837 report of the Boston School Committee that recommended the inclusion of music in the public schools.[64]

Eliot straddled a position between elitist and populist. He did not deny that music provides pleasure, and might do so at all levels of musical sophistication; people who prefer the songs of Henry Russell to those of John Braham, or Billings' anthems to Mozart's *Requiem*, equally share the pleasures of music. He further realized that music other than the most cultivated could not only give pleasure and arouse passion but also be a potent cultural force.

Eliot then surveyed the state of music in Boston. He found it to have been deplorable thirty years earlier, consisting of at best "half a dozen instruments in the orchestra of the theater, and the so-called singing of the several church choirs, with the accompaniment of the violoncello." At about that time Joseph Steven Buckminster had made the first attempt to reform church music. His efforts had little effect, however, and the next step in the development of music in Boston was the formation of the Handel and Haydn Society. Eliot then credited his brother, William, with attempting to improve the style of church music twenty years earlier, through his leadership of the West Church Choir, an effort aborted by Williams's death. According to Eliot, however, none of those earlier efforts compared with events of the past two or three years, which constituted the revolution to which Eliot had referred. The manifestations of the revolution were a greatly increased interest in music, with many more concerts being given in Boston, which in some cases drew audiences of more than a thousand people.[65]

Eliot considered the founding of the Boston Academy of Music the most important step leading to the musical revolution. He listed several contributions the academy had made to the musical life of Boston: it had formed the best-trained choir in the city, refurbished the Federal Street Theatre to create the Odeon, presented a variety of concerts to the public, and secured the adoption of vocal music in the public school curriculum. He considered the last point "the most important thing done by the Academy, or which can be done to promote the progress of music among us."[66]

Eliot saw in music a way of advancing the early republican dream of a unified society. He did not want to exclude the people. He believed that the young would "mould the character of this democracy," and that musical education, with its focus on song, could be a potent tool to effect that end. He spoke of the evil of disunion, of which he was particularly apprehensive, and held aloft the example of music, in which "there is a place for every one, and there ought to be one for every place." Eliot then quoted, with his hearty approval, the report of T. Keeper Davis to the Boston School Committee, on the introduction of music into the public schools: by introducing vocal music into the schools, "you make it what it should be made, the property of the whole people," in which "the taste of all will likewise be cultivated." By this means music helps the educational system "raise up good citizens to the Commonwealth."[67]

Eliot's philosophy did not encompass the populism of the marketplace. He stressed that everyone should accept his proper place, and in musical taste he wanted to bring the people up to his level. Rather than broadening his concept of taste to include music favored by other segments of society, he wished to make the taste of others conform to his. He still believed in taste, progress, cultivation, and a musical hierarchy. He was not ready to abandon the pantheon and justified his position by observing that although the child may enjoy the pleasures of music every step along the way, as one becomes more cultivated one prefers more sophisticated music. He persisted in the notion that some types of music were superior to others, and in the belief that through proper exposure and cultivation the population at large would arrive at the same musical preferences held by Eliot and others of the cultivated class. Whatever the value of fireside melody, music remained to Eliot fundamentally "abstract," "one of the fine arts," and "the great handmaiden of civilization."[68]

Eliot's seemingly contradictory democratizing views and elitism were entirely consistent within the framework of political views held by some members of the upper classes. Eliot was motivated throughout his career by early Federal Whig republicanism and saw his musical revolution as an effort to extend the gentry consensus by bringing the masses into the fold of the eighteenth-century hierarchy via a culture shared in common. He believed equally in progress, education, the preference of the many for cultivated music once given the opportunity, and in a shared social hierarchy of which orchestral music provided a prime metaphor.

Eliot's views were not unusual in early Federal America, but by 1840 Whig republicanism was much out of date; what is unusual is how avidly Eliot worked toward republican goals throughout his life. Although his efforts at the Boston Academy had deep repercussions for American musical culture, politically they represent the last response of a dying social order.

If there was any doubt that Eliot continued to maintain the Whig ideal of a unified society, and that he related this social goal to music, he dispelled them in an 1860 article for *Dwight's Journal of Music* entitled "Music and Politics."[69] He was sixty-two years old at the time and had not been active in musical organizations since the academy folded in 1847. He fervently defended his hierarchical view of the social order by drawing several parallels between musical and political activity, the most important being that each person has a specific part to play and must be willing to play it. Not everyone can be a leader. Individual flights of fancy must be subordinated to the needs of the overall ensemble: "Music is the only art which, requiring the concerted action of numbers, in different spheres, can exemplify and enforce that principle of order and subordination of one thing to another, and of one man to another, without which harmony, whether in music or politics, cannot exist. It is a lesson not unimportant, surely, to young America to learn, that there are rules which must be obeyed." As to how an individual determines his part, Eliot's views had changed little since his days at the academy, when he conceptualized an institution in which the elite, rather than the musicians involved, made decisions: "Every man must be willing to take the place for which nature has fitted him, and for which others, rather than he himself, think him qualified."[70]

Eliot envisaged an ideal order in which every man not only had his place but would, in the interest of good harmony, accept the place assigned. Who determined the places was to Eliot almost self-evident: the few chosen leaders, acting in the interest of the common good. If every man were content to play his assigned part, this would create no problem, and for a man not to accept his role in the hierarchy was to Eliot an egregious blunder: "The fate of him who neglects the part and the place in life for which he is fitted, for one to which he is not adapted, is failure complete and irreparable."[71]

In his discussion of changes that occurred in American society by 1840, Robert Wiebe distinguished two directions. The more radical one led to the revolution in choices and a more individual society. This direction appealed to the middle class and significantly affected the nature of American evangelicalism. Lowell Mason belonged to that movement. His efforts on behalf of music education had been motivated by the pressing religious needs of the newly emergent society. Mason was an evangelical, and to him music had a moral purpose that transcended the artistic.[72] Concurrently a more conservative track sought to maintain the hierarchy by extending its privileges to deserving citizens.[73] Social stability was to be coupled with expanding opportunity. The traditionalists still believed that the integrity of the union required a homogeneous society held together with similar cultural institutions. Eliot belonged to those traditionalists.

Eliot was relatively unique among the descendants of the Colonial gentry in his recognition of music's potential to do more than entertain.

Few of his peers were even interested in the art. Those who were saw it as little more than a frill. Even Jefferson, who admitted that music was "the favorite passion of my soul," considered it essentially an "enjoyment." Only the Presbyterian-Congregational reformers had grasped the significance of the power of music. They had backed into that: if the wrong kind of music could wipe out the minister's most solemn efforts to create the proper atmosphere at a church service, the right kind could enhance that atmosphere. Their concerns were thus more religious than aesthetic.

Eliot considered the symphony orchestra the cornerstone of the musical pantheon he wished to build. As we noted earlier, he began laying plans for the establishment of an orchestra almost from the moment of his installation as president of the academy, and by 1838 he could publicly announce its formation. Yet he chose his vehicle badly, for of all institutions the symphony orchestra was the least compatible with the democratic impulses of the age. This point was not lost on early devotees, who saw in it a troubling conundrum.

In 1840 an anonymous article appeared in the *North American Review*.[74] It began as a review of Stendhal's life of Haydn but consisted mostly of a discussion of national music and it was reprinted in part in the *Musical Magazine* under the title "Prospects for a National Music in America."[75] A handwritten note in one copy of the *Review* attributed the article to Henry R. Cleveland.[76] Cleveland was a graduate of Harvard, an attorney, a respected organist, a writer and translator in several fields, and so well-known for his musical interests that he was asked to give the 1840 lecture before the Harvard Musical Association. He had published a lengthy article on music in *New England Magazine* in 1835 and a review of Gardiner's *Music of Nature* in *New York Review* in 1837.[77] He was known to the *North American Review* editor, who the year before had printed a review of Cleveland's translation of *Sallust's Histories of the Conspiracy of Catiline and the Jugurthine War,* and it is probable that Cleveland was indeed the author of the 1840 *Review* article.

After admitting that America had no national music, because "we have nothing like national taste," Cleveland surveyed the national music of other countries, such as Germany, Italy, and Scotland, and searched for the causes of its existence or lack of it. He explored possibilities such as climate and geography as well cultivation and state support. Cleveland then considered the possibility of a national music arising in America. And herein lay the dilemma: any national music arising in America must be congruent with the democratic spirit of the country. But music as practiced, particularly ensemble music was not democratic: "It may seem a strange assertion, that an art, which has ever been reared and fostered by wealth and aristocracy, can find a genial soil in this republic. Music, it will be said, is peculiarly at war with the spirit of democracy. There is not a more absolute monarch on the earth than the leader of an orchestra. The moment his divine right is disputed, the empire falls to destruction. For musicians, in the practice of their art, there can be none but an absolute autocracy, a pure despotism."[78] In addition, Cleveland observed, an orchestra is an expensive pursuit, better suited to aristocratic state support than the public citizens in a democracy.

Yet music, "to become national, must be received by the people at large." For this reason Cleveland dismissed opera, which appealed to the wealthy class and could not be sustained even in New York. But Cleveland could not admit that national music could come from a simpler, more popular-oriented, folk-related style. He was concerned that music in America would only gratify "a vulgar and depraved taste," a phrase that could have easily come from a psalmodic reformer. His solution was to elevate the taste of the people: "Music must be made popular, not by debasing the art, but by elevating the people."[79]

It is thus not surprising that Cleveland strongly supported the work of the Boston Academy of Music. He shared Eliot's belief in the importance of educating children in music and articulated with considerable precision the republican gentry point of view: "The efforts of the Academy are calculated in the best possible manner to prepare the way for national music among us. Its object is to render music popular; to plant the art among the people; to make it a universal resource for elegant enjoyment." He noted with approval the compositions that the academy performed: works by Haydn, Mozart, Romberg, and Neukomm.[80] Romberg's music was dear to the academy; Eliot's translation of Schiller's "Song of the Bell," highly praised in literary journals, was undertaken for a performance of Romberg's setting. Neukomm's choral music was actually considered on a par with Haydn's in the early nineteenth century. Neukomm almost visited the academy in 1837, and his oratorio *David* was the most frequently performed work at the academy in the late 1830s. Cleveland remained optimistic that the paradox of democratic music and authoritarian musical institutions could be reconciled.

Cleveland was not alone in his awareness of the political dilemma that an orchestra posed. Theodore Hach, in his *Musical Magazine,* confessed that music was still in its infancy in America, and that "our republican spirit, which revolts at any kind of personal restraint, can but ill brook the necessary discipline which the practice of the art requires of us."[81] Neither Cleveland nor Hach, however, provided specific recommendations on how to resolve the dilemma.

The same point about the paradox of a democratic society and elite musical institutions was echoed in the *Musical Cabinet,* edited by George J. Webb and T. B. Haywood. Webb was probably the most versatile musician in Boston in the 1830s and 1840s. Identified primarily with psalmody in the 1830s, as an organist, compiler of sacred anthologies, and professor at the academy, he made the transition to symphonic music in the 1840s, becoming the conductor of the Musical Fund Society's orchestra. Even earlier, however, Webb had not limited his activities to sacred music and was a founder of the Musical Professional Society in 1832. Little is known of Haywood, except that the was associated with Hach in editing the *Musical Magazine.*

The *Musical Cabinet* published an expanded version of a lecture Haywood delivered before the Teachers' Class of the Handel and Haydn Society in August 1841. In it Haywood conceded that the visual arts belonged to the elite: "Painting and sculpture are expensive in their individual encouragement." He considered music to be preeminently social and, in a country where the middle class comprised the bulk of the population, urged that music gain middle-class support. He opposed elitist institutions and identified the middle class with the people: "Her [music's] appeal, therefore, is to the people; not to the rich, nor to institutions got up and endowed with the aristocracy of wealth. If such institutions arise at all, they can only flourish in proportion as they are the people's institutions, in the same manner as our common government is the people's government."[82]

Haywood's structure of class varied considerably from Eliot's and Cleveland's. He identified the upper class with the aristocracy and the middle class with the people. At the same time, he clearly distinguished a middle class from other classes. Like Hach and Cleveland, however, Haywood had no program to secure the middle-class support he believed necessary.

Although Cleveland articulated most directly the paradox of democratic music and authoritarian musical institutions, he remained optimistic that the two could be reconciled. And even though he supported music for the people he remained elitist about taste. He and Eliot shared the same convictions about those issues, both being convinced that only an ignorance of the type of music that they preferred prevented its universal acceptance. Their viewpoint depended on the related beliefs that the art of music was progressive and that the people could be educated in that progress. Through education the people would come to prefer better music: "Once excite a general love of the art in all classes, and the standard of music will rapidly rise. In no art is taste more rapidly progressive."[83]

Eliot and Cleveland cannot be dismissed because of their seemingly naive position on the taste of the people. In his discussion of the symphony orchestra Cleveland pointed to one of the central paradoxes of the genre, and in his work at the academy Eliot did more than anyone else to establish the orchestra as a viable musical idiom in Boston. Rather than perpetrating his vision, however, Eliot's success had the opposite effect of laying the foundation for the orchestra's later elite status. Eliot's attempts to establish the orchestra as a popular or a national medium never succeeded, but Eliot did demonstrate that the symphony orchestra was a highly appropriate vehicle for the type of taste that he and others articulated.

The immediate result of Eliot's effort was its own undoing. The academy succeeded in creating an audience for symphonic concerts. It also succeeded in spawning rival orchestras. In the 1840s Boston erupted in secular instrumental concerts. New organizations of widely divergent character appeared. Some performed music of a more popular character and attracted an even greater audience. Others went toward a more restricted and elitist clientele. Eliot himself became embroiled in a dispute with one of these organizations, which involved not only control of Boston's instrumental resources but also fundamental questions about where such control should lie. The following chapters will trace these events and the new ideas and influences that appeared in New England around 1840.

Chapter Eight

Romanticism and Transcendentalism

By 1840 the view that there was a fundamental incompatibility between classical European music and American society had become widespread. The aristocratic basis of European music had not escaped American observers in the early nineteenth century, for music nurtured in the courts and cathedrals of Europe seemed out of place in the democratic society America was producing. And ideology aside, the very lack of institutions traditionally devoted to patronage prevented a musical culture based upon European models from flourishing. In spite of the best efforts of Eliot, Cleveland, and other members of the republican gentry, early attempts to emulate European practices were looked upon harshly, as unbefitting the new republic.

Members of the republican gentry were aware of the problem of aristocratic pretense from the early days of the republic. When a group of citizens in Boston founded the Tea Assembly, or Sans Souci Club, in the winter of 1784 and 1785, they touched off a heated controversy about the extent to which Americans should emulate European society. The Tea Assembly met every other week for dancing and card playing. There were twenty tables for cards, with the largest allowable bet being twenty-five cents. Each gentleman member was allowed to bring two ladies. Drinks, including coffee, tea, wine, and punch were available. Prior to that Boston had had an Assembly, which met fortnightly, for dancing only.[1]

The Tea Assembly aroused the ire of Samuel Adams in particular. He had long opposed pretension and flagrant displays of wealth, and during the time of the Revolution had hoped that Boston would become a "Christian Sparta." By 1778 he was concerned that a "spirit of avarice" had taken over, and by 1781 he was questioning "whether there is not more Parade among our Gentry than is consistent with sober republican Principles."[2] In 1780 he criticized a series of inaugural balls given by John Hancock, newly elected governor, claiming that the expensive entertainments tended to "dissipate the minds of the people." In 1785 he deplored that the citizens were "imitating the Britons in every idle amusement and expensive foppery which it is in their power to invent for the destruction of a young country."[3] Although Adams and others had reservations about gambling at the Tea Assembly, they were less disturbed by that and the dancing than by the social pretensions associated with the club. They condemned it because of its gentility and because its amusements were too British.[4]

According to a writer, probably Adams, in the *Massachusetts Centinel* who signed himself "Observer," the club represented effete refinement and dissipation, offering amusements designed "to lull and enervate these minds already too much softened, poisoned and contaminated by idle pleasures, and foolish gratifications. . . . We are prostituting all glory as a people, for new modes of pleasure, ruinous in their expenses, injurious to virtue, and totally detrimental to the well being of society."[5] Another writer, "Candidus," probably Benjamin Austin, declared the Tea Assembly "a very dangerous and destructive institution." While it might be suitable to "the long established Courts of Europe," if introduced in the *"infant states of America"* it would "be attended with the most fatal consequences."[6] On the other hand, defenders of the club, particularly Harrison Grey Otis, argued that its purpose was to refine taste. Europeans thought of Americans as crude and lacking in refinement; a club like the Tea Assembly, which was "regulated with propriety, governed by decency, and observant of the nicest and most scrupulous laws of delicacy, . . . bespeaks purity of mind and manners in the highest degree."[7]

Republican principles versus refinement of taste: these were the polar opposites in debates about the arts that would rage for more than a century. They were at the heart of the question about what type of music America should support. The phrase *refinement of taste* came to be used to justify cultural organizations that distanced one segment of society from another, although it had not always had overt elitist connotations. In the earlier part of the nineteenth century refinement of taste was a key objective for the democratizing reformers who were sincerely threatened by new directions in the society about them. They believed that through the elevation of the tastes of the masses society would be united.

John R. Parker and Samuel Eliot recognized that in America the roots of the Platonic or idealistic argument for music lay in sacred music. They also recognized that the ability of music to affect one's emotional and moral state was not limited to sacred music. By 1840 there was little disagreement over that point. Apparent contradictions began to surface, however, between the role that some segments of society wanted music to play and the structure of American society. Although music had the potential to shape citizens in a democracy, the very nature of democracy prevented this from happening: democracy meant individual choice; taste could never be imposed. Nor could anyone expect it to be uniform.

By the 1840s musical idealism had lost some of its appeal. The dream of a culturally monolithic society was fading into the political reality of new waves of immigration and stronger class divisions. As the pluralistic nature of American culture became more apparent, the belief that education would inculcate proper taste in everyone receded, and the dichotomy between an aristocratic musical structure and a democratic society appeared irreconcilable. With these changes, control of the secular musical life of Boston gravitated toward organizations that provided essentially entertainment. This development, however, created a reaction; the upper class retreated into their own cultural world and began to voice the idea of art music for the elite only. Prior to that the upper class of Boston had supported elitist cultural endeavors, such as the Athenaeum or the Massachusetts Historical Society, but their vision of culture had never included music. Eliot and a few others argued that music was very much part of high culture, but they had limited success. If music was to be a part of culture other than entertainment, another, stronger argument for the value of music was needed.

Just such an argument appeared in Boston at that time, finally making a convincing case for music as high culture in America. It viewed music as religious and equated the religious with the abstract: the more abstract a piece of music was, the more sacred, and hence the greater its artistic value. This argument elevated instrumental music, particularly symphonic music, to a position of preeminence. The argument emerged only gradually, a result of significant, concrete changes in musical activity and the synthesis of purely American influences with new intellectual trends from Europe. This chapter and the next trace the emergence of this argument, explore its many subtleties, and seek to explain not only how it came about but also why it was accepted. In this chapter I concentrate on its beginnings up to about 1840. In the next I examine how it evolved in the 1840s to become a predominant force in fundamentally reshaping musical attitudes.

This new argument, which favored abstract instrumental music, was the result of several uniquely American elements: Puritanism, the evangelical reforms, and the gentry concept of republicanism, combined with a new element from Europe, German romanticism. German romanticism is the final influence in the development of the duality that resulted from the appearance of an idealistic attitude toward sacred music in late eighteenth-century America. American musical thought absorbed German romanticism in two ways: directly from German writings about music, and filtered through American transcendentalism. The second of these was by far the more important, as we shall see. German romanticism worked its way into American musical thought so easily because it was so congruent with other intellectual strands; it embodied the same idealistic vision of music that the early hymnodic reformers had advocated, and it complemented the Puritan tradition and a burgeoning utopianism. Moreover, German romanticism was socially acceptable, because it found its strongest adherents in the Harvard-Unitarian axis, a group closely aligned with the socioeconomic elite.

It has become an axiom in American musical historiography to view the second half of the nineteenth century as a time in which German music and musicians dominated American musical activity in urban centers. This tendency is usually traced to the massive German immigration of the nineteenth century, and the positions of musical leadership several prominent German musicians held. The second point is not to be denied: at least two German immigrants, Gottlieb Graupner and H. Theodore Hach, had vital roles in the development of instrumental music in Boston. We have already discussed Graupner's contribution; we shall examine Hach's career later in this chapter. Yet in late eighteenth-century Boston, when the first theatrical orchestras were formed, more instrumental musicians were French and Italian than German.[8] The large influx of German immigrants who arrived in the nineteenth century in fact contributed little to the establishment of American musical values, particularly those pertaining to instrumental music. Simple chronology belies the argument that they did. The large waves of German immigration occurred later in the century, particularly after 1848, and by then the transcendental argument for music was worked out and propagated. In addition, German immigration into Boston remained insignificant, and it was in Boston that German romanticism had its strongest impact.

German immigrants formed a very small part of the community in Boston. Unlike some other areas, Boston did not have a large German population dating from the eighteenth century. According to estimates there were just fifteen hundred Germans in all of New England at the time of the revolutionary war. Between 1821 and 1845, only eleven hundred immigrants entered Boston from Germany. And many of these did not stay. From 1850 on, when statistics are more reliable, the number of Germans remaining in Boston was always considerably below the number of German immigrants arriving.[9]

By 1850 a sizeable but not overwhelming percentage of the musicians in Boston were German. The 1850 census was the first to record both the occupation and provenance of the population. Unfortunately the census grouped actors and musicians into one occupational category. According to the census, thirty-three of the 249 actors and musicians in Boston were German. Most of the thirty-three were probably musicians rather than actors, but even if all were musicians, Germans did not dominate the musical profession in Boston. The total number of actors and musicians was almost certainly higher than 249, and there were probably as many if not more musicians than actors in Boston; the city directory for 1850 lists seventy musicians and ninety-one teachers or professors of music, in addition to seventeen musical instrument dealers, twenty-three organ builders, and 181 in the piano trade, as maker, dealer, manufacturer, or tuner. The totals were certainly higher. We know that some musicians were listed in related occupations, such as teachers and musical instrument makers, while other professional musicians held other jobs totally beyond the world of music. We also know that city directories were notoriously incomplete.[10]

German romantic thought pertaining to music was introduced into Boston in large measure through H. Theodore Hach and John S. Dwight. Both became powerful shapers of opinion in the late 1830s and 1840s. Neither Hach nor Dwight, however, controlled musical events in the 1840s to the extent that Lowell Mason and then Samuel A. Eliot had in the late 1820s and 1830s. Hach never had that kind of authority. Dwight came close. Dwight's fame followed later, after the founding of his music journal in 1852, and throughout much of the 1840s he lived outside Boston at Brook Farm. Yet his writings in transcendental and other journals, his lectures, and his role in the establishment of the Harvard Musical Association made him a central figure in the changing musical world of Boston in the 1840s. At the time some of Dwight's ideas were considered revolutionary, a far cry from the ultra-conservative positions he held about many types of music later in the century.

Hach's principal influence came through his *Musical Magazine*, which he founded in 1839. He was also active as a cellist in the 1830s and 1840s, but not much is known about him. He was of German background, possibly from Lubeck.[11] We first hear of him in Boston in 1837, when the treasurer's books of both the Boston Academy of Music and the Handel and Haydn Society listed him as a member of each organization's orchestra. Hach may have been in Boston prior to 1837, however. He was in Europe in 1837 and apparently planned to tour Germany with Mason, who met him in Hamburg and was disappointed to discover that Hach had been forced to put off his tour. Mason's entry in his journal suggests that he already knew him.[12] Throughout the late 1830s and the 1840s Hach appeared regularly in the Handel and Haydn Society and Boston Academy of Music orchestras, but he was not a member of the Tremont Theatre Orchestra, at least not in 1840. His playing was sufficiently respected that he was the cellist for the Harvard Musical Association's first series of chamber music concerts in 1844. He also acted as spokesman for the performers in their contract negotiations regarding the series, according to a letter from Hach to R. E. Apthorp, the manager of the Harvard Musical Association's chamber-concert series in 1845.

Hach's principal contribution to American music was as a journalist. His *Musical Magazine* was the most sophisticated musical journal yet printed in America; Wunderlich called it "undoubtedly the most scholarly work of its kind during this period."[13] During the first year of its publication, 1839, Hach and Timothy Haywood edited it jointly; after that Haywood withdrew, and Hach edited it alone. The journal survived until April 1842, although the numbers for volume 3 appeared irregularly.

Hach was optimistic about founding a musical journal. He felt that the moment was propitious; he not only sensed a new burst of musical activity in Boston but also felt that music was finally beginning to be accorded its place as a moral and artistic force in America: "The present period is believed to be particularly auspicious for the establishment of a periodical devoted to Music. The public have become so far awake to the importance of its cultivation, that the authorities of the city of Boston have introduced it, as a branch of common education, into the public schools. Throughout the northern and middle States, Music, in its moral and social importance, is evidently fast arising in the public regard."[14] In the prospectus for his journal Hach outlined what he planned to cover. The list included the theory of music, instrumental music, vocal music, the history of music, biography and criticism, news from both North America and abroad, and "musical tales, anecdotes, etc." The journal itself covered instrumental music more than previous journals had, and Hach did not emphasize sacred music in either the prospectus or the journal, although it was occasionally discussed under vocal music.

The *Musical Magazine* was highly cosmopolitan, with a positivistic tone. Articles from many countries were reprinted. Earlier American musical magazines had drawn heavily on European journals, primarily British publications. With his German background, Hach drew more heavily upon Continental sources. Many translations of German and French articles appeared, and not all were limited to European music. One article described "The Music of Oceana," including the various types of Gamelans of Java and Bali, although it must be admitted that such exotic coverage was not unprecedented for an American journal. The magazine stands out for the absence of polemic. Hach attempted to educate the reader by presenting straightforward accounts of musicians, of musical concepts, such as a series of articles on the cadenza, or of genres, such as Haydn's and Mozart's masses. When Hach did review events or pieces he usually took a balanced, considered approach, even though his idealistic bias is apparent. The journal has a level of sophistication and modernity that we do not find in any other of the time. Few American musical magazines from the early nineteenth century can be read by a modern reader without a keen awareness of how dated they are. Hach elicits no such reaction.

Hach fully espoused a view of music as high art. In response to criticism that his standards were too high for the country, he defended his position by invoking an extreme musical idealism: "The art is infinite, and our conception of it will ever soar higher than our earthly means of representation will enable us to bring before the outward senses. It is the critic's office to grasp at the highest conception of what the art can accomplish; he must have art, pure art alone in view, as the ultimate object of what falls under his notice." At the same time, Hach recognized the need to be realistic. He admitted that the critic must "consider in each individual case the particular object aimed or professed," as well the "powers of conception or execution" of those performing.[15]

The *Musical Magazine* regularly ran lengthy articles about musical activity in Boston. From these it is clear that Hach was sympathetic to the goals of Eliot and the academy. He strongly favored instrumental music, and he distinguished music as an art from music as entertainment.[16] In a retrospective article in 1839, entitled "The Late Musical Season," he observed that compared to Europe there was much room for improvement "in the general taste for music, in the knowledge of it both as a science and as an art, and in the practice of it not only among amateurs, but also with professors." He also detected signs that "we are moving in that direction." These signs were the introduction of music into the public schools and the increased interest in instrumental music among amateurs.[17]

Hach's optimism had begun to fade by 1842. In the final issue, April 24, 1842, Hach announced with regret the end of the journal. His disappointment that the public was not ready to support such an enterprise was apparent: "A musical periodical, however much needed for the art, it seems is not yet wanted by the people, and we submit, after three years' perseverance in the unrequited labor." In the final review article, he reiterated many of his earlier positions but sounded decidedly more pessimistic. He allowed himself to comment more fully on the state of music in America as he saw it. Noting first that "we are as yet not a musical people," he compared the situation in America with that of Europe, particularly Germany, where music was revered and honored. He found many reasons for the lack of support for music in America: American institutions di not permit the concentrated patronage necessary for the art to flourish; the pace of life in America and American interest in success did not allow time for the pursuit of artistic activities. But most important were American prejudices. Hach attributed resistance to accepting music to the Puritan antipathy to frivolity. Music was still associated with levity and so was frowned upon: "Our prejudices too are still lingering against the art; they cannot yet fully divest themselves of the idea of levity as connected with it, or of considering music and religion as strangers, if not opposites—an idea inherited from our Puritan forefathers. At any rate, we but too generally consider time spent upon music as time taken from graver pursuits, and use it therefore with an economy fatal to any solid progress."[18]

Hach did not despair completely about the future of music in America. He saw Boston as the key: "There are hardly any efforts made anywhere else to gain a wider influence upon the state of music in the country." Hach admitted that music flourished "more or less" in some of the larger cities like New York, Philadelphia, and New Orleans, and even to an extent in Cincinnati. "Yet the public taste for, and appreciation of music in Boston can well compete with all the other places, with the exception perhaps of Philadelphia; and there is no place whose musical influence extends so far." Hach specifically singled out the Handel and Haydn Society and the Boston Academy of Music for their work. He commented on the academy's efforts to inculcate in the public an appreciation of instrumental music. To Hach this was the basis for the improvement of taste in America: "We hope the Academy will . . . succeed in implanting a taste for classical instrumental music into our public; for we consider this as absolutely necessary for our own progress in the art." As a final bittersweet point he argued that music literature and criticism had to flourish if a solid musical culture was to be built. He declared that none had existed prior to his journal, or what did was "worse than nothing," and now his own efforts were coming to an end. As a solution he suggested that the Boston Academy of Music start a journal.[19]

Hach was an ardent supporter of the academy throughout the life of his journal. He covered its activities in great detail and acted as head cheerleader for most of its efforts, reprinting Eliot's *North American Review* article on national music. But he was not beyond criticizing the academy when its performances were inadequate. In keeping with the European orientation of his magazine, he at one time urged it to model itself upon the Paris Conservatory.[20]

Hach's journal had been adumbrated by Parker's *Euterpeiad* but was more sophisticated: the focus was clearer, the criticism more direct and specific, and the articles chosen from European journals more advanced. It must be remembered, however, that Parker's journal appeared twenty years earlier than Hach's. In fact, Parker was ahead of his time. Although born in America, he had traveled in Europe and was familiar with its musical activity, at least in England. He was hampered by economic necessity, the limitations of the musical activity available to report, and the readers he had to satisfy. The two journals stand head and shoulders above all other musical journals begun before the 1840s, and in spite of the time span separating them, they are remarkably similar in tone, outlook, and orientation. Parker was one of the first to consider instrumental music in the context of Platonic idealism, although he stopped short of ascribing to it the moral values that writers of the 1840s did. He also recognized that instrumental music was the key to the acceptance of music as an art in America. He equated musical progress with the development of instrumental music, and he viewed sacred music as a means to that end. Parker's serious treatment of secular music supported Hach's contention that musical thought in Boston, particularly in regard to the moral potential of secular music, was far ahead of that of any other city in America.[21]

As we noted earlier in connection with Parker's *Euterpeiad*, three years was a relatively good run for a musical magazine in antebellum America. Hach's journal may have failed not because Bostonians were uninterested in music, as he believed, but because they displayed enough interest in it to encourge the founding of other journals. When Hach began his journal, the *Boston Musical Gazette* had recently folded, and the only other musical journal in Boston was the *Seraph*, a monthly publication of church music edited by Lowell Mason. By 1842, however, Hach had plenty of competition. The *American Journal of Music* appeared in 1840, and the *Musical Almanac*, the *Musical Cabinet*, and the *Musical Reporter* in 1841. In contrast to this veritable outbreak of journals, not a single magazine devoted to music other than the *Boston Musical Gazette* and the *Seraph* appeared in Boston between the demise of Parker's *Euterpeiad* in 1823 and the founding of Hach's journal in 1839.

Hach presented German romanticism directly from Germany. Dwight, who ultimately had a more pervasive and protracted influence upon musical developments in Boston, delivered a German romanticism refracted through the prism of New England transcendentalism. Dwight and Mason are often paired as two of the foremost shapers of American musical attitudes in the nineteenth century, and many aspects of their careers are similar. Dwight played the clarinet in his youth but did not give serious consideration to a career in music until late in life. He was deeply interested in religion, enough to become a Congregational minister. He had a strong affinity to the music of the classical masters, and believed in taste, science, and restraint. There, however, the similarities end. The son of a physician, Dwight was a Unitarian. His commitment to organized religion never had the evangelical passion that Mason's did. Mason's religious commitment came abruptly, through a sudden conversion. The closest that Dwight ever came to a conversion experience was when he first heard the symphonies of Beethoven. Dwight's religious beliefs, as well as his musical preferences, were more abstract and universal than Mason's. To Mason, music was a means to an end, that end being the service of evangelical religion. To Dwight, music was religion itself.

Mason and Dwight differed dramatically in personality. Mason was dynamic, energetic, forceful, and practical; Dwight was withdrawn, diffident, and almost prelapsarian in his naïveté. Mason remained very much a populist in his attitudes toward music and the people. For a time Dwight held utterly unrealistic utopian ideals about social class, but throughout his life he aligned himself with the upper class and generally held a relatively narrow elitist point of view about music. In fact he had closer connections with the socioeconomic elite in Boston than any other participant in music, except Eliot.

Dwight, twenty-one years younger than Mason, graduated from Harvard College in 1832 and Harvard Divinity School in 1836. While at

Harvard he played in the Arionic and the Pierian Sodalities. He apparently did not play well enough to be admitted into the Pierian Sodality until his junior year, and he was never a leader in the group. Surprisingly, Dwight remained under the influence of the Presbyterian-Congregational reformers throughout the 1830s. Both an early essay and his divinity dissertation, "On the Proper Character of Poetry and Music for Public Worship," dealt with sacred music, and both were influenced by Mason.

The essay is a thirty-three-page manuscript entitled "Second Annual Report of the Boston Academy of Music . . . Manual of the Boston Academy of Music. . . ." It was never published in its original form, but portions of it were later published in the *American Monthly Magazine* under the title "Sacred Music."[22] The essay almost certainly preceded his divinity dissertation; parts of it seem to be a trial run for the dissertation. As the title implies, it began as a review of the second annual report of the academy and Mason's *Manual of the Boston Academy of Music*. In the first part of the essay, Dwight discussed the place of music in American society. He contrasted music as the language of feeling with words as the language of thought. Even at this stage in his intellectual development, he conceptualized music as a universal, abstract, mystical morality tale. Music occupied realms of thought that language could not penetrate. Man's deepest feelings could be contacted only by music. That "mysterious part of our nature, which binds us to one another, to the beauty of the world, to God and to an hereafter, require a different language from that [of] common sense or intellect," a language supplied by music.

In discussing the oratorio as the highest type of devotional music, Dwight ascribed a moral function even to the harmony: "By its combination of harmony, expressive of commingling emotions; or the introduction of occasional discords, struggling with and at last absorbed in the harmony—(fit image of the triumph of virtue);—the mind may be filled with a sense of all that is sublime in the material or moral universe." Concerned that there was no authority for conscience other than prudence, Dwight thought that music, as the "least exclusive" of the fine arts, could benefit the nation as a whole "by familiarizing men with the beautiful and the infinite. These influences so real, but indescribable, upon a nation's mind should be cherished; because they excite common feeling, create common associations, and unite individuals in common sympathies founded on things eternal; they destroy much of that inherent selfishness in minds wholly bent on business or politics, and giving no thought to the beautiful and the perfect. Music expresses these feelings, and by expressing develops and diffuses them."[23]

Both Mason and Dwight believed that music had a Platonic ethos. It was capable of creating a proper atmosphere, which was fundamentally important in a church service. Mason frequently compared church hymnody with prayer. Each had the same end, to create a devotional spirit, and each was capable of doing so. Mason felt that his contribution to the church service, choosing the music and overseeing the performance, was as important to establishing the spirit of worship as that of the minister in prayer. Yet Mason's vision of the service differed from Dwight's in two fundamental respects. First, Mason believed in the importance of the text and felt that music in church should be subordinate to the text. Second, Mason considered congregational participation of paramount importance. The purpose of hymnody was to unite the collective body in a spirit of praise or prayer. Participation thus superseded musical results.

Mason always judged music by its devotional quality and accessibility. Purely secular music may have interested him intrinsically but (other than glees) never interested him professionally. And even his secular glees had a moral or didactic purpose. Music was always the servant of a religious end. To Dwight, music was an end in itself even at this early stage. The proper type of music performed properly was itself an act of worship. When Dwight discussed the words to be sung in a church service, he was more interested in their sound than their meaning. The message was in the music, not the text. Dwight believed that the words should be poetry and should be suggestive rather than explicit. Protestant hymnody, which repeated several verses to one tune, failed to create a proper spiritual effect. Better to have an often repeated, familiar text like the Catholic Mass. Music should be "the inexhaustible commentator upon the simple words in which are wrapped up infinite feelings and infinite imaginings."[24] Dwight envisioned a church service in which the music, as the central feature, led the worshiper into the realm of the religious, which to Dwight was infinite, indefinable in words.

Dwight attempted to put this theory into practice in the 1840s while at Brook Farm, the transcendentalists' experiment with communal living. It was founded by George Ripley in 1841 and survived until 1848. Dwight became a member in the fall of 1841, and from 1844 until it folded he was an active spokesman for it. He was in charge of music for the services and frequently used parts of the Catholic Mass. He was criticized for this in an article in the *American Review* in May 1847, to which he replied in the *Harbinger* on June 19, 1847. He defended his use of Catholic music on the grounds that it was good music, his only criterion. The music was that of Mozart and Haydn, not the Roman Catholic church. Dwight did not stop there, however. In an important extension, he went on to argue the catholicity of music itself. He claimed that "music is more catholic than all the churches,—the faithful, many-sided servant of the human heart; and whatsoever is good music is a harmony and help to what is most religious, loving, and profound in human souls, whether it was born on Catholic or heretic or even on a heathen soul." According to Dwight, the sacred music of Handel and Mozart, and by implication the music of the classical masters in general, belongs to humanity because music is a universal language; "it knows nothing of opinions, creeds, and doctrines that divide. It knows only the heart of the whole matter, which is one." Dwight believed that the only hope of creating a truly catholic, universal church lay in music.[25]

Dwight absorbed the spirit of romanticism from German literature as well as from German music. His interest in German literature went back to his undergraduate days at Harvard, when he began to study German. In the late 1830s he published several translations of German authors, for which he received considerable acclaim. His first translation, of Schiller's "Ode to Joy," appeared in 1835. His most substantial work was *Select Minor Poems, Translated from the German of Goethe and Schiller*, published in 1839. This was the only complete book ever published under Dwight's name alone. It was commissioned by George Ripley—the founding spirit of the Brook Farm experiment—as part of a series of foreign translations. Ripley's series of translations is considered by some the most important literary work of the Brook Farm transcendentalists.[26]

Dwight's translation of Goethe's and Shiller's poems was dedicated to Thomas Carlyle, who, after examining the work, responded enthusiastically: "With great pleasure I recognize in you the merit, the rarest of all in Goethe's translators, yet the first condition, without which every other merit is impossible, that of understanding your original. . . . I have heard from no English writer whatever as much truth as you write in these notes about Goethe. . . . Your songs seem to me to be the best, far better than one has seen hitherto, than one could have expected to see."[27]

Dwight's volume received a greater response in the American press than such a book would suggest. Reviews appeared in the *Western Messenger*, the *North American Review*, the *Boston Quarterly Review*, the *Christian Examiner*, and the *New York Review*. All of the reviews were favorable, although the *New York Review* found a few of the Goethe translations "very stiff." Some of the reviewers did not know quite what to make of the book, an indication of just how unfamiliar German literature was at the time.[28] More recent critics have also praised Dwight's volume. Walter Fertig claimed that "to this day no set of more satisfactory translations from German lyrics has been produced."[29] In his *Critical Bibliography of German Literature in English Translation*, Bayard Quincy Morgan awarded Dwight a double asterisk, his highest rating, which means "unusually high quality." Lucretia Van Tuyl Simmons claimed that "from the point of view of workmanship and choice of poems, it is far better than anything that had preceded it and most of the attempts which followed it."[30]

Dwight's success seemed to justify his radical theory of poetry, which he explained in the introduction. Even in such a double verbal idiom—translating poetry from one language to another—Dwight sought to transcend language. He looked to Zelter's musical settings of Goethe's songs to find the proper spirit of the poems. For their essence was to be found in music: "The verbal form seemed to defy translation; but being held some time in solution in this subtler element of music, it shaped itself again in his [Dwight's] own language more readily."[31]

The importance that Dwight attached to music may explain why he did not pursue a literary career, which all signs pointed to at this stage in his life. When he was an undergraduate his reputation as a poet was greater than his reputation as a musician. In his senior year he lectured on poetry to the Northborough Lyceum and the Harvard Union. He was chosen class poet, and was honored by having a poem, consisting of thirty Spenserian stanzas, read at graduation.[32] In the 1830s he published several critical reviews of literature, including the first review of Tennyson to appear in America. He had much more extensive contacts with literary figures than with musicians, and was on intimate terms with members of the transcendental movement. Ironically, his two closest friends in the movement were Ralph Waldo Emerson and Theodore Parker, who were known to be at best indifferent and at times antagonistic to music. Emerson helped Dwight considerably in his early career. When Emerson moved from his pulpit at East Lexington, he recommended that Dwight succeed him. He supplied Dwight with the poems of Tennyson, from which Dwight wrote his review. He gave Dwight a letter of introduction to Carlyle. Dwight was invited to attend the "Symposia" at Emerson's in 1836, a nucleus group of transcendentalists. Later Dwight became a member of the Saturday Club. Dwight had attended Harvard with Parker, and in 1837 they exchanged lengthy letters in which each described frankly and in detail the faults and shortcomings of the other.

Dwight made no secret of his interest in music during this time. Between college and divinity school he worked for a year as a tutor for a family in Meadeville, Pennsylvania. Frederick Huidekoper, for whose tutelage Dwight was hired, remembered him as gentle, somewhat lacking in an aptitude for teaching, but with "an admiration for Shakespeare and a strong desire for playing upon the piano."[33] Parishioners in Dwight's first temporary pulpit in East Lexington described him in 1837 as "all music," someone who improvised constantly upon the piano, although they also noted his keen interest in German.[34]

In spite of his ideas about church music and his interest in German romanticism, Dwight remained within the Mason-Webb axis as late as 1838. He was on the editorial board of the *Boston Musical Gazette* along with Mason and Webb. The *Boston Musical Gazette*, founded by Bartholomew Brown, embraced the hymnodic reformers' point of view and was dominated by Mason. One early article compared older sacred composers like Tallis, Ravenscroft, Madan, and Tansur with American-born composers like Read and Billings, and concluded that the music of late eighteenth-century American composers was deficient because it lacked the proper devotional character. The article also acknowledged the greatness of Haydn, Mozart, and Handel but asserted that their music was unsuitable for church because it was more in the style of theater music. The author advocated that tunes intended for divine service be "sweet, flowing, and easy; free from all hard and unnatural skips, intricate melodies, fanciful modulations, and difficult harmonies."

This article, signed "L.," was probably written by Lowell Mason. It reflects his thought precisely: it conforms with Mason's populist approach to the melodic style of church music and represents Mason's views about Handel, Mozart, and Haydn; it also demonstrates Mason's ability to recognize merit regardless of its source. The author admitted that some earlier American music was good, and specifically listed "Jordan" and "Brookfield" by Billings, "Windham" by Read, "Archdale" by Law, and "Coronation" by Holden.

The hand of Lowell Mason is evident elsewhere in this journal. The struggle to get music accepted into the public schools received extensive coverage, including a transcript of the Boston School Committee's report. An article by Mason's brother Timothy, who was a leader in church music in Cincinnati, was published in it. The article is a somewhat vague polemic about the moral value of music and the benefits of having music in the schools, stressing the importance of the enjoyment of music and what music can do to improve the child's attitude toward school.[35]

So far as we know, Dwight wrote only one article for the *Boston Musical Gazette*, "Music, as a Branch of Popular Education." In it he argued that every child should be instructed in the rudiments of music, a sentiment that Mason certainly shared. Dwight's rationale was based upon his general conception of the ability of music to communicate feelings that can be communicated in no other way. Dwight was less interested in sacred vocal music than in the music of the classical masters. He compared Handel, Mozart, and Beethoven to Socrates, Shakespeare, and Newton, feeling that each had something to say to every man, without which "no man can be quite a man."[36]

Dwight's and Mason's differing views of Handel, Haydn, and Mozart symbolize the differences in their concepts of music. Dwight worshiped these composers, along with Beethoven, throughout his life. For Dwight the sacralization of their music was complete. Mason greatly admired their music but was nevertheless troubled by some of it. His most detailed discussion of this problem occurred in the preface to the *Lyra Sacra*, published in 1832. Mason expressed his reservations about the *Messiah*: it required too large an ensemble; it was too difficult for both performers and audiences; it was essentially a theatrical piece, designed for display; it was first performed in a theater, and there is no reason to believe that Handel ever associated it with worship. Mason did later come to admire the *Messiah*. On his first English trip he heard it twice and spoke of its sublimity and expressive power. Mason nevertheless judged the *Messiah* as church music. Whether performed in church or not, he considered the subject sacred, and hence the music religious. Mason felt that religious music should be simple, devotional, and lacking in emotional excess, and he opposed most of all religious music that was theatrical. He walked out of Mendelssohn's *St. Paul* oratorio when he heard it in Birmingham, England, because it was too theatrical.

Dwight interpreted music within the context of the universal and infinite, and he discussed the *Messiah* within that framework. Like Mason's, Dwight's interpretation rested upon the text, but its reasons for doing so were very different from Mason's. The text of the *Messiah* was central to Dwight's conceptualization because of its universality. Dwight considered its theme, "humanity's anticipation of its *Messiah*," the only suitable text for an oratorio. He found the words of the *Messiah* "almost the only words we know, which do not limit the free, world-permeating, ever-shifting, Protean genius of music." As a consequence, the subject matter of the *Messiah* "properly is the one theme of all pure music." From that Dwight connected the *Messiah* with the infinite, the realm in which music resided: "Music is the aspiration, the yearnings of the heart to the Infinite. It is the prayer of faith, which has no fear, no weakness in it. It delivers us from our actual bondage; it buoys us up above our accidents, and wafts us on waves of melody to the heart's ideal home."[37]

After 1838 the careers of Mason and Dwight diverged. Mason's *Lyra Sacra* was published in 1832, just as antebellum evangelicalism peaked.[38] Between then and 1838 Mason was at his busiest. After 1838 his reputation continued to grow nationwide, through his teacher institutes and many publications, but his influence in Boston was already waning. At this time Dwight began to find his own voice, and Mason's influence on his work diminished. Dwight directed his literary efforts into magazines more suitable to his philosophy, and with the appearance in Boston of music more congenial to his orientation, he became much more active in music. His leadership in the founding of the Harvard Musical Association, his writings for the *Dial* and the *Harbinger*, his work at Brook Farm, and his lectures both in Boston and New York began to attract attention. The musical atmosphere in Boston changed dramatically in the ten years between Dwight's graduation from Harvard and his 1841 address to the Harvard Musical Association. In the succeeding ten years it underwent even more dramatic changes, and Dwight, as we will see, had much to do with those changes.

In the 1840s Mason, Eliot, and Dwight began to follow radically different trajectories. The three had been curiously intertwined in the 1830s: Mason and Eliot through the Boston Academy of Music, Mason and Dwight through their writings on church music and their involvement with the *Boston Musical Gazette*, and Dwight and Eliot through their Unitarian-inspired idealistic vision of music. Dwight's distancing from Mason was not at all surprising, given the fundamental philosophical and religious differences between the two. Yet by 1840 the transcendental influence began to lead Dwight away from Eliot also. Dwight's evolvement was typical of transcendentalism: most of the transcendentalists had been trained at Harvard, and several, including Cranch, Dwight, and Emerson, had begun as Unitarian ministers. Dwight's and Cranch's reasons for leaving the ministry had more to do with their unsuitable personalities than theological or moral qualms, but Emerson's departure was directly and consciously a rebellion again Unitarianism. His resignation was precipitated by his inability to reconcile his own beliefs with his sacramental duties as a minister. He could not accept the ministerial role in the administration of the Last Supper. The actual event was of course only the symbolic manifestation of a broader doubt that called into question church doctrine and ritual.

Transcendentalism was more a revolt against Unitarianism than a phase of it. Transcendentalism was, in the words of Perry Miller, "a protest of the human spirit against emotional starvation."[39] The transcendentalists' spiritual guru, Andrews Norton, professor of theology at Harvard, whom Miller called the "Unitarian Pope," castigated the transcendentalists as infidels when he became aware of their leanings. This was a strong statement for someone whose religion taught rationality, consideration, and tolerance. Transcendentalism was not, however, another theological dispute characteristic of New England. The very rationalism of Unitarianism, the foundation upon which it rested, emphasized the importance of the human spirit but left little place for the yearning, soul-hungry, emotional, unconscious, restless side of man. Transcendentalism sought to address that side, and found its deliverance in the arts. Most transcendentalists turned to literature, not surprising in a culture that valued literature so much more highly than any other artistic form. Their principal literary source was unusual, however; they looked to Germany, and there they discovered romanticism and a new brand of idealism. American transcendentalists were well versed in English romanticism, but New England transcendentalism had a strong German accent.[40]

German romanticism emphasized the abstract and the infinite in the spiritual side of man. It thus led easily into the more ephemeral arts, such as lyric poetry, the visual arts, and music, arts that, except for poetry, had never taken hold in New England. Dwight's discovery of German literature while at Harvard was one of the pivotal events of his life, and his beliefs in the universal, the infinite, and the abstract grew directly out of his encounters with German literature and philosophy. Dwight did not fully articulate these ideas until he began writing in transcendental journals in the 1840s, but his 1840 discussion of Handel's *Messiah* demonstrates that they were already in place by the end of the 1830s.

Yet we cannot dismiss the importance of New England Puritanism on Dwight and other transcendental writers; they were, in the words of Harold Clarke Goddard, *"Puritans to the core."* William Clebsch traced an intellectual lineage directly from Jonathan Edwards through Samuel Hopkins and William Ellery Channing to Ralph Waldo Emerson.[41] The transcendental yearing for the spiritual side of man had deep roots in American Puritanism, and although German romanticism provided the shape that transcendentalism took, the revolt against Unitarianism looked back to an emotional absence that had been felt ever since Unitarianism had demolished the terror of unalloyed Calvinism. For all its intellectual rigor, Puritanism had held society together by plunging directly to the deepest and starkest emotions of man. Edwards himself recognized the emotionalism, even mysticism that was the essence of his own spirituality. The Puritan diet may have been acrid, but the emotional side of man did not starve.

The transcendental revolt sought to recover some of the spiritual immediacy and mysticism found in Edwards. No longer fettered by Calvinistic theology, the transcendentalists could seek the spiritual in the broadest terms, in the infinite, and in relation to humanity. Elizabeth Peabody articulated the transcendental position in her attempt to define the term *aesthetic*. She held that art is an "expression of the infinite by means of the beautiful," which occurs in two stages. In its first state it is "national and religious . . . confined in its range but exalted." In its second state it is set free from these limitations, confined only by the bounds of true art, "a second expression of the infinite by the beautiful, in which the beauty and satisfactoriness of the expression balances the less deep significance of the idea."[42]

Although Eliot and Dwight were both products of Unitarianism, Dwight's espousal of transcendentalism led him to follow a decidedly different path from Eliot's. This was not entirely apparent in the 1830s, partly because Dwight's own course was not clear, although hints of it surface. In the 1840s, as we shall see in the next chapter, Dwight's views on music came to resemble closely the general aesthetic position that Peabody articulated. In fact, when Peabody assembled the first (and only) issue of *Aesthetic Papers*, where her general statement appeared, she asked Dwight to elaborate specifically on music. And as Dwight pursued his transcendental vision, his and Eliot's perceptions on the place of music in society diverged considerably.

Curiously, Eliot, Mason, and Dwight were united on an important issue in the 1830s: they all believed that music in America should reach the masses, and that by doing so music was capable of shaping American society. This was of course one of the principal themes of Eliot, probably the motivating force behind his dedication to the cause of music. And although Mason's populism led him into directions different from Eliot's, this same belief was as fundamental to his vision as it was to

Eliot's. Dwight is not normally associated with populist attitudes about music, and indeed in the 1840s he retreated to an out-and-out elitist position. In the 1830s, however, he voiced some of the same principles about the potential place of music in American society that Eliot and Mason did. In his article on "Music as a Branch of Popular Education," Dwight directly asked: "Why may not Music become a popular influence among us?" He responded, in gender-specific language, that all men were musical, and that music could "perform an office for man that no other of the arts can." Dwight's own concept of acceptable music was clearly circumscribed; he advocated that all men be introduced early to Handel, Mozart, and Beethoven. His explanation of the benefits to society were also less specific than Eliot's. Dwight summarized it in the cryptic remark that without Handel, Mozart, and Beethoven, "no man can be quite a man."[43]

Eliot and Mason were both reformers. Mason's goal was specific: he wished to promote evangelical religion. Eliot's goal was more general: he believed American society could be politically transformed through the values fostered by disseminating the proper kind of music. Dwight appears to be a reformer at this time, but, as that final statement above illustrates, his goals are so vague that the term *reformer* has little application. Yet Eliot, Mason, and Dwight were indeed strange bedfellows in the 1830s: all believed in the power of music to move and hence convince; all believed in taste and progress in music; and all believed that through education the taste of the masses, of the average ordinary person, could be raised. In the 1840s, the differences, particularly between Dwight, the transcendental-romantic, and Eliot, the Unitarian-Republican, became more apparent, as each translated further his beliefs into action. Led by these two advocates, secular musical activity exploded in Boston, with reverberations still felt today.

Chapter Nine

Developments of the 1840s: Retraction

By the 1840s Eliot's vision of secular music as high art was firmly in place. It had developed among those idealists who saw in it a way to unite American society. They believed that, through wide exposure, art music would overcome all other types of music and impress on the population at large a common, morally uplifting culture. The only remaining question was to what ends this vision might be put. Who was to share it, and for what purpose? One of the great ironies of American musical culture is that art music came to be used for precisely the opposite purpose: it became a means to separate members of the upper classes from the others. Later in the century the notion of high art would spread to the middle classes in the image of gentility and take on a hollow and pretentious quality. But in 1840 that point was still relatively far off.

The republican vision of using music as a unifying element in society was based on the assumption that Americans had not developed a taste in music. Members of the republican gentry repeatedly said that there was no musical art in America. They were nevertheless buoyed by their staunch beliefs in the moral value of certain kinds of music and the ability of the people to respond positively. Those members of the gentry, such as Eliot and Cleveland, who actively supported music assumed that once the populace had had an opportunity to become familiar with good music they would prefer it.

Events of the 1840s shattered that belief. Cultural homogeneity had been a dubious goal from the start, and by the end of the 1840s American music was more highly polarized than it had ever been. At one end of the spectrum an unabashadly high culture had formed, with the symphony orchestra and in some places opera as its showcase. At the other end popular entertainments like the minstrel show, which made no pretense to gentility, garnered immense public support. In between, festivals and jubilees began to carve a middle ground; often featuring popular singers like Henry Russell, they were early public manifestations of the nineteenth-century genteel tradition, a musical culture that became ubiquitous in American homes in the later part of the century.

Although with hindsight we can see the polarization between high and low culture forming in 1840, it would have been extremely difficult for anyone living then to spot it. By and large the distinctions did not exist. They became evident, however, even to many of the participants, when the concert activities of the Boston Academy of Music were challenged on two fronts in the early 1840s. In October 1843 a group of young musical amateurs formed the Boston Philharmonic Society. (Like the earlier Philoharmonic Society, this was not connected with the later Boston Symphony Orchestra.) And in 1844 the Harvard Musical Association began sponsoring concerts in Boston. The two organizations were utterly different from each other. The new Philharmonic Society had a more popular orientation than either the academy or the Harvard Musical Association. Its programs featured lighter, more accessible music than that offered by the academy, and in the first years the orchestra was essentially a brass band. It catered to a broad general population. The Harvard Musical Association sponsored refined and elitist chamber-music concerts, featuring string quartets, and purposely sought a select audience.

The academy thus found itself threatened from two directions. On the one hand, the popular orientation of the Philharmonic Society cut deeply into the academy's audience. Its success directly challenged Eliot's belief about the musical preferences of the average man or woman. On the other hand, the Harvard Musical Association presented music of an unquestionably high quality, but with elitist trappings that mocked the republican spirit of Eliot and other members of the older gentry. The association's concerts were conceived directly and purposely as a retraction or retreat by members of the upper class, who no longer believed in the presentation of music of a high quality to the population at large.

Eliot's immediate response was to the Philharmonic Society. Here the threat was tangible; it was economic as well as philosophical. The Philharmonic was formed purely as a concert organization, and its founders were probably inspired by the success of the academy. The Boston Academy of Music was caught in a bind: it needed the support of the public while trying to change the public to its tastes. The sponsors of the Boston Philharmonic Society were not hampered by this function. They could meet the public on its own terms. Although the records of the society have not survived, its sponsors clearly had in mind a type of musical presentation closer to that of the academy than, for instance, minstrel shows or folk-style singers. At the same time there is little to indicate that they were motivated by issues of taste, idealism, or any sort of grand vision beyond providing Boston with "good musical en-tertainments," as the *Daily Transcript* reported.[1] The record of the con-certs bears that out.

The Philharmonic Society's concerts featured a large orchestra of be-tween thirty and more than forty musicians. During its first year the orchestra was led by James J. Kendall. His brother, Edward Kendall was featured on the bugle. The presence of the Kendall brothers, who were well known in Boston as band leaders, suggests that the orchestra was more a band than a symphonic ensemble. Three years later, when the *Harbinger* looked back on that season, it confirmed that "what they called an orchestra was only a wind-band, principally of brass instru-ments, which by turns brayed out noisy overtures, or murdered un-meaning solos."[2]

The *Harbinger* faulted everything about the concert. The musicians did not play well, the choice of music was poor, and the hall, the largest in town, was not well suited for concerts. Even the audience was criticized, for being essentially unmusical. The *Harbinger* noted with disgust: "The impression was so sickening to whatever soul of music we had in us, that we have not been able to overcome the associations of the place enough to enter it again, until the late festival of Henri Herz."[3]

The *Harbinger*'s assessment must be viewed with skepticism. It was written by John S. Dwight, who was not known to be sympathetic toward popular idioms. But other contemporary accounts confirm Dwight's assessment. The *Daily Transcript* observed that "it has never been argued in favor of the Society that it has improved the musical taste of the community." The same reviewer was heartened to learn that "it will be in the power of this Society next winter, through some new arrangements, . . . to produce a variety of superior music."[4]

Nevertheless, the Boston Philharmonic Society drew large crowds, as even the *Daily Transcript* was forced to acknowledge. The society's programs were of a lighter and more popular character than the acad-emy's, featuring arias and overtures from bel canto operas, especially those of Rossini and Bellini. The society actively sought to engage touring virtuosi like Vieuxtemps. Equally important was the ticket price of fifty cents for the concerts. One dollar had been the standard price for tickets to similar concerts in Boston since the eighteenth century.

All of this displeased Eliot. Matters came to a head in 1844 when the society replaced James Kendall with Leopold Herwig as leader of the orchestra. That event was probably the *Transcript*'s basis for alluding to "new arrangements" for the coming season. By 1844 Herwig had become one of the most important musicians in Boston. He had been introduced to Boston audiences through a small private violin concert in 1841. Word of his abilities spread so quickly that when he followed the private performance with a public concert at the Melodeon a few weeks later, hundreds were turned away. The *Transcript* called it the "most brilliant affair ever given in this city."[5] Herwig began teaching music in Boston and appeared with the Boston Academy of Music. In 1843 he was appointed leader of the orchestra of the Handel and Haydn Society. In 1844 he played first violin in the string quartet at the Harvard Musical Association's chamber concerts. Although he died suddenly on November 3, 1845, his brief involvement with the Philharmonic Society was a source of consternation to Eliot.

Eliot's papers contain a copy of a lengthy letter that has neither addressee nor date but was almost certainly written by Eliot to Herwig in 1844, a date the letter fixes by mentioning the 1835 opening of the Odeon nine years earlier. The letter refers to attempts of another organization to form a substantial orchestra. The Philharmonic Society hired Herwig to do precisely that, and no other organization was making a similar attempt. Later the Philharmonic Society and the Boston Academy reached a tacit agreement to alternate their concerts so that dates would not conflict, a principal issue in the letter.

In the letter Eliot rejected an earlier proposal, probably by Herwig, that the Boston Academy of Music and the Philharmonic Society share members of the orchestra and cooperate on sponsoring concerts. Eliot objected partly out of pique at a new organization arriving to reap the benefits after the sacrifices made by his organization. In 1840 the academy had staked its future on the presentation of orchestral concerts even though historically such concerts had failed in Boston. The academy had mounted an all-out campaign to win the Boston public over to orchestral music, and by 1844 it appeared to have succeeded. In the letter Eliot acknowledged that the decision of the academy to sponsor orchestral concerts had been risky: "It is well known that the enterprise of getting up instrumental concerts in this city was a bold one at the time when it was commenced, involving considerable labor and expense at the imminent risk of not being repaid for either." Eliot's indignation that the Philharmonic Society should challenge the academy for the audience that the academy had carefully cultivated is clear: "It is now precisely the time when having with much perseverance brought the public taste to appreciate and *require* such performances, a *new society* starts up to enter a field where competition cannot be useful, and indeed can only be mutually destructive." Eliot particularly resented the indirect subsidy that, in his eyes, the academy provided to the Philharmonic Society:

But suppose both go on, cannot the same musicians play for both? There is this pretty serious objection in the minds of the members of the Academy. The probability is that very much the same music would be performed by both societies, as was the case in several instances last winter, and the benefit of rehearsals for which the Academy had exclusively paid would redound to the advantages of another society who have done nothing more than the Academy has done to promote the growth of a public taste for music, and who, under present circumstances at least, can do no more than we can do. There seems to be no reason why we should be so liberal to a society that does not seem likely to favor us much.

Eliot's objections were also practical. Eliot realized that Boston had neither sufficient instrumentalists nor audience to support two rival organizations. "If there were a sufficient number of competent musicians in the city to form two good orchestras, the Academy would most cheerfully meet any competition that might then be really useful to all parties increasing the pay of the performers, and the industry of the societies. But under present circumstances it seems clear that only one such association can exist, and if the friends of the Academy are drawn away, they must stop giving concerts altogether." In that Eliot proved right, as attendance, especially at the academy concerts, went down considerably.

Although not stated in the letter itself, Eliot's displeasure with the Philharmonic Society went beyond questions of precedence and finance. The society differed from the Boston Academy of Music in both composition and philosophy. Not only was it oriented toward popular entertainment, but its government was more open than the academy's. This must have been particularly irritating to Eliot. While he believed strongly in the spread of high culture to the masses, he also believed that the elite should control cultural organizations. Describing the academy in the *North American Review*, Eliot took pride in its governance. He found the constitution of the academy ideal because "the financial and prudential concerns of the society are in one set of hands, and the musical department in another." An organization built on such a separation of powers served the public far better than one in which the musicians themselves ran things. Eliot implied that "desire for attainment in art," "the wish to gain temporary popularity," and "pecuniary advantages" would surely conflict if the musicians themselves had more control.[6]

The officers and directors of the Philharmonic Society included members of the elite, members of the middle class, and musicians. S. Abbott Lawrence was one of the $100 contributors to the refurbishing of the Odeon. Oliver Brewster was a wealthy merchant and also an officer in the Harvard Musical Association. J. F. Marsh was proprietor of the *Daily Bee.* Joseph L. Bates was a musical instrument dealer, and George P. Reed owned a music store. Musicians included Edward Riddle, who was a member of the Tremont Theatre's orchestra, and James Parker, who gave up a law career to pursue music professionally.[7] In 1850 the *Daily Transcript* praised the members of the society for their unselfish efforts: "The Philharmonic Society is composed almost entirely of amateurs, whose simple object is the procurement of good musical entertainments. . . . The only profit or gain, which any member has ever received from the most successful season, has been a free ticket to the concerts; and during *one* season, each member was assessed $1.50, to make up a loss."[8]

In the long run the differences between the Philharmonic Society and the Boston Academy of Music in the musical content of their programs turned out to be relatively superficial. During the 1840s the Philharmonic Society itself was evolving. The efforts to hire Leopold Herwig in 1844 were part of its general trend to improve the quality of its concerts. They were apparently successful. After 1843 the society's programs became more demanding, and the orchestra improved dramatically in both size and quality. By 1845 it consisted of more than forty instruments, with a substantial string section. The *Daily Transcript* reported its composition as follows:

7 first violins	2 clarinets
7 second violins	2 bassoons
2 tenors	4 horns
2 violoncellos	2 trumpets
3 double basses	3 trombones
2 flutes	1 pair timpani
2 oboes	1 triangle

Even by twentieth-century standards this is a respectable orchestral ensemble. The only noticeable weakness is a shortage of violas and cellos.

Reviewers began to notice the better playing and programming. In 1846 the *Harbinger*, acknowledging that the Philharmonic Society had previously catered to a markedly popular taste, detected signs of improvement. The selection of music was better, although the society had not yet attempted symphonies. Its instrumentation was beginning to resemble that of an orchestra. The replacement of Herwig by Henry Schmidt boded well for the future of the ensemble. Schmidt had been the conductor of the Boston Academy of Music's orchestra through 1842, providing critical musical leadership in its pioneering orchestral concerts in 1841 and 1842. When describing those concerts for the *Dial*, J. F. Tuckerman had called Schmidt a "musician of rare taste and steady growth."

Why Schmidt left the academy is not known. His departure certainly had an adverse effect on its orchestra. He was succeeded as leader by William Keyser, who had made a successful debut in Boston as a violin soloist with the academy's orchestra on March 26, 1842. His abilities as a player were recognized, but he was too self-effacing to command the orchestra. He believed that an orchestra should be run democratically and tried to be one of the players rather than the leader set apart. Writers like Cleveland and Hach had begun to realize that a successful orchestra was a despotic, not a democratic, organization, and Keyser's failure with the academy's orchestra only confirmed that.[9]

In January 1847 a review in the *Harbinger* compared the Philharmonic Society's orchestra with that of the academy. The review called the Philharmonic's orchestra one of the best ever heard in Boston. It displayed "unity and beauty as of many made one." The academy's orchestra on the other hand, exhibited "uncertainty and blur and noise and disproportion."[10] Since the two orchestras shared most of the same players, this did not reflect well on the musical leadership of the academy.

By 1845 the Philharmonic Society had doubled the number of concerts it had given in the first season, from four to eight, and programmed a total of sixteen overtures. The concerts continued to attract large audiences. Yet their principal draw was not the orchestra but the soloists. This was graphically demonstrated to the society when, on January 16, 1846, it experimented with a concert that engaged no "foreign stars." Attendance suffered noticeably. It was the only concert of the year that did not enjoy an almost full house. The society did not repeat the experiment.[11]

The Philharmonic Society benefited from its experience with soloists. It reduced the number of concerts that it gave each season and began to program large special concerts, each of which featured several prominent artists. Called festivals, they proved extremely popular.[12] One given on January 30, 1847, featuring Edward L. Walker, the Seguins, and Frazer, drew an audience of twenty-six hundred.[13] These concerts prepared the way for the "monster" concerts of Patrick S. Gilmore and the Strauss festival later in the century. Monster concerts reached their zenith in Boston when Johann Strauss was invited to direct a series of fourteen concerts in 1872, in a special hall designed to seat sixty thousand people. One thousand instrumentalists were reportedly at his disposal, and twenty thousand singers were recruited to sing "The Blue Danube" waltz.[14]

The success of the Philharmonic Society's concerts forced the older advocates of higher-quality music to reconsider one of their fundamental premises: the role of taste in the public's musical preferences. By 1840 the idea of taste had become central in the debate about the nature of music in American society. This was apparent in Eliot's writings, as we saw in the last chapter. Taste began to take on a broader meaning. The specifically religious underpinning that the Presbyterian-Congregational hymnists had given it were loosened, although powerful puritan overtones remained. When stripped of its formal religious connections, however, taste was difficult to define. Yet the very ambiguity of the concept made it useful to a variety of writers with different positions.

Possibly because of the success of the Philharmonic concerts, possibly because of other changes beginning in the 1840s, a defensive note crept into the discourse of writers who believed in the educability of the common man. The change was prompted by questions of taste. A fear began to surface that less tasteful, more vulgar music of the kind the Philharmonic Society produced, or worse, might be preferred by the public. It is detectable in Eliot's 1844 annual report of the Boston Academy of Music.[15]

In the report, Eliot spoke laudably but uneasily of the accomplishments of the past year. Part of the problem was economic. The concerts of the academy were still not breaking even. Eliot praised the audience for its confidence in the academy and its "perception of the superiority of the kind of music presented to them over what they had formerly been accustomed to hear," but at the same time he was not entirely happy about the size of the audience, which he characterized as "a little larger than that of the previous season."[16] Because attendance was less than anticipated, the academy ran a deficit of $948.98 on its concerts. This was an improvemment over previous years, but still below expectations.

Eliot's discomfort was deeper than the immediate financial situation. Although he remained optimistic about the status of music in America,

Developments of the 1840s

doubts had begun to creep in, for the first time. As a result Eliot sounded defensive, his rhetoric shrill. He spoke of the natural capacity of the American people for music and reasserted his belief that in America, as in other countries, "the taste for music, when once cultivated, grows broader and deeper by time, and that no fluctuation of fashion or feeling ever leaves it to be neglected or disregarded."[17] But he did not sound entirely convinced: "Why should we doubt that it will be equally so here? Can we go backwards? Would any one consent for instance to return to the inferior style of church music to which we were formerly accustomed, after having learnt to appreciate the better performances now? Does any one relish the untutored ballad singer, after becoming familiar with the skill of a Caradori, or a Malibran? or prefer the natural music of an African minstrel to the finished performance of a Vieux-temps?"[18]

Eliot was forced to acknowledge that the answer to these questions might be yes. As a consequence he had to reevaluate his positions regarding the acceptability of all types of music and the certainty that better music would be preferred by all who were exposed to it. He continued to adhere steadfastly to the concept of progress in music, but he had to reconcile that with the disturbing tendencies he was beginning to notice. Some listeners were more advanced than others. Eliot's earlier tolerance of those that did not prefer better music was beginning to be strained:

So if, with us, there are crowds who go to hear a rustic ballad, or a solo on the bugle, and hear them with delight, and prefer them to Cinti's singing and Artæt's playing, this is not to be attributed to a want of musical perceptions, but to the absence of cultivation. The natural power is in the audience, but they have not yet learned to distinguish the good from the bad; and with the general preference of untutored persons for strong and decided sensations, they choose the boisterous rather than the delicate. The earliest taste for music is for that which is rough and noisy. But as surely as the desire for any music exists, it will be indulged; and indulgence is practice, and practice is cultivation; and those who began with the ballad will end with the cavatina, and the symphony and the violin will take the place of the military air and the post horn.[19]

Implicit in this statement is a hierarchy of musical taste, a fundamentally elitist concept, but Eliot had not lost confidence that, given enough exposure to art music, audiences would by preference move up the hierarchy. He believed that a significant percentage of the population had already begun to move up the hierarchy, and he detected an increasing momentum for others to follow. And he expressed confidence that there would be no backsliding: "If there be truth in the views just expressed, there is little danger that it will ever diminish again." In an obvious reference to the Philharmonic Society, Eliot threatened: "There is no danger for our being superseded by any who will undertake to provide only an inferior kind of music. Whoever will eclipse the Academy must furnish a high style either of composition, or execution, or of both."[20]

In spite of Eliot's optimism, one cannot help noticing a degree of wishful thinking and a quiet desperation in his comments. They no longer bear the sense of confidence in American society evident in his earlier articles. They reveal a man seeking to buttress his belief in his rightness in the face of gnawing doubts about the course that he has taken.

Eliot's change in position represents a shift toward an attitude that became more prevalent throughout the 1840s. What Eliot had only adumbrated and was struggling vainly to resist, the concept of high art for the privileged few, was advocated openly in the writings of the Harvard axis and articulated explicitly in the activities of the Harvard Musical Association. As such the Harvard Musical Association presented a threat to the Boston Academy of Music that was very different from that posed by the Boston Philharmonic Society. Ultimately it was the Harvard Musical Association's approach to classical music that prevailed in Boston. The association formed a vital link between the 1830s and 1840s, when the role of music in American society was still very much undecided, and later times, when certain types of music had acquired all the trappings and overtones of high culture.

Although the Harvard Musical Association formally dissociated itself from Harvard University in the 1840s, its roots lay deep in the Cambridge institution. Secular music at Harvard can be traced in detail only from 1808, as prior musical activity had focused almost entirely on sacred music. A singing club, for instance, existed from 1786 to 1803, but the account books of the treasurer indicate that the students mainly sang psalmody: most of the books purchased were collections of psalmody, and money was spent for a bass viol, the standard psalmodic accompanying instrument.

The Harvard Musical Association was a direct outgrowth of the Pierian Sodality. Yet the relationship between the two organizations has been curiously distorted in much of the literature about the association. One incident in particular, a critical moment in Pierian history, has drawn considerable attention and is worth revisiting, mainly for what it reveals about the attitudes of the chroniclers of the Pierian Sodality themselves. John S. Dwight, Walter Spalding, and Samuel Jennison all recount a time in 1832 when the Pierian Sodality was reduced briefly to a single member, Henry Gassett, who nevertheless maintained the traditional Thursday-evening rehearsal schedule.[21] According to Jennison, Gassett dutifully posted the requisite announcement of the meeting as the by-laws prescribed "called himself to order," and then faithfully practiced alone on the flute for the allotted time.[22]

The incident is almost certainly fabrication. It is true that Gassett was the only returning Pierian at the beginning of the 1832 fall term, all the others having graduated, and while the records of the society between 1821 and 1832 are lost, a manuscript book of its laws does refer to such an event. The book was compiled at least thirty years later, however. A membership roll printed in 1840 lists eight members graduating in 1832, including Dwight. Gassett was the only 1833 graduate of the society. His name thus appears alone on the membership list, and the Pierian Sodality could not draw on the membership of the Arionic Sodality because it probably no longer existed. The secretary's book of minutes for the Arionic Sodality ended abruptly on June 10, 1831. Blank pages remain in the book, and there is no explanation for the termination, which suggests that the society atrophied rather than dis-solved. Yet by September 25, 1832, when the secretary's records of the Pierian Sodality resume, Gassett had recruited two sophomores. Since graduation Day was on August 29 and the fall semester began in September, Gassett could have met alone, but only very briefly.

The minutes of the society suggest that not even this happened, however. The minutes of July 2, 1833, reflect on the condition of the society in the fall of 1833, and its subsequent growth: "There is quite a contrast between the present flourishing condition of the Pierians and the appearance only a short-year since, when but three individuals wended their way in sadness and silence, to the room appropriated to their use, where they sat brooding over their prospects gloomily, but in *despair*. . . . The Pierians cannot be too grateful to their excellent and skillful President; to whose exertions they are indebted for their very *existence* as a society, since he *alone*, of the former members, was left in the Sodality, at the departure of the Seniors, last commencement. The prospects of the Society are constantly brightening, and are now better than ever." Were Gassett as fastidious as Dwight, Spaldings, and Jennison suggest, surely he would have entered a record of his solitary meetings in the minutes. At the very least the secretary's recollections of July 2, 1833, which discuss the very time the alleged incident occurred, would refer to such an event. Nowhere do the minutes of the Pierian Sodality contain any mention of Gassett ever having met by himself.

If this alleged incident never occurred, why then did the principal chroniclers of the early history of the Pierian Sodality all discuss it? True or not, it fitted perfectly with the image of the Pierians that Dwight, Jennison, and Spalding wished to convey, and within that context it was entirely plausible. They directly connected the Pierian Sodality to the Boston Symphony Orchestra via the Harvard Musical Association.[23] As a consequence, the Pierian Sodality has acquired a status as the birthplace of high musical culture in Boston, and the activities of early Pierians have assumed the dimensions of myth. Thus Spaldings referred to the incident as a time when "the Pierian spring all but ran dry," after which "the spring flowed once more." Gassett was, in Spalding's words, the Pierians' "musical Horatius."[24] According to Jennison, Gassett "kept the sacred flame alive."

The story itself has a legendary quality, and these accounts ascribe to Gassett a responsibility he probably never even imagined. There is no question that the Pierian Sodality meant much to Gassett, as it did to many others who later looked back on their undergraduate years with fond memories of their activities in the organization. That the members considered their activities within the framework of a sacred trust is, however, pure fantasy, contradicted by their own accounts. Furthermore, the Pierian Sodality was neither the direct ancestor of the Boston Symphony Orchestra nor the progenitor of music as high art in Boston. The Harvard Musical Association did spring from the Pierian Sodality, but by the time that it began to assume the mantle of high culture, it had severed its ties not only with the Pierians but also with Harvard itself. And the Harvard Musical Association is related to the Boston Symphony Orchestra only by chronology. The orchestra of the Harvard Musical Association did precede that of the Boston Symphony Orchestra, but when the Boston Symphony was formed in 1882, the Harvard Musical Association was already in its "deathbed struggles," being locked in mortal combat with the Philharmonic Orchestra, which had been formed in 1879 as a spin-off of the Harvard Musical Association's orchestra.[25]

The actual birth of the Harvard Musical Association is itself well documented. In July 1837 three alumni and former members of the Pierian Sodality, John S. Dwight, Henry Gassett, and Henry Pickering, suggested to the Pierians that a "General Meeting of Past and Present Members of the Pierian Sodality" be held on graduation day, August 30. A committee was formed to prepare for the meeting, and was charged with, among other things, determining the purpose of the new group. It worked independently of the Pierians as a whole, and on August 28 met with the immediate members and explained the objectives to be presented at the forthcoming general meeting. Dwight was the spokesman. He was the motivating force behind the idea of forming a new group and wrote the document that was ultimately presented.[26] The undergraduates were more interested in the question of refreshments than the stated objectives; the Pierian minutes for the preliminary meeting on August 28 and the grand meeting on August 30 are silent on objectives but discuss refreshments in great detail. In this matter Dwight was astute. He presented a petition with the signatures of fifteen honorary members pledging financial support for the expenses (like the cost of refreshments) of the general meeting at the same time as he explained his purposes; this virtually guaranteed a favorable reception for his document.

Dwight's document, which became the blueprint for the establishment of the Harvard Musical Association, contained two specific proposals regarding musical activity at Harvard: that musical instruction be offered at Harvard College, eventually with a professorship, and that a musical library be established.[27] Behind these proposals was a broader goal, that Harvard assume leadership in demonstrating the importance of music as an art and as an area of learning. Dwight specifically wished "to raise the standard of musical taste" and to encourage "respectability and seriousness" for the Pierian Sodality and, by extension, for music. He wished to encourage "academic concerts in a pure style." To Dwight the creation of a music library symbolized the recognition that the music of the great masters was literature, that Handel and Beethoven were to be equated with Homer, Plato, Newton, and Shakespeare. "A Sonata should be worth as much as an Oration, a Hymn or a Sacred Voluntary as a Sermon or a Prayer."[28]

These sentiments reveal both Dwight's idealism and his elitism. His references to music in a pure style and his equation of a pantheon of composers with a pantheon of authors reflects a conception of music as high culture. His concern with respectability, musical taste, and the cultivation of music suggests a setting in which musical activity is geared to those who have met the necessary and social and educational conditions.

Dwight also recommended that a permanent organization of members and alumni of the Pierian Sodality be formed, to meet annually on Commencement Day, "if for nothing more, at least to exchange salutations, and revive recollections, and feel the common bond of music and old scenes." This recommendation was adopted and the organization was named the General Association of Members of the Pierian Sodality of Harvard University.

In 1840 the organization changed its name to the Harvard Musical Association and voted to exclude undergraduates. This was the first in a series of actions that weakened its connection to the Pierian Sodality and to Harvard. It next voted to admit some members who had not been Pierians and to sponsor public events like lectures and concerts. The musical library was formed and was housed on Tremont Row in Boston rather than in Cambridge. At first the lectures were held on Commencement Day, but when the association decided to sponsor chamber-music concerts in the mid-1840s, they were held in Boston. Finally, in 1847, the Harvard Musical Association decided to hold its annual meeting in Boston rather than Cambridge, thus breaking the final tie to Harvard.

The Harvard Musical Association turned its back on Harvard partly because Harvard snubbed it. The association's petition to establish musical instruction at Harvard met with stony silence. After receiving no reply, it suggested that the faculty submit the petition to the Harvard Corporation for consideration. Even that suggestion was rejected. It was not until 1856 that instruction in music was officially listed in the catalogue, not until 1863 that the first formal university courses in music were given, and not until 1875 that John Knowles Paine was appointed to the first professorship in music.[29]

The hostility of the Harvard faculty toward music extended over several years. In 1832 the Pierian Sodality first proposed that courses in music be added to the curriculum. The Pierian president, John W. Gorham, discussed this with Harvard's president, Josiah Quincy, who responded favorably. The faculty, however, rejected the idea, on the grounds of expense.[30] The unwillingness of the faculty to support music was confirmed at Exhibition Day on October 16, 1832. When the Pierian Sodality declined to play because they had only three members, Quincy hired the Boston Brigade Band. According to the Pierian minutes, Quincy was forced to pay for the band out of his own pocket because the faculty refused to authorize the expense. The relationship between the Harvard faculty and musical organizations reached a nadir in 1843 when the Pierians were publicly admonished and forbidden to play in the college yard because the members had stayed out all night. In retaliation the Pierians voted not to perform at the coming exhibition, so that "when the Praeses proclaims 'Musica expectatur' either a dead silence may prevail or the audience be charmed with the strains from the damned old organ."[31]

The increasing gap between the Pierians' and the association's concepts of music also may have contributed to the separation between the Harvard Musical Association and Harvard University. After 1840 the Pierian Sodality continued as it had been, an institution devoted to the enjoyment of music, for fun and amusement. In 1843 its instrumentation consisted of one first flute, two second flutes, one third flute, two trombones, and an ophicleide, or serpent. In 1845 it played the following music at exhibition: "Quickstep," "Love Not," "Quickstep," "Jolly Raftsman," "Pot Pourri (*Norma*)," "Worozo Waltzes," "Baden Baden Polka," and "Aurora Waltzes." In the diverging musical world of the 1840s this repertoire represented an entirely different approach from that advocated by the Harvard Musical Association, which was launching a series of string-quartet concerts in Boston. The Pierian Sodality remained a wind band, devoted to light, entertaining music.

The Harvard Musical Association, on the other hand, was advocating, with typical New England evangelical vigor, the ideal of music as a fine art. In doing so, it pursued activities that further defined the nature of music and the type of music presented to the Boston public. In the 1840s the association sponsored two types of events that substantially influenced the future of music in Boston: a series of annual lectures, and a series of chamber-music concerts.

Both the lectures and the chamber-music concerts served to define further the idealistic vision of music that had emerged in the 1830s. That vision, which considered secular instrumental music a fine art rather than an amusement, distinguished the 1830s and beyond from the earlier part of the century. Precedent for the vision may be found earlier, particularly in the writings of Parker in the *Euterpeiad* around 1820, but its full articulation and implementation in successful public concerts did not occur until well into the 1840s. The Harvard Musical Association would radically alter the idealistic vision, but when it began offering lectures in 1840 the direction that the association would take in regard to instrumental music was not yet clear. It still had close ties both to

Harvard and to the Pierian Sodality, whose members continued to pursue music for pleasure and amusement.

The lectures predate the chamber-music concerts by four years. Henry R. Cleveland gave the first annual in 1840. Cleveland was a graduate of Harvard, an attorney, a respected organist, and a writer and translator in several fields. He had published articles on music in *New England Magazine* and the *New York Review*.[32] Although in frial health throughout his life, he traveled extensively, which allowed him to become familiar with European music. His Harvard Musical Association lecture was delivered on Commencement Day at the Cambridge campus. According to the Reverend Dr. John Pierce, who attended, it drew a "small but select audience." Pierce was convinced that attendance would have been greater had there been more advance notice and a larger room. As it was, he was favorably impressed and in his diary accurately summarized some of Cleveland's principal points.[33]

Cleveland's address occupies a middle ground between earlier notions of music as entertainment and later conceptualizations of music as a moral force.[34] Cleveland discussed the time when individuals became aware of "music as an *art*" in contrast to enjoying the pleasures of it. He found that for many this happened in their college days, and that for members of the Pierian Sodality it frequently occurred as part of their activities within the society: "For here it was that many of us first learned the true love of the art; here music was first awakened in our own souls; not recognized merely as a voice from abroad, but as a part and portion of ourselves—a sense—a power of utterance—a living spirit born within us."[35]

Yet Cleveland still spoke within the framework of music as pleasure. The awakening of music in one's soul referred to the discovery of the pleasures of musical performance. He rhetorically asked the Pierian graduates, "Who does not think with pleasure . . . of his gradually increasing power to produce tones which approximated to the musical? of the joy of that moment when with much ado, and many an appoggiature which came in unbidden and undesired, he first succeeded in playing through a real, finished tune?"[36]

Cleveland's position differed from the later sacralized view of music more in emphasis than definition. But his emphasis is important. To Cleveland art meant the power to move one profoundly; it meant the capacity to engender deeply felt emotions. He was aware of the moral dimension of art, recognizing tht true art has a dignity and a "high moral power." It has, he said, the capacity "to elevate the mind and confer a purity and loftiness of sentiment."[37] But while art can be a moral and elevating force, it need not be. It can also provide pleasure. That it affects one emotionally is more important than how it affects one. That it engenders emotions is more important than what emotions it engenders.

Cleveland considered the study of music comparable to the study of literature. Techniques are similiar: the student should become familiar with the works of the great creators and should learn to recognize different styles. He argued that music and poetry have similar forms, as do opera and drama. Even instrumental genres like the sonata have their poetic analogues. Music is a universal language, presenting a "variety and richness of character" that surpasses that of literature of any single language.[38]

Cleveland's address contained much of the rhetoric of later nineteenth-century high culture; he referred to classical music, music as literature, music as art, and the ability of music to elevate and purify. Yet there is a broad-mindedness to Cleveland's conception of music that differentiates it from later concepts of art music. The divisiveness of later propagandists is not apparent here. Cleveland delighted in the pure joy of music making, even when it was tied to no overriding moral end. He was willing to acknowledge the artistic merit of genres and styles that later writers would disparage. Calling the waltz "the most captivating form which music can assume," he placed it on the same level as the oratorio, the opera, the sonata, the odes of Horace, and the sonnets of Petrarch and Shakespeare.[39]

Cleveland did not approve of all music. He disparaged "those performers who descend to the popular taste, low as it is, and amuse the crowd by the most trashy and vapid compilations that ever bore the name of music." He also disparaged the brilliant performances of the great foreign opera singers. Yet he treated the popular singer and the opera singer differently in his criticism. His dislike of the former was based on taste, of the latter on politics. As a representative of the republican gentry viewpoint, Cleveland firmly believed that all members of American society would develop the same love of music and the same discriminating taste that he had, were they only educated to music. He pleaded that even the poorest children be given this education. His Pierian experience led him to argue that presenting concerts and operas did little for a popular taste; they appealed only to the wealthy. He believed that children must be taught to perform; "the people must grow up musical."[40]

Cleveland had voiced similar sentiments in his article on national music in the *North American Review* discussed in the previous chapter. There Cleveland had been even more optimistic than he was in his lecture that music as art would be accepted by the people at large. But in the lecture he added an important element: beneath the "noisy, dusty, rattling shell of Yankee life," a keenness and sensitivity for music existed, fostered and sustained by Americans' love of oratory.[41] Cleveland's linking of music with literature was not an empty analogy. It was at the heart of his image of the future of music in America.

By connecting music and oratory, Cleveland linked his concept of music directly with the Puritan tradition, because rhetoric more than any other art had flourished in Puritan America. Rhetoric was endemic to the Puritan religious experience, touching all classes. It had sustained the early republic when political divisions inflamed passions as they characteristically could only in revolutionary times. It had taken on a new life and a new shape with evangelicalism, and had its secular counterparts in the patriotic celebrations that remained central to many towns and citieis throughout much of the nineteenth century. In 1840 rhetoric was still at the very core of New England life.[42]

Like Eliot, Cleveland firmly believed in progress. There is a retrospective dimension, however, in his concept of musical progress. He considered the time of Haydn, Mozart, and Beethoven the period in which music reached perfection, and the present, still basking in the glow of these masters, a golden age in music. Yet he doubted that their accomplishments would even be equaled, and a decline was inevitable. Indeed, Cleveland sensed that it had already begun: "Even now, perhaps, the symptoms of decline in the art, may be discerned. Handel and Mozart and Haydn and Beethoven are gone; and, though their halo still hovers arounds us, we know that it must finally depart."[43]

Cleveland's attitudes about music were very close to Eliot's. Superficially they were both similar to Dwight's, but beneath the surface lay a fundamental difference, which may be seen in one of Dwight's most important early contributions, a review of musical activities in Boston during the winter season of 1839 to 1840. This appeared in the *Dial*, then a new transcendental journal edited by Margaret Fuller.[44] Dwight agreed with Eliot that while much progress had been made recently on behalf of music in Boston, much more needed to be done. Dwight did not share Eliot's optimism, however: "We cannot flatter ourselves for a moment that we of Boston are, or shall be for years to come, a musical people."[45] Later Eliot would be forced to admit that point, but in 1840 he had not reached such a conclusion.

Part of the difference in perception between Eliot and Dwight may be attributed to their very different personalities. Eliot was a man of action, a shrewd manager of money and an astute politician. He felt at home in Boston. Dwight on the other hand was a dreamy, other-worldly individual wrapped up in music. He did not feel comfortable with the materialistic, enterprising, practical, Yankee personality that typified Boston. He sensed that type's disapproval: "The devoted lover of the art is only beginning to be countenanced and recognized as one better than an idler. He must still keep apologizing to his incredulous, practical neighbors for the heavenly influence which haunts him. He does not live in a genial atmosphere of music, but in the cold east wind of utility; and meets few who will acknowledge that what he loves has anything to do with life."[46]

A larger part of Eliot's and Dwight's different assessments of the future of music in Boston lay in their beliefs. Eliot's attitudes were mainstream Unitarian, and nowhere does Eliot wear his Unitarianism more obviously than in his staunch belief in progress. As we have seen, belief in progress was almost universal in the early nineteenth century, but it reached its apogee and was developed further than anywhere else in Unitarianism. At the heart of progress were the concepts of rational man and the essential goodness of man, which would lead him to a better, more livable society. The essentially good, rational man was the core idea behind the Unitarian rebellion against the foreordained, depraved man of Calvinism.

Dwight, however, did not despair completely of the future of music in Boston. As a transcendentalist he looked to the inner man, and found hope in the association of music and religion. The religious sentiment in the people of Boston demonstrated "a restlessness, which craves more than the actual affords, an aspiration and yearning of the heart for communion, which cannot take place through words and thoughts, but only through some subtler medium, like music."[47] Dwight's twin beliefs in the universality of religion and of music were the cornerstone of his aesthetic.

Dwight made the connection between music and religion explicit in his comparative description of Handel, Haydn, and Beethoven. Haydn's music is "the perfection of art," a Grecian temple. It "stands complete in itself and fully executed, and suggests no more." A work of Handel's or Beethoven's is "a Gothic cathedral, which seems never finished, but becoming, growing, yearning and striving upwards, the beginning only of a boundless plan, whose consummation is in another world."[48]

Dwight recognized that, even though unarticulated aspirations might exist among the people of Boston, the development of musical sensibilities had to be cultivated. He was, however, ambivalent about some recent efforts in that direction, particularly Lowell Mason's work. He acknowledged that the teaching of the rudiments of music in the public schools was a good thing, and that it might create an interest in oratorios and concerts, but the entire educational process as it was practiced occurred without "much consciousness . . . of the higher meaning of music." In like manner he differed with Eliot about the value of popular music in society: "The Psalmody of the country choir and the dancing master's fiddle, the waltzes and variations of the music-shop, Russell's songs, and 'Jim Crow,' and 'Harrison's Melodies,' are not apt to visit the popular mind with the deep emotions of true music."[49] While Eliot, Cleveland, and other members of the older gentry recognized the difference between popular, or vulgar, and true art, they saw the value of popular and folk art for those whose tastes were not, in their opinion, sufficiently refined. With Dwight a true duality emerged: popular art was different, not a stepping-stone to higher things.

Dwight elaborated on his purist vision of music in his 1841 Harvard Musical Association address.[50] This address is an important statement in the development of American music for two reasons: it was one of Dwight's most complete statements about his concept of the nature of music, and in it Dwight clearly and unequivocally explicated a sacralized musical culture. In it the difference between Dwight's and both the Presbyterian-Congregational reformers' and the republican gentry's viewpoints is even more apparent than in his earlier writings.

Dwight had little time to prepare his address, as he was not the intended speaker. He was not even the designated replacement. The association had originally selected G. B. Emerson as the speaker, followed by Rev. Henry Ware after Emerson declined. George L. Hillard was chosen to be Ware's substitute. For some reason none of these speakers was able to appear. Dwight himself admitted that his thoughts were put together at the eleventh hour, and that he was speaking from the heart. Possibly for this reason his address has a directness, completeness, and clarity that contrasts with his often elliptical, opaque prose.

Dwight's explicit purpose was "to show the dignity of music, as an art, and to establish the power, so often claimed for it, of elevating the feelings and ennobling social life." He despaired that music was generally not recognized as an art in America. For Dwight the distinction between music as an art and music as an amusement was much more categorical than it was for Eliot or Cleveland, or even Mason. Dwight admitted that music used for amusement could serve "to while away an idle hour, to refresh a weary mind, or extract the sting of sorrow." Nevertheless, in a manner reminiscent of the eighteenth-century Puritans, he rejected music meant to be entertaining or amusing. Such music was indulgence. It "belongs to the ornamental, not the indispensable." It "represents a wandering away from the earnest business of life, and not acquaintance with a higher life." It "cannot enrich, ennoble, purify and perfect the powers and sensibilities of man." It has "the weakness of the flesh."[51]

Most of Dwight's address was an exploration of the distinction between sacred and secular music. He discussed the two types at length, partly because his definitions were themselves radical, and partly because they had even more radical implications. Dwight believed that the prevailing distinctions between sacred and secular music accounted for the lack of appreciation of music as an art in America. Secular music was identified with the trivial or profane and was considered amusement or recreation. Sacred music was limited to a monotonous and dull form of church music whose worth was based on associations rather than intrinsic merit. "Thus is Music clipped at both ends; secular and sacred run away in opposite directions, each with its half, and Art is left a minus quantity in the middle. That is to say; the music of the church, in its dread of the secular spirit, grows lifeless, dull and cold; the music of the parlor and the street, in its dread of solemn dullness, grows altogether trivial and gay; while true music, conceived in the exalted sense of art, is tolerated in neither place, since it falls under neither head."[52]

Dwight then proceeded to redefine sacred music. He first reiterated an opinion he had expressed since the mid-1830s, that music was a language in itself, with a meaning of its own. He defined sacred music as "elevating, purifying, love and faith-inspiring." Absolute instrumental music represented the highest type of sacred music, because it existed purely on its own terms, uncorrupted by language. In Dwight's view absolute music was superior to music that imitated nature or specific events, like *The Battle of Prague*, Neukomm's fantasia representing a storm on a lake (that is, program music), or even vocal music like Haydn's *Creation*. To Dwight the more abstract a piece was, the more sacred. He thus considered practically all instrumental music of the great masters sacred, more so than much of the music sung in church: are not some of the adagio movements of Beethoven's instrumental music "almost the very essence of prayer?—not formal prayer, I grant, but earnest, deep, un-speakable aspiration? Is not his music pervaded by such prayer?"[53] Dwight then drew on a common religious metaphor, the sense of awe one feels on a starry night. Beethoven's music evoked the same sense of awe to him.

Dwight thus provided a definition of instrumental music that placed it in a realm it had never before occupied in American culture. He did it within a context that was readily understood in the early nineteenth century, the distinction between the sacred and secular. He adopted the Presbyterian-Congregational reformers' rhetoric about the dignity inherent in sacred music but then subverted their position regarding the relationship between music and text by identifying the sacred with the abstract. In doing so he transformed their ideas into a new doctrine that was closely aligned with romanticism, which from the time of E. T. A. Hoffmann had elevated abstract instrumental music to a position of preeminence within the arts. Dwight thus extended the gentry's views about art far beyond their intentions, both by his reverential treatment of abstract instrumental music, and by sarcastic rejection of the very foundation of the gentry's aesthetic judgment, taste. To him ornamental music "occupies a place in neither of the recognized departments of Labor, of Learning, or of Wisdom; but is consigned, with little ceremony, to that uncertain limbo, never accurately surveyed, where men run to and fro irresponsible, called Taste."[54]

Dwight's devotion to the abstract concept of art, his sincerity, his enthusiasm, and fervent appreciation of secular instrumental music added another voice to the chorus of recognition that was beginning to build in America, that some types of music have a worth beyond mere amusement. But Dwight did more than give a new status to instrumental music or connect Puritanism with German romanticism. While be built on the ideas of both the Presbyterian-Congregational reformers and the republican gentry, he did not simply redefine sacred music, placing certain instrumental music within its sphere. Dwight conceived of all music as sacred: "I hazard the assertion, that *music is all sacred*; that music in its essence, in its purity, when it flows from the genuine fount of art in the composer's soul, when it is the inspiration of his genius, and not a manufactured imitation, when it comes unforced, unbidden from the heart, is a divine minister of the wants of the soul. . . . To me music stands for the highest outward symbol of what is most deep and holy, and most remotely to be realized in the soul of man. It is a sort of Holy Writ; a prophecy of what life is to be; the language of our presentiments; the rainbow of promise translated out of seeing into hearing."[55]

With the articulation of this argument, the split between music as art and music as entertainment became irreconcilable. The implications of Dwight's definition are profound: if music is sacred by nature, then whatever does not aspire to the pure and the abstract, and therefore does not enrich and ennoble, is not simply different; it is a corruption of the holy art itself. By definition it is not music and thus not worthy of consideration. It must not be tolerated, because it represents a threat to the very concept of music.

Dwight was not overtly elitist when he delivered this lecture, but his ideas lead in that direction. If music is considered a sacred object, then respect for its sanctity precludes tolerance of frivolous or entertaining musical activity. The canon must be enhanced and intensified, a worshipful atmosphere evoked, and the superiority of certain types of music stressed. Music that does not fit the canon can only be vulgar at best, with the implication that those who listen to such music are also. Little concession is made to the audience. Although in the 1840s Dwight was very much under the sway of the Brook Farm experiment with its philosophy of utopian socialism, there is little of the social reformist element in his vision of music. His views were, however, entirely consistent with his transcendental orientation, which emphasized the abstract, spiritual quality of art.

The next Harvard Musical Association lecture was given by William W. Story in 1842.[56] Story was an 1838 graduate of Harvard and had been a member of the Pierian Sodality, although he had not held office. He was not on the committee that recommended the founding of the Harvard Musical Association, but he was active as a Pierian at the time. Dwight's idealism is evident in Story's lecture, which also confirms that the symphonic experiment of the Boston Academy of Music was beginning to bear fruit. Story's lecture, however, did not share the transcendental proclivity for the infinite and abstract.

Story concentrated on Beethoven for most of the lecture, in part because Beethoven was becoming known. For that he credited orchestral concerts of the academy, which on March 26, 1841, had presented the first Boston performance of the Fifth Symphony. Story was extremely moved by this event. In ornate rhetoric he provided a highly romantic and detailed program for the symphony: he referred to it as "the work of his [Beethoven's] complete manhood" and "the story of genius strug-

gling with nature for expression." He then gave a specific program to
each of the movements:

> In the first grand division is developed the limitation and prohibition
> which nature asserts to the aspirations of the spirit, and that blind
> struggle between the soul and fate, as of one in the folds of a snake.
> Here is painted the spasmodic effort and failure,—the aimless seek-
> ings—the panting as for breath within a confined atmosphere—the
> fatal approximation to despair—the doubts—the fears—the disap-
> pointment. It is, as Beethoven himself said, 'as if fate was knocking
> at the door.' In the second movement is the morning landscape of a
> new era, whereon the beams of faith and hope are dawning through
> the cloudy bars of doubt and distrust, which circle the horizon. Hope
> as yet is stronger than Faith, and that superstitious child hath not yet
> left her mother's side. Still the cold wearisome limit, the weakened
> prohibition, and the echo of a former despair, are heard, like the
> suppressed growling of a lurking thunderstorm. Aspiration often, in
> its soaring, changes to doubt and falls. The two elements of faith and
> distrust are in conflict, and nothing is accomplished, though all is
> hoped. . . .[57]

Story continued with similar metaphors for several pages. There are
echoes of E. T. A. Hoffmann here, less in the program than in the tone
and rhetoric. And Story's equating Beethoven's struggle with masculinity
bears an obvious relationship to Dwight's comment that without Han-
dle, Mozart, and Beethoven, "no man can be quite a man." Both Story
and Dwight seem to be selling Beethoven as a masculine counterfoil to
an unspecified fear that music might be perceived as too feminine. The
topic itself cries out for a much fuller investigation and would, I believe,
provide further insights into the age.[58] My point here in quoting Story
has less to do with the specific program that he used than to illustrate
his choice of method—elaborate pictorial descriptions—to make Beethoven understandable to the Boston public.

Lest Story be dismissed as a musical innocent, however, his lecture,
compared to most other talks and articles in America about music at the
time, is quite technical in spots. For instance, he discussed Beethoven's
harmony in some detail, asserting that if any one chord characterized
Beethoven it was the flat seventh, the secondary dominant.

Story was not alone in providing a poetic description of Beethoven's
Fifth Symphony. In a lecture delivered at approximately the same time,
Samuel Eliot described the first movement of the symphony:

I have imagined, then, a conversation to be carried on between two parties in this symphony, one urging the other to some attempt which seems too difficult for him to undertake. After a statement of the project in the opening of the first movement at some length, the listener replies in the plaintive notes of the lighter instruments, "I can't. I can't, it is too difficult and dangerous. I shall fail." The other answers with a predominance of the stronger tones of the heavier instruments, "You can, I am sure of it. Be a man. Screw your courage to the sticking point, and you'll not fail." This goes on in a somewhat similar strain of alternate doubt and urgency several times, till toward the close of the first allegro, the hesitating man seems to yield, and agrees to undertake the almost desperate scheme.[59]

Eliot's metaphor is different from Story's, but the principle behind both is the same: enhance the listening experience through specific extramusical association. Eliot was well aware that he was not dealing with program music. He explicitly stated that the symphony itself was abstract, and that any story or dialogue was the listener's invention. He further admitted that his purpose was overtly didactic, to allow the truly naive listener to follow what at the time was a challenging piece.[60]

In his recognition of the moral value of music and his attempts to provide concrete associations to help the listener—in essence, in his desire to elucidate and educate—Story is closely aligned to Eliot. Story believed that art could "purify the morals and strengthen the character," that it embodied "the highest and noblest cravings of our nature," and he viewed music as part of that. For this reason he was not content with music that aimed at providing recreation and a way to fill leisure time.[61] Story's position, like Eliot's, reflects Unitarianism's belief in the moral, didactic value of art, and the Whig principle of educating the population to higher moral ends.

Even though Story was not a transcendentalist, some echoes of transcendentalism surfaced in his lecture. He looked on the classical masters from Bach to Beethoven in terms of a mystic whole: "In our age these greats [Bach, Handel, Haydn, Mozart, and Beethoven] would have successively risen in a perfect growth, each representing a different phase of one great whole,—'four faced to four corners of the sky.'"[62] In his mystical approach to classical music Story aligned himself closely with Dwight. In his aversion to music as entertainment he also placed himself more in the camp of Dwight than that of Eliot and Cleveland.

The difference between the Whig point of view, represented best by

Eliot, and the transcendentalist point of view, represented best by Dwight, is illustrated in a comment made by another transcendentalist, George William Curtis. Curtis was not a transcendentalist proper, as his most important work, particularly the editorship of *Harper's Weekly*, lay outside the movement. He was at Brook Farm between 1842 and 1844, however, where he came under the musical influence of Dwight. In 1843 he heard Beethoven's *Wellington's Victory* in New York. He was offended that Beethoven would use so trivial a tune; he had expected a symphonic piece. He was also troubled that Beethoven could have used the orchestra itself for such a "purely external" composition. Eliot would have probably welcomed the use of "Malbrook, s'en va t'en guerre," although he might have agreed with Curtis about the orchestra. Both groups considered the symphony orchestra a serious and exalted medium.

Although some ideas, such as the moral value of orchestral music, ran consistently through the Harvard Musical Association lectures, enough variance was expressed to make it difficult to ascertain the exact direction of the association. To what extent did the Whig Unitarian ideas of Eliot or the transcendental idealism of Dwight determine its activities? Any ambiguity about that was removed when in 1844 the association entered its second phase of public activity, the presentation of chamber-music concerts, controlled by Dwight. They are historically significant for several reasons: they were the first successful chamber-music concerts in Boston (and probably in America) to be built around the string quartet; they presented instrumental music for the first time within the idealistic, reverential context advocated by Dwight; and, finally, they signaled a new phase in the social evolution of instrumental music, concerts that were unapologetically elitist.

The Harvard Musical Association was not the first group to attempt a chamber-music series in the Boston area. In November 1842 George J. Webb and A. U. Hayter, pianists, William Keyzer, violinist, H. Theodore Hach, cellist, and an unidentified flutist announced a series of four chamber-music concerts to be given in Cambridge, beginning on November 18. The first concert consisted of music from "Mozart, Haydn, Beethoven, and other eminent classical composers."[63] Whether the concert was a success (indeed, whether it even occurred) is unknown, but the series itself apparently did not receive sufficient support to justify its continuation. No announcements of the three other concerts appeared. It is also unclear whether the Harvard Musical Association had anything to do with this particular series. According to Paul Eric Paige, the association sponsored it, but there is neither mention of the association in the advertisement nor reference to the concert in its minutes. Any relationship between the association and the musicians presenting the concert was at the most informal.

The Harvard Musical Association's chamber-music concerts represent the coming of age of the string quartet in America, although they were not the first public string-quartet performances in America; isolated presentations of string quartets are found as early as 1810 in Boston.[64] Probably the first attempt to establish a string-quartet series occurred in New York in 1843, when U. C. Hill presented a series of four fortnightly string-quartet concerts beginning on March 4 and ending April 15. But like the 1842 Cambridge chamber-music offerings, Hill's series apparently was not well received. He was forced to offer half subscriptions after the first two concerts, which suggests a thin house.[65] The absence of any further similar ventures corroborates the series' poor reception. In fact, neither Hill nor any other New York musician attempted similar chamber-music programs until 1849. In contrast to Hill's short series, the Harvard Musical Association's first series (of eight concerts) extended through the entire season and was successful enough to have prompted further series throughout the 1840s, although not in every year.[66] The association's chamber series also stimulated the formation of other chamber-music groups, most notably the Mendelssohn Quintet Club, which was founded in 1849. And although attendance at the association's concerts began to slack off by 1849, this was at least partly attributable to the greater competition from these rival organizations. By 1850 the Harvard Musical Association had, in three relatively successful seasons, established the string quartet as a viable public medium.

Interest in the string quartet as a chamber ensemble closely paralleled the emergence of an idealistic attitude toward instrumental music. Theodore Hach, in his *Music Magazine*, began lobbying in 1839 for the inauguration of string-quartet concerts in Boston. He called the string quartet "the most perfect instrumental music that can be imagined" and observed that the most eminent recent composers had "thrown their genius" into the genre. After acknowledging Haydn as the founder of the string quartet, he cited Mozart, Beethoven, A. Romberg, B. Romberg, Fesca, Ries, Onslow, H. Mendelssohn (sic), and Schubert for their contributions. He also argued that the string quartet was a fashionable genre, at least in Continental Europe. It was particularly so in Germany, where most of the large cities had inaugurated string-quartet concert series. To Hach fashion and taste were not separable, although fashion had a definite Teutonic flavor.[67]

In 1840 Dwight concluded his *Dial* review of the concerts of the past winter with a plea that "a few of the most accomplished and refined musicians institute a series of cheap instrumental concerts, like the Quartette Concerts, or the 'Classic Concerts' of Moscheles in England."[68] He specifically suggested that Schmidt, Hach, and Isenbech undertake it. Dwight realized that such a project would not attract a large audience, at most two or three hundred, and the effort probably would not be profitable at first. Dwight's euphemism for the financial undesirability of the project was, it "might be a labor of love at the outset." More important than numbers, however, was the role that the audience for the concerts would play in the musical life of Boston. Dwight believed that the concerts could eventually secure an audience that would serve as a nucleus for the development of taste in Boston.

In 1842 the *Musical Cabinet* took note of a number of concerts given by string players in Boston, by the violinists Nagel and Herwig, and by the cellist Knoop. The *Cabinet* urged the Boston Academy of Music to present string quartets when such players were available. It called the quartet a "most rich and varied species of music, [which] we as yet know but little," and observed that even in Europe the most eminent solo artists did not consider it beneath them to participate in quartet performances.[69]

The first concert sponsored by the Harvard Musical Association occurred on November 13, 1844, in the music room of Mr. Chickering. The performers were Leopold Herwig, violin, H. Theodore Hach, cello, John Lange, piano, and Anthony Werner. The program consisted of Beethoven's Trio in C minor, Op. 1, No. 3, Mozart's String Quartet in D minor, K. 421, and two solos, a "Polonaise for Piano Forte," by Herz, performed by Lange, and "La Melancholie," for violin, by Prume, performed by Herwig. The exact composition of the quartet must be inferred. We know that Herwig led it, and that Hach played the cello. Werner probably played second violin, as he had appeared several times in Boston as a violinist and flutist. Lange may have doubled on viola, as the Harvard Musical Association correspondence states explicitly that these four individuals did form a quartet. One work on the program, however, Schmitt's "Rondo for Piano with Quartet Accompaniment," suggests a fifth member. The viola part could have been performed by an amateur, although some acknowledgement would have probably been made. The payment receipts also list John Lange, who is otherwise unknown, rather than the better known Nicholas Lange, as one of the performers.[70]

The eight concerts in the Harvard Musical Association's series for the first season were presented from November into March every two to three weeks on Tuesday evenings, except for the first, which was on a Wednesday. Altogether fourteen string quartets were performed, five by Mozart, four by Haydn, and one each by Beethoven, Fesca, Kalliwoda, Romberg, and Spohr. Five piano trios were played, including three by Beethoven and one each by Hummel and Reissiger. Most of the other pieces consisted of various solos and duets. The concerts were strictly instrumental.

Tickets were priced at $2 for the series, which sold out. The audience was limited to 150, the size of Chickering's room. John S. Dwight implied that this size limitation was intentional. According to Arthur W. Hepner, Dwight played a significant role in organizing the series, including accepting responsibility for their success.[71] Dwight was the vice-president of the Harvard Musical Association at the time and president of its board of directors, the body that oversaw day-to-day operations. Management of the concerts was placed in the hands of Bernard Roelker and Robert E. Apthorp, who negotiated with the musicians regarding both salary and programming. Roelker headed a standing committee on concerts, and Apthorp was treasurer. Dwight probably served on the standing committee, although there is no record of the committee's membership.

Dwight discussed the philosophy behind the Harvard Musical Association's concerts in two articles that he wrote for the *Harbinger*. In a laudatory review of the first series, he portrayed them as more a religious assembly than entertainment. Religious metaphors abound. He called the string quartet the "quintessence of music" and among German musicians "the purest and favorite form of musical communion." In it music stands "in its naked beauty," in which "no original sin or weakness . . . can escape detection." When hearing Mozart's quartets "you are in the celestial world, disembodied. . . . The material world which separated him from the world of spirits, was the thinnest possible." He argued that for such presentations "the audience must be small and select, since the music is not on a scale sufficiently grand for great halls, nor must its sphere be disturbed by the presence of incongruous and unsympathizing elements."[72]

When Dwight published Christopher P. Cranch's 1845 Harvard Musical Association lecture in the *Harbinger* the following year, he included a lengthy introduction, in which he discussed the objectives of the association and the manner in which the concerts addressed that objective. Dwight indirectly confirmed the class aspect of the association's public presentations. Included on his list of objectives was the elevation of taste, hardly an unexpected goal. Dwight, however, connected the elevation of taste with class. The means of achieving it in American society were by "making it an avowed and corporate interest of men of intelligence and education, by attaching respectability to the musical profession." These were the same ideas and some of the same key words that Dwight had used in his 1841 Harvard Musical Association address. He continued to speak in religious terms, referring to the association's efforts toward the "deepening, and purifying and informing of the general taste for music" and of the "ministry of music," through which would come "more and more believers." He described the small, select audiences of the association's chamber music as "those best qualified to enjoy it in Boston," by which he meant those with proper taste and understanding.[73]

Cranch's 1845 address fully supported the view of music and society that the chamber-music concerts attempted to promulgate. The address was mostly a eulogy to Haydn, Mozart, and Beethoven. Cranch disparaged the tendency toward display found in many virtuoso concerts that were becoming common in Boston and lamented the popularity of performers like Henry Russell and the Hutchisons, as well as Italian opera. He called for performers to be content with "smaller audiences and fewer dollars, with better music." He characterized the association's effort as "a marked exception to this superficial standard of musical cultivation." Cranch felt that the music of those concerts would "inevitably elevate the general standard of taste in the community, and banish from refined and cultivated circles the trashy and commonplace things which find their way into so many fashionable parlors."[74]

Like Dwight, Cranch believed that music would be best served if such concerts addressed a limited circle, not the population at large. This was the position of the Harvard Musical Association in the 1840s. And if there were any question about that point, Dwight dispelled it some years later: "We never have believed that it was possible to educate the whole mass of society up to the love of what is classical and great in Art: we know that all the great loves, the fine perceptions and appreciations belong to the few."[75] Instead of the easygoing tolerance of Samuel Eliot, we find in the Harvard Musical Association the acerbic disparagement of John S. Dwight, William Story, and Christopher Cranch.

We see a retraction, as Dwight, Story, and Cranch turned inward and distanced themselves from society as a whole. Music assumed a role completely different from the one assigned it in the vision of Eliot and the republican gentry: music became more a means to separate rather than unite various levels or segments of society. High culture came to be perceived, as it would be in the late nineteenth century, as the province of the privileged few.

With this retraction came a bitterness about American society, although Dwight, Story, and Cranch each went on to important careers in the arts: Dwight as a writer on music, Story and Cranch as painters. Cleveland did not live long enough to experience the retraction, as he died in 1844 at the age of thirty-four. Both Cranch and Story became disillusioned about America. Story found Boston an impossible city in which to live: "Every twig is intensely defined against the sky. The sky itself is hard and distant. Earth takes never the hue of its heaven. The heart turns into stone."[76] He became a permanent expatriate in 1856. When Cranch returned to the United States after a European journey, he found New York a dreary inhospitable place, lacking in manners, urbanity, and elegance. Broadway, which he had once found impressive, seemed "shorn of its glory."[77]

As early as 1842 Story doubted that musical talent could flourish in America: "I have little to hope from the music which America shall compose. I seek in vain for indications of a native and spontaneous genius for this art; and it seems to me as if Music were never the offspring of the Anglo-saxon mind, though she may well be its friend and intimate."[78] By 1856 his pessimism about music had deepened. Shortly before leaving the United States he was asked to deliver an address as part of the dedication of Crawford's statue of Beethoven at Boston Hall. Story lamented that "it is an indisputable truth, that music, as an art, does not exist in this country; that is, among Americans. . . . When shall we have musicians who shall be as much distinguished in their profession as Longfellow, Bryant, and Prescott are among the writers, or as Allston and Crawford among the artists, of all ages?" Story tried to be optimistic, noting that "we are beginning to be discriminating in our taste," even though "our range is not yet very wide." He was forced to admit, however, that the emergence of American musical talent was "almost too wild a dream."[79]

Dwight, Cranch, and Story shared a similar background typical of members of the Harvard Musical Association at this time: New England Unitarianism, Harvard, and the Pierian Sodality. Story and Cranch were from prominent legal families; Cranch's father was chief justice of the United States circuit court of the District of Columbia, and Story's was the youngest associate justice ever appointed to the Supreme Court, after which he became the most important law professor at Harvard. Dwight's father was a Harvard-trained physician, although he was only moderately successful in his field. Both Cranch and Dwight played the flute, and each had unsuccessful careers as Unitarian ministers. In 1841 Cranch wrote a letter to Dwight about his extreme discomfort in the ministry, a letter that expressed precisely sentiments Dwight himself had articulated a few years earlier: "Nothing is whole, bright, and perfect to me. I have no inspirations. Thought, eloquence, and poetry desert me. Preaching and praying are fallen into traditions, and things for routine. I live—that is all. Nothing interests me but what excites or amuses. Music and drawing I can enjoy. . . . One want I feel here is music. There is a flute in the house. And I have seen a couple of pianos since I have been in Bangor—but more unmusical people I have seldom met."[80]

The pessimism about American society that these men shared was not unique to them. As we saw earlier, even Eliot, who maintained his Whig beliefs throughout his life, began to doubt that his vision of music in American life would be realized. Yet the failure of Eliot's vision should not obscure the important contribution that he made to American music. Eliot's historical position can best be understood by viewing his work in tandem with that of Mason and Dwight. Mason, Eliot, and Dwight represent three different segments of society. Each had radically different views about the nature of music and society. Yet the shape that musical attitudes took in Boston in the 1830s and 1840s depended on the convergence and the interaction of their disparate views. All three shared common influences and a similar New England heritage. As a result, the attitude that ultimately emerged was uniquely American. Even Dwight reflected as much Puritanism as German romanticism in his views. In later years he would be known for his extreme conservative positions, particularly regarding modern (late nineteenth-century) composers, as well as his aloofness to trends in popular music. In the 1840s his attitudes about the sacred and secular and the universality of music were more important. Dwight and Eliot had similar opinions about the universality of music, but by connecting more closely with the stream of mysticism inherent in American Puritanism, Dwight was able to present an argument for the value of music that was more acceptable for American consumption.

Eliot's vision was too divorced from cultural and political reality to have any chance of success. Yet Dwight's position depended on Eliot's work. Eliot's efforts represented the first serious breach in the hegemony of the Presbyterian-Congregational reformers' vision of music. Eliot established the ensembles that would allow the music of which Dwight spoke to be heard. Eliot was not the first to introduce serious instrumental music to the Boston public, but he was the first to combine an acceptable philosophical justification of instrumental music with a practical organization to explicate it. Earlier attempts to establish instrumental music of quality had engendered an almost immediate reaction when the music became too serious or too challenging. Eliot had argued that the seriousness was a merit not a fault, that familiarity combined with the proper education would win over a reluctant public.

Eliot bought breathing room for serious instrumental music by expanding the distinction between art and entertainment to include instrumental music. When his achievement was in danger of being eroded by a more popular approach to orchestral music, which the success of his own orchestra had spawned, even those orchestras that catered more to the popular taste could not ignore the idea of music as art. Yet in cloaking a decidedly populist strain in the mantle of high art, those quasi-popular institutions represented a more subtle and serious threat to the older gentry than unabashedly vernacular music had. Rather than turning against the vision of Eliot, they threatened to corrupt it. The problem was inherent in the republican gentry point of view. It was its fatal flaw. If music for the masses differed only in the sophistication of the listener, if such music had the capacity to move the listener just as art music did, the necessity of educating the masses to higher forms of art was less pressing. If there was nothing inherently wrong with the masses' music, why should they not prefer it? Eliot could not answer that question and remain consistent to the republican gentry ideal.

For the vision of music as high art to take hold, music as art needed to be more forcefully separated from music as entertainment. Dwight provided the rationale for doing that, in intellectually radical but politically reactionary terms. He dressed his argument in language that any New Englander could understand, in the context of sacred and secular music. He expanded sacred music to include all that was abstract and serious, which meant that the Presbyterian-Congregational hymnists' strictures about sacred music could be applied to instrumental music as well. That Dwight's own definition of abstract and serious music was extremely limited did not prevent his view from ultimately shaping the fundamental notion of high musical culture in America.

Mason had prepared the way for both Dwight and Eliot. Desiring to upgrade church music, he realized the importance of music education as well as Platonic idealism. Eliot not only shared both of these goals but was also as ready as Mason to support them actively. That Eliot and Mason shared the same platform, the Boston Academy of Music, only confirms the congruence of their positions about the potential of music, in spite of their fundamental differences regarding the use of that potential.

Yet not only Mason and Eliot shared a similar philosophy. For a brief time in the mid-1830s the three visions of the place of music in American society converged: the Presbyterian-Congregational-hymnist outlook of Mason, the Whig republican view of Eliot, and the transcendentalist-romantic perspective of Dwight. All three visions rested on a commonality of heritage, which for each of the participants led to the Boston Academy of Music. By 1840 the differences among them had become more apparent, and each of the three principals was pursuing his own path. The persistence of all three visions, however, contributed much of the uniquely American concept of high culture that came to dominant American society later in the century.

Chapter Ten

Bands, Opera, Virtuosi, and the Changing of the Guard

In 1883 Frederic Louis Ritter looked back with disdain on the efforts of the psalmodic reformers. In a chapter in his history of American music entitled "The Last Representative Psalm-Tune Teachers," Ritter examined the philosophy and the contributions of the three psalm-tune teachers he considered the most influential in the early nineteenth century: Thomas Hastings, Lowell Mason, and N. D. Gould. Ritter was particularly critical of Hastings' philosophy as reflected in his *Dissertation on Musical Taste.* He reckoned Hastings' views to be almost schizoid. What good things about the beauty of music Hastings the musician said were nullified by the antiquated, amateurish pronouncements that Hastings the psalm-tune teacher uttered. According to Ritter, Hastings was forced to contradict himself because he could not acknowledge the aesthetic value of music independent of religious considerations. Thus while Hastings could not help but admire the "Hallelujah Chorus," he could not condone the genre from which it came, because it was tainted with profane associations and was frequently performed in opera houses.[1]

Ritter found Hastings' stand on contrapuntal music unacceptable, interpreting it to mean a complete rejection of "all higher forms of musical composition, based upon rich, varied, contrapuntal means." He ridiculed Hastings' attitude toward the symphony and the concerto. After characterizing his comments on the larger forms as "cold, formal explanations," Ritter annotated Hastings' words with his own acerbic commentary. In the following quotation Ritter's comments are in italics; the brackets are Ritter's:

Such sentences as that concerning symphonies "that they are excellent subjects for study to professional men, but possess few attractions for the community at large," will excite no one's curiosity to attend symphonic performances. In the same vein our author thinks that "concertos and songs of execution are useful as tasks for learners, and convenient for the exhibition of talent; and when they pretend to nothing more we can ocassionally [!] listen to them with satisfaction.

[*O shades of Mozart and Beethoven!*] Parlor-music, when not intended for the mere exercise of talent, should be adapted to promote moral principles, refined sentiments, and sympathetic emotions." *All this is a pretty difficult task, especially the promoting, by means of a sonata, of moral principles "à la Hastings."*[2]

I believe that Ritter misread Hastings. Hastings was more indifferent than antagonistic toward instrumental music. Ritter was writing at a time when the symphony occupied a preeminent place in the musical pantheon. Practically no one in Federal America viewed the symphony that way in 1822, when Hastings published his *Dissertation*. Hastings recognized that some instrumental music was designed to do nothing more than amuse, which he did not oppose so long as it pretended nothing more. But Hastings also called some instrumental pieces a "high species of art" and "refined specimens of composition," and in his 1853 revision of the *Dissertation* distinguished them from "those [compositions] which continue most in favor with the middling classes and the illiterate." Hastings' own populist tendencies, however, characteristic of the Presbyterian-Congregational reformers, prevented him from endorsing the more refined instrumental compositions, because they were too inaccessible: "The ideas are too abstruse for ordinary apprehension," he wrote in 1822. When he revised his *Dissertation* he added the sentence, "They are as the higher classics of the art, intended only for the initiated few." Hastings' views actually changed little in his 1853 revisions. He simply acknowledged new tendencies in music since the original publication.[3]

The elitism implicit in the inaccessibility of complex instrumental music does not seem to have bothered Ritter. Yet the difference of opinion between Ritter and Hastings cannot be attributed completely to the political stances of the two writers. Between the time of Hastings' *Dissertation* and Ritter's book, a fundamental rethinking about the nature or purpose of music occurred in America. To Hastings music was the servant of religion, and he equated religious value with moral principles. To Ritter music was an intrinsic art, and he equated moral principles with aesthetic value. Ritter specifically rejected the evangelical function of music and saw its liturgical value purely in aesthetic terms: "Music's function is not to preach the gospel of religious creeds and morality, but to beautify and make more expressive certain religious emotions: the more artistic excellence it brings, be it simple or rich, to the support of this function, the more effective will be its office." Ritter had his own religious agenda, however: he distinguished between the psalm-tune teacher, who thought that the ability to quote the Bible and lead a revival meeting was more important than playing a musical instrument, and the professional musician, who considered music purely the help-mate of religion and "preached the gospel of true art."[4]

Ritter's discussion was driven by a view of music as high art, in which artistic merit was an ideal in itself. It contradicted the views of the Presbyterian-Congregational reformers, who considered the moral im-plications of music more important than its artistic qualities. Lowell Mason, whom Ritter praised for valuing music as art, explicitly acknowl-edged the Presbyterian-Congregational reformers' distinction between the artistic and moral. In a letter written to his son William, Mason summarized his music aesthetic by classifying music according to the reasons it is cultivated—that is, according to its ends and purposes. He delineated four categories: the sensuous, the intellectual, the artistic, and the moral. There is no doubt about a hierarchy here; Mason's own metaphor was ascending a ladder. And although he valued the artistic highly, claiming that only a few composers had reached that plateau, he nevertheless found the moral a rung above that. Mason's aesthetic cat-egories were no mere sudden improvisation, quickly dashed off and forgotten. In a lengthy letter to W. W. Killip in 1860 he repeated them once again, with slight variants. With reference to teaching singing, he exhorted Killip to reach beyond the sensuous and the physical in his to aspire to the moral as well as the intellectual.

Yet Mason did recognize that secular music could have a moral pur-pose. In his 1826 address on church music, he carefully indicated that his criticism of church music did not extend to secular music outside the church. He allowed that secular music could not only provide amuse-ment but could also contribute "to the happiness and moral improve-ment of mankind." Such effects, however, assumed a man of "taste and cultivation."[5] Mason's views resembled those of Hastings; he had no objection to the cultivation of secular music, but was concerned because sacred music was not similarity cultivated.

Ritter's position on the moral and aesthetic value of music was typical of the late nineteenth century. It was virtually synonymous with that of Mason's son William, who was not convinced by his father's aesthetic. In his memoirs William said virtually nothing about religion beyond recounting anecdotes of his father's church career. He was acutely em-barrassed when his father pressed him to present a copy of one of Lowell Mason's anthologies to Moritz Hauptman. His embarrassment sprang from the apparent musical naïveté that he felt the volume displayed. He was astounded when Hauptman reacted positively to it: "At the moment I could not understand how such a big contrapuntist could express himself in such strong terms of approval." William Mason accepted the idea of progress, noting a distinct improvement in the aesthetic climate of his day compared to that of his father, but he inverted completely his father's position regarding sacred and secular music. William spoke of the "crudity of musical taste in the early days [the 1830s and 1840s]," and he observed that his father would drill the participants in his musical conventions mostly "in church music, but also, where he found sufficient advancement, in music of a higher order."[6]

Ritter's own concept of art was quasi-religious. Ritter spoke of "the gospel of pure art" and believed that music had an unmistakable moral component. Yet both early and late nineteenth-century musical thought recognized the importance of the moral quality of music. Mason and Ritter differed only in that Mason separated the "artistic" from the "moral." For Ritter, and indeed many in the late nineteenth century, the two terms were not separable. The moral meant nothing less to Ritter than it did Mason, but to Mason the artistic had not yet acquired the moral dimension that it later did.

Mason defined composers who pursue music for artistic purposes in terms of the relative purity of their pursuit. Such composers "labor for the discovery of new forms of beauty and truth in the numbers, successions, or combinations of tones and for the mental and physical power necessary to communicate or bring up these forms to the conception of others." Their aim is to "press forward into the region of beauty, and to bring up taste to its appreciation in its highest and most powerful forms." As might be expected, Mason named Mozart and Beethoven as composers who had reached the level of the artistic, but he also added that Schumann definitely, and Liszt and Wagner possibly, belonged there.

In spite of the Platonic idealism inherent in his concept of the artistic, Mason still considered the moral to be a rung higher in his artistic hierarchy. He did not limit the moral category to religious music, however. He contrasted the differences in purpose between the composer of artistic and of moral music: "The artist aims at the discovery and at the communication of new forms of beauty—but he who views the subject from the highest point, sees in it a most powerful instrument for the perfecting of man's emotional or moral nature."

The last part of that sentence could well have been written by Ritter,

William Mason or Dwight. It embodies fully the concept of a sacralized culture. Yet there was a fundamental difference. Mason was not ready to abstract his religion. His vision of God was too specific, and his concern with earthly morality too concrete. Part of his concept of the religious was that it "unites man to his Maker, or the human to the divine." Apparently Mason did not see the divine even in Mozart or Beethoven. Dwight in contrast heard in Beethoven's music a religious quality seldom surpassed anywhere else. Mason was silent in his list of composers that had reached the level of the moral, probably because his criteria for determining the moral level were not musical at all. He considered religious sincerity and communication more important than musical sophistication. Such a concept resembles Ives' distinction between substance and manner, although Ives, like Dwight, was much more abstract about his concept of moral value than Mason was.

The difference between the positions of Ritter, Dwight, and William Mason on the one hand and of Lowell Mason on the other represents a fundamental shift in the nature and purpose of instrumental music. In Lowell Mason's world instrumental music could aspire only to the level of the artistic. Mason had no professional interest in instrumental music. Dwight, in contrast, had no interest in Puritan psalmody; he described it as "monotonous and barren" and denied that it had "any significant relation to the growth of music or of musical taste and knowledge here."[7] In the late nineteenth century, instrumental music, particularly symphonic music, occupied the apex of a pyramid of musical values. It was artistic, moral, and intrinsically sacred.

In considering the positions of the Masons, Dwight, and Ritter, I have discussed the shift in the way instrumental music was viewed in America in relation to social and political developments mostly unique to America. The shift must also be considered as part of a broader tendency common to both sides of the Atlantic. Between the start of Lowell Mason's career and the time Ritter surveyed it, the idea of a canon of great musical works emerged in both Europe and America. William Weber described the canon as "a body of works that are defined as the summit of achievement in an artistic field; they are studied and emulated by practitioners and honored in ritual and iconography."[8] The canon (or pantheon) consisted primarily of instrumental music, with orchestral compositions occupying the central positions on both sides of the Atlantic. Haydn, Mozart, and Beethoven formed the core.

Even though there were precursors, such as Corelli's concertos or Handel's vocal works in eighteenth-century England, the idea of a canon took shape only in the nineteenth century. Haydn was venerated on his two English visits, but his late symphonies and string quartets, the featured works in his English concerts, were seldom subsequently performed. By the early nineteenth century, however, the principal classical-era composers were held in awe, and their compositions became staples on concert programs. They were considered models of perfection, providing standards of excellence against which all other composer's efforts could be assessed. And once the concept of a canon was established, it was only a matter of extension to admit other composers. This process occurred throughout the nineteenth century, with Bach, Schumann, Mendelssohn, and later Brahms and Wagner being admitted. Wagner's admission into the pantheon aroused considerable controversy, but the controversy itself only confirmed that the pantheon did indeed exist.

The elevation of the symphony to a position of preeminence in Europe was closely related to the recognition that the music of Beethoven expressed an artistic depth hitherto unknown. Shortly after 1800, Beethoven's compositions became more individual and more personal, and to some writers contained an ethical quality not apparent in his earlier music.[9] At the same time, Beethoven channeled most of his compositional energy into orchestral works, to a degree that was unprecedented. Eight of his nine symphonies were written between 1800 and 1812, as were five of his seven concerti and his most important overtures, including *Prometheus*, the second and third *Leonore* Overtures, and the Overtures to *Coriolan* and *Egmont*. And of all the works that he composed during this period, the symphonies became the most well-known and revered. By the late nineteenth century Beethoven's symphonies had become the innermost core of the musical canon.

Beethoven's symphonies and overtures provided the starting point for E. T. A. Hoffmann to explore the nature of romantic instrumental music. More than any other writer, Hoffmann established the theoretical basis for the canon. He was the first to avow the transcendent quality of Beethoven's orchestral music. In several reviews in the *Allgemeine musikalische Zeitung*, the first of which appeared in 1810, Hoffmann took the view that music was the most romantic art. He believed that Beethoven's compositions best embodied that view, and he considered the symphonies Beethoven's crowning achievement. To Hoffmann the Fifth Symphony in particular resonated with a sublimity that set it and the genre apart.[10] Approximately thirty years later, the Fifth would assume the same position in American musical thought that it had in Hoffmann's.

The rise of the symphony to the genre nonpareil began in the last fifteen years of the eighteenth century. The symphony was the centerpiece around which Haydn's London concerts of the 1790s pivoted. At the same time, his compositions in other genres took on symphonic characteristics. Throughout most of his career Haydn had carefully distinguished his symphonic works stylistically from those of other instrumental genres. After 1790 virtually all of his instrumental genres became symphonic, including the piano sonata, which until then he had considered the epitome of the sonata, or nonsymphonic, style. Mozart regarded the symphony as a special type of composition by the early 1780s. Like Haydn's late symphonies, all of Mozart's composed after 1782 were for public rather than private performance, and all were large-scale, complex, and serious.

In Germany the symphony orchestra had a dual role. All of the larger orchestras gave symphonic concerts. They were not, however, the orchestra's raison d'être. The symphony orchestra was primarily an opera orchestra. Its place in the opera pit both enhanced the status of opera in Europe and provided a common linkage in audience interest between the operatic and the symphonic styles. It also put the orchestra in a secondary position, as the orchestra's lack of independent identity hampered its capacity as a cultural symbol.

In America the orchestra was not identified with opera.[11] Although theaters provided employment for orchestral musicians, the symphony orchestra developed as an independent entity. To many Americans opera was an uncertain medium; it meant many things, from light musical entertainment to more grandiose romantic spectacles, but in general its association with the theater tainted it. Opera was viewed suspiciously by the upper and middle classes in Boston, its acceptance hindered by a perception of rowdiness in the theater itself and vestiges of an earlier Puritan distrust of theatrical presentations. At times, as in New York in the 1820s and 1830s, opera producers catered to the upper classes and sought to market opera as an elitist alternative to the theater. Most of the time, however, opera meant the ballad opera of England, which was everyday theatrical fare, and for which orchestral demands were light.

In spite of the ambiguous way opera and other cultural presentations were received, a distinction between a popular and a high culture did exist in the early nineteenth century. The distinction, however, is difficult to see today because it is masked by a fundamental difference between then and now in the manner in which musical objects—that is, compositions—were perceived. Beginning in the mid-eighteenth century, a fundamental realignment of the relationship between composer and audience occurred; this affected profoundly both the manner in which the composer recorded his thoughts and the role and prestige of the composer himself. In the eighteenth and early nineteenth centuries musical compositions were resources on which musicians could draw in a variety of ways to create musical experiences of considerably differing natures. A Bellini opera could be an enriching, high-art experience or it could become the basis for a set of contra dances. Shakespeare's plays functioned in a similar manner. Shakespeare was much esteemed in the early nineteenth century, and although audiences may have been rowdy, they did expect a high level of performance from their Shakespearean actors. Shakespeare's works appeared in a twelvemo edition in Boston in 1802. The run of three thousand was considered a success, which meant it was probably sold out.[12] Shakespeare could be parodied or burlesqued at the same time, however, precisely because of the high esteem in which he was held, just as Italian opera could be a source for contra dances.

There is little difference in the aesthetic integrity of the theatrical parodies of Shakespeare, sets of quadrilles based on operatic themes, and the Presbyterian-Congregational reformers' adaptation of European compositions. Whether the Presbyterian-Congregational reformers chose European or other tunes was an issue within the prevailing framework of their time; whether they modified the tunes they chose was not (at least not early in the ninteenth century). Adaptation was accepted with little question of the rightness of doing so. A new attitude toward adaptation emerged only later in the century, and only then were such practices condemned in the name of art.

Ritter's view of art greatly limited his understanding of the Presbyterian-Congregational reformers' use of classical music. The almost casual dismemberment of "classical" compositions to create new pieces, as the Presbyterian-Congregational reformers did, offended the very premise of the sanctity of the music of the classical masters. Ritter's position, derived from European romanticism, has influenced much later writing about the reformers. Yet the Presbyterian-Congregational reformers saw no disparity between musical idealism and their adaptation of classical compositions for religious purposes. Mason and other reformers believed that their religious mission far transcended any aesthetic considerations. And their quest for music that was dignified, enriching, and chaste could be thoroughly satisfied by the music of Haydn, Mozart, and Beethoven, if it was used in accordance with their own standards.

The change in atmosphere regarding the limits of adaptation came when the sources themselves—the compositions—became sacred artifacts. Before this situation, certain types of music had been recognized as pure, ennobling, or enriching, but such a characterization depended as much on the setting in which a composition was presented and the manner in which it was performed as on the nature of the work itself. Musical culture was stratified, but the strata cut transversely through different types of compositions. All were available for whatever purpose musicians chose, and a single composition could exist simultaneously on several strata. A fundamental change occurred as the fault lines shifted and the strata paralleled pieces or genres. In consequence, compositions perceived as high art were placed off-limits to less serious uses.

With romanticism came a new attitude toward the piece: a composition existed as an external entity, inviolable. Three developments made this new attitude possible: a tendency by composers to notate compositions more precisely, a significant expansion of the music publishing industry, and a shift in the roles of composers and performers. The three developments are closely related. Music in the late eighteenth century was notated much more precisely than it had been in the early part of the century, but the difference is less attributable to technical developments than to changes in composers' attitudes toward composition. By the early eighteenth century our modern notational system was fully in place. A baroque composer, however, expected the performer to contribute to the piece in two ways: by filling in the continuo, and by providing ornamentation. The extent of improvisation allowed by the continuo was, relative to melodic decoration, rather small. But the melodic line of the composer was only a skeleton, dependent on the performer to breath life into it. It was possible of course to write out a version with complete ornamentation, as J. S. Bach often did, but this practice was frowned upon, as the reaction of Bach's colleagues attests. They clearly recognized what he was doing and roundly criticized him for it.

In the second half of the eighteenth century composers began to insist that their music be played as written. The continuo was abandoned in favor of obbligato accompaniment parts. Melodic nuance and detail became the composer's responsibility. C. P. E. Bach could publish not only a set of sonatas with *verandete reprise* (varied repeats) but also a second version with different verandents.[13] By publishing the variants Bach invited the performer to add variations on the reprise. By publishing two different sets, presumably equally valid, Bach revealed an open-ended attitude toward musical composition. Some years later Mozart struggled with singers who took too much liberty with his arias, although this probably tells us more about license on the opera stage than about any hard-nosed insistence on unquestioning loyalty to his score. But when Beethoven railed against Carl Czerny for adding ornamentation to his Quintet for Piano and Winds, Op. 16, he clearly was disturbed not to hear the piece precisely as he wrote it.[14]

The dissemination of music through published scores increased geometrically in the second half of the eighteenth century. As a consequence, musical compositions became more independent of the composer's direct control over the performance. An interest in instrumental music by amateurs created a burgeoning demand for printed instrumental music. In the early eighteenth century only a small fraction of the instrumental compositions of even the best known composers were published; by 1800 the publication of important instrumental compositions had become the norm.[15]

The change in the role of the composer between C. P. E. Bach's time and Beethoven's is fundamental, affecting our perception of the nature of music as far back as there are tracks of notation. It is no less than the relationship between a *piece* as existing on paper, there, external, and a piece as a model for music making, and as such it is closely related to the problem of notation, which until recent times served as the only means to fix and preserve a musical work. Musicologists have probed this particular problem from the early stages, dealing with early chant notation.[16] In recent years composers have explored this relationship with a variety of experimental music, ranging from new notational devices to graphic compositions in which notation functions as simply a loose guide to give improvisational inspiration to the performer. The problems associated with defining earlier music and the interest of recent composers in questions of notation demonstrate the extent to which we now identify the piece as an object in itself.

It should be noted that literacy itself does not define musical type. In fact, literacy versus nonliteracy does not define the duality that existed in nineteenth-century America. The dichotomy between a written and an oral tradition predates the division of musical practices in the nineteenth century. It may be found in the attempts to reform congregational singing in the eighteenth century, riven by the differences between the advocates of regular singing and those of singing from memory. The clergy lost control in the late eighteenth century to a type of music, the fuging tune, that is considered part of the vernacular tradition but was transmitted through notation. Performance of fuging tunes depended upon at least a degree of musical literacy. The vernacular tradition was transmitted essentially through written sources in the nineteenth century as well. The shape-note tune books, the music of the minstrel stage, the many waltz and quadrille collections all depended upon written transmission, and all were at the heart of the vernacular tradition.

As the transmission of music through the printed score assumed a more central place in European and American musical life, a specialization of roles within the musical community began to occur. The composer could communicate to the performer only through the printed page. Naturally, what he put on paper became more detailed. At the same time, the composer emerged in his own right. He was a name identified on the top of the score. Beethoven was known throughout Europe, far beyond the range of those who actually heard him perform. In later years he sustained himself almost completely through the publication of his compositions. Schubert and, some years later, Chopin eschewed the role of professional performer almost completely. Both lived primarily on their published compositions. That Schubert remained in poverty is more a commentary on copyright laws and his own lack of business acumen than on the economic viability of the music printing industry.

With the physical separation of composer from composition as well as composer from audience, a mystique about the composer could develop. Apocryphal stories about the meaning of a piece could arise, frequently planted by the publishers themselves. Biographies or memoirs by friends of the composer found ready audiences. Such publications, dependent upon the recognition of the unique or special quality of the works of the composer in question, sought to bolster the mystique. From that a growing consensus emerged in the early nineteenth century that certain composers possessed a quality of genius that others did not.

The concept of genius had already found a place in writings on music in the late eighteenth century, when writers attempted to plumb the emotional basis of musical compositions. Failing in virtually every case, they would then fall back on the notion of genius. They defined a musical genius in terms of his ability to feel music and to transmit this feeling, rather than in terms of his virtuosity, technical facility, fantastic ear, or keen memory. Certain composers, because their music expressed deeply felt emotions, were labeled geniuses, and their music was considered superior to that of merely good composers. From such a designation it was only a small step to place these composers off-limits to tampering. Closely associated with romanticism, in which the inexplicable was stressed, the notion of genius only reinforced the prevailing attitude that the works of some composers were to be set apart and considered with awe and reverence.

The concept of organic form that emerged in the late eighteenth century further fed the notion of the inviolability of the piece. It was a time of fundamental change in the structural models by which European man explained the world, and new models that emerged late in the century had a profound effect on the way in which music was conceptualized. The work of Isaac Newton had provided the principal model for earlier eighteenth-century conceptions of nature. Although Newton's *Principia* and *Optics* were probably as difficult for the eighteenth-century reader to understand as Einstein's theory of relativity is for most twentieth-century lay persons, writers like Fontenell and Voltaire did much to popularize Newton's ideas. The Newtonian world view was essentially mechanical, and at the heart of the Newtonian synthesis were two concepts that would in large measure shape eighteenth-century ideas about the structuring of nature. The first was the emphasis on individual parts rather than the entity as a whole. As Newton demonstrated with his prism, the proper way to understand a phenomenon was to break it down into its components and then minutely study them. The second concept was the tendency to view structure as essentially static. The entire universe was reducible to mathematical formulae, and form or structure referred to the passive configuration of a phenomenon, unrelated to the internal forces that determined its shape or activity.

Even the nonmechanistic sciences like biology and chemistry had aspects of this mechanistic model imposed on them. Biology was characterized by a rigid classification system that precluded any possibility of variation and hence of internal change. The development or function of an organism was less important than where it fitted into the classification scheme. A similar point of view was reflected in the very name given to chemistry, *Scheidekunst*, which meant the art of separating.

In the latter part of the eighteenth century, the limitations imposed by the mechanized outlook become more apparent. The most far-reaching changes occurred in biology, where it became apparent that the static quality of the ordering schemes was not adequate. Living structures exhibited characteristics whose explanations required nonmechanistic models. Biologists, in search of a better model for living structures, revived the concepts of organism and organic form. The notion of organic form had been suggested by Plato and Aristotle, but had had minimal influence on the post-Christian world.[17] When science became a fundamental shaper of Western thought in the sixteenth and seventeenth centuries, mechanics predominated.

The concept of the organism became a crucial aspect in the doctrine of romanticism. The organic metaphor found a central place in the writings of Herder, Goethe, and Friedrich and August Wilhelm von Schlegel in Germany and was transmitted to England by Coleridge, who was intimately familiar with German writings of his time. As developed by writers in the late eighteenth and early nineteenth centuries, organic form had several important characteristics. First, it was dynamic rather than static, containing an inner force that motivated the organism. Study of a structure was not simply study of an unchanging configuration. An organism was constantly in the process of development, mutation, and change, a form of becoming rather than being. Second, the whole was all important and was more than the sum of its parts. The organism was a unity, with every detail contributing; all parts were mutually connected, and the removal of one part would destroy the essential unity. Third, the organism was teleological. It evinced goals and directions generated from within.

Goethe's description of Strasbourg Cathedral illustrates how this concept was applied directly to works of art: "How freshly it shone in the morning rays, how joyfully I stretch out my arms toward it, surveying its vast harmonious mass, animated by countless details of structure! As in works of eternal nature, every form, down to the smallest fibril, alive, and everything contributing to the purpose of the whole."[18]

Musical works were viewed the same way. In a piece composed according to the principles of organic form, every note had its place and functioned to contribute to the whole. This was especially true if the piece was composed by a genius like Haydn, Mozart, or Beethoven. Their compositions were considered perfect, down to the last detail. Their perfection gave them the aura of a sacred object, and distanced the listener from them. They were to be revered more than enjoyed.

Although the application of the concept of organic form to instrumental music developed in Europe, it profoundly affected musical attitudes in the United States. The justification of instrumental music was premised on the perfectibility of a composition. This attitude was universal among the many apologists for instrumental music. It is apparent as early as John Rowe Parker, editor of the *Euterpeiad*, and other progressives who associated instrumental music with taste and progress. We see it in men like Eliot and Cleveland, for whom taste was a central defining element. And it is especially noticeable in the transcendental writers, who transferred much of the mysticism of Puritanism to instrumental music.

It was thus only natural that the development of the canon would occur on both sides of the Atlantic. In spite of widening political differences in the eighteenth century, American music continued to follow British models closely well into the nineteenth century, as we have observed. The principal American composers of fuguing tunes used British tune books as their models, and the American theater was populated and run by Britons. American journals borrowed heavily from British journals, and the veneration of Handel and Haydn, the impetus for the founding of many choral societies in America and an important precursor of the full emergence of the canon, arose originally in eighteenth-century England. In most cases these developments appeared roughly a generation earlier in England than America.

Yet for all the many similarities between Europe and America, the development of the canon followed different paths in America and Europe. Puritanism, evangelicalism, republicanism, Unitarianism, and transcendentalism had European parallels, but no exact European counterparts. Each of these movements developed independently in America and, as we have seen, each contributed to the distinctive course of American music. On a more concrete level, different organizations were crucial to the establishment of the canon, and some influences that were critical in Europe were peripheral in America. The singing societies and the virtuoso played roles in the development of the canon in America for which there are no precise European correspondences. According to William Weber, the establishment of the canon in Europe was largely in response to the popularity of the virtuoso. Weber divided musical activity in early nineteenth-century Europe according to audiences, or "taste publics." Around each taste public a style developed. He delineated three: the operatic style, created by Rossini and adapted by Germans like Meyerbeer; the virtuosic style, built out of national sources into an international idiom and culminating in the dazzling performances of Liszt and Thalberg; and the German classic style, based on the music of Haydn, Mozart, Beethoven, and Schubert and emphasizing orchestral music.[19]

The proponents of the German classical style conceptualized music of the classical masters in relatively ascetic terms and viewed the activities of the two other groups with antagonism. The canon that emerged in Europe in the 1830s and 1840s was in reaction to the commercialization of musical life. It was a self-conscious foil to the prevailing salon music and the cult of the virtuoso. Weber specifically addressed the division between the proponents of the classical style on the one hand and the operatic and virtuosic styles on the other as a conflict between high and popular culture.

The virtuoso did not receive the same reception in America as in Europe. In Europe the virtuoso's reception had progressed from astonishment to adulation and finally antagonism, as Weber has documented. This sequence began early in the nineteenth century, and the third phase was evident by the 1830s. A corresponding pattern occurred in the United States, but with important differences. The entire sequence happened later and was much more compressed. Instead of being spread out over a period of twenty to thirty years, the pattern unfolded in less than five, between 1840 and 1845, and the final phase was limited to a small segment of the populace. As a consequence, the role that the virtuoso played in establishing musical idealism was quite different in America. In Europe the adulation of the instrumental works of the classical masters, particularly the symphonies of Haydn, Mozart, and Beethoven, was in large measure a reaction against the virtuoso school. In America the classical canon was in place before the reaction against the virtuoso set in. In fact, the virtuoso contributed in no small way to the establishment of the canon in America.

Instrumental virtuosi opened the eyes of many Americans to what instruments, particularly string instruments, could do. Good instrumentalists were too infrequent in America to allow the development of practices parallel to those in Europe. Thomas Jefferson, emulating European models, wished to create a private orchestra at Montecello but was constrained by practical and economic problems. More generally, American audiences were ignorant of the potential of most types of instrumental ensembles simply because they had no opportunity to hear competent performances. Most Americans, even professional musicians, had only a limited perception of the expressive and technical possibilities of musical instruments. The virtuoso changed all of that. He significantly raised the level of instrumental musical activity in America, in part by demonstrating the power of the instruments themselves.

Virtuoso concerts were relatively uncommon in America throughout much of the Federal period. When they did occur, audiences were not receptive. In 1817 John Rowe Parker, an early supporter of instrumental music, attempted to describe musical activity in Boston. In his first column in the *Boston Intelligencer and Morning and Evening Advertiser*, he observed that "music is rapidly cultivating in this country and many foreign publication and foreign virtuosos [are] constantly arriving from Europe." He recalled with pleasure many of the performances, "several specimens of musical exhibitions wherein much talent, genius and execution were conspicuous." He then referred to concerts given by "Messrs Gilles and Etienne, gentlemen whose musical education in the best Parisian Schools gave them the means of excelling upon their respective instruments." Denis-Germain Etienne was a pianist and Peter Gilles an oboist and hornist; Gilles' son Peter, Jr., was a cellist and his son Henri-Noël an oboist. Parker also singled out for praise the concert of Louis Ostinelli, whose first public performance established him as one of the pre-eminent musicians in Boston, a position he held for the next twenty years: "This gentlemans [sic] performances on Monday Evening, gave greater satisfaction than we ever recollect to have witnessed on any former occasion." The *Columbian Centinel* also praised Ostinelli's performance: "Mr. Ostinelli satisfied the expectations of the company, which is saying very much in favor of his performance." Both Parker and the *Centinel* also spoke highly of another instrumental virtuoso who appeared in Ostinelli's concert, Gottlieb Graupner. Parker referred to "the incomparable and masterly execution of Mr. Graupner's double Bass," and claimed Graupner to have no equal in America and few superiors in Europe. The *Centinel* observed that the concert did as much honor to Graupner as Ostinelli, and that both Ostinelli's "execution on the Violin, and Mr. Graupner's on the oboe, drew repeated applause from the company."[20]

Yet in spite of Parker's optimism about the future of instrumental music in Boston and the quality of the performances, Parker was not pleased with the reception given Ostinelli and Graupner: "We anticipated a more crowded audience, and have to regret that many amateurs in musick were not present, to witness the transcendent talents that were exhibited in the inimitable performance of the above mentioned gentlemen." In 1820 Parker confirmed that instrumental concerts in general did not draw well in Boston. By then he was writing in his own journal, "Is there not some reason to doubt whether we are alive to refined music? That this doubt is not altogether unfounded, may be proved by appealing to the success of several concerts of Instrumental music which have been offered the public; not one of the individuals has been substantially benefited by the exercise of those talents. It may be said this was partly owing to their own folly and excess of conduct. . . . Regular concerts have never succeeded well, in this metropolis, and although there exists other causes of failure, beside the want of knowledge of music, yet this last is clearly the reason why patronage is so sparingly bestowed upon professors."[21] The following year Parker acknowledged that instrumental virtuosi were still relatively rare. He attributed the lack of audience support for instrumental music to that situation: "Candidates for solo performances are so few in this metropolis, that Instrumental music has not been cherished to that extent which has attended the vocal branch of this science."[22]

Other evidence corroborates the fact that the virtuoso received a lukewarm reception in Federal America. William Bentley recorded in his diary in 1798 that a "celebrated Teacher on the Fortepiano has appeared in Town [Salem], but with slender encouragement." Some twenty years later S. Mocenig presented the first violin concert in Salem. It was not a success, which Mocenig attributed to insufficient notice. He attempted to organize a second concert but received so little encouragement that it probably did not even take place.[23] Admittedly, Mocenig did do better in Boston when he presented a concert in December 1817, aided by the Philharmonic Society. Parker claimed that the audience was large, and positive in its response. Yet we hear little of Mocenig after that.[24]

When Lowell Mason went to Europe in 1837 he was notably unimpressed with the choirs that he heard, finding many of them inferior and only a few equal to those in America. Most of the better choirs were in Germany, yet he criticized many aspects of even their performance. His reaction to instrumental virtuosi was entirely different, however. He was astounded at what he heard; nothing in America even approached Europe's level of instrumental performance. This disparity encompassed both orchestral and keyboard instruments. It is noteworthy that Mason was particularly amazed at the level of organ playing in Europe, since Boston supposedly had had several good European organists, including George K. Jackson, George J. Webb, and Charles Zeuner.

As late as 1839 an instrumental virtuoso concert was still a novelty in Boston. Theodore Hach reported that a piano concert by C. Kossowsky was unique for the 1839–1840 season because it was all instrumental. He reviewed its virtuosic aspect favorably, praising Kossowsky for undertaking "the arduous task of playing alone eight times, each time performing pieces every one of which would be sufficient to tire the physical or mental powers of any one in Boston except himself." While complaining that the concert was longer than Boston audiences were accustomed to, Hach addressed its unusual nature: "Concerts wholly instrumental, should always be short, for our public are only just beginning to appreciate them."[25]

Virtuoso concerts blossomed in Boston in the next year. The difference between the offerings of 1839–1840 and 1840–1841 was dramatic. In reviewing the 1840–1841 season Hach was delighted to report the "unusual number of foreign artists, and especially instrumentalists, who have produced their art before us." In that year, Herwig, Nagel and William Keyser appeared on the violin, George Knoop on the cello, Jane Sloman, Louis Rakemann, and Kossowsky on the piano, G. Paggi and Ribas on the oboe, and Delores Nevares de Gony on the guitar. Although not all of these artists appeared in strictly instrumental concerts, Hach observed that they found ready audiences, to the extent that vocalists suffered because of the sudden popularity of instrumentalists. Hach did sound a warning that foreshadowed reactions later in the century when he expressed concern that the audiences might have been motivated more by "fashion and caprice" for the foreign performers, than out of true love of music." Nevertheless, audiences' positive responses to instrumental concerts were "cheering, and we think a decided progress."[26]

Of all virtuosi appearing in the early 1840s, George Knoop made the deepest impression. Hach called him "the best performer on any instrument whom we have had here for a great while." The *Musical Cabinet*, edited by George J. Webb and T. B. Haywood, reviewed in detail the concert of Knopp on the cello and de Gony on the guitar. The reviewer stated that "as a virtuoso he [Knoop] stands higher than any other, of whatever description, who has visited this country; and on his particular instrument, there are few in Europe who excel, or even equal him." The reviewer referred to de Gony as not only a "most delightful performer" on the guitar but also an "*artiste* of high merit." He singled out her performance for its "neatness, beauty, grace, sweetness, power, variety, finish, expression, and pathos" and concluded, "We have never heard anything like it."

The *Musical Cabinet* considered Knoop's and de Gony's enthusiastic reception a matter of civic pride. The reviewer characterized the audience as one of "the first taste and respectability," and expressed considerable satisfaction that a concert consisting wholly of cello and guitar should be received so favorably by a full house. The audience's reaction "speaks better of the musical taste of our city than we could have dared to expect." The reviewer also made it clear that this was a virtuoso concert. Focusing on the technical ability of the performers, he referred to Knoop as a virtuoso and described his playing with a detail seldom found at this time: "His tone is of exquisite sweetness, yet full of fire and power; his intonation is most accurate; his bowing is very effective, his style of playing extremely neat and finished; and his power of expression very great. His themes are given with great pathos, beauty, and expression; his adagios and singing passages are full of feeling and passion; his double stops, in thirds, sixths, and octaves, are highly finished and effective; and he exhibits many of the difficulties of the instrument in a style which shows himself to be a master of it."[27]

The reviewer did not mention a single piece that was played, and other than to characterize the performers' expressive ability, he did not once comment on the music itself. Yet there was no disdain or disapproval of the concert's virtuosic nature; he considered the performers to be artists. He wholly approved of the full house and exuberant response that they elicited.[28]

In a lecture before the Teacher's Class of the Handel and Haydn Society in 1841, T. B. Haywood lamented that America had produced no great composers, no native artists, like Mendelssohn, Spohr, or Neukomm. He was also concerned that America had produced no "*virtuosos* in music, like Thalberg, Chopin, Liszt, De Beriot, Ole Bull, who are chiefly distinguished for astonishing the world by the greatness of their musical talents, as exhibited in their performances on some particular instrument; who have extended the capabilities of that instrument; and who, if they have written at all, have written chiefly for it."[29] Although Haywood equated artist with composer, he discussed the virtuoso on equal footing with the composer. There is no reference to the emptiness or undesirability of the virtuoso's activities. He described what virtuosos do in a straightforward and matter-of-fact manner and included them in his categorization of great musicians. Haywood's lack of criticism of the virtuoso contrasts markedly with both contemporary European and later American attitudes.

A reaction against the virtuoso school surfaced in America around 1845. That year John S. Dwight wrote a lengthy two-part article in the *Harbinger* on "the virtuoso age in music," in which he compared the virtuoso to a gladiator who has "to contend with that most formidable foe, the extravagant demand of a pampered public taste for some new miracle that shall swallow up the miracle of yesterday, like Aaron's rod." Dwight equally deplored the tendency of the virtuoso to make music "secondary to the fashion and display of the thing," and the audiences who come "to see a great deed performed, to admire and applaud a wonderful achievement." Yet Dwight was not unqualified in his criticism on the virtuoso school. He conceded that the profession of the solo artist could be a noble calling and a "very distinct and legitimate province of the art," when not corrupted by the temptation for personal display and adulation.[30]

William W. Story had voiced similar concerns about the virtuoso school in his address before the Harvard Musical Association in 1842. Story categorized the virtuosi from France and Germany as "dexterous instrumentalists" rather than "great creators and originators." He connected their popularity among Boston audiences with the "passion for novelty" that he found "typical of the taste of his age," and he lamented that pieces were performed "solely to display the power of the instrument or the skill of the player." In consequence, "music [is] sacrificed entirely to attain that end." Story did recognize that even though the music of the virtuoso school was not profound, it was "graceful and accomplished." He acknowledged that one could enjoy it, and he was perfectly willing to pay homage to it. He warned, however, against confusing it with the real thing. It was folly to compare the waltzes of Strauss or the piano music of Chopin, Liszt, Henselt, or Thalberg with Handel, Beethoven, or even Bellini, Weber, Gluck, Hummel or Spohr. Story's list of classical composers was broader than Dwight's, encompassing Italian opera as well as German instrumental composers, and he verged on approval of the virtuoso school itself by including Spohr and Hummel in the list. Unlike Dwight, who found German music superior, Story distinguished more between the newer and older generations. His tolerance of different types of music resembled the older gentry attitude: even though he considered the music of the classical masters superior, he acknowledged the worth of other types. He even conceded that there was value in the waltz.[31]

Story's lecture was given three years before Dwight's *Harbinger* article appeared, when attitudes toward the virtuoso were in transition. If we look back to the beginning of the 1840s, we find that Dwight's position toward the virtuoso was considerably different from what it had become by 1845. In July 1840 Dwight reviewed the Boston concerts of the past season for the *Dial*, discussing at some length two concerts of Rackeman and two of Kossowski, both pianists. He explicitly stated that they performed music of the "new school of Piano Forte playing," which included compositions by Thalberg, Dohler, Chopin, Henselt, and Liszt. He acknowledged that their compositions "have given new meaning to the Piano Forte," and that they are designed to display the virtuosic ability of the performer. He described the pieces enthusiastically, calling them "rich, brilliant, wild, astonishing"; "they are everything marvellous and exquisite." He singled out favorites, referring to Liszt's "Gallope chromatique" as the "wildest and most original thing of all." And lest there be any doubt that Dwight was thoroughly enraptured by these performances, he added: 'It was a satisfaction to hear them," and "it is with pleasure that we record these things."[32]

Dwight's 1840 position on the virtuoso school was similar to Story's. Dwight accepted the new school, so long as the listener did not confuse it with the music of the classical masters, whom he still held in higher repute. He cautioned the listener to accept compositions of the new school "for what they are, without complaining that they are not something else." He nevertheless wished that the pianists had played more music of Weber or Beethoven. He was particularly pleased that two trios of Beethoven were included in the programs, and that the audiences responded favorably. He encouraged such music: "Let us have more of this." Yet although Dwight's 1840 position on Beethoven was consistent with his later views, the full implications of the virtuoso school for a sacralized musical standard were not yet clear to him.

Positions about the virtuoso school hardened in the mid-1840s, prompted by two related events: the appearance of a growing number of well-known European virtuosi in Boston and the emergence of the Boston Philharmonic Society as a shaper of musical taste. The Philharmonic itself sponsored several of the concerts by foreign virtuosi. As we saw in chapter 9, the society had no pretension about the moral benefits of its presentations. It was interested in good musical entertainment, and attendance at its concerts vindicated its approach. Its success also sent shudders through those members of the upper class who envisaged instrumental music as a tool of moral reform. It questioned the very premises of their position.

The most important foreign virtuoso to come to Boston in the early 1840s was Ole Bull, who made his first tour of America between 1843 and 1845. Bull proved a particularly vexing case for those concerned with the status and integrity of instrumental music. His taste had been suspect in Europe for years. Even Mason was struck by the shallowness of his music, while recognizing the genius of his playing, in 1837.[33] Yet to most Americans who heard him, Bull's virtuosity had no parallel. In addition, he proved a charming visitor even to those who were prone to dismiss him.

Dwight was ambivalent about Ole Bull. In a concert review in the

Harbinger of June 28, 1845, he was by no means critical of Bull's playing. On the contrary, he not only acknowledged Bull's ability as a violinist but even found his improvisations inspiring. Most of the article, however, discussed Bull as a composer, and here Dwight was critical. He faulted Bull's pieces for their lack of unity, although he realized that their purpose as virtuosic vehicles dictated their somewhat free, rapidly changing form.

Dwight's discussion of Bull was part of a larger propagandist effort on behalf of the doctrine of Fourierism, to which the *Harbinger* was dedicated. It was around the Fourierian type of utopian socialism that Brook Farm was originally organized. At the heart of Fourier's theory was his concept of universal unity, in which the individual, by following his natural instincts, would be attracted to those activities that would allow him to fulfill his role in a perfect, harmonious society. This was Dwight's understanding of Fourierism, which was shared by George Ripley, the first editor of the *Harbinger*.[34]

Dwight interpreted Bull's compositions within the framework of Fourierism. He considered them emblematic of the times, their lack of unity reflecting the "individualism of the age." Dwight viewed his time as a period of transition "to a new order of society," in which individualism would give way to a "Unitary Concert" and an "orchestra of genius." Rather than condemning the competition and individualism of the age, however, he saw it as a valuable and necessary step. The virtuosity that resulted from it served to "develop the powers of the individual instrument." Thus, in utopian terms, Dwight defended the virtuoso on the grounds that he was raising the general performance level of his instrument.

Dwight's criticism flew in the face of much popular opinion that elevated Bull to a minor deity. Part of Bull's attraction was a magnetic personality. In November 1845 Christopher P. Cranch wrote to Dwight about Bull's reception in New York. Cranch complimented Dwight for putting Bull's music in sober perspective, a perspective that Cranch fully shared. He then observed that others were angry with Dwight for not making him "the God he is here." "There is such a nimbus of light around him at present, that few persons are clear-sighted enough to speak moderately of him."[35] Later that same day Cranch met Bull. His attitude changed dramatically. The next week he wrote to Dwight again: "The deep impression the man made upon me was hardly in harmony with the very moderate tone in which I have been speaking of his music. . . . He is the most delightful person I almost ever met. He attracted me at once. . . . I parted from him with deep regret, for it was the first and last time I met him in society."[36]

In spite of Dwight's increasing unease with the virtuoso school, he remained susceptible to its charms throughout much of the 1840s. His description of the first season of the Boston Philharmonic Society in 1843, for instance, was almost entirely negative. He disapproved of the ensemble, the choice of music, the hall, and the audience. Yet he vigorously defended the playing of Vieuxtemps, whose virtuosic performance obviously moved him. He referred to Vieuxtemps' "divine solos," which were lost on both the "braying" players and the "most unmusical of audience."[37] And Dwight was writing this from the perspective of three years later, in 1847.

Even Dwight's reserved attitude toward Ole Bull came only after lengthy reflection. His original reaction was quite different. In 1844 Lydia Maria Child sought to enlist him to write an article on Bull for the *Democratic Review*. Dwight replied that he was interested but uncertain of his ability to do so. He was deeply involved with Brook Farm at the time and could only promise to attempt to write the article. He was also in one of his period fits of depression, which may have affected his assessment of his own abilities. In his letter to Child, Dwight did offer his opinion of Bull, writing that he was deeply moved the first time he had heard him: "The most glorious sensation I ever had was to sit in one of his audiences, and to feel that all were elevated to the same pitch with myself, that the spirit in every breast had risen to the same level. My impulse was to speak to any one and to every one as to an intimate friend. The most indifferent person was a man—a living soul—to me. The most remote and proud I did not fear nor despise. In that moment they were accessible,—nay, more, worth reaching. This certainly was the highest testimony to his great art, to his great soul." Dwight then admitted that, "excepting only a symphony of Beethoven or a mass of Mozart, nothing ever filled me with such deep, solemn joy." He called Bull a genius who, compared to Vieuxtemps, was "the stronger and greater man," "the most original," and "the most never-failing and commanding." Bull "does inspire as the other does not."[38]

Dwight's attitude is typical of American reaction to the virtuoso school. The first wave of virtuosi found relatively virgin audiences, unaccustomed to the skill, the power, and the mastery of such performers. The effect was understandably overwhelming. Only after this initial phase had passed did writers and listeners begin to raise doubts about the musical value of what the virtuosi were doing. At that point reaction to the merits of the virtuosi began to parallel that of Europe, with segments of the public falling into opposing camps.

The new years between the original virtuoso invasion and the reaction, roughly from 1841 to 1845, was a critical time for instrumental music in America. In 1840 it faced an uphill battle, with little public support, especially in Boston. Then appearances by numerous virtuosi from 1841 on began to bring the public to the concert hall to hear instrumental music, a feat the Boston Academy of Music was having difficulty doing. Once there and once introduced to the expressive range of instruments, the audience could begin to form preferences for specific types of instrumental music. Critics could argue the merits of different styles and genres. Yet until audiences were enthusiastic about the idea of instrumental concerts, distinctions between different types of instrumental music existed in a relative vacuum, an atmosphere devoid of significant public support.

By the time a reaction against the virtuoso school appeared, the classical canon was well in place. The emergence of the canon in Boston can be dated from Eliot's efforts to feature orchestral music at the Boston Academy of Music's concerts, beginning in 1840. The five years from 1840 to 1845 were crucial in the formation of the canon in Boston. During that time Beethoven symphonies became known to the public through frequent repetition by the academy, regular chamber concerts were introduced (although on only a small and purposely limited scale), orchestral music became popular enough to encourage rival ensembles, and instrumental music in general began to be favored by the public. All of this preceded the reaction to the virtuoso school, which occurred almost entirely after 1845.

Another significant difference between the emergence of the canon in Europe and in America was the role that choral societies played in America. When Weber considered the various groups that contributed to the fracturing of the musical world of early nineteenth-century Europe, he found that the choral societies stood apart from the others. Although they aligned themselves with the conservatives, their repertoire being essentially the music of Handel, Haydn, Beethoven, Mendelssohn, and a few contemporaries, they were outside the mainstream of European concert life. Members of the choruses had no other links to the classical musical world, and their audiences consisted mainly of friends and relatives. The few attempts to broaden the choral audience were not successful.[39]

Precisely this group, the choral societies, has been considered the backbone of the classical-music movement in America. Virtually all scholars have recognized the historical importance of the Boston Handel and Haydn Society in the establishment of the cultivated tradition. Similar societies in other cities played comparable roles. Their background as an outgrowth of the singing-school movement afforded them a place in society at variance with similar institutions in Europe. And, as we have seen, they were closely associated with orchestral societies. This earned them a role in the musical life of most American cities for which there was no European parallel.

With the emergence of the canon in America the role of the wind band changed dramatically. Although wind bands were popular in Europe, they had nowhere near the historical importance that they did in America. In the early Federal period military bands were the most common (and in many places the only) large instrumental ensemble. And as late as the 1830s wind bands were considered on a par with symphonic ensembles. They played the same music and were welcome to share the stage. In fact, the presence of a wind band was considered a plus by anyone organizing a concert.

Public perception of wind bands changed markedly between 1830 and 1845. By 1845 they were considered distinctly inferior to symphony orchestras. Signs of the change are foreshadowed in a campaign Theodore Hach mounted in his *Musical Magazine*, beginning in 1839, which associated bands with bad taste. Describing the 1838–1839 season, Hach observed that band concerts were the most well-attended musical events of the season, demonstrating "how gaudy the public taste for music still is." And in reviewing a concert by Edward Kendall in 1840, Hach stated forthrightly that "music by the brass band in a concert room is not and will never be to our taste."[40]

To support his position on bands in the concert hall, Hach made a distinction between indoor and outdoor music: "We like to hear their music in its proper place; that is, in the open air, at the head of one of our handsome volunteer companies, for instance: for we know that they have some very good performers among them. Neither do we blame them for making money when they can. But that performances on such instruments, in the concert room, where they cannot but be heard to the greatest disadvantage, should meet with greater success than any others offered to the public, presents indeed a humiliating picture of the public musical taste."[41] Hach's view was hardly new. The distinction between indoor and outdoor instruments had existed for centuries in Europe. Hach's invocation of this distinction, however, was new to

American music, where wind instruments had formed the core of instrumental ensembles since the earliest records of such ensembles, and bands like Kendall's were still very popular.

Part of the change in perception of the band had to do with repertoire. Through the mid-1830s the band repertoire differed little from the orchestral repertoire. A typical band concert consisted of one or more overtures, in all likelihood by Rossini or Auber, several solos, and some dances. The principal differences between band and other concerts were the prominence of dances and the tendency to feature instrumental rather than vocal solos. Band concerts actually represented the most sustained attempts to present all-instrumental concerts in Boston.

The association of bands with dance was a damaging connection in the minds of many Bostonians, even in the early nineteenth century. Bostonians loved to dance, and dances as well as dancing schools had flourished in Boston throughout the eighteenth and nineteenth centuries. As late as the 1840s, however, Bostonians remained reserved if not antagonistic toward dances. In 1842 J. R. Lowell wrote to Emelyn Eldredge in New York about the prospects of visiting Boston: "You are very gay, I hear, in New York, balls. etc., being the standard amusements provided for every evening. . . . Ah! we poor puritanical Boston people will seem quite tame and flat, I am afraid."[42] As bands proliferated in the 1830s, dances became one of their principal sources for income. Most of the bands were available not only as a large ensemble but also in various smaller combinations, depending on the demand. These smaller groups, frequently known as "Quadrille Bands," became the desired ensembles for dances in Boston in the 1830s and 1840s. It is highly unlikely that some of the bands in Boston in the early nineteenth century could have survived economically were it not for dances.

It was common early in the century to have concerts conclude with a dance. With the attempts to raise the level of instrumental music to an idealistic plane, the separation of instrumental concert music from dance music became more pressing. The *Boston Musical Gazette* was appalled that this separation was not occurring in New York in 1838. In all fairness, so were some New Yorkers. The *Gazette* reprinted a report from the *New York Musical Review* criticizing a recent concert of the Euterpean Society of New York, which the reviewer considered possibly the oldest musical society in the United States. The Euterpean Society was founded in the late 1790s, at approximately the same time that the Philoharmonic Society was found in Boston. Because of its pedigree, the reviewer considered the Euterpean Society an object of veneration and felt that it should be providing proper models. The reviewer was therefore dismayed that the society followed its concerts with a ball. In doing so, he concluded, "we opine that its members look upon it more as a social and convivial circle than a society for the cultivation of musical taste."[43]

Advocates of the idealistic view of instrumental music faced the same problem with band music that the Presbyterian-Congregational hymnodic reformers had faced with secular tunes: their prior associations tainted them. Both groups of reformers needed to endorse music that was consistent with their goals and free of improper associations. The music of Haydn, Mozart, and Beethoven was relatively unknown, and where it was known it was associated with exalted sacred choral music. The symphony as an idiom had only a sketchy history in early Federal America. I do not believe that Hach, Dwight, and Eliot chose the music they did in such a calculated manner; Mozart, Haydn, and Beethoven truly moved them. I do believe, however, that they rejected certain instrumental music in full cognizance of the associations it carried in the mind of the public. Band music fitted that category.

Yet the change in perception regarding orchestral and band music around 1840 depended on another change, a change in the way string and wind instruments themselves were regarded. Prior to 1840 wind instruments were favored. As we have seen, the military band had much to do with that. The flute was considered the favorite instrument of gentlemen. In his "Reminisces of an Ex-Pierian" Samuel Jennison observed, "At that time [the late 1830s] the flute was almost the only instrument played by gentlemen."[44] The membership lists of the Pierian Sodality confirm the essential, although somewhat exaggerated, truth of Jennison's remark. Flutes were more common than any other instrument.

The violin, in particular, was held in disrepute. It was associated with popular dance. In a review of the concerts of the 1839–1840 season, Dwight referred to the "dancing master's fiddle" and connected it with Jim Crow, Harrison's melodies, waltzes, and Russell's songs.[45] In the proposal to form the Harvard Musical Association, Dwight distinguished the proposals of his group, "the serious promoters of the best interests of the young," from "the killers of time only and those who scrape the fiddle for bread."[46] A German resident in the United States from 1827 (or earlier) to 1836, Francis Grund, observed that he did not hear a single amateur performer on the violin in the entire time he was in the country.[47] Men confined themselves to playing the flute.

Jennison reported that during his four years at Harvard, from 1835 to 1839, he knew of only two string players, one violinist and one cellist. The Pierians persuaded the violinist to set his instrument aside and take up the flute. He was lucky. Earlier, in 1830, the Arionic Sodality, according to its records, "voted that a nondescript freshman, who was heard scraping a fiddle be neglected." We recall that in his 1826 address on church music Mason wanted to advocate the use of the violin in church but was constrained from doing so because of its too many "irrelevant associations." To Mason irrelevant meant secular, profane, or vulgar.[48]

It was a bold step in 1836 for Samuel Eliot to hire Joseph Keller to teach violin and form an orchestra at the Boston Academy of Music. Eliot stressed that the orchestra was subordinate to the chorus, but the very act of offering instruction on the violin placed instrumental music on a par with vocal music. Eliot's hiring of Henry Schmidt the next year as leader of the orchestra was an even stronger affirmation of the importance of string instruments. Eliot wrote to Keller that the board of directors "would be highly gratified to obtain a violin played in so superior manner as Herr Schmidt exhibits.[49]

Although the academy's effort to generate an interest in the violin as a serious instrument of study was unusual, it was not unprecedented. Louis Ostinelli had labored since 1818 to educate Bostonians to the violin. His first concert in 1818 (described at the beginning of this chapter) was considered an important musical event. The *Euterpeiad* called it "the most genteel thing of the kind we ever witnessed in Boston."[50] *Genteel* was still a term of praise in the early nineteenth century, acquiring the pejorative connotation that it carries today only in the second half of the century. For at least the next ten years Ostinelli was considered the finest violinist in Boston, and one of the finest in the country. He was keenly aware of the reputation the violin had as a vernacular instrument in New England. According to several anecdotes, he was furious when his violin was referred to as a fiddle or when he was requested to play dance music. Once when asked by a lady if he was to play for a dance following a concert, he deliberately cut his violin strings and said, "Veree story, veree story, madam, you see I can no play."[51]

The prevailing attitude about the violin changed totally in the 1840s. The Boston Academy of Music had begun the process, but two other factors contributed significantly to it. Musical journals like the *Musical Magazine* and the *Musical Cabinet* emphasized the importance of string instruments, both as solo instruments and in ensembles. They championed the orchestral push of the academy and advocated the introduction of string-quartet performances. More important, however, was the flood of concerts featuring string instruments. It is no coincidence that string virtuosi become common in the same year that the academy began its orchestral concerts. The virtuoso movement thus advanced materially the cause of classical instrumental music in Boston by providing Bostonians with a first-hand demonstration of the potential of the violin. The style and ability of these foreign performers were unprecedented, and for many listeners provided an entirely new dimension to the potential of the instrument. Bostonians heard other virtuosi also, ranging from Ribas on the oboe to de Gony on the guitar, but the concentration of violin virtuosi in the critical years between 1840 and 1843 probably did more than any other single development to establish the viability of a musical style based on string instruments.

The *Musical Cabinet* recognized the concerts of 1840 to 1842 to be of a different order to any previous ones. The journal praised in particular the presentation of Beethoven's Fifth and Sixth Symphonies by the Boston Academy of Music and the concerts of Knoop, Nagel, and Herwig. All were string players; Knoop a cellist, and Nagel and Herwig violinists. The *Musical Cabinet* claimed the concerts "furnished a musical entertainment of a much higher character than has ever before been presented to the lovers of music in Boston," and saw in them the beginning of a new and better era: "We regard both of these classes of concerts [the virtuoso and the orchestra] as marking a new era in the history of music in Boston; and the degree in which it is superior in character to former eras, is very gratifying, and affords much encouragement for the future."[52]

When the Boston Academy of Music programmed Beethoven's Fifth Symphony for the first time, in 1841, all of the musical journals were lavish in their praise of both the music and the performance. The *Musical Magazine* saw it as another step in the advancement of musical progress. The *Musical Reporter*, a much less sophisticated journal and so a better reflection of public opinion, acknowledged that the performance probably helped educate many Bostonians to what instrumental music could do: "The deep harmonies of Beethoven receive from his touch a richness and sweetness of tone, that surpasses all our former conceptions of the instruments."[53]

In this heady atmosphere of change band music and sacred vocal music, both at the very center of Boston musical life only some ten years earlier, were simply overwhelmed. Neither disappeared, but each assumed a place different to that it previously had in the musical milieu of Boston. Except for the Handel and Haydn Society, sacred vocal music moved to the peripheries, no longer attracting large audiences or generating much press. Band music continued to enjoy a strong following through-out the nineteenth century but suffered from the emergent duality that had become apparent by 1840. After the criticism of the Boston Philharmonic Society for hiring Kendall as the leader of its orchestra in 1843, band music no longer shared the principal concert halls with other genres. At times bands would be in the limelight, as when Gilmore assembled his "monster concerts" in 1869 and 1872 but only an extraordinary personality like Gilmore could command wide support for bands, and not even he was accepted by the increasingly insular and elitist Boston musical establishment.

Band music itself did not change. Public perception about instrumental music changed, and band music was left behind or, depending on one's point of view, remained true to its roots. We are familiar with the way bands were viewed in the late nineteenth century, as popular, vernacular entertainment, evoking pleasure and a little bit of awe, so long as they were not too serious or pretentious. That is precisely the way orchestral music was regarded in Federal America, and that is why little distinction was made between a band and an orchestra, and why military bands could share the same program with orchestral ensembles. Hach, Dwight, Eliot, and others needed to convince audiences that instrumental music was capable of serious, ethical expression. Dwight's regarding parts of Beethoven's symphonies as a religious experience was only the most extreme example of this problem. Eliot's and Story's descriptions of Beethoven's Fifth Symphony, for all their fantasy, fitted this same pattern (as we saw in chapter 8). It was difficult for them to argue, however, that band music was capable of similar interpretation. Band music was familiar, and it was considered entertainment. Prior to 1840 that was sufficient for any instrumental ensemble. Only after 1840, when orchestral music was draped in new idealistic clothing, did band music seem something separate.

The campaign to elevate the status of orchestral music was so successful that abstract instrumental music became not only the core of the canon but also the basis on which other, at times quite disparate, genres were judged. Even opera, a vocal, dramatic, representative, theatrical genre, totally at odds with the abstract symphonic ideal, came under the symphonic ethos of the extent that the symphony more than the stage set the tone and the attitude with which opera would be perceived in America. And here I do not mean simply Wagnerian opera, which is symphonic in nature. By the late nineteenth century, Italian operas like Verdi's were presented and received as if they were abstract musical compositions. This development illustrates vividly the extent to which the arguments Bostonians advanced in the early nineteenth century took hold of and influenced American culture.

Early in the century opera had an image very different from the one it later acquired. The musical idealism that shaped Bostonian attitudes toward instrumental music profoundly affected the way in which opera was conceptualized later in the century, even though during the early Federal period Boston was clearly behind New York in staging opera. Although Boston had had theatrical entertainment from 1793, and the presence of the theater certainly affected the musical life of Boston in many ways, the theater was much more central to New York's musical culture than to Boston's. Opera, first in the form of English ballad opera and English adaptations of Italian opera, then later pure Italian opera as well, drew larger audiences and remained a fashionable attraction for the upper classes to a much greater extent in New York than in Boston.

From the moment Italian opera was first introduced in New York in 1825 by the Park Theatre, which had engaged Manuel Garcia's company, it was identified as a fashionable entertainment for the upper class. Prices for box seats and the pit were doubled, to $2 and $1 respectively, although the gallery price remained at twenty-five cents. Prior to opening night the New York newspapers had described the opera as a "source of rational and refined enjoyment," which "ranked as the most elegant and refined among the amusements of the higher classes of the old world." The press also mounted a strenuous campaign to educate the public, less about opera than about conventions of dress and behavior expected of the audience. One writer urged that the theater management impose a dress code. This was strongly opposed by other writers, not on the grounds that a wider variety of dress should be allowed but because such limitations should be voluntary in a republic; that is, society itself should enforce the code. Reports of the opening night indicate that the efforts at self-policing were successful; a large number of women, "elegant and well-dressed," were present, and the audience behaved decorously, in marked contrast to prevailing theatrical standards.[54]

When Francis Grund visited New York between 1827 and 1836, he was baffled by American reaction to opera. He reported opera on a scale commensurate with that anywhere in Europe but observed that opera never really caught on, and he attributed its failure to the high price of tickets and Yankee shrewdness about value. He argued that opera was essentially drama and that if one could not understand the language one would miss the entertainment and be left with only the other half, the music. Thus "the good people of New York . . . were obliged to pay for the remaining half double of what they were accustomed to pay for a whole night's amusement at another theater. The ratio was as one to four when compared to the other plays, and was, consequently, too unreasonable to satisfy such nice calculators as the Americans." Grund entirely missed the point, that the high price of tickets was part of a calculated effort at exclusion.[55]

The Garcia company's stay in 1825 was brief, but a pattern had been set. Italian operra was an elitist and fashionable form of entertainment. A second attempt to establish Italian opera in New York, in 1833, was even more elitist. The perpetrators of the second attempt, a group of shareholders or proprietors who formed the Italian Opera Association, separated opera from the theater and built a grandiose opera house. Ticket prices were again double those of the theater, except those for seats in the gallery, which were tripled to seventy-five cents. Proprietors could purchase boxes for $6,000 and decorate them as they wished. As might be expected, each tried to outdo the other in the lavishness of the decor. Not surprisingly, opera engendered considerable resentment and debate about the place of such exclusive and opulent activities in American society. This particular opera venture was not supported for long, however. It closed in 1835 after only two season.

There was no serious attempt to establish Italian opera in Boston prior to 1847, although anglicized Italian operas had been staged irregularly after the Tremont Theatre opened in 1827. These anglicized versions were more than translations; they were adaptations that allowed considerable departure from the original, including the interpolation of substitution of English ballads for the original arias. Anglicized Italian opera represented a hybrid between pure Italian opera and the popular stage. Because it was more accessible than pure Italian opera, it attracted all classes. The presentation of anglicized Italian opera in Boston depended on imported stars. When an important singer or troupe appeared in Boston, opera briefly became fashionable. Most notable were the appearances of the Woods, beginning in 1833. Joseph and Mary Ann (Patton) Wood made several brief engagements of about one month each during the 1830s, performing many of the operas popular at the time: *Cinderella, Guy Mannering, The Barber of Seville, Love in a Village, Massaniello, The Marriage of Figaro*. But as soon as they departed, opera, left to local talent, languished.

Regardless of the type of opera presented in Boston, general interest in the genre never reached the levels that it did in New York; other types of musical entertainment proved more attractive. The large singing societies, such as the Handel and Haydn Society, for example, had a prestige far beyond that of their counterparts in New York, and when taste shifted in the 1840s, it was toward instrumental music rather than opera. The theater's loss was instrumental music's gain, however. Because secular concerts did not have to compete with opera for prestige, they held a position of prominence in the Boston musical world that they had nowhere else in America.

The differences in attitude between Bostonians and New Yorkers about music is apparent as early as 1826, when prominent citizens in Boston and New York made parallel attempts to establish new musical organizations. At the very time that some of the most prominent citizens of Boston released a circular calling for the creation of a society to promote secular concerts, a group of New York citizens attempted to create a company that would produce Italian opera. The two proposals were similar in many respects: each was to depend on a group of subscribers who would contribute a substantial sum of money, $100 each in Boston and $250 each in New York. The New York group's goals were more ambitious, to raise $100,000 from four hundred subscribers, as opposed to $10,000 from one hundred subscribers in Boston. In each case the wealthy individuals would retain control, although they would participate only as patrons.

The proposals had equivalent rationales, cast in remarkably similar wording. The New York proposal spoke of opera as "a source of rational and refined pleasure, imparting a purer character to public amusements, and elevating the public taste." The Boston circular promised that its proposed concerts would be "of the purest and most refined character" and defined its objective as being "to promote the cultivation of the Science of Music . . . and to advance the growth and diffusion of an *enlightened* taste in this department of the Fine Arts." The New York proposal claimed that opera, "an admirable school of instruction in the science of music," would "aid the public morals, counteracting the influence of less innocent pleasure." The authors of the Boston circular "conceive[d] public amusements indispensable in large societies, and they think it no trifling service to good morals, to aid in rendering those attractive which are perfectly innocent, which are of a nature to polish the manners . . . and the enjoyment of which leaves no regret behind." Thus both the Boston circular and the New York proposal emphasized the moral effect of music and extolled music for its purity and science. But they still viewed it within the realm of innocent pleasure.[56]

The two proposals were motivated by similar events and suffered similar fates. Both came soon after the demise of previous musical organizations: in Boston the Philharmonic Society and the Apollo Society had ended their public activities; in New York the third Philharmonic Society was in a weakened condition that would soon prove fatal, and the management of Park Theatre had declined to renew the Garcias' contract. New Yorkers, significantly, put their efforts into reviving opera rather than the Philharmonic. But the attempts to create new musical organizations failed in both cities.

By the late nineteenth century, New Yorkers had thoroughly identified musical culture with opera. The political and social establishment in New York and Boston each compiled a large, four-volume memorial history of its city in the 1890s. Both histories contained a chapter devoted to music. John D. Champlin, writing about New York, stated flatly that "the real beginning of New-York's musical development must be conceded to the coming among us of Italian opera." Champlin backed up his statement in the organization of his presentation: he crammed into one and one-quarter pages his discussion of all the musical societies that existed in the first half of the nineteenth century—the Apollo Society, the St. Cecilia Society, the Euterpean Society, the Philharmonic Society (1824), the Musical Fund Society, the Concordia, The New-York Choral Society, the Sacred Music Society, the "second Philharmonic Society" (1842), the Vocal Society, the American Musical Institute, and the New York Harmonic Society. He then devoted twelve pages to the development of opera. In another multivolume history of New York City written at about the same time, Martha J. Lamb and Burton Harrison viewed the city as a musical magnet, calling it with more pride than verbal elegance "the present goal toward which strains the genius of the world." They then spoke mostly of the recently renovated Metropolitan Opera.[57]

New York writers on music in the first half of the century also considered opera more important than instrumental music. In 1830 Charles Dingley, editor of the *The Euterpeiad: An Album of Music, Poetry, and*

Prose, discussed the state of music in America. His article was actually about music in New York, and it emphasized opera, stating that "drama in all its branches flourishes most." Dingley reviewed the activities of the leading theaters, the Park and Bowery, and discussed the Italian opera venture of Manuel Garcia and his company. He scarcely mentioned instrumental music, observing only at the end of his article that "at the Park Theatre, the band plays well together." In 1834 an article in the *American Music Journal*, probably by James Dunn, stated flatly that opera was "the highest branch of the art."[58] These views contrasted markedly with Bostonian ideas of the late 1830s and 1840s, which sought to elevate instrumental music to a position of supremacy.

The puritan hold on New England artistic life not only inhibited the development of the musical arts in Boston, specifically the theater and concert activity, but also gave to Boston's musical life a unique orientation. As we recall, the most successful concert organization early in the century, the Handel and Haydn Society, had deep roots in the singing school and psalmody. Early attempts at instrumental concert activity failed until Dwight and others provided a justification for instrumental music that owed much to that puritan tradition. Music that was abstract, and pure because it was abstract, became the desired standard in Boston. And when instrumental music was finally accepted, it assumed a significance far greater than that in other American urban centers.

It was precisely the Bostonian orientation toward abstract instrumental music that ultimately became the model for musical attitudes in later nineteenth-century America. The model was derived from New England puritanism, with its emphasis on the moral, edifying, and spiritual and its aversion to the frivolous and bacchanalian, and found its ideal realization in the orchestral music of the classical masters, Haydn, Mozart, and Beethoven. In consequence, the symphony orchestra assumed a special place in the American musical hierarchy, and a community's orchestra became a matter of civic pride. The quality of an orchestra became a litmus test for the community, as the orchestra reflected its moral as well as artistic fiber. In such circumstances it was only natural that support of the orchestra devolved on the leaders of the community, the elite, and became their responsibility and domain.

The Boston model significantly affected American attitudes toward opera. How to conceptualize opera was an issue that arose repeatedly throughout much of the nineteenth century. In the mid-1800s a heated debate erupted between William Henry Fry and John S. Dwight about the nature of opera. Fry and others argued fervently for a national opera. They believed that American composers should turn to American subjects and create a uniquely American idiom. Dwight on the other hand believed that music was universal, so that it mattered little whether American or European themes were used. Standards were universal, and if an opera was good enough it would win its way. Fry's arguments for a national opera never met acceptance. They have a certain allure today because they were neither as consciously elitist nor as narrowly sanctimonious as Dwight's purism. And Fry's eloquent appeal to a pride in America strikes a harmonious chord. But his case fell essentially on deaf ears, in part because Fry and his colleagues could never meet the fundamental challenge: show me.[59]

There were other reasons for the American public's resistance to Fry's argument. As we have seen, the attempt to establish Italian opera in New York was one of the clearest and most consciously elitist acts in American musical history. Yet the early attempts to use opera in that manner failed. Opera still bore the stigma of a theatrical genre and could not be dissociated from other theatrical elements, in spite of conscious efforts by its supporters. The content of the plays could not be ignored, at least at the time. Karen Ahlquist has shown that opera audiences in the first half of the century were troubled by what passed for a plot on the opera stage. The morality of some of the libretti themselves was disturbing. Operas that were successful in the 1820s like *Guy Mannering* and *The Devil's Bridge*, were melodramas with exaggerated characterizations of good and evil. Successful operas in the 1830s, like *Cinderella*, *La sonnambula*, and *Clari* emphasized women whose virtue was tested but survived intact. They remained essentially theater, seen and judged for their theatrical content, which included the plot.[60]

In the second half of the century attitudes toward what was presented on the opera stage changed dramatically. Even operas as morally offensive (to nineteenth-century America) as Verdi's *Rigoletto* and *La traviata* became acceptable not because the plot was palatable but because the music transcended it. Audiences came to hear music, not drama. A plot could be immoral so long as the music was elevating.[61] The presentation of opera in a foreign language eventually proved a benefit, because it removed the plot that much further from the audience's consciousness. Musical absolutism had permeated audience reaction. The successful establishment of opera in New York in the second half of the nineteenth century owed much to a purist, abstract approach to music, which was essentially the Boston model. Thus the victory of opera as high culture in this country ironically represented a victory for Dwight and the symphonic standard that he and other New England writers articulated in the 1830s and 1840s.

Chapter Eleven

Boston and Beyond

When Samuel Jennison was asked to give the Harvard Musical Association address in 1851, he began by summarizing the changes that had occurred in the Boston musical world in the preceding half-century. He could look back with pride on many accomplishments. Italian opera had been established on Boston soil, the Harvard Musical Association itself had sponsored several series of successful chamber-music concerts, and weekly "rehearsals" of a new association for orchestral music drew large crowds. Foreign musicians, whose ranks filled the orchestras, were arriving daily, and American musicians regularly departed for study abroad. American composers were producing symphonic pieces, and music dissertations were being allowed in higher education.

Jennison described a musical world vastly different from the one of only ten years earlier. Then orchestral music was still a novelty, Italian opera was untried, chamber-music concerts were unknown, instrumental virtuosi had yet to make a significant impact, and Harvard had firmly rejected any role for music. Yet as we read Jennison's description we think less of the early than the late nineteenth century. In his retrospective view, Jennison was describing with remarkable accuracy the American musical scene for the rest of the century. Even more important, his history stands as a striking witness to the deep division that separates the two half-centuries in musical matters.

If we look ahead to 1870, we can see just how different the musical landscape of Boston had become. Except for Dwight, the old triumvirate was gone. Samuel Eliot was no longer alive, and his institution, the Boston Academy of Music, had been extinct for twenty-three years. Lowell Mason, who had permanently left Boston in 1850, still cast a deep shadow nationally but had little impact on the Boston music world. Only John S. Dwight remained a force in musical Boston. He had found in *Dwight's Journal of Music* an ideal medium through which to propagate his vision of music. The extent of Dwight's influence, however, is unclear. The precise circulation of the journal has never been ascertained. And Dwight himself was becoming isolated. His purist, Germanic view of music never really reflected the tastes of the Boston public. As his views hardened, he became increasingly distanced from the reality of Boston concert life.

Dwight nevertheless remained a powerful figure in Boston music circles. His power base came from his connection to elite society, which was centered in two organizations: the Saturday Club and the Harvard Musical Association. As a member of the Saturday Club Dwight was admitted into the inner sanctum of the elite. The club joined literature and power; its membership included some of the richest, most prominent men in Boston, such as Thomas G. Appleton, Charles Francis Adams, and James Elliot Cabot, as well as some of the age's most important literary figures, such as Ralph Waldo Emerson, Henry W. Longfellow, and Nathaniel Hawthorne. Its stated purpose was to provide a forum for the exchange of ideas.

The Saturday Club could command the support of the elite because of the continuing respect accorded rhetoric in New England. In the minds of most New Englanders literature easily eclipsed all the other arts. And it was Dwight's literary rather than his musical gifts that earned him a place in the Saturday Club. His friendship with Emerson and Parker, his principal entree into intellectual society, had been forged when his work in German literature far outweighed his musical accomplishments. No other musician was a member of the Saturday Club, although by the 1880s there were other potential candidates in Boston, such as William Mason and B. J. Lang.[1] No painter, sculptor, or other visual artist was a member.

Dramatic changes occurred in the musical power structure of Boston in the late nineteenth century. By the 1860s the Harvard Musical Association had assumed an even wider role in Boston's musical life than it had enjoyed in the 1840s. But its influence began to wane soon thereafter. The old guard, composed of the Harvard Musical Association, the Handel and Haydn Society, and other similar institutions, gave way to new efforts to bring a more enlivened and financially secure musical programming to Boston. The struggle had serious historical implications, the most direct being the formation of the Boston Symphony Orchestra out of the wreckage produced by too many organizations that had become too complacent and ossified.

Yet the struggle, which was for control of orchestral and chamber music in Boston, was purely internal, limited to a relatively small group of musicians and dilettantes interested in a fairly narrow musical world. Many varieties of popular music and parlor music lay wholly outside this arena. The factions or cliques interested in orchestral and chamber music were all led by members of the elite. By this time these two types of music had become the province of the upper class. Samuel Eliot had originally initiated the elite into the musical world in Boston and had successfully established the symphony orchestra as the most prestigious forum for music. Dwight had completed the task. In an environment in which puritan prejudices about frivolity were still widespread, he had provided the moral justification that enabled secular music to be accepted. By viewing music as a type of abstract religious expression, he had provided a direct link between it and the world of puritan rhetoric.

In his argument that all music was inherently sacred—the more abstract the music, the more manifest its sacred qualities—Dwight had not only taken the notion of taste one step further than earlier propagandists but had also provided a means to allow Eliot's more flexible notion of taste to serve an elitist political agenda. Orchestral and chamber music were set apart. They possessed a quality that no other music did. From that principle a musical hierarchy, with a clear apogee, was established. The struggle then for control of the orchestral world of Boston became the struggle for control of the top rung of that hierarchy. That struggle, a complex problem deserving intensive study, awaits further scholarly investigation.[2] In its breadth and complexity it will reveal much about many aspects of turn-of-the-century America.

Yet one issue overrides the struggle, independent of the intricacies that still need to be sorted out. None of the battles over musical organizations among the elite of Boston ever challenged the premise of the moral nature of music. By the late nineteenth century certain types of music were assumed to be superior to others because they reflected moral values that set them apart from those that aimed at nothing more than entertainment. It thus mattered little who won the orchestral war. The terms of peace were the same: the symphony orchestra deserved to be patronized by the very best (most elite) citizens of Boston because it provided the very best (most moral) music.

This position was limited neither to Boston nor the nineteenth century. It still dominates the cultural landscape of most American cities, and debates about the place of music in American society that began in Boston in the 1830s and 1840s continue. For example, when Congress deliberated the establishment of a national arts foundation and a national humanities foundation in the 1960s, the arguments were remarkably similar to Eliot's. Morton Sosna described the mid-1960s as a "uniquely critical moment in the history of American cultural nationalism." According to Sosna cultural nationalism, as opposed to national culturalism, "views the arts within the context of highbrow and lowbrow and seeks to use high culture to provide a unifying identity for the nation as a whole. High culture is used to define the role of the nation in the world as well as present to the world a superior society. It is meant to foster external as well as internal pride."[3]

In the mid-1960s the cold war had entered a new phase, in which the imminent military threat gave way to renewed economic, scientific, and cultural competition. Many members of American society were questioning the disparity between America's prosperity and scientific accomplishments on the one hand and its cultural products on the other. America was perceived as lacking in spiritual commitment, a deficiency attributed directly to the poverty of its artistic and literary life. Howard Conant testified before joint hearings of Congress that "America has gained practically the whole world of material welfare and scientific progress, but it has failed to develop the soul of its civilization, which is culture." Senator Edward Kennedy declared that, in spite of America's scientific accomplishments, we would be remembered as "dull and listless men, amid all these wonders, if we do not also expand the human mind and spirit."[4]

America's leading role in the world at that time was assumed. This laid a special responsibility on American culture and hence on the development of American culture. In 1964 the Commission on the Humanities, created by the American Council of Learned Societies, the Council of Graduate Schools, and the United Chapters of Phi Betta Kappa, issued a report, which Sosna called a "cultural nationalist manifesto." The report spoke of America's "cultural responsibilities," which were no less than the guardianship of Western high culture itself: "To know the best that has been thought and said in former times can make us wiser than we otherwise might be, and in this respect the humanities are not merely ours, but the world's best hope."[5] We of course no longer hubristically assume that Western culture represents the last great hope of civilization.

The goal of the report was to create a humanities foundation that would "correct the views of those who see America as a nation interested only in the material aspects of life." This charge of materialism has resonated throughout American history. It was first leveled in the seventeenth century; Tocqueville provided only one of the best known of many nineteenth-century expressions of it. Americans acknowledged it. Emerson, in his famous essay "The American Scholar," admitted that America lagged woefully behind in the arts and letters. His essay was more a call for Americans to do something about it than a defense of the status quo. Whitman's "Democratic Vistas" likewise denounced America as a cultural desert.[6]

When the Rockefeller Commission issued its report on the arts in America in 1965, it took as its point of departure the creation of Lincoln Center in New York. The commission considered it *the* model for arts development in America. Since then many cities have followed suit. Civic pride and the creation of an architectural monument to the performing arts now go hand in hand. These edifices are used for many events, but in virtually every case a symphony orchestra is at the center.[7] This development has occurred in spite of pointed warnings from critics and artists. Richard Franko Goldman called the Rockefeller report the "summa theologica," extending the religious metaphor. He also called it a "lexicon of misuse of the English language" and, observing that it was "immensely *significant*, without ever being serious," castigated it for its "confusion of the vocabularies of art and marketing, and in its substitution of statistical cliches and easy pieties for any real notions of art." The object of Goldman's ire was the premise that art is something to be measured and consumed, culture itself thus being transformed into a commodity to be exploited for the benefit of the community. Goldman does not say this, but in the end the Rockefeller report is another 1960s version of cultural nationalism. The moral imperative in that instance was couched in the crasser but more politically acceptable language of marketing.[8]

Events such as the founding of Lincoln Center and the many other arts centers throughout the country reflect Samuel Eliot's early Federal Republicanism as much as John S. Dwight's puritan-derived transcendentalism. Eliot's ideal of a society unified at least in part by art music was the first of many attempts to use music in the service of cultural nationalism.

Throughout the one and a half centuries of the debate that began in Boston in the 1830s about the place of music in American society, one problem has surfaced repeatedly: reconciliation of the premises of a high culture with the democratic nature of American society. Eliot, Dwight, and many others struggled with it. Emerson and Whitman recognized the same forces at work in literature. Van Wyck Brooks attributed the unhealthy state of the arts in the early twentieth century to a polarization into high and low, with no "genial middle ground." Like others before him, however, he saw no way out.[9]

Congress in the 1960s thought it saw a way out: the creation of national endowments for the arts and for the humanities. Few people today would claim that this solution solved the problem. The two endowments have been subjected to criticism from all quarters and in the early 1990s have come under siege, as their sponsorship has once more precipitated a national debate about what the arts are or should be in American society.

This debate has not only raised again the question of the moral value of art but has also indicated the extent to which artists themselves have adopted the sacralized point of view. Many consider the artist to occupy a special place in society, because he or she has a duty to produce something that transcends entertainment. His or her works are perceived as the moral conscience of society. The debate over the NEA has proceeded strictly from that assumption. The gulf separating the two points of view regarding such issues as freedom of expression and obscenity results from widely divergent beliefs about what is moral, not about differences in the moral potential of art.[10]

The role of moral guardian has not been thrust upon the artist. He or she has seized it. In worst cases the artist has been given a license to produce much that is empty. In best cases, however, the artist has given us a vision that can penetrate a world of dissonance, searing one's very core. In this respect the artist with vision is no different from his or her counterpart in previous times. Yet in both the best and worst cases today the artist views his or her role as that of making society better. In that sense his or her standard is almost always a moral one.

We hear less and less directly of the moral value of an orchestra, but the ghost of Dwight is still with us. The message is still there, only disguised in other terms. Morality as a word has been usurped, as it has acquired a more narrow, religious meaning. When we speak of art we use only the word *art*, because art has been equated with morality (in the broadest sense of the term *morality*). Art is something to be valued because it makes us better. Our values about what we should be have changed, so we allow different art into the pantheon. We program sacred music, but under the guise of a secular artistic standard. We still cling to our past, so we program a traditional repertoire made comfortable by familiarity. We nostalgically look back on a time in which individualistic idealism mattered, so we program artistic products of heroic scope. We live in a global, ethnically pluralistic society and want to expand our horizons, so we program music from many world cultures. Narrow elitism is now a most serious charge, so we program many events because we value ethnic diversity.

At the close of the twentieth century the concepts of highbrow and lowbrow have undergone radical transformation. Artists now cross over from one style to another as nimbly as they once changed clothes. Distinctions between highbrow and lowbrow have not been rejected, however. Art is no longer the limited term it once was, but in principle the duality remains: art is more than entertainment. Little actual debate is heard about that point; instead, we listen sympathetically to the claims of many divergent types of music for admission in to the pantheon of art. Jazz, Broadway musicals, and much popular music have gained entrance.

We may now actually be closer to the reconciliation of a democratic and a moral view of art than ever before. Our institutions are still premised on an idealistic concept of art, but we are ready—indeed, we actively seek—to justify any and all types of music by its standards. The pantheon is now wide open, and few argue for its closure. But it remains intact. We have taken what was originally a relatively narrow standard, a view of art as moral argument, and in a process that reflects an inherently democratic process have made it accessible to all. Whether this limits music and the concept of art or serves them well is another issue.

Instrumental Musicians in Boston, 1796–1842

In the course of this book we have watched symphony overtake psalmody. We have seen Boston audiences, at first indifferent if not hostile to instrumental music, come to embrace it enthusiastically. But we have mostly ignored a cognate question: When did a critical mass of instrumental musicians appear? More specifically, were there enough musicians in Boston prior to the mid-1830s to allow an instrumental musical culture to flourish? This question has colored what studies have been done of the musical life of antebellum Boston. John S. Dwight claimed that not even a half-score of professional musicians lived in Boston at the time of the founding of the Philoharmonic Society, which he believed occurred in 1810 or 1811. H. Earle Johnson suggested that one of the reasons for the demise of the Philharmonic Society was the small repertoire and the quality of the performances, both indications that not enough competent musicians were available.[1]

The many records of the activities of musicians in antebellum Boston allow us to assemble a relatively complete picture of who was in Boston when, what they were paid, and how they were viewed. In some cases we have considerable information about the contract negotiation process itself. This can reveal much about the status of the negotiators as well as the results of the negotiations.

A list of instrumental musicians in Boston between 1796 and 1842 appears at the end of this appendix. These dates were chosen because prior to 1796 records are too scanty to have any meaning and by 1843 instrumental music was established and flourishing. The names in the list are drawn from a variety of sources, the most important being programs of concerts and payment records of various performing organizations. In some cases programs from the concerts themselves have survived; more often, programs are taken from newspaper advertisements or articles. Treasurers' receipts provide one of the most reliable and detailed sources of instrumental musical activity. They enable us to determine the size of the ensemble and the relative status of musicians within it. The receipts or payment records are more accurate about who actually performed than newspaper advertisements, as details could change between the advertisement and the event. Unfortunately, payment records invariably leave out one important fact, the instrument the musician played.[2] For this reason the instrument is unspecified on the master list for many musicians. We know for certain that these musicians played in an orchestra, because treasurers' records are usually clear about the purpose of such payments. But there is frequently no mention of the player in any other source.

A third source, city directories, is notoriously unreliable. The directories are flagrantly incomplete. Boston's directory of 1809, for instance, lists a total of five persons who classified themselves as either musicians or teachers of music; the directory of 1831 lists twenty-two persons under that category. But at least twice that number were active in both 1809 and 1831. Also, the city directories usually do not differentiate between instrumental and vocal musicians. William Billings is listed in the city directories through 1798 as a "singing master," the only person so designated. Other singing-school teachers, if listed at all, probably used "teacher of music" or "music master." Since a music teacher had more prestige than a musician, some instrumental musicians also used that designation.

Peter R. Knights, whose work dealt specifically with antebellum Boston, discussed in detail the problem of using city directories.[3] Knights detected a distinct economic and ethnic bias in the inclusion of names. White heads of households were much more likely to be included than other groups, as were those with property of more than $1,000. Inclusion of the latter group approached 100 percent, compared with inclusion of one in seven in the predominantly black Ward 6.[4] In addition, the same names tended to be perpetuated. Once a directory was printed, canvassers would prepare later editions by taking with them unbound pages from the previous one, writing in any necessary corrections. Finally, as the publication of directories were money-making ventures aimed at the business community, the desire or sense of obligation to be complete was less than compelling, particularly for individuals with little connection to the business world. One pass through a neighborhood probably sufficed, which may have worked against musicians with irregular and itinerant working schedules.

Other records include private accounts and secondary sources, such as books. I have included only those secondary sources that contain plausible firsthand material available nowhere else. If a secondary source quotes an eyewitness, and if there is no reason to doubt the reliability of the quotation, then the information is included. In some instances primary sources have disappeared since the time a nineteenth-century writer examined them. The first volume of the secretary's records of the Handel and Haydn Society no longer exists, but Perkins apparently had access to it when he wrote his history in 1883.

Table A.1 provides an overview of instrumentalists in Boston, subdivided by instrument. By way of summary I have grouped the instrumentalists into five-year units. This does not mean that every instrumentalist was in Boston for the entire five years. If a name appears at any time during that five-year period, it is included in the listing. The totals thus represent larger numbers than were available at any one time. I have used five-year groupings partly to compensate for fluctuations in individual years because of the variance in available records, and partly to allow a summary view of the number of instrumentalists available. Much of the considerable yearly variation in the number of musicians is due to the fortuitous survival of records. Most of the concert programs of 1831, for instance, list the entire membership of orchestras and bands, an event seldom found in programs of other years. It is highly unlikely that the bulk of these musicians disappeared from Boston in 1832. A five-year total thus may actually be closer to the number of musicians available than the count of any single year.

Even the five-year groupings are subject to the luck of records surviving, although part of the overall fluctuation reflects actual changes in the employment situation in Boston. At times it is clear which is which and at times it is not. For instance, many more musicians are listed in the 1830–1834 period than any other because of the 1831 programs, which give the names of the members of the orchestras. James Kendall's military band appeared on three of the programs, giving us complete information about one large wind ensemble. The presence of the band on those programs accounts for the relatively many woodwind and brass players that appear in the totals for that period. In a similar manner the more than two-fold increase in musicians from 1815 to 1819 is attributable to the survival of the treasurer's records of the Handel and Haydn Society. It is doubtful that the increase corresponds to a comparable change in the number of musicians in Boston. While the Handel and Haydn Society represented a new opportunity for instrumental musicians, the number of concerts it presented was insufficient to provide full-time employment. It is more likely that most of the musicians who played in the society were already in Boston, and for the first time we have specific information on them.

On the other hand, the large increase in musicians in the 1825–1829 period probably does reflect the situation in Boston. The Tremont

Table A.1

Instrumental Musicians in Boston, 1796–1842

Instrument*	1796–99	1800–04	1805–09	1810–14	1815–19	1820–24	1825–29	1830–34	1835–39	1840–42
Violin/Viola**	3	4	6(1)	4(1)	7(1)	8	16	18	11(1)	11
Cello	0	0	1(1)	0(1)	1(1)	1	3(1)	3(1)	2	1(1)
Double bass	1	1	1	1	1	1	3	4(1)	2(1)	2
Flute	1	0(1)	0	2	3(1)	4(1)	6	6(2)	2(1)	1
Oboe	1(2)	0(1)	0(1)	0(1)	0(1)	0(1)	0(2)	0(1)	0(2)	1(1)
Clarinet	2(2)	3	5	5	6(1)	5	4(1)	12(1)	9	4(1)
Bassoon	1	1(1)	1	1	1	1	3	4	2(1)	2
Trumpet	1	0	1	1	0(1)	1(1)	2(1)	7(1)	2(1)	2
French horn	1	0	0	1	1	1	6	5(1)	5	2
Trombone	0	0	0	0	0	0	0(1)	8(1)	5(1)	4(1)
Percussion								2(3)	1(1)	0(2)
Unspecified	21	3	2	0	16	3	6	8	27	11
Total	32	12	17	15	36	25	49	77	68	41

* Numbers in parentheses indicate players who doubled on the instrument listed. These numbers are not counted in the total number of musicians.

** Most violinists of the time doubled on violin and viola.

Theatre opened in 1827, and its orchestra was not only the largest ever assembled in Boston but also one of the largest regular orchestras in America. It alone provided steady employment for approximately twenty-four instrumental musicians. The much smaller number of musicians from 1800 to 1804 than from 1796 to 1799 is probably due to a combination of the survival of records and changes in the employment picture. In the 1790s there were two active theaters, the Boston (or Federal Street) Theatre and the Haymarket Theatre. By 1803 only one survived, and there are indications that a smaller orchestra was used. We have the treasurer's records of the Boston Theatre from 1796 to 1798, which list orchestra players for each year, but no such records exist for the 1800–1804 period.

Because of the types of sources available, we do not know the instruments of many musicians in the periods from 1796 to 1799, 1815 to 1819, and 1835 to 1839. In each case the principal sources are the treasurers' records: for 1796 to 1799 those of the Boston Theatre, for 1815 to 1819 the Handel and Haydn Society, and for 1835 to 1839 the Handel and Haydn Society and the Boston Academy of Music.

In assessing the availability of musicians the question of professional versus amateur is particularly elusive. The Olympic Games definition, that a professional is anyone who has accepted compensation for performing, is more useful than one that defines a professional as someone who earned his living primarily by playing in an orchestra, because it is easier to determine and because it provides more pertinent information. Many musicians combined instrumental performance with entirely different means of livelihood. Yet these musicians were paid, and their income for performing may not have been trivial to their living standard. When musicians' names appear in programs, as in the case of the many in the 1831 programs, we cannot tell whether they were professional. Most of the musicians listed in the 1831 programs were professionals, as most of them were connected with the Tremont Theatre, all of whose performers were paid. Some of the players in the wind band may not have been. Sometimes we can tell through the city directories whether a musician considered himself a musician or something else by profession. Frequently we cannot, and many musicians almost certainly had other sources of income about which we know nothing.

A professional status is important only to the extent that some tension between professional and amateur musicians developed around 1820, and this affected the way in which professional musicians were perceived. Yet since the primary purpose of this book is to determine the presence of instrumental musicians in Boston, the degree to which they relied upon public performance for their source of livelihood is less important than evidence that they were there and active. If they meet the criterion of activity, their names are included on the master list even if their professional status cannot be explicitly confirmed.

Sometimes even the identity of a musician is not clear. Handwritten records for which there is no external confirmation are subject to uncertainties of spelling. And some records provide only the musician's last name. A particularly thorny problem occurs when two or more musicians have the same last name. This is not uncommon, as the profession tended to run in families. Often the distinction is clear. The brothers James and Edward Kendall were two of the best known musicians in Boston, and references to them usually included at least a first initial. Two names that illustrate a multitude of problems are Niebuhr and White. Beginning in 1832, an L. White and an A. White appear in the violin section of several concerts. The A. White was Azell White, who played in the Handel and Haydn Society's orchestra from 1832 to 1842, and who had a benefit concert given for him by the Boston Brass Band in 1840. A Loring White also appeared as a vocalist once, and as a flutist. One of the programs, which included both an orchestra and a military band, listed a Loring White as a flutist in the band. The two references are undoubtedly to the same person. The city directory lists an Azell White and a Lorenzo White, both as musicians. Are Loring White and Lorenzo White the same person? Probably not. The program for E. R. Hansen's concert on November 26, 1831, mentions three Whites. The violin section lists, in this order, "L. White, A. White, L. White, and two Amateurs." If this was not a printer's error, then three Whites existed, and they were all professionals. And all played violin. Thus when only the name L. White is given, the problem of determining which man is meant is insoluble.

The name Niebuhr is complicated by an inconsistency of spelling. According to the records of the Handel and Haydn Society, a Niebuhr played in the orchestra from 1816 to 1828 and again from 1832 to 1842. Various treasurers entered the names Neihbuhr, Niebuhr, and Nibuhr. Hansen's concert of November 26, 1831, listed a Neihbuhr as cellist. Sharp indicated that a Neibuhr played first horn in the Handel and Haydn Society's orchestra from 1817–1822. The Handel and Haydn Society treasurer's books of 1837 and 1838 frequently included the name of the instrument, a rarity for these records. In June 1837 Henry Niebuhr was listed as a drummer. The treasurer's report of the

Boston Academy of Music indicated payment to an H. Nibuhr in 1837 and an E. H. Niebuhr in 1838. Finally, the city directory of 1831 lists a Henry Niebuhr as a piano tuner. These all probably refer to the same person. All references to a first name give either Henry or an initial that could reflect it, and it was common for a musician to double on several instruments, even covering three major sections of the orchestra. Yet we cannot be sure that the name variants referred to only one musician. The same is true of the names Pearce and Pierce in the many programs for 1831. Pearce or Pierce is listed as a bassoonist, except in military bands, where he is listed as a bass hornist. It is probably the same person, even though both spellings are used on the same program. There is never an indication of both a Pierce and a Pearce appearing simultaneously in the same ensemble, and when both variants are recorded, one is used for the band, the other for the orchestra. There is no consistency about which name was used for which ensemble, however, strongly suggesting that the same person used both spellings.

The pivotal event that made the assemblage of a critical mass of professional musicians possible was the founding of the Haymarket Theatre and the Boston Theatre in the 1790s, although little is known about the original orchestras of the two theaters. The theater offered instrumentalists their only opportunity for regular and steady employment. The program of the opening night of the Boston Theatre on February 3, 1794, contained "A Grand Symphony by Signor Charles Stametz [sic]; Grand Overture by Signor Vanhall; Grand Symphony by Signor Haydn; do. by Charles Ditters." After the financial failure of the 1794 season, Col. J. S. Tyler assumed the management of the theater. On October 22, 1795, he published an advertisement in the newspapers which promised a larger and stronger cast and a "more numerous orchestra."

"More numerous" must be viewed in historical perspective. The term *orchestra* or *band* was a loose one in eighteenth-century America, applicable to any miscellaneous array of instruments, regardless of size. In his memoirs Joseph Buckingham describes a summer theatrical company in Salem and Providence in 1803 formed by Bates and Harper, actors of the Boston Theatre. Buckingham depicts the orchestra as follows: "Old Doctor Schaffer, as he was called, long known as the second violin player in the Boston Theatre, was the leader of the orchestra, which consisted of one fiddler beside himself, and occasionally a couple of students in Brown University, who volunteered as amateurs, with a violin and a flute or clarionet."[5]

This was of course a summer venture, not the regular season of the Boston Theatre. Yet two fiddles qualified as an orchestra. And even when supplemented by the amateurs, the ensemble completely lacked any bass. The amateurs probably doubled the violin parts. Even more revealing is Buckingham's reference to Schaeffer as "the second violin player in the Boston Theatre." Whether Buckingham's account can be taken literally is an open question. Buckingham was a journalist, not a musician. Yet Schaeffer may have been the only second violin in the orchestra. Later in the nineteenth century orchestras containing three or four violins are not uncommon. An orchestra of between six and ten players for the theater in the 1790s would not be unusual, especially in difficult financial times. Even as late as the 1840s some theaters had orchestras of that size. The orchestra of the Boston Museum (a theater, in spite of the name), which opened in 1841, consisted of between nine and eleven players. While this is small by the standards of the 1830s and 1840s, the orchestra was directed by Thomas Comer, one of the leading theatrical musicians in Boston at the time.

European ensembles visiting Boston were sometimes no larger. In 1837 the "Celebrated Prague Company" gave a series of concerts in Boston. It consisted of "nine Professors of Music, from Europe." The instrumentation was as follows:

3 violin
1 viola
1 double bass
1 clarinet
1 flute
2 horn and trumpet[6]

We know much more about the theater orchestras beginning in 1796 because the account book of the Boston Theatre for the years 1796 and 1797 has survived. It lists the players of the orchestra (called "The Band") and their weekly salaries, in dollars. For 1796 the list was:

Mr. Leaumont	14
Mr. Scavoye	14
Mr. Brook	12
Mr. Much	12
Mr. Priest	12
Mr. Austin	10
Mr. Stone	10

Mr. Schethy [Schaffer?]	10
Mr. Granger	10
Mr. L'Epousé	10
Mr. Glaan	10
Mr. Anderson	10
Mr. Layeme	10
Mr. Boullay	15
Mr. Labarre	16

There were thus fourteen members in the orchestra, and their weekly salaries came to $175. The salary range is comparable to the low end of the actors' scale. The highest-paid actors, the stars in a company, received $54 and $40. Actors' salaries ranged down to $10, with many in the $10 to $15 range.

Leaumont was the leader of the orchestra. Labarre received a higher salary because he was employed as an arranger as well as a performer.[7] Boullay's salary may reflect solo activity. An advertisement in the *Columbian Centinel* for March 29, 1797, listed "A Concerto on the Violin [composed by Jarnavick], by Mr. Boullay."

The orchestra remained relatively stable in both size and personnel in 1797, as the list for that year confirms:

Mons Leaumont	14
Scavoye	14
Brook	12
Much	12
Mallet	10 Left the theatre
Barbotheau	10 Left the theatre
Austin	10
Stone	10
Granger	10
L'Epousé	10
Shethy [Schaffer?]	10
Anderson	10
Layeme	10
Boullay	15
Graupner	[left blank]
Labarre Composer	16

In the 1797 list Labarre is specifically referred to as a composer. Graupner is included, but no salary is attached to his name. He may also have played in the orchestra in 1796, although he is not listed. His wife was one of the actresses in the theater, and there is a notation in the 1796 records of owing "M. Graupner" $45. The Graupners probably signed a package contract. In 1798, when cost-cutting measures became necessary, management drew up a list: "Managers, Performers, Prompters, Writers etc. as they stood before the Reduction." This list does not enumerate the members of the band, but beside the salary of several of the actors and other members of the company a second, lower figure has been penciled in. One line reads:

Mr. & Mrs. Graupner   26 12

Other musicians probably augmented the orchestra when needed. We know that at least one, William Rowson, was available. Rowson became familiar to Boston audiences as a trumpeter in the early years of the nineteenth century, playing in various benefit concerts and with the Handel and Haydn Society. A native of England, he had been a member of the Royal Guard Band in England. He and his wife were both engaged with the Boston Theatre in 1796, she as an actress and he as a prompter and occasional actor. He played several roles, including that of "Trumpeter" in *Jubilee*.[8] How much other trumpet playing he did in the theater is not known.

For at least two years the orchestra had a stable membership of fourteen. We do not know what happened in the reduction. The document about the reduction mentions "14 musicians, including Leader and Composer, $140" before the reduction, but $140 suggests that some reduction in salary had already occurred. Given the financial difficulties of the principal theaters in the early nineteenth century, and the known size of the other orchestras in Boston slightly later, it is highly unlikely that the orchestra was ever much larger than it was for the 1796–1797 season.

Practically nothing is known about the Haymarket Theatre's orchestra, except that Peter Von Hagen sometimes provided accompaniments and may have conducted. At least one advertisement in the *Columbian Centinel*, on July 29, 1797, bills the orchestra as a special situation, implying that one was not always used: "An opera called Highland Reel. Then after the opera a tragedy, ARIADNE ABANDONED, by THESIUS in the Isle of Naxos. Between the different Passages spoken by the Actors, will be FULL ORCHESTRAL ACCOMPANIMENTS, Expressive of each Situation and Passion. The Music composed by Pelisier."

The Haymarket Theatre burned down in February 1798 but had been rebuilt and opened again before the year was out. It closed permanently in 1803. The Boston Theatre remained the only legitimate theater in Boston until 1823, when the City Theatre was formed. In 1827 the Tremont Theatre opened. There were also other regular orchestras or bands in the early nineteenth century. Some military bands probably dated back to the revolutionary war (see chapter 5), and various types of entertainment employed instrumental ensembles. On October 28, 1797, for instance, Mr. Spinacuta announced an elaborate program of fireworks at "Mr. Ricket's Ampitheatre."[9] The advertisement specifically stated that a band would perform. The fireworks were apparently a success, as they were repeated frequently after that, and one may assume that some sort of instrumental performance continued to accompany the event. Circuses and equestrian shows were also common and often used an orchestra.

Theatrical employment, although steady, was seasonal. The theatrical season generally ran from October to May, leaving musicians unemployed for four months of the year. Some theaters tried to present a summer season, and several attempts were made to establish outdoor gardens with music. Most of these efforts were either unsuccessful or short-lived until the Washington Gardens becme a fixture in 1815.

Frustratingly little is known of the orchestra of the first semipermanent ensemble in Boston, the Philoharmonic Society. Information about the society itself has been elusive, although evidence suggests that (at least in its early years) it was more private than public; hence its orchestra was not a money-making ensemble. With the founding of the Handel and Haydn Society in 1815, however, our information about orchestral musicians is much more complete, because its records have survived. They include the minutes for the meetings of the board of directors and the treasurer's record books. Given the small number of musicians that lived in Boston at the time, and the symbiotic relationship between the Handel and Haydn Society's orchestra and other organizations, these records probably mention most of the professional orchestral musicians in Boston. This is especially true in the early years, before the founding of the Tremont Theatre in 1827. The records also provide unique insight into negotiation processes.

It is clear from the minutes of board meetings of the Handel and Haydn Society that the orchestra was a significant item in its budget, so that they constantly sought ways to reduce costs.[10] The amount paid per year varied greatly. It was dependent not only on the number of concerts given each year and the size of the orchestra but also on the nature of the musicians' contracts. The directors bargained hard with the musicians, frequently pitting one group against another.

Table A.2 lists the composition of the orchestra of the Handel and Haydn Society between 1816 and 1829. The first program to list members of the orchestra for a Handel and Haydn Society concert dates from 1829. The composition of earlier orchestras can be determined principally by the treasurer's reports, supplemented with other information where available. Since the reports only indicate money paid out, they reflect a minimum size. Amateurs are not included, and in some instances the reports are either incomplete or unclear. A directive from the board of directors in 1821 confirms that amateurs played in the orchestra, and that they were needed to supplement it: "Any member of this Society refusing or neglecting to take his proper situation in the Orchestra when requested thereto by the President or any Committee appointed for that purpose shall at the discretion of the Board of Trustees be discontinued as a member of said Society."[11] We know from other sources that some professional musicians performed with the Handel and Haydn Society but do not appear in the treasurer's records. Payment may have come from other funds or have been hidden in other entries. Sometimes it is unclear if a bill was paid for orchestral performance or other services like copying music or repairs. Thus we can say that the orchestra contained at least the instrumentation indicated.

According to table A.2 the orchestra, of moderate size in the first years, began to shrink after 1817, reached a low point in 1820, and then increased unevenly until 1829, when it grew dramatically. These differences in size are due to two factors: the availability of musicians in Boston and the changing financial situation of the Handel and Haydn Society.

In 1819, the first year for which the directors' minutes are extant, the society was in financial trouble. A committee appointed to examine its financial condition for the previous year reported that the organist was paid $140 and the orchestra $1,077. All other expenses—bills, rents, printing, and so forth—came to $1,126.36. Thus more than half of the budget of the Handel and Haydn Society went to cover the costs of hiring instrumentalists. In anticipation of that report, the society had voted the previous April to do away with the services of the orchestra. Apparently this did not happen, for the program of the June 22, 1819, concert begins with "Symphony—by the Orchestra." Cost-cutting measures went beyond the orchestra, however. On September 11 the society voted to "dispense with the performance of public Oratorios, except on

Table A.2
Handel and Haydn Society Orchestra, 1816–1829

	1816	1817	1818	1819
	2 vl	4 vl.	3 vl.	3 vl.
	2 vla.	1 vla.	1 vla.	1 vla.
	1 db.	1 db	1 db.	1 db.
	1 fl	1 fl.	1 cl.	1 cl.
	2 horn	2 cl.	1 fg.	1 fg.
	1 cl.	1 ob.	1 horn	1 horn
	2 unknown	1 fg.	4 unknown	4 unknown
		2 horn		
		3 unknown		
Total	10	17	12	12

	1820	1821	1822	1823
	3 vl	3 vl.	4 vl.	6 vl.
	1 vla.	1 vla.	1 vla.	1 vla.
	1 cl.	1 vc.	1 vc.	1 vc.
	1 fg.	1 cl.	1 db.	2 db.
	2 horn	1 fg.	1 cl.	2 cl.
	1 fg.	1 unknown	1 unknown	1 fl.
				1 horn
Total	8	9	9	14

	1824	1825	1826	1827
	3 vl.	2 vl.	4 vl.	3 vl.
	2 vla.	1 vla.	3 vla.	1 vla.
	1 db.	1 db.	2 fl.	2 db.
	1 fl.	1 fl.	1 ob.	2 fl.
	1 cl.	1 cl.	2 horn	2 cl.
	1 horn	2 horn	1 unknown	1 fg
			1 unknown	
Total	9	9	13	11

	1828	1829		
	2 vl.	7 vl.		
	1 vla.	2 vla.		
	2 db.	2 vc.		
	1 fl.	2 db.		
	2 cl.	2 fl.		
	1 fg.	2 cl.		
	2 horn	1 fg.		
	1 tb	1 tpt.		
		1 tb.		
		drum		
Total	12	24		

charitable or other special occasions." And on January 8, 1820, S. P. Taylor, the organist, resigned, feeling that "the increased duties incumbent on the Organist . . . [are] incompatible with my professional avocations." Such increased duties were probably related to the curtailed use of the orchestra, necessitating more organ accompaniment at rehearsals and possibly performances. In accepting the resignation Amasa Winchester, the president, and John Dodd, the treasurer, acknowledged that Taylor's request was reasonable, but that the current state of finances would not permit it; Taylor probably wanted more money. Throughout the season there is no mention of an orchestra in the programs.

A limited orchestra was used, however. At its May 13, 1820, meeting the board instructed the treasurer to borrow $250 for defraying the costs of the orchestra. It voted $200 to be distributed among the professional gentlemen of the orchestra for their assistance at rehearsals and the oratorios. The board also instructed the secretary to communicate its thanks to Gottlieb Graupner, who had probably assembled and led the orchestra. The $200 was distributed as follows:

Asa Warren	violin	28
H. Niebuhr	horn	18
Samuel Wetherbee	horn	18
Wm. Bennett	viola	18
F. Granger	clarinet	36
Ostinelli	violin	36
Wood	bassoon	28
Jno. Hart	clarinet	18
Total		200

How and how much Graupner was paid is not clear.

The society also realized that it needed an organist, and on September 16, 1820, tried to induce S. P. Taylor to resume the position at $200 per year. Taylor apparently wanted $300 and declined. The post was then offered to Sophia Hewitt, the daughter of James Hewitt, and after 1822 to the wife of Louis Ostinelli. The salary for the organist remained stable at $200 for the next ten years, even after Charles Zeuner replaced Hewitt in 1830. In 1820 the members of the orchestra were offered the same terms as the previous year, with one addition, a public benefit whose proceeds would go to the orchestra. From that benefit, the orchestra received $174. The records for 1820 also indicate that for at least one oratorio each member of the orchestra would receive $2.50.

This probably represents a rock-bottom price for an orchestral performance. It was comparable to what a theater musician received for one night's performance but was less than the remuneration the society paid in later years, which hovered around $5.00 minimum. And it may have been less than the society had paid out in earlier years.

In 1822 Graupner's connection to the Handel and Haydn Society was broken. Graupner had apparently demanded too much. The records of January 11, 1822, state that he had communicated his terms for future assistance to the society, which voted that "owing to the present situation of the Society his terms could not be complied with." By the following season Graupner was back on the account book, however, and the orchestra was larger than ever. Orchestral expenses almost doubled, to $382 from $200 in 1820, and, judging from the pay scale, Graupner was the leader.

Over the years the Orchestra Committee of the Handel and Haydn Society attempted various strategies for assembling an orchestra. In the early years especially the committee negotiated with individual players. Usually a flat fee was offered and accepted. Fees were listed as annual fees, and since the players were paid for rehearsals as well as performances, it is impossible to calculate the precise amount per evening. Some of the more prominent musicians were more difficult to secure. As we saw, Graupner sat out at least one season because his terms could not be met. Louis Ostinelli proved especially difficult. The minutes for September 13, 1827, record that a number of musicians agreed to play at the previous year's fee. This list included Graupner. The minutes continue: "Voted . . . that the [Orchestra] Committee be authorized to treat with Mr. Ostinelli discretionary, and that relative to the other professional gentlemen they have further time."

With the founding of the Tremont Theatre in 1827 and the continuance of the Boston Theatre, two assembled orchestras existed in Boston. In 1828 the Handel and Haydn Society took advantage of this situation. They first obtained a separate agreement for Graupner, Granger, and Geitner to assist at rehearsals for $4 per evening. Then they sought to strike a special deal with one of the leaders of the two orchestras: half the proceeds of an oratorio would go to the orchestra for assistance at the rehearsals and performance of the oratorio. Granger, speaking for Graupner, Geitner, and Peile, refused outright. Ostinelli stated his preference for specific compensation, but agreed to the proposal. For the first concert the orchestra collected $205.50, from an attendance of 411. The repeat of that concert netted the orchestra only $103.50, however.

After that Ostinelli and the Tremont Theatre Orchestra apparently changed their minds. The same offer was made for the next concert but was then suddenly rescinded by the directors with the instruction that the Orchestra Committee "engage an Orchestra for the remainder of the season on the best terms that may be practicable." That offer was then rescinded and the original one reinstated.

The following year, 1829, the Orchestra Committee again attempted the same offer, and it again met with resistance. The directors were forced to pass the following resolutions: "Voted—That the Orchestra Committee have discretionary power relative to the selection of an orchestra provided they cannot effect an arrangement with the gentlemen who performed last season: reserving however a privilege to a set of those members of the Society who have heretofore assisted in the orchestra at the Society's performances" (October 13, 1829) and "Voted—That the Orchestra Committee have power to engage additional assistance to the present Orchestra, as they may deem expedient, this vote was taken by yeas and nays" (passed by six votes to three, December 14, 1829). The precise terms are not contained in the minutes.

The Handel and Haydn Society suffered a fate common to musical organizations in America: ticket receipts did not meet expenses. The financial situation was so grave in the early 1820s that the society was forced to assess each member $10. The problem persisted into the late 1820s. In 1828 the treasurer's report expressed concern that "the ordinary expenses of the Society have exceeded by a great amount the ordinary receipts of the past year," and explained that the reason was due to "a deficiency in the number of purchasers of Season tickets." In 1829 the treasurer reported that ordinary expenses exceeded ordinary income by more than $600.

Yet by 1828 the financial picture of the Handel and Haydn Society had improved dramatically. In 1824 a committee was appointed to examine finances. It could report that "the balance on the Organ has been paid, and the Society is now able to meet every demand that may be brought against it." It could do this even though no assessment had been necessary for five years. This success was diplomatically attributed in part to the support of subscribers, but in fact ticket receipts no longer had to cover expenses. In 1824 the society was receiving remuneration from two publications, *Boston Handel and Haydn Society Collection of Sacred Music* and *Boston Handel and Haydn Society Collection of Church Music*. Of these the collection of church music was by far the more important;

Table A.3

Sales of Boston Handel and Haydn Society Collection of Church Music,
from Treasurer's Report of the Handel and Haydn Society

Edition	Year	Copies	Comments
1st	1821	3,000	Richardson & Lord paid Society $500 for right to distribute it
	1824		received from Church Music, $601.09
	1825		
4th	1826		received from Church Music, $964.28 "so extensive a circulation"
5th	1827		Society expected to realize in one year $800
6th	1828	10,000	received from Church Music, $820
7th and 8th	1829		Society expected to realize in one year $1,000
9th	1830	12,000	Society expected to realize $1,000
10th	1831		received from Church Music, $1,166.67

table A.3 indicates its given revenues and sales figures. Lowell Mason's collection probably saved the society, securing for it a financial base that permitted it to survive not only these early years but also the even more competitive 1830s and 1840s, when several other musical organizations sprang up in Boston and taste shifted away from choral toward instrumental music.

Apart from the theaters, the Handel and Haydn Society provided the most sustained and visible opportunity for the Boston public to hear orchestral music, especially after both the Philoharmonic Society and the Apollo Society stopped presenting concerts in the mid-1820s. The orchestra itself existed only because of the renewed financial solvency of the society. And that was almost entirely because of Lowell's church-music collection, which essentially subsidized the orchestra. Thus in Boston in the 1820s symphony still depended on psalmody.

An orchestral musician in Boston between 1800 and 1840 could expect to earn roughly between $400 and $600 a year from his trade. As we recall, the most steady employment, indeed the only employment sufficient to provide a living, came from the theater. Theater musicians normally earned between $10 and $15 a week throughout this period. Because the theater season only ran from October to May, annual income from that source would be approximately between $300 and $400. Many of the theatre musicians performed with other organizations, like the Handel and Haydn Society or the Boston Academy of Music, which brought in another $20 to $40 a year. That sum varied considerably because of the range in the number of performances as well as the various negotiating strategies that the organizations employed.

As the theater usually had performances at least five nights a week, there was little opportunity for the theater musician to engage in free-lance work, such as playing at dances. There was some opportunity for summer employment, especially after 1815, when the Washington Gardens opened, but for much of the time summer employment was highly uncertain. The income that the average musician earned from teaching is unclear. The going rate for private lessons was between seventy-five cents and $1 an hour, so if a musician averaged only a half-dozen lessons a week, his annual income could increase by about $200. Better known musicians like Louis Ostenilli, Gottlieb Graupner, or Thomas Comer probably earned more than $1,000 a year. Their salaries in the theater were highter, as they usually served as leader of the orchestra, and they were in more demand for outside activities. When the Tremont Theatre opened in 1827 the salaries of Comer, as musical director, and Ostinelli, as leader of the orchestra, were $40 a week; the other musicians were paid between $11 and $14 a week.

An income of between $400 and $600 a year placed musicians at the high end of the income range for skilled workers and roughly equal to the earnings of a small artisan shop owner. Sean Willenz has calculated that in New York City in 1850 workers annually earned from $84 for females and $117 for males in the clothing and tailoring trades to $580 in shipbuilding. The average annual income for all trades was $297.[12] Bruce Laurie, Theodore Hershberg, and George Alter discovered that workers' wages in Philadelphia closely resembled those in New York.[13] It is unlikely that those of Boston were much different. Clarence Long specified an average annual wage of $297 for industrial workers in America in 1860.[14] Because wages and prices rose between 1840 and 1850, musicians earning a similar amount earlier in the century were relatively better off. According to Robert A. Margo and Georgia C. Villafor, wages rose an average of 32 percent from 1820 to 1856.[15] Income of nonmanual workers is more difficult to determine, but according to Blumin most were above the $500–$600 range.[16] Laurie, Hershberg, and Alter, however, discovered that the average gross profit for small artisan shops in Philadelphia in 1850 was $482, from which expenses like rent and operating costs must be deducted. Many clerks and professionals earned $1,000 or more annually; those that prospered or opened their own businesses probably earned several times that. Musicians like Gottlieb Graupner who had their own music businesses no doubt derived considerable additional income from them. The $1,000 or more that a few musicians in Boston earned probably placed them on a par with at least the lower echelons of the professional class.

Only a few musicians accumulated significant property. The record of persons taxed $25 or more in 1848 listed three musicians: Lowell Mason, George J. Webb, and Shadrach Pearce. Mason's total estate, personal and real estate, was valued at $41,000, Webb's at $5,500, and Pearce's at $5,600. The list only confirms what most scholars have known about Mason, that he was far and away the wealthiest musician in Boston. Webb is no surprise; he had taught at the Boston Academy of Music, conducted several orchestras, was active as an organist, and co-authored publications with Mason. How Pearce acquired his wealth is unknown. He was a bassoonist with the Boston Brass Band, the Handel and Haydn Society, the Boston Academy of Music, and possibly the Tremont Theatre in the 1830s and 1840s. If he had another liveli-hood, he did not advertise it; he listed himself in the city directories as a musician.[17]

One of the principal problems plaguing musicians was the absence of a fund or organization to provide a pension for a musician's family in the event of his death or for the musician himself in old age. Some sporadic efforts were made in individual cases, usually in the form of benefits. The Philoharmonic Society sponsored a benefit concert for Frederick Granger, Sr., on April 8, 1820. The announcement in the *Euterpeiad* acknowledged the approbation Granger had received for many years and observed that, having "outlived his abilities," he was "descending the vale, and may be denominated a *decayed musician.*" Granger was one of the more well-known and well-loved musicians in Boston. He may have been a Hessian who remained in Boston after the Revolution. He was in Boston at least from 1785, when he married, and for many years was leader of the orchestra at the Boston Theatre. He played for both the Philoharmonic Society and the Handel and Haydn Society, and the Pierians turned to him when they wanted some professionally arranged music in 1811.

The 1826 circular letter proposing a concert society included the es-tablishment of a fund to aid musicians' widows, the first attempt to address the problem in a systematic manner. No other organization tried to do so until 1847, when the Boston Musical Fund Society was founded. It was unique in being organized and run by musicians. One of its principal purposes was the establishment of a relief fund. In 1841 Hach had suggested that such a fund was strongly needed, and he argued that it would come into being only if the musicians took matters into their own hands. The success of the Boston Musical Fund Society proved Hach right. Musicians flocked to sign up and agreed to almost unlimited rehearsal time. They also agreed not to play in other orchestras without the consent of the society, guaranteeing a full orchestra on performance nights. As a result, the orchestra quickly established itself as the largest and most competent ensemble in town, and soon both the Boston Academy of Music and the Boston Philharmonic Society orchestras disbanded. The Boston Musical Fund Society orchestra remained popular until it was eclipsed by the smaller but more artistic Germania Music Society orchestra in the 1850s.

Although many musicians had an economic status that placed them at least above the level of most of working-class people, their acceptance in society was more problematic. The New England suspicion of the arts as frivolous or morally suspect influenced many New Englanders' opinions of professional musicians. Lowell Mason's own attitude was typical of New England society. As a young man he was interested in little besides music, but he did not even consider it a possible career choice. When he published the *Boston Handel and Haydn Society Collection of Church Music*, he left his name off of the title page for fear that it would harm his banking career. And even though he was guaranteed an income of $1,500 a year for directing church choirs when he returned to Boston in 1828, he nevertheless worked briefly in a bank, possibly as a hedge against the uncertainties of a career in music. Mason's position as a church musician was more prestigious than that of orchestral musicians who, among other things, were connected with the theater. And as we noted earlier, many musicians were not included in the city directories, which reflects their lack of status, even when one allows for inaccurate canvassing methods. The publishers of the city directories did, however, make a much more strenuous effort to include citizens of greater wealth and status. Those musicians that were included often chose to be listed as a professor or teacher of music rather than as a musician, because professors had more status.

New Englanders kept their social distance from musicians for reasons other than wariness about the arts. John Rowe Parker confirmed that the musician was looked down upon in Boston society in the early nineteenth century. His 1821 article in the *Euterpeiad* urged aspiring professional musicians to seek a better education and advocated a college devoted to the study of music, which would provide not only musical training but also a more general education. It would train the intellect, develop character, and produce a refined person attuned to the more elegant pursuits. In antebellum terms Parker was advocating a traditional liberal-arts education.

Parker's perception of the status and situation of the musician in his society impelled him to write the article. He voiced concern that many young men became musicians through necessity or because of a natural facility. Most received only a "loose and vague" education. The nature of the profession allowed the admittance of many persons of "infinitely lower standing in intellectual refinement." This created problems because the profession entailed associating with people of class and refinement, and the musician was ill equipped to do so. He knew only his art. As a consequence, he was snubbed: "The polite and the informed who are induced to enter into conversation with him, discover at once that his recommendations are confined to his fiddle or his voice, and they quit him under that hopeless conviction; while he himself is doomed to experience for evermore the mortification of a neglect the more cutting, as he conceives the insolence of wealth, or the hard heartiness of pride. Of his own defects unhappily it is a part of his portion to remain ignorant."

A more insidious problem was the perceived moral dissolution to which a lack of education led. Parker equated a general education with moral dignity. He viewed the formation of character as an essential part of a proper education. Since most musicians lacked this education, they could only relieve their "labour of practice" with "some coarse or dissolute species of dissipation." They would be reduced to associating with other musicians, thus reinforcing their moral corruption. He quoted an earlier statement of his that musicians were generally excluded from "genteel society" because their character was "clouded and obscured by facts and prejudices, owing to the existence of a laxity of principal."[18]

Parker held a typical merchant-class view of both the average musician and society. The formation of character was the crucial factor in the education of a young man, and conversely education was critical to the development of proper character and values. (Because women were not normally professional musicians Parker's point was gender specific). Since most musicians did not come from the segment of society that received the proper general education, their character flaws and lack of refinement were presumed inevitable. But because the work of the musician allowed, even forced, him to associate with members of the upper classes, he was forever knocking at the door for admittance into the higher levels of society. His own limitations, however, would keep him out. There is no question that Parker was referring to the orchestral musician. He pointed out that many professional musicians were associated with orchestras, and he entitled his article "The Orchestra."

The social status of orchestral musicians began to change in the 1840s, as attitudes about instrumental music changed. If instrumental music had a moral quality then the musicians that played it must also, at least in the public eye. The appearance of foreign virtuosi enhanced this perception. Whatever their artistic taste, these virtuosi appeared serious, and they were masters of their instruments. They comported more as artists than as entertainers. Even those leery of Ole Bull's artistic taste were impressed by his commanding personality. And Leopold Herwig, shy and diffident, his personality completely different from Bull's, was hailed immediately for his dignity and great spirit, a far contrast from the difficult campaign Louis Ostinelli had waged earlier in the century to be recognized as an artist rather than simply as a fiddler. Finally, when the Germania Music Society orchestra arrived in 1852, the citizens of Boston were prepared to give its members the best reception they had ever received in any city in North America.

Individual List of Instrumental Musicians
in Boston, 1796–1842

Note. When inclusive dates are given, the earliest and latest are confirmed, and there is evidence to suggest that the performer was in Boston in the intervening time. Not every year in the interim is necessarily confirmed. If widely spaced early and late dates are found with no intervening confirmation, those dates are not listed as inclusive. The musicians' instruments are not always known.

Aimes; basn., bass horn; 1831.
Anderson; 1796–97.
Anguera, J. E.; tb.; 1835–42.
Armour, Thomas; tpt.; 1835–41.
Austin; 1796–97.
Badger, Thos., Jr.; 1817–22.
Barbotheau; 1797.
Barnett; vla.; 1825–31.
Barret, Jonas P.; clar., ob., fl., bsn.; 1802, 1839.
Bartlett, John; tpt.; 1828–42.
Bauer, Charles F.; vla.; 1837–42.
Beatty, Robert; clar., ob.; 1825, 1835–42.
Belcher; fl.; 1829.
Belread, William; 1796
Bennet, William; vl., vla.; 1816–42.
Bohoursers, E. H.; 1837.
Bonnemort; 1796–1801.
Boquet; 1817.
Boullay; vl.; 1796–97.
Bowe, G. F.; 1838.
Boyd, David; clar.; 1831.
Brockaway, H. A.; 1840.
Brook; 1796–97.
Brooks, L.; bugle; 1831.
Burdakin, Joseph; 1837–41.
Burditt, Benjamin A.; 1836–41.

Burt, C. F.; 1818.

Callender, William; 1796–1800.

Caster, Henry S.; 1837.

Charlton, F.; 1836–42.

Chevaliar; 1834–36.

Clapp, W. W.; 1835.

Clark, James; bsn., 1831.

Clark, Lemuel; vl., vla., trb.; 1826–41.

Clark, Richard; 1816.

Clark, Samuel; cb.; 1827–37.

Clemens, J. M.; 1836.

Coffin, William; vl.; 1829–31.

Colburn, Marcus; clar.; 1831–37.

Comer, Thomas; vl.; 1828–42.

Cushing, George, fl.; 1824–31.

Cutting, Gilbert; 1831–42.

D'Hattentot, Lewis; 1789.

Darnegre; bsn.; 1825.

Delano, J.; trb.; 1834–38.

Denzi; cb.; 1825–29.

Dickson, James; 1816.

Dorn, Valentine; horn; 1836–41.

Downe, John; fl.; 1831.

Downes; vc., fl.; 1825–29.

Downs, Ephraim; trb., 1831.

Dubois; ob.; 1797.

Eberle, Frederick; horn, tp., timp.; 1825–31.

Everdell, James; vl.; 1805–07.

Everet, Henry; vl.; 1831–33.

Fillebrown, Asa; clar.; 1822–42.

Flagg, Eben; clar.; 1831–40.

Frederick; 1836.

Friedheim, I.; 1836–42.

Fuller, G.; 1837.

Garbelt(s), R.; 1837.

Gear, Joseph; cb., vc.; 1825–42.

Geitner, Charles; vl., vla.; 1826–40.

Gertins, Wm.; 1837.

Glaan; 1796.

Granger, Frederick; clar.; 1796–1824.

Granger, Thomas; vl., vla.; 1810–1831.

Grant, William; 1816.

Graupner, Gottlieb; cb., ob.; 1797–1831.

Green, Isaac; vl., vla.; 1825–31.

Green, J. C.; 1838.

Greene, B.; 1837–39.

Hach, Henry Theodore; vc.; 1837–41.

Hanna; fl.; 1825–29.

Hansen, Edward Richard; vl., vla., fl.; 1831–33.

Hanson, Joseph; tpt.; 1825–31.

Hanson, W.; 1825–32.

Harbonet, Charles; 1840.

Hart, John; clar., fl., tpt.; 1812–1823.

Hay, J. D.; 1821.

Heinrich, A. P.; vl.; 1823–25.

Hewitt, James; vl.; 1808–16, 1824–26.

Hill, U. C.; 1834.

Hill, Uri K.; vl.; 1805–10.

Holloway, John; vl.; 1832–36.

Hooper; clar.; 1831.

Hooten, James; 1831.

Hufman, John; 1806.

Huntington, Jonathon; fl.; 1813.

Isenbeck, W.; 1838–40.

Jackson; fl.; 1825.

Jenks; vc.; 1829.

Jones, E.; trb.; 1831.

Keller, J. A.; vl.; 1825–40.

Kendall, Edward; tpt.; 1831–42.

Kendall, James; clar.; 1831–42.

Keyzer, William; vl.; 1842.

Kibary; horn; 1825.

Knaeble; horn; 1829–39.

Knight, Abel F.; clar.; 1831–40.

Kyberz, B.; tpt., horn; 1831.

Kymbig, D.; 1837.

L'Epousé, Henry; 1796–97.

Labarre, Trill; 1796–97.

Layeme; 1796–97.

Leaumont; vl., clar.; 1796–97.

Lehethy; 1797.

Lemaine, L.; 1836–40.

Lewis, Philip; vl.; 1817–29.

Loring, Josiah; fl.; 1816–31.

Mallet, Francis; vl., vla.; 1796–1831.

Mann, Joel R.; clar.; 1831–36.

Mann, Moses; timp., drums; 1830–37.

Mann, W. W.; clar.; 1831.

Manning, William; 1806.

Marek; vl.; 1831.

Masi, Francis; clar., vc., vl.; 1807–19.

Maulin [?]; 1835.

Meyer, Carl; vl.; 1837.

Milon; vc.; 1825.

Moffat; clar.; 1806–11.

Moorhouse, Isaac; 1834–42.

Much; 1796–97.

Mumler, John F.; vc.; 1806.

Muscarelli; vl.; 1825.

Myers, Edward; clar.; 1825–32.

Neihbuhr; vc.; 1816–31.

Newall, A.; trb.; 1831.

Niebuhr, Henry; horn, drums; 1822–42.

Nolcini; 1825.

Nolen; drums; 1829.

Nolton, Henry; 1816.

Norbor; 1815.

Norton; fl., clar.; 1817.

Ostinelli, Louis; vl.; 1818–42.

Papanti, Lorenzo; horn; 1826–31.

Passage, A.; vl., vla.; 1823–24.

Pearce, J. N.; clar.; 1831–38.

Pearce, Shadrach S.; bsn.; 1827–42.

Pearce, S. H., fl.; 1836.

Peele; 1829.

Peile; vc.; 1828.

Perkins; 1819.

Perry; 1817.

Phillips, N.; 1816–21.

Pick, John; 1796–98.

Pierce, Joseph M., bsn., clar.; 1825–41.

Pollock, George; fl.; 1817–40.

Pray, William; fl.; 1825–42.

Priest; 1796.

Prince, George; fl.; 1823.

Raymond, F. L. [S?]; trb., cymbals; 1831–38.

Reed, William; horn; 1825–31.

Reid, John W.; 1825.

Reinhart; 1830.

Ribas, Antonio L.; ob.; 1842.

Ribes; vl.; 1814.

Richards; clar.; 1831.

Rosleo; drums; 1831.

Rowson, William; tpt.; 1796–1831.

Rozier, Etiene; 1798.

Rozier, M. M.; horn; 1797.

Ruggles, Nathaniel; fl.; 1811.

Rundberg, John N.; 1816.

Sandborn, L. L.; 1834–39.

Schaeffer, George Jr.; vl.; 1803–10.

Schaffer, Francis; clar.; 1797–1820.

Schmidt, Henry; vl.; 1837–40.

Schott; vl., clar.; 1825–30.

Schubart, G.; 1838–40.

Scripps; 1839.

Seible; trb.; 1831.

Seipp, H.; 1841.

Shaw, Isaac J.; trb.; 1837–40.

Shaw, Ralph; bsn.; 1805–07.

Sibley, H.; trb.; 1831–40.

Smink, Peter; bsn.; 1798–1801.

Smith, T.; drums; 1831.

Stone; fl., clar., ob.; 1796–97.

Sweeny, George; 1796–97.

Taylor; 1826.

Torp; vl.; 1825.

Trajetta, Fil; vl.; 1800–1802.

Turner, James; clar.; 1810–17.

Vechner, Joseph; 1798–1800.

Von Hagen, P. A.; vl.; 1796–1803.

Von Hagen, P. A. Jr.; vl., vla.; 1800–1807.
Warren, Asa; vl.; 1816–42.
Weatherbee, Samuel; horn; 1810–28.
Weintz, Chas. J.; 1839.
Wheelock, A.; 1819.
White, Azell; vl.; 1831–32.
White, I. M.; 1826, 1838.
White, Lorenzo; vl., fl.; 1831.
White, Loring; fl.; 1831.
Whitemore, J.; cb.; 1833–40.
Widtl; horn; 1825–30.
Withington, E.; 1817–28.
Wivild; vc., cb.; 1828–37.
Wood, Simeon; bsn.; 1810–24.
Wood, Thomas; 1816, 1831.
Woodliff; fl.; 1825.
Worsley, Joseph; vl., vla.; 1825–31.
Wyman, William M.; 1837.
Young; 1818.

Notes

Introduction

1. In this context the term *classical music* is used without a precise definition. Most often it refers to music of the European art tradition. I shall attempt to define the duality through other terminology.
2. Hitchcock, *Music in the United States*, 44.
3. DiMaggio, "Cultural Entrepreneurship," 33–50, and "Cultural Entrepreneurship, Part II," 303–22. Levine, *Highbrow, Lowbrow*, 83–168.
4. Levine, *Highbrow, Lowbrow*, 134.
5. Levine, *Highbrow, Lowbrow*, 130.
6. Chase, *America's Music*, 164–67. Hamm, *Music in the New World*, 159–72.
7. Elson, "Musical Boston," 2.
8. *North American Review* 52 (April 1841); *Musical Magazine* 2 (Jan. 18, 1840); *Musical Review and Record* 1 (July 1838); *Herald*, Feb. 17, 1888; and *Atlantic Monthly* 26 (September 8, 1870), contained articles in which Boston's intellectual leadership in music was either asserted or acknowledged.

Chapter One
Boston's Place in the Musical World

1. Mason kept a detailed diary, noting the distance covered each day. He calculated 1,088 miles for the journey. The diary is inferred from a detailed letter to his parents dated Jan. 21, 1813. The letter is in the Lowell Mason Papers in the John Herrick Jackson Music Library at Yale University; it is also quoted in Pemberton, *Lowell Mason*, 13–14.
2. Adams, *United States in 1800*, 43–44.
3. Larkin, *Reshaping of Everyday Life*, 234–37.
4. *New England Magazine* 1 (1835): 120.
5. Lawrence, *Strong on Music*, 111.
6. Paige, "Musical Organizations," 344–45
7. Cranch, "Music in New York," 59.
8. Dwight, "Music in Boston," 155.
9. Dwight, "Music as a Means of Culture," 322.
10. Dwight, "History of Music," 426–27.
11. Dwight, "Boston a Musical Center," 1.
12. *North American Review*, April 1839, 17.
13. *Musical Review and Record* 1 (July 1838): 129.
14. "Music in America," *Musical World*, Dec. 2, 1837.
15. While this statement is based on my own assessment of American journals before 1845, it agrees with the view of most other scholars. Fellinger and Shepard single out Parker's *Euterpeiad*, Hach's *Musical Magazine*, and Dwight's *Journal*, which appeared in 1852, as the most important nineteenth-century musical

journals ("Periodicals," 503–05). Wunderlich, "Early American Musical Periodicals," 1:63–123, 138, considered Parker's *Euterpeiad* superior in almost every respect to other musical magazines published before 1830 and characterized Hach's *Musical Magazine* as "undoubtedly the most scholarly work of its kind during this period [to 1852]."

16. *Musical Magazine* 2 (October 1840): 365–67.
17. *New York Musical Chronicle and Advertiser* was in one sense a trade journal, admittedly one of the first of its kind. Its purpose was to carry information and advertisements of interest to professional musicians. According to Spillane it was sustained principally through advertising patronage from several piano manufacturers, with the consequent emphasis of forming a link between piano manufacturers and musicians. As no copies have been found, it is impossible to judge its contents. Wunderlich, "Early American Musical Periodicals," 2:547–49, quotes a prospectus of the journal and a discussion of the journal in Spillane, *History of the American Pianoforte*, 348–49. The *Musical Album* hardly qualifies as a journal; it was "A Collection of Concerted Pieces for Soprano" and had a run of two issues.
18. *New York Daily Tribune*, Mar. 25, 1846.
19. *Semi-Weekly Courier and Enquirer*, Mar. 25, 1846.
20. The various letters are quoted in Cooke, *John Sullivan Dwight*, 116–18.
21. *Tribune*, Mar. 25, 1846.
22. Culver, *Horace Mann and Religion*, 39–40, cites contemporary comment regarding the considerable impact that Mann's annual reports had nationwide.
23. Mann, *Life of Horace Mann*, 553. Mary Mann was Horace Mann's second wife.
24. Pemberton, *Lowell Mason*, 89.
25. Horace Mann, letter to Lowell Mason, Nov. 24, 1845. Quoted in Pemberton, *Lowell Mason*, 132.

Chapter Two
Sacred-Music Reforms in Colonial and Federal America

1. *Arrow against Profane and Promiscuous Dancing*, attributed to Increase Mather, 29–30.
2. The most detailed compendium of musical activities in Puritan New England is Scholes, *The Puritans and Music*. In arguing that the Puritans were not antimusic, Scholes cites many examples of musical activity, but the very sparseness of his citations also supports the conclusion that music was not widely practiced.
3. Quoted in Howard, *Our American Music*, 21.
4. Winslow, *Hypocrisie Unmasked*. Quoted in Pratt, *Music of the Pilgrims*, 6, and in Howard, *Our American Music*, 5.
5. Hitchcock, *Music in the United States*, 5, makes this argument.
6. Temperley, "Old Way of Singing," 520.
7. Mather, *Diary*, 373, 560, 606, 624.
8. Mather, *Accomplished Singer*, 10.
9. Mather, *Accomplished Singer*, 22–23.
10. Symmes, *Utile Dulci*; Walter, *Grounds and Rules of Musick Explained*; Walter,

Sweet Psalmist of Israel; Dwight, *Essay to Silence the Outcry*: [Anon.], *Brief Discourse concerning Regular Singing*; Thacher, Danforth, and Danforth, *Essay*.

11. Thacher explicitly states that women should sing in church.
12. Thacher, Danforth, and Danforth, *Essay*, 3–4.
13. Walter, *Sweet Psalmist of Israel*, 6.
14. Mather, *Diary*, 623.
15. The microprint copy at the American Antiquarian Society bears the comment that this is probably not by Mather.
16. Weisberger, *They Gathered at the River*, 8.
17. Walter, *Grounds and Rules of Musick Explained*, 4.
18. Gould, *Church Music in America*, 78–84; Andrew Law to Ashbel Green, Oct. 23, 1797, quoted in Crawford, *Andrew Law*, 137; McKay and Crawford, *William Billings*, 39, discuss the social dimension of American psalmody.
19. Hubbard, *Essay on Music*, 19.
20. Crawford, "'Ancient Music,'" 230–31.
21. Gould, *Church Music in America*, 59.
22. Mason, *Address on Church Music*, 13.
23. Mason, *Address on Church Music*, 14–15.
24. Emerson, *Discourse on Music*, 9–10.
25. Harris, *Artist in American Society*, 2.
26. Allen, *Jonathan Edwards*, 25. Quoted in Parrington, *Main Currents in American Thought*, 1:157.
27. Parrington, *Main Currents in American Thought*, 1:162.
28. Arminianism was the doctrine that salvation was available to all, rather than only the elect. Methodism espoused arminianism, which in part accounts for its popularity in the early nineteenth century.
29. Hammond, "Music in Urban Revivalism," 68–69, states that Leavitt wrote to Finney.
30. Finney, *Lectures*, 126.
31. Finney, *Lectures*, 127.
32. Law, *Musical Primer*, 5. Quoted in Crawford, *Andrew Law*, 105.
33. Crawford, *Andrew Law*, 165.
34. Mason and Mason, eds., *Sacred Harp*. The original version was published in standard notation. The shape-note version was published contrary to the editors' wishes, but apparently they did allow its publication.
35. McKay and Crawford, *William Billings*, 193.
36. Hubbard, *Essay on Music*, 17.
37. Temperley, *Music of the English Parish Church*, is the standard work on this subject. Lowell Mason referred to the idea, using the terms *parish church* and *cathedral*, in the first edition of *Boston Handel and Haydn Society Collection of Church Music*, iv. In the preface to the 1832 edition Mason rephrased the argument without changing the point, by distinguishing between music for "common use" as opposed to pieces "suitable for exhibitions and concerts" (iv).
38. Temperley, "Old Ways of Singing," 533; Crawford, *Andrew Law, 260*.
39. Bentley, *Diary*, 2:185–86.

40. *Musical Magazine* 1 (May 1835): 6. The "Practical" section appeared in all of vol. 1 and the first seven issues of vol. 2.
41. Broyles, *Yankee Musician in Europe*, 30.
42. Hastings, *Sacred Lyre*, 3.
43. Trollope, *Domestic Manners of Americans*, 78–81.
44. Reed and Matheson, *Narrative of Visit to American Churches*, 2:8.
45. Wiebe, *Opening of American Society*, 146.
46. Wiebe, *Opening of American Society*, 265; see also Cott, *Bonds of Womanhood*, 84–92.
47. Wiebe, *Opening of American Society*, 255.
48. Halttunen, *Confidence Men and Painted Women*, passim.
49. Nagel, *This Sacred Trust*, 73.
50. Nagel, *This Sacred Trust*, 73.
51. Bailyn, *Peopling of British North America*, 113–14.
52. Zeuner, *American Harp*. Quoted in Metcalf, *American Writers and Compilers of Sacred Music*, 222–23.
53. Cushing, *Salem Collection*, iii. Quoted in McKay and Crawford, *William Billings*, 192.
54. Hubbard, *Essay on Music*, 19.
55. Hastings, *Sacred Lyre*, 26–27.
56. *Boston Musical Gazette* 1 (Dec. 26, 1838): 140.
57. *Musical Magazine* 1 (July 1835): 84.
58. Gould, *Church Music in America*, 58.
59. *Musical Magazine* 1 (May 1835): 6–7.
60. *Musical Magazine* 1 (October 1835): 170.
61. Freeman, *Psalmodia*, 141–42. Quoted in Rasmussen, *Musical Taste as a Religious Question*, 42.
62. *Musical Magazine* 1 (June 1835): 58–59.
63. *Musical Magazine* 2 (May 1836): 17.
64. "National Musical Convention," *Musical Cabinet* 1 (October 1841): 49–50.

Chapter Three
Lowell Mason: Hymnodic Reformer

1. Chase, *America's Music*, 151; Hitchcock, *Music in the United States*, 56; Hamm, *Music in the New World*, 163.
2. Eskew, "Lowell Mason," 749, and Paige, "Musical Organizations in Boston," 41, present mostly critical views. Ross, "Lowell Mason, American Musician," 411, referred to Mason as "the founder of national music." Matthews, *Hundred Years of Music in America*, 40, asserted that "in Dr. Mason's labors were founded the germinating principles of a national musical intelligence and knowledge, and afforded a soil upon which all higher musical culture has been founded."
3. Aikin, *Christian Minstrel*, 3.
4. Quoted in Ellingwood, *History of American Church Music*, 109.
5. Ellingwood, *History of American Church Music*, 108–09; Eskew, "Lowell Mason," 749.

6. He did remain a member of the Boston Academy of Music from its founding in 1832 until it folded in 1847. Mason's years of active leadership lasted only until 1838, however.

7. Much of the teaching done at the Boston Academy of Music actually occurred in private schools, as Mason and Webb would visit different schools each week for classes.

8. Johnson Mason, Lowell Mason's father, was engaged in various business endeavors. He owned a dry-goods store, from which the straw-hat business originated. His status in the community is attested to by several political offices he held, including one term in the state legislature (Pemberton, *Lowell Mason*, 3–4).

9. Mason described his youth in a letter to Abby Maria (Wood) Bliss dated Jan. 7, 1864, now in the Lowell Mason Papers at Yale University. In reminiscing about his youth, Mason observed: "At that time I was nearly as much interested in dancing as in music." Henry Lowell Mason, Lowell Mason's grandson, worked for many years on a biography of Lowell Mason but never completed it. He left a 545-page manuscript ("Lowell Mason"), which contains much information available nowhere else. For intance, it reports an account (p. 88), possibly taken from a diary of Mason's, of how amazed the citizens of Savannah were when, in a demonstration of church music, Mason simultaneously sang an air and accompanied himself on the bass-viol.

10. Lowell Mason's father, Johnson Mason, in a letter written to Lowell just prior to his departure, hints about the discouraging situation in Medfield, and in his first letter arriving in Savannah, Lowell Mason refers to an apparently optimistic account that he had earlier received from a Mr. Bosworth about Savannah prospects. The letters are in Mason, "Lowell Mason," 79, 82.

11. Mason, "Lowell Mason," 90.

12. Letter to Abby Maria (Wood) Bliss, Jan. 7, 1864.

13. Mason, "Lowell Mason," 90.

14. Loveland, *Southern Evangelicals*, 5–7.

15. From Brooks, ed., *Diary of Michael Floy, Jr.*, 14–17.

16. In New England Mason's denomination was called Congregationalism. South of New England it was called Presbyterianism.

17. Quoted in Loveland, *Southern Evangelicals*, 86–87.

18. Mason, *Boston Handel and Haydn Society Collection of Church Music*; Gardiner, *Sacred Melodies*. Volume 1 of *Sacred Melodies* was reprinted in the United States in 1818, although Mason apparently had a copy of vol. 2 also.

19. Weyman, *Melodia Sacra*, no. 27.

20. For examples of Gardiner's use of instruments in vol. 1 of *Sacred Melodies*, see "Shine Mightly God," p. 122; "The Spacious Firmament on High," p. 10; "Let Ev'ry Creature Join," p. 18.

21. Arnold and Callcott, *Psalms of David*; Costellow, *Selection of Psalms and Hymns*; Whittaker, *Seraph*. The letter of Parker is in the Lowell Mason Papers at Yale University.

22. Broyles, ed., *Yankee Musician in Europe*, 32–33.

23. Mason, *Address on Church Music*, 11.

24. Mason, *Address on Church Music*, 14.
25. Mason, *Address on Church Music*, 19.
26. Weisberger, *They Gathered at the River*, 120.
27. *Western Recorder*, Aug. 30, 1831, 139.
28. Hastings would later come to tire of Mason's constant efforts to promote his own work. Stevenson, *Protestant Church Music in America*, 81–82, quotes some of Hastings' later remarks about Mason.
29. *Western Recorder*, Feb. 13, 1827, 28. The previous reference appeared in *Western Recorder*, July 25, 1826, 120. Both are discussed in Dooley, "Thomas Hastings," 51–52.
30. The original prospectus announcing it appeared in *Western Recorder*, July 5, 1831. An announcement that it had already been issued appeared in *Western Recorder*, Aug. 16, 1831.
31. Dooley, "Thomas Hastings," 52–63, summarizes the publishing history.
32. It is impossible to know for certain whether this came from Hastings' or Mason's pen, but the similar phraseology here and in an article that Hastings wrote for the *Western Recorder* points to him as the author.
33. *Quarterly Christian Spectator* 3 (1831): 666–67.
34. *Western Recorder*, Aug. 30, 1831, 139.
35. *Western Recorder*, Aug. 30, 1831, 139.
36. *Western Recorder*, Aug. 30, 1831, 139.
37. Bacon, *Sermon Commemorative of Lowell Mason*. Quoted in Pemberton, *Lowell Mason*, 167.
38. Information from Alexander, *Forty Years' Familiar Letters*. Cited by Elfrieda A. Kraege, letter to Eva J. O'Meara, Jan. 2, 1972, Lowell Mason Papers, Yale University.
39. Crawford, *Andrew Law*, 29; Mason's references to chanting while in Europe in 1837 are found in Broyles, ed., *Yankee Musician in Europe*, 37, 100, 130. Haydn's London Notebook is quoted by Landon, *Haydn: Chronicle and Works*, 3:173–74.
40. Mason, *Book of Chants*, iii.
41. Mason, *Book of Chants*, iii.
42. Crawford, *American Musical Landscape*. I would like to thank Richard Crawford for sharing with me a prepublication copy of this work.

Chapter Four
Class and Concert Life in Early Nineteenth-Century Boston

1. Hodgson, *Remarks during a Journey*, 82–84; Tocqueville, *Journey to America*, 86–87. Tocqueville recognized that older gentry class had been swept away by the industrial revolution, and when he met Charles Carroll, the last surviving signer of the Declaration of Independence, he realized Carroll was an almost extinct type. Tocqueville considered him "the exact counterpart of the European gentleman."
2. Haywood, "The Musical Profession," 130; Blumin, *Emergence of the Middle Class*, 1–16; Wilentz, *Chants Democratic*, 1–11. The literature on class structure in

antebellum America is extensive. Jaher, *Urban Establishment*, and Story, *Forging of an Aristocracy*, have discussed the upper class specifically in Boston. Rose, *Transcendentalism as a Social Movement*, 18, distinguished a middle class consisting of small manufacturers, clerks, and other white-collar workers from a working class including both skilled and unskilled laborers.

3. Wiebe, *Opening of American Society*, 11. Most of the discussion in this paragraph is taken from Wood, *Creation of the American Republic*, 59, 53.

4. Wood, *Creation of the American Republic*, 70–73; Persons, *Decline of American Gentility*, 30, discusses the implications of Johnson's definition; Wiebe, *Opening of American Society*, 12.

5. James Madison. Quoted in Wood, *Creation of the American Republic*, 410.

6. Martineau, *Society in America*, 260. Hamilton, *Men and Manners in America*, 1:120, also noted the aristocratic leanings of members of the older, wealthier families in Boston.

7. Both quotations come from Dalzell, *Enterprising Elite*, 122.

8. Buckingham, *Personal Memoirs*, 2:83–84.

9. The term *patriarchal* has been used in recent literature to designate any family system in which the male or father dominates. I am using it in a more limited way, following Wiebe, *Opening of American Society*, 265–67, to refer to an extended family in which the father governs even the adult males. This is in opposition to a nuclear-family model, in which the authority of the father extends only until the offspring become adults and strike out on their own. Hamilton, *Men and Manners in America*, 1:249, comments on the persistence of the patriarchal family system.

10. Story, *Forging of an Aristocracy*, 163.

11. Pease and Pease, *Web of Progress*, 82–89.

12. Trollope, *Domestic Manners of the Americans*, 154–55.

13. See Nagel, *This Sacred Trust*, 73, for a discussion of Horace Mann's views on this subject.

14. Crawford, "Musical Learning," 2, points out references to the use of the term *priggery* in connection with Lowell Mason.

15. Wiebe, *Opening of American Society*, 265–90, discusses these issues.

16. Rose, *Transcendentalism as a Social Movement*, 20.

17. Quoted in Jaher, *Urban Establishment*, 20.

18. Sonneck, *Early Concert-Life in America*, 285–309. Most of the important documents about concert activity in Boston prior to 1800 are either included or summarized in Sonneck's study.

19. *Massachusetts Centinel*, Nov. 22, 1788; Sonneck, *Early Concert-Life in America*, 281.

20. Pierce, "Extracts from the Diary of John Rowe," 29.

21. Sonneck, *Early Concert-Life in America*, 260, 273.

22. Sonneck, *Early Concert-Life in America*, 259.

23. Pierce, "Extracts from the Diary of John Rowe," 29.

24. Sonneck, *Early Concert-Life in America*, 286.

25. Sonneck, *Early Concert-Life in America*, 281.

26. Sonneck, *Early Concert-Life in America*, 259; *Boston Directory*, 1798.

27. Sonneck, *Early Concert-Life in America*, 275–76.
28. Sonneck, *Early Concert-Life in America*, 277.
29. Sonneck, *Early Concert-Life in America*, 277.
30. Sonneck, *Early Concert-Life in America*, 285.
31. Officially named the Boston Theatre, it was frequently referred to as the Federal Street Theatre.
32. The antitheater law of 1750 is reproduced in Clapp, "Drama in Boston," 2–3.
33. Clapp, *Record of the Boston Stage*, 20.
34. Sonneck, *Early Concert-Life in America*, 294.
35. Clapp, *Record of the Boston Stage*, 48–49; *Columbian Centinel*, Feb. 3, 1798.
36. Quoted in Clapp, "Drama in Boston," 358–9.
37. Clapp, *Record of the Boston Stage*, 3–4.
38. Sonneck, *Early Opera in America*, 137.
39. Letter from Belknap Society, 1796, to the trustees of the Theatre in Federal Street, Boston Theatre Records.
40. Clapp, *Record of the Boston Stage*, 49.
41. Sonneck, *Early Opera in America*, 138.
42. Wansey, *Excursion in the United States*. Quoted in Nevins, ed., *American Social History*, 47–48.
43. Clapp, *Record of the Boston Stage*, 26.
44. Clapp, *Record of the Boston Stage*, 284.
45. Clapp, *Record of the Boston Stage*, 331, lists the nightly receipts for the Woods' run of *La sonnambula*, one of the most successful runs in the history of the Tremont Theatre. The final day produced receipts of $820, a figure obtained only because tickets were sold at auction.
46. This varied little between 1796, when records are first available, and 1840. Boston Theatre Records, 1796–1797; Tremont Theatre Records, 1839–1840.
47. Clapp, *Record of the Boston Stage*, 337, 339, 347–48, 360.
48. Clapp, *Record of the Boston Stage*, 79.
49. Clapp, *Record of the Boston Stage*, 146; Buckingham, *Memoirs*, 171.
50. Broyles, ed., *Yankee Musician in Europe*, 74–75.
51. *Daily Evening Transcript*, Sept. 2, 1843.
52. This practice was not uncommon in the nineteenth century. It was frequently used as a publicity trick when popular performers were scheduled. The most famous example is P. T. Barnum's use of it to stimulate interest in Jenny Lind.
53. Clapp, *Record of the Boston Stage*, 185–93.
54. The copyright was taken out by William Haliburton, presumed to be the author. Clapp, *Record of the Boston Stage*, 15, and Sonneck, *Early Opera in America*, 139–40, discuss it.
55. Haliburton, *Effects of the Stage*, 38–39.
56. Haliburton, *Effects of the Stage*, 36–37.
57. Haliburton, *Effects of the Stage*, 11, 35–36.
58. Perry, *Intellectual Life in America*, 181.
59. Dunlap, *History of the American Theatre*, 402–04.
60. Dunlap, *History of the American Theatre*, 403.
61. Dunlap, *History of the American Theatre*, 404–05.

62. Sonneck, *Early Concert-Life in America*, 305.
63. *Columbian Centinel*, Sept. 23, 1809.
64. *Columbian Centinel*, June 10, 1810.
65. *Columbian Centinel*, May 19, 1810.
66. *Columbian Centinel*, Mar. 3, 1798, and subsequent weeks. *Clapp, Record of the Boston Stage*, 60.
67. *Columbian Centinel*, June 26, 1823.
68. *Boston Gazette*, June 26, 1815; June 29, 1815.

Chapter Five
Private Music Making and Amateur Musical Organizations

1. Rhodes, "English at Home," 776.
2. Bentley, *Diary*, 2:185.
3. Hodges, *History of Watertown, Massachusetts*, 80; Loring, "Arthur Bird, American," 78–91; I wish to thank Mr. Loring for generously allowing me to examine and use the many papers and documents of the Bird family that are in his possession.
4. Gould, *Church Music in America*, 74–75. Perkins, *History of the Handel and Haydn Society*, 33–34, quoted Gould as calling the Park Street Choir "undoubtedly the best of its kind in Boston," but the citation is incorrect.
5. Perkins, *History of the Handel and Haydn Society*, 33; *Columbian Centinel*, Feb. 25, 1815.
6. McGlinchee, *First Decade of the Boston Museum*, 18. George Ticknor was one of the most educated, urbane, and cultured persons in antebellum Boston. As a young man he traveled extensively in Europe and spent twenty months in residence at the University of Göttingen. He was received by Byron, Châteaubriand, Humphry Davy, Mme. de Staël, Goethe, Alexander W. and Friedrich Schlegel, Scott, Wordsworth, Southey, and other prominent figures. According to Nathaniel Hawthorne, "You recognized in him at once the man who knows the world, the scholar, too." Quoted in Johnson et al., *Dictionary of American Biography*, 9:526–28.
7. Pearson, "Frederic Tudor, Ice King," 171.
8. Pearson, "Frederic Tudor, Ice King," 172–73.
9. Tudor, *Letters on the Eastern States*, 173–95.
10. Bentley, *Diary*, 2:254.
11. Bentley, *Diary*, 2:175, 190, 264.
12. Bentley, *Diary*, 1:107, 2:255, 3:68; Pearson, "Frederic Tudor, Ice King," 173.
13. Bentley, *Diary*, 2:63.
14. Bentley, *Diary*, 2:246, 292.
15. Quoted in Dwight, "History of Music in Boston," 417.
16. Announcement in *Boston Evening Post*, Sept. 5, 1774. Quoted in Sonneck, *Early Concert-Life in America*, 268–69.
17. Camus, "Military Music in Colonial Boston," 1:101. The quotation is from Pichierri, *Music in New Hampshire*, 112.
18. Bentley, *Diary*, 2:255, described a "little band" as consisting of "2 Bass Viols, 3

german flutes and 6 Violins." The ninth annual report of the Handel and Haydn Society, in discussing the need of an orchestra in Boston, used the term *band*, when clearly symphonic music was meant: "We esteem nothing more desirable, in the present state of musical taste in Boston, than to establish permanently a band capable of performing music of the high character which was given at our concerts the last season."

19. Goldman, *Wind Band*, 35. Quoted by Camus, "Military Music in Colonial Boston," 1:103.

20. Paige, "Musical Organizations in Boston," 203–4.

21. Bugbee, "Boston under the Mayors," 234–35. Paige, "Musical Organizations in Boston," 213–14.

22. At the time, Dwight played the clarinet, although he is better known as a flute player. He acknowledged that he played the clarinet in the Arionic Sodality in "Musical Clubs at Harvard," 363–74.

23. Dwight, "Musical Clubs at Harvard," 369.

24. This summary is taken from the Pierian Sodality records, "Book No. IV. Containing The Laws of the Society, and a List of Members from its Foundation, in 1808." The Arionic Sodality has no such summary, but those rules recorded in the minutes indicate that it operated in a manner virtually identical to that of the Pierians.

25. "Records of the Arionic Sodality," entry for July 13, 1821.

26. All of the entries from the minutes of the Pierian Sodality are from two manuscript books entitled "Records of the Pierian Sodality" (books 1 and 3). Book 1 runs from 1808 to 1822; book 3 begins Sept. 25, 1832. A notation in book 3 (entry for Aug. 15, 1821) states that book 2 is lost. Harvard University Archives.

27. "Records of the Pierian Sodality," book 3.

28. Dwight, "Musical Clubs at Harvard," 365–66.

29. Jennison, "Reminiscences of an ex-Pierian."

30. Records of the Pierian Sodality," book 1.

31. The principal document heralding the full assault of the Presbyterian-Congregational reformers' efforts was Hubbard, *Essay on Music.*

32. Emerson, *Discourse on Music*, 4–6.

33. Hubbard, *Essay on Music*, 5. The airs of Scotland were generally considered the finest of any country.

34. "Modern Music," *Euterpeiad* 1 (Apr. 15, 1820): 10.

35. The Philoharmonic Society was sometimes called the Philharmonic Society, the Philo-Harmonic Society, or the Phil Harmonic Society. The society itself used different spellings in various documents and announcements.

36. Letter from Elish Ticknor to Andrew Law, July 1802. Quoted in Crawford, *Andrew Law*, 159.

37. Johnson, *Musical Interludes in Boston*, 53–56, surveys some of these organizations.

38. Perkins, *History of the Handel and Haydn Society*, 31–32.

39. Perkins, *History of the Handel and Haydn Society*, 32–33.

40. Perkins, *History of the Handel and Haydn Society*, 29–30.

41. Perkins, *History of the Handel and Haydn Society*, 37, (22), (85). The latter two numbers are the pagination for Perkins' list of members at the back of the book.
42. Grund, *Americans*, 84.
43. Dwight, "History of Music in Boston," 419.
44. Fertig, "John Sullivan Dwight," 73–4, 140.
45. Perkins, *History of the Handel and Haydn Society*, appendix, 22–96, gives a complete list of members and officers of the Handel and Haydn Society, based on the secretary's records of the society. The act of incorporation is published in Johnson, *Musical Interludes in Boston*, 145–46.
46. Dwight, "History of Music in Boston," 419.
47. The information in table 2 is taken from the *Boston Directory* of 1816. According to Spear, *Bibliography of American Directories*, 48, no directory was issued in 1815.
48. Johnson, *Hallelujah*, 34. Johnson provides a list of occupations of original members that varies somewhat from table 2 but in general corroborates it. Johnson lists no source for his information about discharges and resignations, and it is not known whether he had access to the original records, which are no longer extant. Book 1 of the secretary's records, from 1815 to 1819, has disappeared since Perkins and Dwight wrote their history in the 1880s. Perkins' complete membership list of the Handel and Haydn Society indicates whether each membership was terminated by resignation, discharge, or death. These names can be checked against the city directory, and they do confirm, with only slight variance, the accuracy of Johnson's summaries. They also indicate that several other original members were discharged. Perkins does not say, however, when or why the discharges and resignations occurred; they could have happened many years later.
49. Dwight, "History of Music in Boston," 421; Sonneck, *Early Concert-Life in America*, 309; Johnson, *Musical Interludes in Boston*, 121; Layman, "Philharmonic Society," 2–3; *Boston Intelligencer*, Dec. 27, 1817. This is Parker's first column entitled "The Euterpeiad." *Boston Intelligencer*, Mar. 20, 1819; *Euterpeiad* 1 (Nov. 18, 1820): 133.
50. Sonneck, *Early Concert-Life in America*, 60; Johnson, *Musical Interludes in Boston*, 172; Seilhammer, *History of the American Theatre*, 3:345.
51. *Euterpeiad* 2 (Oct. 27, 1821): 124.
52. George Cushing to Rev. Luther Farnham, Dec. 1871, quoted in Perkins, *History of the Handel and Haydn Society*, 37.
53. The population estimate is taken from Chickering, *Statistical View of the Population of Massachusetts*, 44. Perkins reports that 1,600 tickets were printed, 412 were given away, and 496 were sold at $1 each. Total proceeds for the evening were $533. The difference in numbers probably includes admission paid at the door.
54. It is not clear whether this was a public announcement or was sent to selected individuals. It is quoted in *Lyre* 1 (Jan. 1, 1825): 141.
55. The act of incorporation is quoted in *Lyre* 1 (Jan. 1, 1825): 141–44, and in Perkins, *History of the Handel and Haydn Society*, appendix, 1.
56. Handel and Haydn Society records, Sept. 11, 1819.

57. Mason, *Address on Church Music* (1851), 14. Paige, "Musical Organizations in Boston," 43.

58. In his *Address on Church Music* (1826), 17, Lowell Mason observed that "among the wealthy, every parlour must be furnished with a piano." According to Wolverton, "Keyboard Music and Musicians," 173–76, piano manufacturers who established their business before 1830 include Benjamin Crehore, Lewis and Alpheus Babcock, John Osborn, William and Adam Bent, John Dwight, William M. Goodrich, Lemanuel and Timothy Gilbert, one Shaw, and the most important manufacturer, Jonas Chickering. According to Loesser, *Men, Women, and Pianos,* 458–65, Boston was probably the leading center for piano manufacture in the early Federal period. Many European pianos were sold, too, as advertisements in newspapers indicate. American makers had a difficult time in the early nineteenth century because of a preference for European instruments.

59. *Columbian Centinel,* Apr. 14, 1798, Sept. 13, 1797.

60. Advertisement in *Boston Gazette,* June 1, 1801.

61. Although Catherine Graupner was born in Europe before her mother, then Catherine Hellyer, came to America, she used her stepfather's name.

62. *Columbian Centinel,* Apr. 3, 1799.

63. Handel and Haydn Society records, Aug. 5, 1828; Johnson, *Hallelujah,* 40–41.

64. Guild, "Samuel Atkins and Mary Eliot."

Chapter Six
Crisis in Secular Concert Activity: Disputes and Divergences

1. Lowell Mason letter to Abbey Maria Wood Bliss, Jan. 7, 1864, Lowell Mason Papers, Yale University. Mason describes teaching a band in his youth and refers to it specifically as a military band.

2. Alexis Eustaphieve, the Russian counsel, frequently played the violin in orchestras in Boston. He was only the most conspicuous of the amateurs.

3. *New England Galaxy,* Jan. 26, 1821, 62.

4. *Euterpeiad* 2 (Aug. 4 and 18, 1821): 76, 84.

5. *Euterpeiad* 2 (Aug. 4 and 18, 1821): 76, 84.

6. *Columbian Centinel,* Jan 2, 1819. Quoted in Johnson, *Musical Interludes in Boston,* 142.

7. *Euterpeiad* 2 (Oct. 27, 1821): 124.

8. *Euterpeiad* 2 (Oct. 27, 1821): 124.

9. Johnson, *Musical Interludes in Boston,* 145, prints part of the act of incorporation.

10. *Columbian Centinel,* Apr. 16, 1817.

11. *New England Galaxy,* Jan. 19, 1821; *Euterpeiad* 1 (Jan. 20, 1821): 171.

12. *Euterpeiad* 2 (Mar. 2, 1822): 196.

13. *Euterpeiad* 1 (Apr. 8 and May 20, 1820): 7, 31.

14. *Euterpeiad* 1 (June 10 and Oct. 7, 1820): 43, 111.

15. *Euterpeiad* 1 (June 24, 1820): 51.

16. *Euterpeiad* 1 (Jan. 27, 1821): 175.

17. *Euterpeiad* 1 (June 3, 1820): 39.

18. *Euterpeiad* 1 (July 29, 1820): 70.

19. *Euterpeiad* 1 (Apr. 15, 1820): 10.
20. *Euterpeiad* 2 (May 26, 1821): 36.
21. *Euterpeiad* 2 (Jan. 27, 1821): 175.
22. *Literary and Musical Magazine*, Apr. 26, 1819, 3.
23. Wunderlich, "Early American Musical Periodicals," 1:70.
24. Johnson, "John Rowe Parker Letters," 80.
25. "The Euterpeiad—No. 1," *Boston Intelligencer*, Dec. 27, 1817.
26. "The Euterpeiad—No. 10," *Boston Intelligencer*, Apr. 11, 1818.
27. "The Euterpeiad—No. 2," *Boston Intelligencer*, Jan. 3, 1818.
28. "The Euterpeiad—No. 20," *Boston Intelligencer*, Oct. 10, 1818.
29. *Boston Intelligencer*, Mar. 20, 1819.
30. Wunderlich, "Early American Musical Periodicals," 2:361–485.
31. Johnson, "John Rowe Parker Letters," 75–85.
32. Johnson, "John Rowe Parker Letters," 81.
33. Wunderlich, in the introduction to the reprint edition of *Euterpeiad*, states that it provided the model for thirty later magazines.
34. Wunderlich, "Early American Musical Periodicals," 1:121.
35. Johnson, "John Rowe Parker Letters," 73–74.
36. *Euterpeiad* 1 (July 29, 1820): 70.
37. *Euterpeiad* 1 (Sept. 23, 1820): 106.
38. Lawrence, *Strong on Music*, xxxv–xxxvi, describes the New York Handel and Haydn Society.
39. Beethoven, "Hallelujah to the Father," from *Christ on the Mount of Olives*; Handel, "Worthy Is the Lamb That Was Slain," from *Messiah*; Haydn, "The Heavens Are Telling," from *The Creation*.
40. This letter is quoted in Johnson, "John Rowe Parker Letters," 84.
41. *Euterpeiad* 2 (Aug. 18, 1821): 84.
42. According to the records of the society, the precise amounts were: 1824: $601.90; 1826: $964.28; 1827: $800 (estimate); 1828: $820; 1829: $1,000 (estimate); 1830: $1,000 (estimate); 1831: $1166.67. The figures are from the treasurer's annual report presented at the board of directors' meeting.
43. Layman, "Philoharmonic Society," 3.
44. *Euterpeiad* 3 (January 1823): 166.
45. *Columbian Centinel*, May 24, 1825.
46. *Columbian Centinel*, May 18, 1825.
47. *Columbian Centinel*, May 25, 1825.
48. "As the terms [for season tickets] do not appear to be understood, the Society intends to give an additional Concert in the course of the season." *Columbian Centinel*, Nov. 27, 1824.
49. *Columbian Centinel*, Apr. 30, 1825; May 21, 1825.
50. Circular, "Promotion of a Taste for Music," 1.
51. The Athenaeum had opened Boston's first art gallery that same year. Raising funds proved a problem.
52. Circular, "Promotion of a Taste for Music," 10.
53. Circular, "Promotion of a Taste for Music," 7.
54. Israel Thorndike, Jr., and William H. Eliot are not in the dictionary.

55. Jaher, *The Urban Establishment*, 51.
56. For a discussion of the role of the academy in eighteenth-century Europe see Broyles, "Ensemble Music Moves out of the Private House," 97–122.
57. Circular, "Promotion of a Taste for Music," 11.
58. Perkins' chronological membership list (starting in 1815) of the Handel and Haydn Society, in his *History of the Handel and Haydn Society*, appendix, reaches no. 311 by the end of 1826. This list does not indicate termination of membership; given normal dropouts, it is virtually certain that the membership did not exceed three hundred. The records of the Handel and Haydn Society prior to 1819 have disappeared since Perkins' research. Attendance at the concerts is determined from the concert receipts reported in the treasurer's records. Members were allowed a certain number of free tickets, varying from year to year. Concert tickets were sold for one dollar.
59. Clapp, *Record of the Boston Stage*, 260; "Music in Boston," 176; "Programs of Concerts in Boston 1817–1863," in the Boston Public Library.
60. *Daily Evening Transcript*, Sept. 29, 1830.
61. *Daily Evening Transcript*, Nov. 4, 1830.
62. *Daily Evening Transcript*, Apr. 27, 1831.
63. *Daily Evening Transcript*, July 14, 1832.

Chapter Seven
Samuel Eliot and the Boston Academy of Music

1. Quoted in the *First Annual Report of the Boston Academy of Music*, 3.
2. *First Annual Report of the Boston Academy of Music*, 8.
3. *First Annual Report of the Boston Academy of Music*, 4; Eliot, *Address before the Boston Academy of Music*, 4.
4. *First Annual Report of the Boston Academy of Music*, 8. The academy issued an annual report from 1833–1844 and a combined report for 1845–1846.
5. *Second Annual Report of the Boston Academy of Music*, 4, 7, 22.
6. *Second Annual Report of the Boston Academy of Music*, 14–15.
7. The quotation is from Johnson et al., *Dictionary of American Biography*, 6:81–82. Other material is also from Eliot, *Sketch of the Eliot Family*, 50–51.
8. *Our First Men*, 21.
9. Eliot, *Sketch of the Eliot Family*, 51. Genzmer, *Dictionary of American Biography*, 6:80.
10. Spalding, *Music at Harvard*, 11–12.
11. The Library of Congress contains a copy of Gardiner's *Sacred Melodies* signed, "Saml Eliot Organ Loft of West Boston Society."
12. Letter to George Ticknor, Oct. 6, 1821, in the Samuel Atkins Eliot Papers, Harvard University Archives.
13. These letters are in the Samuel Atkins Eliot Papers, Harvard University Archives.
14. Letter to J. A. Keller from Samuel A. Eliot, July 14, 1836, Samuel Atkins Eliot, "Letterbook, 1825–1842," Harvard University Archives. According to Lawrence, *Strong on Music*, 32, Schmidt was in New York in 1836.
15. "Academy of Musick and Boston Theater," manuscript booklet.

16. One of the names on the treasurer's list is illegible. The information for table 2 is taken from *List of Persons, Copartnerships, and Corporations Who Were Taxed Twenty-Five Dollars and Upward*. City Document No. 12.

17. Members of both the Handel and Haydn Society and the Boston Academy in 1835 were Joseph Brown, Abel W. Bruce, Jonas Chickering, L. S. Cragen, Bela Hunting, Lowell Mason, George Pollock, George James Webb, and Increase S. Withington.

18. Weisberger, *They Gathered at the River* 138–39.

19. "Billings and Holden Society," *Boston Musical Gazette* 1 (May 30, 1838):19; Paige, "Musical Organizations in Boston," 92–104, summarizes the activities of the Billings and Holden Society.

20. *Daily Evening Transcript*, May 10, 1834. Italics original.

21. Paige, "Musical Organizations in Boston," 92.

22. Gould, *Church Music in America*, 190.

23. Bentley, *Diary*, 3:469. Entry for June 22, 1809.

24. Pease and Pease, *Web of Progress*, 154.

25. Samuel Eliot letter to Mary Lyman Eliot, Aug. 9, 1834, Samuel Atkins Eliot Papers, Harvard University Archives.

26. Guild, "Samuel Atkins and Mary Eliot," Samuel Atkins Eliot Papers, Harvard University Archives.

27. When the *First Annual Report* was reissued in 1835, Gordon's name at the end was deleted.

28. *Third Annual Report of the Boston Academy of Music*, 4.

29. *Third Annual Report of the Boston Academy of Music*, 5.

30. *Fourth Annual Report of the Boton Academy of Music*, 3.

31. *Fourth Annual Report of the Boston Academy of Music*, 4–6.

32. *Fifth Annual Report of the Boston Academy of Music*, 9–10, 4.

33. *Sixth Annual Report of the Boston Academy of Music*, 4–5.

34. *Sixth Annual Report of the Boston Academy of Music*, 5.

35. *Sixth Annual Report of the Boston Academy of Music*, 11–12.

36. *Seventh Annual Report of the Boston Academy of Music*, 7.

37. *Eighth Annual Report of the Boston Academy of Music*, 5.

38. "The Concerts," *Musical Magazine* 1 (Mar. 30, 1839): 111.

39. "The Late Musical Season," *Musical Magazine* 1 (July 20, 1839): 236.

40. "Eighth Annual Report," *Musical Magazine* 2 (Aug. 29, 1840): 278–80.

41. "Eighth Annual Report," *Musical Magazine* 2 (Aug. 29, 1840): 280–81.

42. "The Late Musical Season," *Musical Magazine* 2 (Aug. 29, 1840): 236.

43. *Ninth Annual Report of the Boston Academy of Music*, 4.

44. "Music in Boston," *Musical Magazine* 3 (June 5, 1841): 174–75.

45. "Concerts," *Musical Reporter* 1 (Mar. 1, 1841): 127–30.

46. *Ninth Annual Report of the Boston Academy of Music*, 4.

47. *Musical Cabinet* 1 (May 1841): 184.

48. Dwight, "History of Music in Boston," 425–27.

49. *Musical Magazine* 3 (May 1842): 417; *Musical Cabinet* 2 (February 1842): 115.

50. *Boston Daily Evening Transcript*, Jan. 9, 1843.

51. *Eleventh Annual Report of the Boston Academy of Music*, 5.

52. *Report of the Government of the Boston Academy of Music*, 4.
53. Samuel Atkins Eliot Papers, Harvard University Archives.
54. Eliot, "First Annual Report," 53–85.
55. Eliot, "First Annual Report," 53.
56. Eliot, "First Annual Report," 75.
57. Eliot, "First Annual Report," 75.
58. Eliot, "First Annual Report," 76–78.
59. Eliot, "First Annual Report," 79.
60. Eliot, "First Annual Report," 81–83.
61. Eliot, "First Annual Report," 83.
62. Eliot, "Annual Reports," 320–38.
63. Eliot, "Annual Reports," 320–22. The song was written by Alexander Coffman Ross, a jeweler from Zanesville, Ohio, who set it to the tune "Little Pig's Tail." According to Lawrence, *Music for Patriots*, 269, it "became the theme song of the most singing campaign in American history."
64. Music soothes the ferocity in humans and excites "kind and gentle feelings" without weakening strength or character. It promotes social interaction, encourages precise thinking, and teaches discipline and the necessity of order and authority. Its study through singing enhances elocutionary abilities and promotes physical well-being through the exercise of the lungs. The committee's report was published in the *Boston Musical Gazette*, Nov. 28, 26, and Dec. 26, 1838. It is given in Pemberton, Lowell Mason, unpub. diss., University of Minnesota, 1971, 517–24.
65. Eliot, "Annual Reports," 329.
66. Eliot, "Annual Reports," 332.
67. Eliot, "Annual Reports," 332, 334, 337.
68. Eliot, "Annual Reports," 337.
69. Eliot, "Music and Politics," 344–46. The article is signed "E.," but Eliot's papers confirm his authorship.
70. Eliot, "Music and Politics," 345.
71. Eliot, "Music and Politics," 345.
72. Lowell Mason to his son William, Lowell Mason Papers, Yale University. Lowell and William differed sharply on this point. See William Mason, *Memories*, 10 and 25.
73. Wiebe, *Opening of American Society*, 129.
74. [Cleveland], "Life of Haydn," 1–19.
75. *Musical Magazine* 2 (1840): 17–22.
76. Copy at Cornell University. I wish to thank William Austin for pointing this out to me.
77. Cleveland, "Origin and Progress of Music," 58–65, 106–17; "Gardiner Music of Nature," 157–97.
78. [Cleveland], "Life of Haydn," 14.
79. [Cleveland], "Life of Haydn," 14–16.
80. [Cleveland], "Life of Haydn," 17–18.
81. *Musical Magazine* 2 (1840): 365–66.
82. Haywood, "Lectures Before the Boston Academy of Music," 130.
83. [Cleveland], "Life of Haydn," 16.

Chapter Eight
Romanticism and Transcendentalism

1. Warren, "Samuel Adams and the Sans Souci Club," 322.
2. Wood, *Creation of the American Republic*, 421.
3. Letter to John Adams, July 2, 1785, *Writings of Samuel Adams*, 4:315. Quoted in Warren, "Samuel Adams and the Sans Souci Club," 320.
4. Warren, "Samuel Adams and the Sans Souci Club," 323.
5. *Massachusetts Centinel*, Jan. 15, 1785. Quoted in Warren, "Samuel Adams and the Sans Souci Club," 322–23.
6. *Independent Chronicle*, Jan. 27, 1785. Quoted in Warren, "Samuel Adams and the Sans Souci Club," 328.
7. *Massachusetts Centinel*, Jan. 19, 1785. Quoted in Warren, "Samuel Adams and the Sans Souci Club," 325–26.
8. The statement is based partly on the known ancestry of some musicians, such as Philip Trajetta, Francis Masi, and Francis Mallet, and partly on the admittedly less reliable inferences based on surnames of members of the Federal Street Theatre orchestra, about whom little is known.
9. Information on German immigration is taken from "Arrivals of Alien Passengers and Immigrants in the United States from 1820 to 1892," prepared by the Bureau of Statistics and published in 1893 by the Government Printing Office. It is quoted in Schrader, *Germans in the Making of America*, 29.
10. Known musicians frequently appeared as teachers, instrument dealers, or in completely unrelated occupations in city directories. See appendix 1 for further discussion of the numbers and professional status of musicians. These statistics were compiled by Paige, "Musical Organizations in Boston," 34.
11. In the *Musical Magazine*, Jan. 5, 1839, Hach states that he is German. In 1837 Lowell Mason wrote to Hach in Lubeck and later met him in Hamburg (Broyles, ed., *Yankee Musician in Europe*, 31).
12. Broyles, ed., *Yankee Musician in Europe*, 58.
13. Wunderlich, "Early American Musical Periodicals," 1:138.
14. "Prospectus," *Musical Magazine* 1 (January 1839): 2–3.
15. *Musical Magazine* 2 (October 1840): 365.
16. *Musical Magazine* 3 (January 1841): 19.
17. *Musical Magazine* 1 (July 1839): 220.
18. *Musical Magazine* 3 (April 24): 420, 415. This was the final issue of the journal.
19. *Musical Magazine* 3 (April 24): 416, 418, 420.
20. *Musical Magazine* 1 (August 1839): 254.
21. *Musical Magazine* 3 (April 24): 416.
22. *American Monthly Magazine* 7 (November 1836): 447–57.
23. Dwight, "Second Annual Report of the Boston Academy of Music," 14–15.
24. Fertig, "John Sullivan Dwight," 39.
25. *Harbinger* 5 (June 19, 1947): 29–30.
26. Fertig, "John Sullivan Dwight," 64.
27. Carlyle to Dwight, Mar. 14, 1839, in the Harvard University Library. Reprinted in Cooke, *John Sullivan Dwight*, 26–30.
28. Fertig, "John Sullivan Dwight," 61–63.

29. Fertig, "John Sullivan Dwight," 58.
30. Fertig, "John Sullivan Dwight," 58; Morgan, *Goethe's Lyric Poems*, 56. Fertig quotes both Morgan and Simmons.
31. Quoted in Fertig, "John Sullivan Dwight," 57.
32. Cooke, *John Sullivan Dwight*, 7.
33. Moore and Tiffany, *Harm Jan Huidedoper*, 257. Quoted in Fertig, "John Sullivan Dwight," 15.
34. Cooke, *John Sullivan Dwight*, 18–19. Cooke implies that he got his information direct from members of Dwight's congregation.
35. *Boston Musical Gazette* 1 (Jan. 23, 1839): 156.
36. *Boston Musical Gazette* 1 (May 16, 1838): 9–10.
37. Dwight, "Concerts of the Past Winter," 124.
38. Weisberger, *They Gathered at the River*, 130–34.
39. Miller, ed., *Transcendentalists*, 8.
40. English writers like Carlyle and Coleridge were important influences on the transcendentalists. They were themselves heavily influenced by German romanticism and thus reinforced the Germanic element in the transcendentalists.
41. Goddard, *Studies in New England Transcendentalism*, 188, italics Goddard's; Clebsch, *American Religious Thought*, 66–68.
42. Peabody, "The Word Aesthetic," *Aesthetic Papers* 1 (1849): 1–4. Reprinted in Miller, ed., *Transcendentalists*, 372–74.
43. Dwight, "Music, as a Branch of Popular Education," 9–10.

Chapter Nine
Developments of the 1840s: Retraction

1. *Daily Evening Transcript*, Jan. 18, 1850.
2. *Harbinger* 4 (Jan. 9, 1847): 77.
3. *Harbinger* 4 (Jan. 9, 1847): 77.
4. *Daily Evening Transcript*, Jan. 26, 1844.
5. *Daily Evening Transcript*, Oct. 18, 1841.
6. Eliot, "Annual Reports," 334.
7. The annual election of officers, held each year in October or November, was reported in the *Daily Evening Transcript*.
8. *Daily Evening Transcript*, Jan. 18, 1850.
9. "Life of Haydn," *North American Review* 50 (1840): 14–16; *Musical Magazine* 2 (1840): 365–66; see chapter 7 for a further discussion of Cleveland's and Hach's views. *Harbinger* 3 (Mar. 7, 1846): 204. Paige, "Musical Organizations in Boston," 419–22, discusses Keyser's career.
10. *Harbinger* 4 (Jan. 9, 1847): 77. Paige, "Musical Organizations in Boston," 265, discusses the implications of this review.
11. *Daily Evening Transcript*, Jan. 24, 1846. *Musical Gazette* 1 (Mar. 2, 1846): 22.
12. *Harbinger* 8 (Jan. 6, 1849): 79, referred to them as "splendid winter festivals."
13. *Daily Evening Transcript*, Feb. 1, 1847.
14. *New York Times*, June 16, 1872. The figure of twenty thousand is from Nettl, *Story of Dance Music*, 269.

15. *Twelfth Annual Report of the Boston Academy of Music*, 3.
16. *Twelfth Annual Report of the Boston Academy of Music*, 3.
17. *Twelfth Annual Report of the Boston Academy of Music*, 4.
18. *Twelfth Annual Report of the Boston Academy of Music*, 4.
19. *Twelfth Annual Report of the Boston Academy of Music*, 5.
20. *Twelfth Annual Report of the Boston Academy of Music*, 5.
21. Part of the problem with membership may have been the extraordinary increase in the initiation fee in 1829. From 1808 to 1824 the initiation fee had been fifty cents. In 1824 it was raised to $1 and in 1829 to $13. It was reduced to $4 in 1839 and to $2 in 1847.
22. Spalding, *Music at Harvard*, 53; Dwight, "Musical Clubs at Harvard," 371; Jennison, "Reminensces of an Ex-Pierian," in scrapbook at Harvard Musical Association.
23. Spalding, *Music at Harvard*, 42.
24. Spalding, *Music at Harvard*, 53.
25. Fox, "Cliques, Clubs and Catholicity," 1–3.
26. The minutes of the Harvard Musical Association state that Dwight was spokesman. They are in a large, bound manuscript, "Records of the Harvard Musical Association. 1840. From its formation in 1837," at the Harvard Musical Association. Dwight himself acknowledged that he wrote the proposal, in a five-page manuscript at the association, "Brief Historical Sketch by J. S. Dwight, 1852." The title itself is not by Dwight. Dwight's title was "H.M.A."
27. The Pierian Sodality had already attempted to establish a musical library. The minutes of Oct. 9, 1832, refer to opening a subscription to the *Harmonicum* (London) for the library and to "the advancement of the Society in Musical Science."
28. "Report Made at a Meeting of the Honorary and Immediate Members of the Pierian Sodality, 1837." The report was reprinted in the *Boston Musical Gazette*, June 27 and July 11, 1838, 33–34 and 42.
29. Spalding, *Music at Harvard*, 160–63. The instruction in 1856 was given by Levi Parsons Homer of Boston; the 1862 lectures were delivered by John Knowles Paine.
30. Pierian Sodality minutes, Sept. 25, 1832. This is the view of the Pierians who received their information from President Quincy.
31. Pierian Sodality minutes, June 22, 1843.
32. Cleveland, "Origin and Progress of Music," *New England Magazine* 9 (1835): 58–65, 106–17; Cleveland, "Gardiner Music of Nature," *New York Review* 3 (1837): 157–97. Cleveland, ed., *Caii Crispi Salustii de Catilince Conjurtione Belloque Jugurthino Historiae*, 1838. Cleveland's translation was reviewed in the *North American Review*, April 1839.
33. Smith, "Commencements at Harvard," 5 (1889–1890): 230.
34. Cleveland's address was printed in the *Musical Magazine*, Sept. 26, 1840, 305–18, under the title "Mr. Cleveland's Lecture Before the Pierian Sodality at Cambridge." Cleveland had it reprinted with a special title page that referred to it as *An Address Delivered Before the Harvard Musical Association at the Annual Meeting on Commencement Day, Aug. 26, 1840*. The copy in the Loeb Music

Library at Harvard bears the inscription "H. W. Longfellow, with the regard of his friend, H. R. Cleveland."

35. Cleveland, *Address*, 305.
36. Cleveland, *Address*, 306.
37. Cleveland, *Address*, 307.
38. Cleveland, *Address*, 309–11.
39. Cleveland, *Address*, 310.
40. Cleveland, *Address*, 313.
41. Cleveland, *Address*, 314.
42. In her discussion of opera in antebellum New York, Karen Ahlquist contrasted the preference, almost the need, of American audiences for simple tunes in operas to the audience's acceptance of, indeed fondness for, the verbally sophisticated plays of Shakespeare (Ahlquist, "Opera, Theatre, and Audience in Antebellum New York," 171).
43. Cleveland, "Origin and Progress of Music, No. 2," 116.
44. Dwight, "Concerts of the Past Winter," 124–34.
45. Dwight, "Concerts of the Past Winter," 124.
46. Dwight, "Concerts of the Past Winter," 124.
47. Dwight, "Concerts of the Past Winter," 124.
48. Dwight, "Concerts of the Past Winter," 127–28.
49. Dwight, "Concerts of the Past Winter," 124–25.
50. Printed as "Address, Delivered before the Harvard Musical Association, August 25, 1841," *Musical Magazine* 3 (Aug. 28, 1841): 257–72.
51. Dwight, "Address," 258, 259.
52. Dwight, "Address," 259.
53. Dwight, "Address," 263–64.
54. Dwight, "Address," 259.
55. Dwight, "Address," 264–65, italics Dwight's.
56. Story, *Address*.
57. Story, *Address*, 6–7.
58. Fox, "Cultural Counterpoint," 6–8.
59. Manuscript entitled "Lecture on Symphonies, particularly Beethoven No. 5." Papers of Samuel Atkins Eliot, Harvard University Archives. There is no date on the lecture, but it was almost certainly given in the early 1840s.
60. Donald Francis Tovey's analytical approach was based on the idea of the "naive listener," by which he meant a listener with some but not extensive background or knowledge. Tovey was constantly concerned with what the naive listener would or could hear. A Boston audience in the early 1840s, composed of listeners with little musical knowledge and even less knowledge of Beethoven, would be an extreme case.
61. Story, *Address*, 10.
62. Story, *Address*, 4.
63. *Daily Evening Transcript*, Nov. 17, 1842. Paige, "Musical Organizations in Boston," 232.
64. A "Quartetto by Pleyel" was performed at a benefit concert for Gottlieb Graupner

on May 5, 1801. Another Pleyel quartet was performed on June 13, 1810. *Boston Gazette*, May 4, 1801; *Columbian Centinel*, June 10, 1810.

65. Lawrence, *Strong on Music*, 221–22.
66. Concert series were presented in the 1844–45, 1846–47, and 1849–50 seasons. The absence of the series in the 1845–46 season may have been due to the sudden death of Herwig, although no evidence exists to support such a hypothesis. There is no explanation for the absence of the series in the 1847–49 season.
67. *Musical Magazine* 1 (Feb. 2, 1839): 46–47.
68. *Dial* 1 (July 1840): 134.
69. *Musical Cabinet* 1 (May 1842): 184.
70. Paige, "Musical Organizations in Boston," 234, states incorrectly that Nicholas Lange was the pianist. The program only lists "Mr. Lange."
71. Hepner, *Harvard Musical Association*, 11.
72. Dwight, "Music in Boston," 123–24.
73. Cranch, "Mr. Cranch's Address," 98–100, 109–10, 123–24. Dwight's comments occurred on pp. 98–99.
74. Cranch, "Mr. Cranch's Address," 124.
75. *Dwight's Journal of Music* 22 (1862): 271.
76. Quoted in Harris, *Artist in American Society*, 295.
77. Christopher Pearse Cranch to the Misses Myers, New York, Aug. 7, 1849. Quoted in Scott, *Cranch*, 172. The issue of Cranch's and Story's alienation from American society is discussed by Harris, *Artist in American Society*, 294–95.
78. Story, *Address*, 9–10.
79. Story, "Poem," *North American Review* 83 (July 1856): 94.
80. Cranch to John S. Dwight, Feb. 12, 1841. Quoted in Scott, *Cranch*, 69.

Chapter Ten
Bands, Opera, Virtuosi, and the Changing of the Guard

1. Ritter, *Music in America*, 169–70.
2. Ritter, *Music in America*, 172–73.
3. Hastings, *Dissertation*, 1822 ed., 82, 153; 1853 ed., 129, 188.
4. Ritter, *Music in America*, 171, 183.
5. Mason, *Address on Church Music*, 17.
6. Mason, *Memories*, 46, 25, 10. William does not specify which of Mason's works he presented to Hauptman.
7. Dwight, "History of Music in Boston," 413.
8. Weber, "The Rise of the Classical Repertoire," 362.
9. Kerman and Tyson, "Beethoven," 381–83.
10. Hoffman's review of Beethoven's Fifth Symphony appeared in the *Allgemeine musikalische Zeitung* in two parts, July 4 and July 11, 1810.
11. Theodore Thomas noticed the difference between the orchestras of Europe and America when he traveled to Europe in 1867 (Schabas, *Theodore Thomas*, 34–35).
12. Boston: Munroe and Francis, 1802; Clapp, *Record of the Boston Stage*, 78.
13. Newman, *Sonata in the Classic Era*, 424–26, discusses the history of these sonatas.

14. Beethoven wrote to Czerny the next day, "But you must pardon that [his outburst] in a composer who would have preferred to hear his work exactly as he wrote it" (Forbes, ed., *Thayer's Life of Beethoven*, 640–41).
15. There are of course many important exceptions: Corelli's sonatas were widely published before 1700, and many of Schubert's instrumental pieces were not published.
16. Treitler, "Early History of Music Writing in the West," 237–79.
17. Orsini, "Ancient Roots of a Modern Idea," 25–60.
18. Spingarn, ed., *Goethe's Literary Essays*, 5.
19. Weber, *Music and the Middle Class*, 19.
20. *Boston Intelligencer*, Dec. 27, 1817; *Columbian Centinel*, Oct. 17, 1818.
21. *Euterpeiad* 1 (May 20, 1820): 31.
22. *Euterpeiad* 2 (May 26, 1821): 36.
23. Hehr, "Musical Activities in Salem," 272.
24. "The Euterpeiad—No. 1," *Boston Intelligencer*, Dec. 27, 1817.
25. *Musical Magazine* 2 (Mar. 28, 1840): 111–12.
26. *Musical Magazine* 3 (Apr. 24, 1842): 418–19.
27. *Musical Cabinet* 1 (Feb. 1, 1842): 115.
28. *Musical Cabinet* 1 (Feb. 1, 1842): 115.
29. Haywood, "Lectures," *Musical Cabinet* 1 (February 1842): 114.
30. Dwight, "Virtuoso Age," 362–64.
31. Story, *Address*, 20–21.
32. Dwight, "Concerts of the Past Winter," 124–34.
33. Broyles, ed., *Yankee Musician in Europe*, 133.
34. *Harbinger* 1 (June 1845): 16; Fertig, "John Sullivan Dwight," 123–30.
35. Scott, *Cranch*, 89–90.
36. Scott, *Cranch*, 90–91.
37. Dwight, "Musical Review," 77.
38. Dwight's letter is quoted in Cooke, "John Sullivan Dwight," 80–82. The date of the letter, which Cooke does not give, is October 1844.
39. Weber, *Music and the Middle Class*, 21.
40. *Musical Magazine* 1 (July 20, 1839): 238; 2 (Mar. 28, 1840): 112.
41. *Musical Magazine* 1 (May 5, 1839): 159.
42. J. R. Lowell to Miss Evelyn Eldredge, Boston, Apr. 12, 1842. Quoted in James, *William Wetmore Story*, 1:48.
43. *Boston Musical Gazette* 1 (May 30, 1838): 20. The *Gazette* is quoting the *New York Musical Review*, May 8, 1838.
44. Jennison, "Reminensces of an Ex-Pierian," in scrapbook at Harvard Musical Association.
45. Dwight, "Concerts of the Past Winter," 125.
46. The committee's report is quoted in Nutter, *Harvard Musical Association*, 124.
47. Grund, *The Americans*, xix, 85.
48. Records of the Arionic Sodality, Sept. 12, 1830.
49. Samuel A. Eliot to Joseph Keller, July 14, 1836. In Eliot, "Letterbook, 1825–1842," Harvard University Archives.
50. *Euterpeiad* 2 (May 26, 1821): 36.

51. Edward, *Music and Musicians of Maine*, 427.
52. *Musical Cabinet* 1 (May 1842): 164.
53. *Musical Reporter* 1 (Mar. 1841): 127–28.
54. Ahlquist, "Opera, Theatre, and Audience," 82–85.
55. Grund, *The Americans*, 81–82.
56. The New York proposal appeared in the *Evening Post*, Apr. 1, 1826, and is quoted in Ahlquist, "Opera, Theatre, and Audience," 133. The Boston proposal was printed as a "Circular," 4, 6–7; see chapter 6 for a more detailed discussion of it.
57. Champlin, "Nearly Two Centuries of Music," 169–82; Lamb and Harrison, *History of the City of New York*, 3:855.
58. *American Musical Journal* 1 (November 1834): 18. Quoted in Wunderlich, "Early American Musical Periodicals," 1, 169.
59. Chmaj, "Fry versus Dwight," 63–84.
60. Ahlquist, "Opera, Theatre, and Audience," 30–55.
61. Ahlquist, "Opera, Theatre, and Audience," 282–312.

Chapter Eleven
Boston and Beyond

1. This is not to assume that any of these musicians would have even wanted to join, had they been asked.
2. Pamela Fox has addressed this issue in "Cliques, Clubs, Catholicity." She is further investigating the topic in a forthcoming study of music in late nineteenth-century Boston.
3. Sosna, "NEH," 13.
4. Sosna, "NEH," 12.
5. Sosna, "NEH," 12.
6. Sosna, "NEH," 12, 7.
7. Rockefeller panel report, "The Performing Arts."
8. Goldman, "Wonderful World of Culture," 245–49.
9. Brooks, *Coming-of-Age*, 6–7.
10. Many artists do not use such terms as morality or sacred, but they perceive their mission as a sacred one: to challenge, whether it be political issues or individual complacency. A common goal is to make individuals or society as a whole better.

Appendix 1
Instrumental Musicians in Boston, 1796–1842

1. Dwight, "History of Music in Boston," 417; Johnson, *Musical Interludes*, 150–52.
2. This is included only very rarely, as in the Handel and Haydn Society's records for 1837.
3. Knights, "Using City Directories."
4. Knights' statistics were derived by comparing the city directories of 1830 and 1840 with the census records.

5. Buckingham, *Personal Memoirs*, 1:52.
6. "Programs of Concerts," Boston Public Library.
7. *Columbian Centinel*, Mar. 25, 1797.
8. Seilhamer, *History of the American Theatre*, 3:143, 334, 351.
9. *Columbian Centinel*, Oct. 28, 1797.
10. The records of the Handel and Haydn Society, including the treasurer's books and minutes of the directors' meetings, are in the Boston Public Library.
11. Professional musicians were not members of the society, with the exception of one or two honorary members, because the by-laws stipulated that no member would be compensated for his services.
12. Wilentz, *Chants Democratic*, 405. Wilentz lists average monthly wages, which I have multiplied by twelve.
13. Laurie, Hershberg, and Alter, "Immigrants and Industry," 105. Quoted in Blumin, *Emergence of the Middle Class*, 109–10, which discusses the statistics of Wilentz and Laurie et al. and compares them with other information.
14. Long, *Wages and Earnings in the United States*, 68. Quoted in Blumin, *Emergence of the Middle Class*, 343.
15. Margo and Villaflor, "Growth of Wages in Antebellum America," 873–95. Quoted in Blumin, *Emergence of the Middle Class*, 343.
16. Blumin, *Emergence of the Middle Class*, 112.
17. *List of Persons, Copartnerships, and Corporations Who Were Taxed Twenty-Five Dollars and Upward.*
18. *Euterpeiad* 2 (Aug. 4 and 18, 1821): 76, 84.

Works Cited

Primary Sources

"Academy of Musick and Boston Theatre." Small manuscript booklet in the Allen A. Brown Collection of the Boston Public Library.

Aikin, J. B. *The Christian Minstrel*. 152d. ed. Philadelphia: S. C. Collins, 1846.

Annual Reports of the Boston Academy of Music. Boston: Isaac R. Butts, 1833; Perkins, Marvin, 1834–1840; T. R. Marvin, 1840–1846. The academy issued an annual report from 1833 to 1844 and *Report of the Government of the Boston Academy of Music, for the Years 1845 and 1846*. The *First Annual Report* was written by George Wm Gordon, all others by Samuel A. Eliot.

Arnold, Samuel, and John W. Callcott. *The Psalms of David, for the Use of Parish Churches*. London: John Stockdale and George Goulding, 1791.

Bacon, George Blagden. *Sermon, Commemorative of Lowell Mason*. New York: Cushing, Bardus, 1872.

Bentley, William. *The Diary of William Bentley, D. D.* 4 vols. Salem, Mass.: Essex Institute, 1905–1914.

The Billings and Holden Collection of Ancient Psalmody. Boston: Marsh, Capen, and Lyon, 1836.

The Boston Directory. Boston: E. Cotton, 1816.

Boston Theatre (Federal Street Theatre) Records. Harvard University Archives, Harvard University.

A Brief Discourse concerning Regular Singing, Shewing from the Scriptures, the Necessity and Incumbency thereof in the Worship of God. Boston: B. Green. 1725.

Buckingham Joseph Tinker. *Personal Memoirs and Recollections of Editorial Life*. 2 vols. Boston: Ticknor, Reed, and Fields, 1852.

Chickering, Jesse. *A Statistical View of the Population of Massachusetts, from 1765 to 1840*. Boston: Charles C. Little and James Brown, 1846.

"Circular" ["Promotion of a Taste for Music" added in pencil]. Boston: Dutton and Wentworth, dated 15 May, 1826.

Cleveland, Henry R. *An Address Delivered Before the Harvard Musical Association at the Annual Meeting on Commencement Day, August, 26, 1840*. Boston: Published by request, 1840.

———. "Gardiner Music of Nature (Boston: J. H. Wilkins and R. B. Carter, 1837)." *New York Review* 3 (1837): 157–97.

———. "The Origin and Progress of Music. No. 1 and No. 2." *New England Magazine* 9 (1835): 58–65, 106–16.

[Costellow, Thomas.] *A Selection of Psalms and Hymns with Favorite and Approved Tunes for the Use of Bedford Chapel*. Music connected and revised and several tunes composed by Mr. [Thomas] Costellow. Compiled by William Parry. London: Wm. Crace, 1791.

Cranch, Christopher P. "Mr. Cranch's Address: Address, Delivered before the Harvard Musical Association, in the Chapel of the University at Cambridge, August 28, 1845." *Harbinger* 3 (1846): 98–100, 109–10, 123–24.

William Dunlap, *A History of the American Theatre*. New York: J. & J. Harper, 1832.

Dwight, John S. "Address, Delivered before the Harvard Musical Association, August 25, 1841." *Musical Magazine* 3 (1841): 257–72.

———. "Boston a Musical Center." *Herald*, Feb. 17, 1888, supplement.

———. "The History of Music in Boston." In vol. 4 of *The Memorial History of Boston*, edited by Justin Winsor. 4 vols. Boston: James R. Osgood, 1881.

———. "Music as a Means of Culture." *Atlantic Monthly* 26(September 1870): 322.

———. "Music in Boston during the Past Winter." *Harbinger* 1:155.

———. "Music in New York." *Harbinger* 1:59.

———. "Musical Clubs at Harvard: The Pierian Sodality." In *The Harvard Book*, compiled by F. O. Vaile and H. A. Clark, 2:363–74. Cambridge, Mass.: Welch, Bigelow, 1875.

Dwight, Josiah. *An Essay to Silence the Outcry That Has Been Made in Some Places against Regular Singing. A Sermon Preach'd at Framingham*. Boston: John Eliot, 1725.

Eliot, Samuel A. *Address before the Boston Academy of Music, on the Opening of the Odeon, August 5, 1835*. Boston: Perkins, Marvin, 1835.

———. "1. Annual Reports of the Boston Academy of Music. . . . 2. Address on the Opening of the Odeon. . . . 3. Report to the School Committee of Boston. . . . 4. The *Musical Magazine*. Conducted by H. T. Hach. . . ." *North American Review* 52 (1841): 320–38.

———. "1. First Annual Report of the Boston Academy of Music. . . . 2. Second Annual Report. . . . 3. Third Annual Report. . . ." *North American Review* 43 (1836): 53–85.

———. "Lecture on Symphonies, particularly Beethoven No. 5." Manuscript in the Papers of Samuel A. Eliot, Harvard University Archives.

———. "Music and Politics." *Dwight's Journal of Music* 18 (1860): 344–46.

———. Papers of Samuel Atkins Eliot. Harvard University Archives, HUG 1322, Harvard University.

Eliot, Walter Graeme. *A Sketch of the Eliot Family*. New York: Livingston Middleditch, 1887.

Elson, Louis. *The History of America Music*. New York: Burt Franklin, 1925. Reprint. 1971.

Emerson, Caleb. *A Discourse on Music, Pronounced at Amherst, N.H., Before The Handellian Musical Society, September 13, 1808*. Published at the Request of the Society. Amherst, N.H.: Joseph Cushing, 1808.

Finney, Charles G. *Lectures on Revivals of Religion*. 2d. ed. New Yorkj: Fleming H. Revell Company, 1868.

[Floy Michael.] *The Diary of Michael Floy, Jr., Bowery Village, 1833–1837*. Edited by Richard Albert Edward Books. Introduction, annotations, and postscript Margaret Floy Washburn. New Haven: Yale University Press, 1941.

Freeman, F[rederick]. *Psalmodia or the Pastor's Plea for Sacred Psalmody*. Philadelphia: J. Whethman, 1836.

Gardiner, William. *Sacred Melodies, from Haydn, Mozart, and Beethoven, Adapted to the Best English Poets, and Appropriated to the use of The British Church.* 2 vols. London: Clementi, 1812, 1815.

Gould, Nathaniel D. *Church Music in America.* Boston: A. N. Johnson, 1853. Reprint. New York: AMS Press, 1972.

Grund, Francis J. *The Americans in Their Moral, Social, and Political Relations.* Boston: Marsh, Capen, and Lyon, 1837. Reprint. New York: Johnson, 1968.

Guild, Mary E. "Samuel Atkins and Mary Eliot: A Memory Sketch by Their Oldest Daughter." Unpub. manuscript in the Papers of Samuel Atkins Eliot, Harvard University Archives.

Haliburton, William. *Effects of the Stage on the Manners of the People; and the Propriety of Encouraging and Establishing a Virtuous Theater: By a Bostonian.* Boston: Young and Etheridge, 1792.

Hamilton, Thomas. *Men and Manners in America.* 2 vols. Edinburgh: William Blackwood, 1833. Reprint (2 vols. in 1). New York: Augustus M. Kelley, 1968.

Hastings, Thomas. *Dissertation on Musical Taste.* Albany, N.Y.: Websters and Skinners, 1822. Rev. and enl. ed. New York: Mason, 1853.

————. *The Sacred Lyre.* New York: Daniel Fanshaw, 1840.

Haywood, T. B. "Lectures Before the Boston Academy of Music." *Musical Cabinet* (1841–1842): 66–67, 82–83, 98–99, 114–15, 130.

Hodgson, Adam. *Remarks During a Journey Through North America in the Years 1819, 1820, and 1821.* New York: J. Seymour, 1823. Reprint. Westport, Conn.: Negro Universities Press, 1970.

Hubbard, John. *An Essay on Music.* Boston: Manning and Loring, 1808.

Jennison, Samuel. "Reminensces of an Ex-Pierian." In scrapbook at library of Harvard Musical Association.

Law, Andrew. *The Musical Primer.* Cheshire, Conn.: William Law, 1793.

Leavitt, Joshua. *The Christian Lyre.* 2 vols. New York: Joshua Leavitt, 1831.

List of Persons, Copartnerships, and Corporations Who Were Taxed Twenty-Five Dollars and Upward, in the City of Boston, in the Year 1847, Specifying the Amount of the Tax and Real and Personal Estate, Conformably to an Order of the City Council. City Document No. 12. Boston: Jh. H. Eastburn, 1848.

Mann, Mary. *Life of Horace Mann.* New York: Lee and Shepherd, 1865.

Martineau, Harriet. *Society in America.* Edited by Seymour Martin Lipset. Garden City, N.Y.: Doubleday, 1962.

Mason, Lowell. Papers, MS 33. John Herick Jackson Music Library, Yale University.

————. *Address on Church Music: Delivered by Request, on the Evening of Saturday, October 7, 1826. . . .* Boston: Hilliard, Gray, Little, and Wilkins, 1827.

————. *Book of Chants: Consisting of Selections from the Sacred Scriptures, Adapted to Appropriate Music, and Arranged for Chanting. Designed for Congregational Use in Public or Social Worship.* Boston: J. H. Wilkins and R. B. Carter, 1842.

————. *The Boston Handel and Haydn Society Collection of Church Music.* Boston: Richardson & Lord, 1822. Reprint with introduction by H. Wiley Hitchcock. New York: Da Capo Press, 1973.

———— and Timothy B. Mason, eds. *The Sacred Harp of Eclectic Harmony.* Cincinnati: Truman and Smith, 1834.

———— and Thomas Hastings, eds. *Spiritual Songs for Social Worship*. Utica, N.Y.: Hastings and Tracy and W. Williams, 1832.

Mason, William. *Memories of a Musical Life*. New York: Century, 1901.

Mather, Cotton. *The Accomplished Singer. Instructions First, How the Piety of Singing with a True Devotion, May Be Obtained and Expressed; the Glorious God after an Uncommon Manner Glorified in It, and His People Edified. And Then, How the Melody of Regular Singing, and the Skill of Doing It, according to the Rules of It, May be Easily Arrived unto*. Boston: B. Green, 1721.

[————.] *Diary of Cotton Mather, 1709–1724*. Massachusetts Historical Society Collections, seventh series, no. 8. Boston: Published by the society, 1912.

[Mather, Increase?] *An Arrow against Profane and Promiscuous Dancing. Drawn out of the Quiver of the Scriptures by the Ministers of Christ at Boston in New England*. Boston: Samuel Green, 1684.

Musical Review and Record of Musical Science, Literature, and Intelligence 1, no. 11:129.

"Our First Men": A Calendar of Wealth, Fashion, and Gentility; Containing a List of Those Persons Taxed in the City of Boston, Credibly Reported to be Worth One Hundred Thousand Dollars, with Biographical Notices of the Principal Persons. Boston: D. H. Ela, 1846.

Peabody, Elizabeth. "The Word Aesthetic." In vol. 1 of *Aesthetic Papers*. 1849. Reprinted in *The Transcendentalists: An Anthology*, edited by Perry Miller. Cambridge, Mass.: Harvard University Press, 1970.

"Programs of Concerts in Boston, 1817–1863." Manuscript collection in Boston Public Library, Boston.

"Programs of the Handel and Haydn Society." Scrapbook in Allen A. Brown Collection of the Boston Public Library.

Ravenscroft, Thomas. *The Whole Booke of Psalmes: With the Hymnes Evangellical and Songs Spirituall. Composed into four parts by Sundry Authors*. . . . London, 1621.

"Records of the Arionic Sodality. Cambridge: N.E. 1813." Manuscript book, Harvard Musical Association Library, Boston.

"Records of the Harvard Musical Association. 1840. From Its Formation in 1837." Manuscript book, Harvard Musical Association Library, Boston.

"Records of the Pierian Sodality [No. 1 and No. 3]," and "Book No. IV. Containing The Laws of the Society, and a List of Members from its Foundation, in 1808." Book 1 runs from 1808 to 1822, book 3 begins September 25, 1832. A notation in book 3 states that book 2 is lost. Harvard University Archives, Harvard University.

Reed, Andrew, and James Matheson. *A Narrative of the Visit to the American Churches*. 2 vols. London: Jackson and Walford, 1835.

Report Made at a Meeting of the Honorary and Immediate Members of the Pierian Sodality . . . Cambridge, August 30, 1837, with a Record of the Meeting. Cambridge: Folsom, Wells, and Thurston, 1837. Reprint. *Boston Musical Gazette* June 27 and July 11, 1838, 33–34 and 42.

Rhodes, Albert. "The English at Home." *The Galaxy: A Magazine of Entertaining Reading* 13 (1872):776.

Ritter, Frederic Louis. *Music in America*. New York: B. Franklin, 1890.

The Salem Collection. Salem, Mass.: Joshua Cushing, 1805.

Spalding, Walter Raymond. *Music at Harvard*. New York: Coward-McCann, 1935.

Sternhold, Thomas, and John Hopkins. *The Whole Booke of Psalms*. London: John Day, 1562.

Story, William W. *An Address Delivered before the Harvard Musical Association in the Chapel of the University at Cambridge, August 24, 1842*. Boston: S. N. Dickinson, 1842.

Symmes, Thomas. *Utile Dulci: Or, a Joco-Serious Dialogue, Concerning Regular Singing : Calculated for a Particular Town, (Where It Was Publickly Had, on Friday October 12. 1722.) but May Serve Some Other Places in the Same Climate*. Boston: B. Green, 1723.

Thacher, Peter, John Danforth, and Samuel Danforth. *An Essay, By Several Ministers of the Gospel: For the Satisfaction of Their Pious and Consciencious Brethren, as to Sundry Questions and Cases of Conscience, concerning the Singing of Psalms, in the Publick Worship of God, under the Present Evangelical Constitution of the Church-State*. Boston: S. Kneeland, 1723.

Tocqueville, Alexis de. *Democracy in America*. 2 vols. Translated by Henry Reeve. Edited by John T. Morgan and John T. Ingalls. New York: Colonial Press, 1899.

Trollope, Frances. *Domestic Manners of the Americans*. Edited by Donald Smalley. New York: Alfred A. Knopf, 1949. Orig. pub. 1832.

Walter, Thomas. *The Grounds and Rules of Musick Explained: Or, an Introduction to the Art of Singing by Note. Fitted to the Meanest Capacities*. Cornhill, Mass.: J. Franklin, 1721.

———. *The Sweet Psalmist of Israel, a Sermon Preach'd at the Lecture Held in Boston by the Society for Promoting Regular . . . and Good Singing, and for Reforming the Depravations and Debasements Our Psalmody Labours under, in Order to Introduce the Proper and True Old Way of Singing*. Boston: J. Franklin, 1722.

Wansey, Henry. *Excursion in the United States of North America in the Summer of 1794*. Quoted in *American Social History as Recorded by British Travelers*. Edited by Allan Nevins. New York: Henry Holt, 1923.

Weyman, David. *Melodia Sacra; or the Psalms of David . . . with Hymns, Anthems, and Chorusses*. 2 vols. Dublin: Allen, 1814, 1816.

Whittaker, John. *The Seraph: A Collection of Sacred Music*. 2 vols. London [1818, 1819].

Winslow, Edward. *Hypocrisie Unmasked*. London: Printed by R. Coates for J. Ballamy, 1646.

Zeuner, Charles, arranger and composer. *The American Harp: Being a Collection of New and Original Church Music, under the Control of the Musical Professional Society in Boston*. Boston: Hilliard, Gray, 1832.

———, arranger and composer. *The Ancient Lyre: A Collection of Old, New, and Original Church Music, under the Approbation of the Professional Musical Society in Boston*. Boston: Crocker and Brewster, 1833.

Newspapers and Journals

Note. Many newspapers and journals in the early nineteenth century carried short, usually unattributed articles or advertisements. Those newspapers and journals that have actually been cited are listed here. More substantial articles are listed in the section above.

Allgemeine musikalische Zeitung
American Musical Journal
Boston Daily Evening Transcript
Boston Evening Post
Boston Gazette
Boston Intelligencer and Morning and Evening Advertiser
Boston Musical Gazette
Columbian Centinel
Euterpeiad; or Musical Intelligencer
Harbinger
Independent Chronicle
Lyre
Massachusetts Centinel
Musical Cabinet
New York Daily Tribune
Semi-Weekly Courier and Enquirer
Musical Magazine
Musical Reporter
New York Musical Chronicle and Advertiser

Secondary Sources

Adams, Henry. *The United States in 1800.* Ithaca, N.Y.: Cornell University Press, 1955. Originally published as chapters 1–6 of Henry Adams, *History of the United States of America during the First Administration of Thomas Jefferson.* New York: Charles Scribner's Sons, 1889.

Ahlquist, Karen Ethel. "Opera, Theatre, and Audience in Antebellum New York." Unpub. diss. Univ. of Michigan, 1991.

Alexander, James Waddel. *Forty Years' Familiar Letters.* Edited by John Hall. Trenton, N.J., 1860.

Allen, Alexander Viets Griswold. *Jonathan Edwards.* Boston: Houghton, Mifflin, 1889.

Bailyn, Bernard. *The Peopling of British North America: An Introduction.* New York: Knopf, 1986.

Blumin, Stuart. *The Emergence of the Middle Class: Social Experience in the American City, 1760–1900.* Cambridge, U.K.: Cambridge University Press, 1989.

Brooks, Van Wyck. *America's Coming-of-Age.* New York: Viking Press, 1930.

Broyles, Michael. "Ensemble Music Moves out of the Private House: Haydn to Beethoven." In *The Orchestra: Origins and Transformations,* edited by Joan Peyser, 97–122. New York: Charles Scribner's Sons, 1986.

———, ed. *A Yankee Musician in Europe: The European Journals of Lowell Mason.* Ann Arbor, Mich.: UMI Research Press, 1990.

James M. Bugbee, "Boston under the Mayors." In vol. 2 of *The Memorial History of Boston,* edited by Justin Winsor. 4 vols. Boston: James R. Osgood, 1881.

Camus, Raoul François. "Military Music in Colonial Boston." In *Music in Colonial Massachusetts, 1630–1820. I: Music in Public Places.* Boston: Colonial Society of Massachusetts, 1980.

Champlin, John D. "Nearly Two Centuries of Music." In vol. 4. of *The Memorial History of New York*, edited by James Grant Wilson. 4 vols. New York: New-York Historical Society, 1892–1893.

Chase, Gilbert. *America's Music: From the Pilgrims to the Present.* New York: McGraw-Hill, 1966.

Chmaj, Betty E. "Fry versus Dwight: American Music's Debate over Nationality." *American Music* 3, no. 1 (Spring 1985): 63–84.

Clapp, William. "The Drama in Boston." In vol. 4 of *The Memorial History of Boston.* edited by Justin Winsor. 4 vols. Boston: James R. Osgood, 1881.

———. *A Record of the Boston State.* Boston: James Munroe, 1853.

———. *"The Life of Haydn, in a Series of Letters Written at Vienna; Followed by the Life of Mozart, with Observations on Metastasio, and on the Present State of Music in France and Italy.* Translated from the French of L. A. C. Bombet, with Notes by William Gardiner. . . ." *North American Review* 50 (1840): 1–19.

———. *A Record of the Boston Stage.* Boston: James Monroe, 1853. Reprint. New York: Greenwood Press, 1969.

Clebsch, William A. *American Religious Thought: A History.* Chicago: University of Chicago Press, 1973.

Cooke, George Willis. *John Sullivan Dwight, Brook-Farmer, Editor, and Critic of Music.* Boston: Small, Maynard, 1898.

Cott, Nancy F. *The Bonds of Womanhood: "Woman's Sphere" in New England, 1780–1835.* New Haven: Yale University Press, 1977.

Richard A. Crawford, *The American Musical Landscape.* Los Angeles: University of California Press, forthcoming.

——— *Andrew Law, American Psalmodist.* Evanston, Ill.: Northwestern University Press, 1968.

———. "'Ancient Music' and the Europeanizing of American Psalmody, 1800–1810." In *A Celebration of American Music: Words and Music in Honor of H. Wiley Hitchcock*, edited by Richard Crawford, Carol J. Oja, and R. Allen Lot. Ann Arbor, Mich.: University of Michigan Press, 1989.

——— "Musical Learning in Nineteenth-Century America." *American Music* 1, no. 1 (Spring 1983): 1–11.

Culver, Raymond B. *Horace Mann and Religion in the Massachusetts Public Schools.* New Haven: Yale University Press, 1929. Reprint. New York: Arno Press and the *New York Times*, 1969.

Dalzell, Robert F. *Enterprising Elite: The Boston Associates and the World They Made.* Cambridge, Mass.: Harvard University Press, 1987.

DiMaggio, Paul. "Cultural Entrepreneurship in Nineteenth-Century Boston: The Creation of an Organizational Base for High Culture in America" and "Cultural Entrepreneurship in Nineteenth-Century Boston, Part II: The Classification and Framing of American Art." *Media, Culture and Society* 4 (1982): 33–50, 303–22.

Dooley, James Edward. "Thomas Hastings: American Church Musician." Unpub. diss. Florida State University, 1963.

Edward, George Thornton. *Music and Musicians of Maine.* Portland, Maine: South-worth Press, 1928.

Eliot, Walter Graeme. *A Sketch of the Eliot Family.* New York: Livingston Middleditch, 1887.

Ellingwood, Leonard. *The History of American Church Music.* New York: Morehouse-Gorham, 1953.

Elson, Louis. "Music in Boston." *Music and Drama,* New York, June 3, 1882.

Eskew, Harry. "Lowell Mason." In *The New Grove Dictionary of Music and Musicians,* edited by Stanley Sadie. London: Macmillan, 1980.

Fellinger, Imogen, and John Shepard. "Periodicals." In *The New Grove Dictionary of American Music,* edited by H. Wiley Hitchcock and Stanley Sadie. New York: Grove's Dictionaries of Music, 1987, 3:503–05.

Fertig, Walter L. "John Sullivan Dwight: Transcendentalist and Literary Amateur of Music." Unpub. diss. University of Maryland, 1952.

Forbes, Eliot, ed. *Thayer's Life of Beethoven.* Princeton: Princeton University Press, 1967.

Fox, Pamela. "Cliques, Clubs and Catholicity: The Founding of the Boston Symphony Orchestra and Its Aftershocks." Unpub. paper delivered at the Annual Meeting of the Sonneck Society, Danville, Ky., April 1989.

———. "Cultural Counterpoint and Historiographical Challenges: Reexamining the Later 19th Century." Unpub. paper delivered at the Annual Meeting of the Sonneck Society, Hampton, Va., April, 1991.

Goddard, Harold Clarke. *Studies in New England Transcendentalism.* New York: Hillary House Publishers, 1960.

Goldman, Richard Franko. *The Wind Band: Its Literature and Technique.* Boston: Allyn and Bacon, 1961.

———. "The Wonderful World of Culture, Or: A Strictly Highbrow and Artistic Subject." *American Scholar* 35, no. 3 (Summer 1966). Reprinted in *Richard Franko Goldman: Selected Essays,* edited by Dorothy Klotzman. I. A. S. M. Monographs 13: 245–49. Brooklyn, N.Y., 1980.

Halttunen, Karen. *Confidence Men and Painted Women: A Study of Middle-Class Culture in America, 1830–1870.* New Haven: Yale University Press, 1982.

Hamm, Charles. *Music in the New World.* New York: W. W. Norton, 1983.

Hammond, Paul Garnett, "Music in Urban Revivalism in the Northern United States, 1800–1835. Unpub. diss. Southern Baptist Theological Seminary, 1974.

Harris, Neil. *The Artist in American Society: The Formative Years, 1790–1860.* New York: George Braziller, 1966.

Hepner, Arthur W. *Pro Bono Artium Musicarum: The Harvard Musical Association, 1837–1987.* Boston: Harvard Musical Association, 1987.

Hitchcock, H. Wiley. *Music in the United States: A Historical Introduction.* Englewood Cliffs, N.J.: Prentice-Hall, 1969.

Hodges, Maud deLeigh. *Crossroads on the Charles: A History of Watertown, Massachusetts.* Edited by Sigrid R. Reddy. With an epilogue by Charles T. Burke. Canaan, N.H.: Phoenix, 1980.

Howard, John Tasker. *Our American Music: A Comprehensive History from 1620 to the Present.* 4th ed. New York: Thomas Y. Crowell, 1965.

Jaher, Frederic. *The Urban Establishment: Upper Strata in Boston, New York, Charleston, Chicago, and Los Angeles*. Urbana, Ill.: University of Illinois Press, 1982.

James, Henry. *William Wetmore Story and His Friends, From Letters, Diaries, and Recollections*. 2 vols. Boston, 1903. Reprint (2 vols. in 1). New York: Da Capo Press, 1969.

Johnson, Allen, et al. *Dictionary of American Biography*. 20 vols. New York: American Council of Learned Societies, 1928–1937. Reprint. 11 vols. New York: Charles Scribner's Sons, 1963.

Johnson, H. Earle. *Hallelujah, Amen! The Story of the Handel and Haydn Society of Boston*. Introduction by Richard Crawford. Boston: Bruce Humphries, 1965. Reprint. New York: Da Capo Press, 1981.

————. "The John Rowe Parker Letters." *Musical Quarterly* 62 (1976): 72–86.

————. *Musical Interludes in Boston, 1795–1830*. New York: Columbia University Press, 1943. Reprint. New York: AMS Press, 1967.

Kerman, Joseph, and Alan Tyson. "Beethoven." *The New Grove Dictionary of Music and Musicians*, edited by Stanley Sadie. London: Macmillan, 1980.

Knights, Peter R. "Using City Directories in Ante-Bellum Urban Historical Research." *Historical Methods Newsletter* 2 (September 1968): 1–10. Revised and included as appendix A in Knights, Peter R. *The Plain People of Boston, 1830–1860: A Study in City Growth*. New York: Oxford University Press, 1971.

Lamb, Mrs. Martha J., and Mrs. Burton Harrison. *History of the City of New York: Its Origin, Rise, and Progress*. 3 vols. New York: A. S. Barnes, 1896.

Landon, H. C. Robbins. *Haydn: Chronicle and Works*. Vol. 3 of *Haydn in England, 1791–1795*. 5 vols. London: Thames and Hudson, 1976.

Larkin, Jack. *The Reshaping of Everyday Life, 1790–1840*. New York: Harper and Row, 1988.

Laurie, Bruce, Theodore Hershberg, and George Alter. "Immigrants and Industry: The Philadelphia Experience, 1850–1880." In *Philadelphia: Work, Space, Family, and Group Experience in the Nineteenth Century: Essays Toward an Interdisciplinary History of the City*, edited by Theodore Hershberg. New York: Oxford University Press, 1981.

Lawrence, Vera Brodsky. *Music for Patriots, Politicians, and Presidents: Harmonies and Discords of the First Hundred Years*. New York: Macmillan, 1975.

————. *Strong on Music: The New York Music Scene in the Days of George Templeton Strong, 1836–1875*. New York: Oxford University Press, 1988.

Layman, Daniel. "The Philoharmonic Society: Newcomers and the Nucleus of Boston's Orchestral Tradition." Unpub. paper read at the Annual Meeting of the Sonneck Society, Danville, Ky., April 1988.

Levine, Lawrence. *Highbrow, Lowbrow: The Emergence of Cultural Hierarchy in America*. Cambridge: Harvard University Press, 1988.

Long, Clarence D. *Wages and Earnings in the United States, 1860–1890*. Princeton: Princeton University Press, 1960.

Loring, William C., Jr. "Arthur Bird, American." *Musical Quarterly* 29, no. 1 (January 1943): 78–91.

Loveland, Anne. *Southern Evangelicals and the Social Order*. Baton Rouge, La.: Louisiana State University Press, 1980.

McGlinchee, Claire. *The First Decade of the Boston Museum*. Boston: Bruce Humphries, 1940.

McKay, David P., and Richard Crawford. *William Billings of Boston: Eighteenth-Century Composer*. Princeton: Princeton University Press, 1975.

Margo, Robert A., and Georgia C. Villaflor. "The Growth of Wages in Antebellum America: New Evidence." *Journal of Economic History* 47 (1987): 873–95.

Mason, Henry Lowell. "Lowell Mason, His Life and Works." Manuscript in the Lowell Mason Papers, Yale University.

Mason, William. *Memories of a Musical Life*. New York: Century, 1901. Reprint. New York: Da Capo Press, 1970.

Matthews, William S. *A Hundred Years of Music in America*. Chicago: G. L. Howe, 1889.

Metcalf, Frank J. *American Writers and Compilers of Sacred Music*. New York: Abingdon Press, 1925.

Miller, Perry. *The Transcendentalists: An Anthology*. Cambridge: Harvard University Press, 1960.

Moore, Nina, and Francis Tiffany. *Harm Jan Huidedoper*. Cambridge, Mass.: Riverside Press, 1904.

Nagel, Paul C. *This Sacred Trust: American Nationality, 1798–1898*. New York: Oxford University Press, 1971.

Newman, William. *The Sonata in the Classic Era*. New York: W. W. Norton, 1972.

Nutter, Charles R. *The Harvard Musical Association, 1837–1937*. Boston: Anchor, 1937.

Orsini, N. Giordano. "The Ancient Roots of a Modern Idea." In *Organic Form: The Life of an Idea*, edited by G. S. Rousseau. London, 1972.

Paige, Paul Eric. "Musical Organizations in Boston, 1830–1850." Unpub. diss. Boston University, 1967.

Parrington, Vernon L. *Main Currents in American Thought: Volume 1, The Colonial Mind*. New York: Harcourt, Brace, and World, 1927.

Pearson, Henry G. "Frederic Tudor, Ice King." *Proceedings of the Massachusetts Historical Society* 65 (1940): 169–215. Paper read in November 1933.

Pease, William H., and Jane H. Pease. *The Web of Progress: Private Values and Public Styles in Boston and Charleston, 1828–1843*. New York: Oxford University Press, 1985.

Pemberton, Carol. *Lowell Mason: His Life and Work*. Rev. ed. of diss. University of Minnesota, 1971. Ann Arbor, Mich.: UMI Research Press, 1985.

The Performing Arts: Problems and Prospects. Rockefeller panel report on the future of theatre, dance, and music in America. New York: McGraw-Hill, 1965.

Perkins, Charles C., and John S. Dwight. *History of the Handel and Haydn Society, of Boston, Massachusetts, from the Foundation of the Society through Its Seventy-fifth Season, 1815–1890*. Boston: A. Mudge and Sons, 1883–1898.

Perry, Lewis. *Intellectual Life in America: A History*. New York: Franklin Watts, 1984.

Pichierri, Louis, *Music in New Hampshire, 1623–1800*. New York: Columbia University Press, 1960.

Pierce, Edward L. "Extracts from the Diary of John Rowe." *Proceedings of the*

Massachusetts Historical Society, 2d series, 10 (1895): 11–108. Boston: Published by the Society, 1896.

Rasmussen, Jane. *Musical Taste as a Religious Question in Nineteenth-Century America.* Studies in American Religion. Vol. 20. Lewiston, N.Y.: Edwin Mellen Press, 1986.

Rose, Ann. *Transcendentalism as a Social Movement, 1830–1850.* New Haven: Yale University Press, 1981.

Ross, James J. "Lowell Mason, American Musician." *Education* 14 (March 1894): 411–16.

Schabas, Ezra. *Theodore Thomas: America's Conductor and Builder of Orchestras, 1835–1905.* Urbana, Ill.: University of Illinois Press.

Scholes, Percy. *The Puritans and Music in England and New England.* London: Oxford University Press, 1934.

Schrader, Frederick Franklin. *The Germans in the Making of America.* Boston: Stratford, 1924.

Scott, Leonore Cranch. *The Life and Letters of Christopher Pearse Cranch.* Boston: Houghton Mifflin, 1917.

Seilhammer, George O. *History of the American Theatre: New Foundations.* 1888–1891. Reprint. New York: Benjamin Bloom, 1968.

Simmons, Lucretia Van Tuyl. *Goethe's Lyric Poems in English Translation Prior to 1860.* University of Wisconsin Studies in Language and Literature, no. 6. Madison: University of Wisconsin Press, 1919.

Smith, Charles C. "Commencements at Harvard, 1803–1848: Some Excerpts from the Journal of the Rev. Dr. John Pierce." *Proceedings of the Massachusetts Historical Society*, 2d series, 5 (1889–1890): 167–263. Boston: Published by the Society, 1890.

Sonneck, Oscar. *Early Concert-Life in America, 1731–1800.* Leipzig: Breitkopf and Hßrtel, 1907. Reprint. New York: Da Capo Press, 1978.

———. *Early Opera in America.* New York: 1915. Reprint. New York: Benjamin Bloom, 1963.

Sosna, Morton. "The NEH and American Cultural Nationalism." Unpub. paper delivered at the Annual Meeting of the Organization of American Historians, Washington, D.C., March 1990.

Spalding, Walter Raymond. *Music at Harvard.* New York: Coward-McCann, 1935.

Spear, Dorothea. *Bibliography of American Directories through 1860.* Worcester, Mass.: American Antiquarian Society, 1961.

Spillane, Daniel. *History of the American Pianoforte; Its Technical Development and the Trade.* New York: D. Spillane, 1890.

Spingarn, J. E., ed. *Goethe's Literary Essays.* New York, 1921.

Stevenson, Robert M. *Protestant Church Music in America.* New York; W. W. Norton, 1966.

Story, Ronald. *The Forging of an Aristocrcy: Harvard and the Boston Upper Class, 1800–1870.* Middletown, Conn.: Wesleyan University Press, 1980.

Temperley, Nicholas, *The Music of the English Parish Church.* Cambridge, U.K.: Cambridge University Press, 1969.

———. "The Old Way of Singing." *Journal of the American Musicological Society* 34, no. 3 (Fall 1981): 511–44.

Treitler, Leo. "The Early History of Music Writing in the West." *Journal of the American Musicological Society* 35, no. 2 (Summer 1982): 237–79.

Warren, Charles. "Samuel Adams and the Sans Souci Club in 1785." *Massachusetts Historical Society Proceedings*, 3d series, 60 (1927): 322–28.

Weber, William. *Music and the Middle Class: The Social Structure of Concert Life in London, Paris, and Vienna.* New York: Holmes and Meier, 1975.

———. "The Rise of the Classical Repertoire in Nineteenth-Century Orchestral Concerts." In *The Orchestra: Origins and Transformations*, edited by Joan Peyser. New York: Charles Scribner's Sons, 1986.

Weisberger, Bernard A. *They Gathered at the River: The Story of the Great Revivalists and Their Impact upon Religion in America.* Boston: Little, Brown, 1958.

Wiebe, Robert. *The Opening of American Society: From the Adoption of the Constitution to the Eve of Disunion.* New York: Alfred A. Knopf, 1984.

Wilentz, Sean. *Chants Democratic: New York City and the Rise of the American Working Class, 1788–1850.* New York: Oxford University Press, 1984.

Wood, Gordon S. *The Creation of the American Republic, 1776–1787.* Chapel Hill: University of North Carolina Press, 1969.

Wunderlich, Charles. "A History of Bibliography of Early American Musical Periodicals, 1782–1852." Unpub. diss. University of Michigan, 1962.

Index